Lecture Notes in Computer Sc

Commenced Publication in 1973
Founding and Former Series Editors:
Gerhard Goos, Juris Hartmanis, and Jan van Leeu..._

Sašo Džeroski   Jan Struyf (Eds.)

Knowledge Discovery in Inductive Databases

5th International Workshop, KDID 2006
Berlin, Germany, September 18, 2006
Revised Selected and Invited Papers

 Springer

Volume Editors

Sašo Džeroski
Jožef Stefan Institute
Department of Knowledge Technologies
Jamova 39, 1000 Ljubljana, Slovenia
E-mail: saso.dzeroski@ijs.si

Jan Struyf
Katholieke Universiteit Leuven
Department of Computer Science
Celestijnenlaan 200A, 3001 Leuven, Belgium
E-mail: jan.struyf@cs.kuleuven.be

Library of Congress Control Number: 2007937944

CR Subject Classification (1998): H.2, I.2

LNCS Sublibrary: SL 3 – Information Systems and Application, incl. Internet/Web and HCI

ISSN   0302-9743
ISBN-10   3-540-75548-9 Springer Berlin Heidelberg New York
ISBN-13   978-3-540-75548-7 Springer Berlin Heidelberg New York

Springer is a part of Springer Science+Business Media

springer.com

© Springer-Verlag Berlin Heidelberg 2007
Printed in Germany

Typesetting: Camera-ready by author, data conversion by Scientific Publishing Services, Chennai, India
Printed on acid-free paper   SPIN: 12171675   06/3180   5 4 3 2 1 0

Preface

The 5th International Workshop on Knowledge Discovery in Inductive Databases (KDID 2006) was held on September 18, 2006 in Berlin, Germany, in conjunction with ECML/PKDD 2006: The 17th European Conference on Machine Learning (ECML) and the 10th European Conference on Principles and Practice of Knowledge Discovery in Databases (PKDD).

Inductive databases (IDBs) represent a database view on data mining and knowledge discovery. IDBs contain not only data, but also generalizations (patterns and models) valid in the data. In an IDB, ordinary queries can be used to access and manipulate data, while inductive queries can be used to generate (mine), manipulate, and apply patterns. In the IDB framework, patterns become "first-class citizens", and KDD becomes an extended querying process in which both the data and the patterns/models that hold in the data are queried.

The IDB framework is appealing as a general framework for data mining, because it employs declarative queries instead of ad-hoc procedural constructs. As declarative queries are often formulated using constraints, inductive querying is closely related to constraint-based data mining. The IDB framework is also appealing for data mining applications, as it supports the entire KDD process, i.e., nontrivial multi-step KDD scenarios, rather than just individual data mining operations. The goal of the workshop was to bring together database and data mining researchers interested in the areas of inductive databases, inductive queries, constraint-based data mining, and data mining query languages.

This workshop followed the previous four successful KDID workshops organized in conjunction with ECML/PKDD: KDID 2002 held in Helsinki, Finland, KDID 2003 held in Cavtat-Dubrovnik, Croatia, KDID 2004 held in Pisa, Italy, and KDID 2005 held in Porto, Portugal. Its scientific program included nine regular presentations and two short ones, as well as an invited talk by Kiri L. Wagstaff (Jet Propulsion Laboratory, California Institute of Technology, USA). This volume bundles all papers presented at the workshop and, in addition, includes three contributions that cover relevant research presented at other venues. We also include an article by one of the editors (SD) that attempts to unify existing research in the area and outline directions for further research towards a general framework for data mining.

We wish to thank the invited speaker, all the authors of submitted papers, the program committee members and additional reviewers, and the ECML/PKDD organization committee. KDID 2006 was supported by the European project IQ ("Inductive Queries for Mining Patterns and Models", IST FET FP6-516169).

July 2007

Sašo Džeroski
Jan Struyf

Organization

Program Chairs

Sašo Džeroski   Department of Knowledge Technologies
Jožef Stefan Institute
Jamova 39, 1000 Ljubljana, Slovenia
`saso.dzeroski@ijs.si`
`http://www-ai.ijs.si/SasoDzeroski/`
Jan Struyf   Department of Computer Science
Katholieke Universiteit Leuven
Celestijnenlaan 200A, 3001 Leuven, Belgium
`jan.struyf@cs.kuleuven.be`
`http://www.cs.kuleuven.be/~jan/`

Program Committee

Hiroki Arimura, Hokkaido University, Japan
Hendrik Blockeel, Katholieke Universiteit Leuven, Belgium
Francesco Bonchi, ISTI-C.N.R., Italy
Jean-François Boulicaut, INSA Lyon, France
Toon Calders, University of Antwerp, Belgium
Luc De Raedt, Katholieke Universiteit Leuven, Belgium
Minos N. Garofalakis, Intel Research Berkeley, USA
Fosca Giannotti, ISTI-C.N.R., Italy
Bart Goethals, University of Antwerp, Belgium
Jiawei Han, University Illinois at Urbana-Champaign, USA
Ross D. King, University of Wales, Aberystwyth, UK
Giuseppe Manco, ICAR-C.N.R., Italy
Rosa Meo, University of Turin, Italy
Ryszard S. Michalski, George Mason University, USA
Taneli Mielikäinen, University of Helsinki, Finland
Shinichi Morishita, University of Tokyo, Japan
Siegfried Nijssen, Katholieke Universiteit Leuven, Belgium
Céline Robardet, INSA Lyon, France
Arno Siebes, Utrecht University, The Netherlands
Takashi Washio, Osaka University, Japan
Philip S. Yu, IBM Thomas J. Watson, USA
Mohammed Zaki, Rensselaer Polytechnic Institute, USA
Carlo Zaniolo, UCLA, USA

Additional Reviewers

Annalisa Appice
Marko Bohanec
Emma L. Byrne
Hong Cheng
Amanda Clare

Francesco Folino
Gemma Garriga
Kenneth A. Kaufman
Elio Masciari
Riccardo Ortale

Jimeng Sun
Janusz Wojtusiak

Table of Contents

Invited Talk

Value, Cost, and Sharing: Open Issues in Constrained Clustering   1
Kiri L. Wagstaff

Contributed Papers

Mining Bi-sets in Numerical Data   11
Jérémy Besson, Céline Robardet, Luc De Raedt, and
Jean-François Boulicaut

Extending the Soft Constraint Based Mining Paradigm   24
Stefano Bistarelli and Francesco Bonchi

On Interactive Pattern Mining from Relational Databases   42
Francesco Bonchi, Fosca Giannotti, Claudio Lucchese,
Salvatore Orlando, Raffaele Perego, and Roberto Trasarti

Analysis of Time Series Data with Predictive Clustering Trees   63
Sašo Džeroski, Valentin Gjorgjioski, Ivica Slavkov, and Jan Struyf

Integrating Decision Tree Learning into Inductive Databases   81
Élisa Fromont, Hendrik Blockeel, and Jan Struyf

Using a Reinforced Concept Lattice to Incrementally Mine Association
Rules from Closed Itemsets   97
Arianna Gallo and Rosa Meo

An Integrated Multi-task Inductive Database VINLEN: Initial
Implementation and Early Results   116
Kenneth A. Kaufman, Ryszard S. Michalski,
Jarosław Pietrzykowski, and Janusz Wojtusiak

Beam Search Induction and Similarity Constraints for Predictive
Clustering Trees   134
Dragi Kocev, Jan Struyf, and Sašo Džeroski

Frequent Pattern Mining and Knowledge Indexing Based on
Zero-Suppressed BDDs   152
Shin-ichi Minato and Hiroki Arimura

Extracting Trees of Quantitative Serial Episodes   170
Mirco Nanni and Christophe Rigotti

IQL: A Proposal for an Inductive Query Language 189
    Siegfried Nijssen and Luc De Raedt

Mining Correct Properties in Incomplete Databases 208
    François Rioult and Bruno Crémilleux

Efficient Mining Under Rich Constraints Derived from Various
Datasets 223
    Arnaud Soulet, Jiří Kléma, and Bruno Crémilleux

Three Strategies for Concurrent Processing of Frequent Itemset Queries
Using FP-Growth 240
    Marek Wojciechowski, Krzysztof Galecki, and Krzysztof Gawronek

Discussion Paper

Towards a General Framework for Data Mining 259
    Sašo Džeroski

Author Index 301

Value, Cost, and Sharing:
Open Issues in Constrained Clustering

Kiri L. Wagstaff

Jet Propulsion Laboratory, California Institute of Technology,
Mail Stop 126-347, 4800 Oak Grove Drive, Pasadena CA 91109, USA
kiri.wagstaff@jpl.nasa.gov

Abstract. Clustering is an important tool for data mining, since it can identify major patterns or trends without any supervision (labeled data). Over the past five years, semi-supervised (constrained) clustering methods have become very popular. These methods began with incorporating pairwise constraints and have developed into more general methods that can learn appropriate distance metrics. However, several important open questions have arisen about which constraints are most useful, how they can be actively acquired, and when and how they should be propagated to neighboring points. This position paper describes these open questions and suggests future directions for constrained clustering research.

1   Introduction

Clustering methods are used to analyze data sets that lack any supervisory information such as data labels. They identify major patterns or trends based on a combination of the assumed cluster structure (e.g., Gaussian distribution) and the observed data distribution. Recently, semi-supervised clustering methods have become very popular because they can also take advantage of supervisory information when it is available. This supervision often takes the form of a set of pairwise *constraints* that specify known relationships between pairs of data items. Constrained clustering methods incorporate and enforce these constraints. This process is not just a fix for suboptimal distance metrics; it is quite possible for different users to have different goals in mind when analyzing the same data set. Constrained clustering methods permit the clustering results to be individually tailored for these different goals.

The initial work in constrained clustering has led to further study of the impact of incorporating constraints into clustering algorithms, particularly when applied to large, real-world data sets. Important issues that have arisen include:

1. Given the recent observation that some constraint sets can *adversely* impact performance, how can we determine the utility of a given constraint set, prior to clustering?
2. How can we minimize the effort required of the user, by active soliciting only the most useful constraints?

S. Džeroski and J. Struyf (Eds.): KDID 2006, LNCS 4747, pp. 1–10, 2007.

3. When and how should constraints be propagated or shared with neighboring points?

This paper begins with a description of the constrained clustering problem and surveys existing methods for finding satisfying solutions (Section 2). This overview is meant to be representative rather than comprehensive. Section 3 contributes more detailed descriptions of each of these open questions. In identifying these challenges, and the state of the art in addressing them, we highlight several directions for future research.

2 Constrained Clustering

We specify a clustering problem as a scenario in which a user wishes to obtain a partition $\mathcal{P}$ of a data set $\mathcal{D}$, containing n items, into k clusters or groups. A *constrained clustering* problem is one in which the user has some pre-existing knowledge about their desired $\mathcal{P}^*$. Usually, $\mathcal{P}^*$ is not fully known; if it were, no clustering would be necessary. Instead, the user is only able to provide a partial view $\mathcal{V}(\mathcal{P}^*)$. In this case, rather than returning $\mathcal{P}$ that best satisfies the (generic) objective function used by the clustering algorithm, we require that the algorithm adapt its solution to accommodate $\mathcal{V}(\mathcal{P}^*)$.

2.1 Pairwise Constraints

A partition $\mathcal{P}$ can be completely specified by stating, for each pairwise relationship (d_i, d_j) where $d_i, d_j \in \mathcal{D}$ and $d_i \neq d_j$, whether the pair of items is in the same cluster or split between different cluster. When used to specify requirements about the output partition, we refer to these statements as *must-link* and *cannot-link* constraints, respectively [1,2]. The number of distinct constraints ranges from 1 to $\frac{1}{2}n(n-1)$, since constraints are by definition symmetric. It is often the case that additional information can be automatically inferred from the partial set of constraints specified by the user. Cluster membership is an equivalence relation, so the must-link relationships are symmetric and transitive. Cannot-link relationships are symmetric but not necessarily transitive. When constraints of both kinds are present, an *entailment* relationship permits the discovery of additional constraints implied by the user-specified set [2,3].

The first work in this area proposed a modified version of COBWEB that enforced pairwise must-link and cannot-link constraints [1]. It was followed by an enhanced version of the widely used k-means algorithm that could also accommodate constraints, called COP-KMEANS [2]. Table 1 reproduces the details of this algorithm. COP-KMEANS takes in a set of must-link ($Con_=$) and cannot-link ($Con_{\neq}$) constraints. The essential change from the basic k-means algorithm occurs in step (2), where the decision about where to assign a given item d_i is constrained so that no constraints in $Con_=$ or $Con_{\neq}$ are violated. The satisfying condition is checked by the VIOLATE-CONSTRAINTS function. Note that it is possible for there to be no solutions that satisfy all constraints, in which case the algorithm exits prematurely.

Table 1. Constrained K-means Algorithm for hard, pairwise constraints [2]

COP-KMEANS(data set D, number of clusters k, must-link constraints $Con_= \subset D \times D$, cannot-link constraints $Con_{\neq} \subset D \times D$)

1. Let $C_1 \ldots C_k$ be the k initial cluster centers.
2. For each point $d_i \in D$, assign it to the closest cluster C_j such that VIOLATE-CONSTRAINTS($d_i, C_j, Con_=, Con_{\neq}$) is false. If no such cluster exists, fail (return {}).
3. For each cluster C_i, update its center by averaging all of the points d_j that have been assigned to it.
4. Iterate between (2) and (3) until convergence.
5. Return $\{C_1 \ldots C_k\}$.

VIOLATE-CONSTRAINTS(data point d, cluster C, must-link constraints $Con_= \subset D \times D$, cannot-link constraints $Con_{\neq} \subset D \times D$)

1. For each $(d, d_=) \in Con_=$: If $d_= \notin C$, return true.
2. For each $(d, d_{\neq}) \in Con_{\neq}$: If $d_{\neq} \in C$, return true.
3. Otherwise, return false.

A drawback of this approach is that it may fail to find a satisfying solution even when one exists. This happens because of the greedy fashion in which items are assigned; early assignments can constrain later ones due to potential conflicts, and there is no mechanism for backtracking. As a result, the algorithm is sensitive to the order in which it processes the data set D. In practice, this is resolved by running the algorithm multiple times with different orderings of the data, but for data sets with a large number of constraints (especially cannot-link constraints), early termination without a solution can be a persistent problem. We previously assessed the hardness of this problem by generating constraint sets of varying sizes for the same data set and found that convergence failures happened most often for problems with an intermediate number of constraints, with respect to the number of items in the data set. This is consistent with the finding that 3-SAT formulas with intermediate complexity tend to be most difficult to solve [4].

In practice, however, this algorithm has proven very effective on a variety of data sets. Initial experiments used several data sets from the UCI repository [5], using constraints artificially generated from the known data labels. In addition, experimental results on a real-world problem showed the benefits of using a constrained clustering method when pre-existing knowledge is available. In this application, data from cars with GPS receivers were collected as they traversed repeatedly over the same roads. The goal was to cluster the data points to identify the road lanes, permitting the automatic refinement of digital maps to the individual lane level. By expressing domain knowledge about the contiguity of a given car's trajectory and a maximum reasonable separation between lanes in the form of pairwise constraints, lane-finding performance increased from 58.0% without constraints to 98.6% with constraints [2]. A natural follow-on to this work was the development of a constrained version of the EM clustering algorithm [6].

Soft Constraints. When the constraints are known to be completely reliable, treating them as hard constraints is an appropriate approach. However, since the constraints may be derived from heuristic domain knowledge, it is also useful to have a more flexible approach. There are two kinds of uncertainty that we may wish to capture: (1) the constraints are noisy, so we should permit some of them to be violated if there is overwhelming evidence against them (from other data items), and (2) we have knowledge about the *likelihood* that a given constraint should be satisfied, so we should permit the expression of a probabilistic constraint. The SCOP-KMEANS algorithm is a more general version of COP-KMEANS algorithm that treats constraint statements as soft constraints, addressing the issue of noise in the constraints [7]. Rather than requiring that every constraint be satisfied, it instead trades off the objective function (variance) against constraint violations, penalizing for each violation but permitting a violation if it provides a significant boost to the quality of the solution. Other approaches, such as the MPCK-means algorithm, permit the specification of an individual weight for each constraint, addressing the issue of variable per-constraint confidences [3]. MPCK-means imposes a penalty for constraint violations that is proportional to the violated constraint's weight.

Metric Learning. It was recognized early on that constraints could provide information not only about the desired solution, but also more general information about the metric space in which the clusters reside. A must-link constraint (d_i, d_j) can be interpreted as a hint that the conceptual distance between d_i and d_j is small. Likewise, a cannot-link constraint implies that the distance between d_i and d_j is so great that they should never be clustered together. Rather than using a modified clustering algorithm to enforce these individual constraints, it is also possible to use the constraints to learn a new metric over the feature space and then apply regular clustering algorithms, using the new metric. Several such metric learning approaches have been developed; some are restricted to learning from must-link constraints only [8], while others can also accommodate cannot-link constraints [9,10]. The MPCK-means algorithm fuses both of these approaches (direct constraint satisfaction and metric learning) into a single architecture [3].

2.2   Beyond Pairwise Constraints

There are other kinds of knowledge that a user may have about the desired partition $\mathcal{P}^*$, aside from pairwise constraints. Cluster-level constraints include existential constraints, which require that a cluster contain at least c_{min} items [11,12] and capacity constraints, which require that a cluster must have less than c_{max} items [13].

The user may also wish to express constraints on the features. *Co-clustering* is the process of identifying subsets of items in the data set that are similar with respect to a subset of the features. That is, both the items and the features are clustered. In essence, co-clustering combines data clustering with feature selection and can provide new insights into a data set. For data sets in which the features have a pre-defined ordering, such as a temporal (time series) or spatial ordering, it can be useful to express interval/non-interval constraints on how the features are selected by a co-clustering algorithm [14].

3   Open Questions

The large body of existing work on constrained clustering has achieved several important algorithmic advances. We have now reached the point where more fundamental issues have arisen, challenging the prevailing view that constraints are always beneficial and examining how constraints can be used for real problems, in which scalability and the user effort required to provide constraints may impose an unreasonable burden. In this section, we examine these important questions, including how the utility of a given constraint set can be quantified (Section 3.1), how we can minimize the cost of constraint acquisition (Section 3.2), and how we can propagate constraint information to nearby regions to minimize the number of constraints needed (Section 3.3).

3.1   Value: How Useful Is a Given Set of Constraints?

It is to be expected that some constraint sets will be more useful than others, in terms of the benefit they provide to a given clustering algorithm. For example, if the constraints contain information that the clustering algorithm is able to deduce on its own, then they will not provide any improvement in clustering performance. However, virtually all work to date values constraint sets only in terms of the number of constraints they contain. The ability to more accurately quantify the utility of a given constraint set, prior to clustering, will permit practitioners to decide whether to use a given constraint set, or to choose the best constraint set to use, when several are available.

The need for a constraint set utility measure has become imperative with the recent observation that some constraint sets, even when completely accurate with respect to the evaluation labels, can actually decrease clustering performance [15]. The usual practice when describing the results of constrained clustering experiments is to report the clustering performance averaged over multiple trials, where each trial consists of a set of constraints that is randomly generated from the data labels. While it is generally the case that average performance does increase as more constraints are provided, a closer examination of the individual trials reveals that some, or even many, of them instead cause a drop in accuracy. Table 2 shows the results of 1000 trials, each with a different set of 25 randomly selected constraints, conducted over four UCI data sets [5] using four different k-means-based constrained clustering algorithms. The table reports the fraction of trials in which the performance was lower than the default (unconstrained) k-means result, which ranges from 0% up to 87% of the trials.

The average performance numbers obscure this effect because the "good" trials tend to have a larger magnitude change in performance than the "bad" trials do. However, the fact that any of the constraint sets can cause a decrease in

Table 2. Fraction of 1000 randomly selected 25-constraint sets that caused a drop in accuracy, compared to an unconstrained run with the same centroid initialization (table from Davidson et al. [15])

	Algorithm			
	CKM [2]	PKM [3]	MKM [3]	MPKM [3]
	Constraint	Constraint	Metric	Enforcement and
Data Set	enforcement	enforcement	learning	metric learning
Glass	28%	1%	11%	0%
Ionosphere	26%	77%	0%	77%
Iris	29%	19%	36%	36%
Wine	38%	34%	87%	74%

performance is unintuitive, and even worrisome, since the constraints are known to be noise-free and should not lead the algorithm astray.

To better understand the reasons for this effect, Davidson et al. [15] defined two constraint set properties and provided a quantitative way to measure them. *Informativeness* is the fraction of information in the constraint set that the algorithm cannot determine on its own. *Coherence* is the amount of agreement between the constraints in the set. Constraint sets with low coherence will be difficult to completely satisfy and can lead the algorithm into unpromising areas of the search space. Both high informativeness and high coherence tend to result in an increase in clustering performance. However, these properties do not fully explain some clustering behavior. For example, a set of just three randomly selected constraints, with high informativeness and coherence, can increase clustering performance on the `iris` data set significantly, while a constraint set with similarly high values for both properties has no effect on the `ionosphere` data set. Additional work must be done to refine these measures or propose additional ones that better characterize the utility of the constraint set.

Two challenges for future progress in this area are: 1) to identify other constraint set properties that correlate with utility for constrained clustering algorithms, and 2) to learn to predict the overall utility of a new constraint set, based on extracted attributes such as these properties. It is likely that the latter will require the combination of several different constraint set properties, rather than being a single quantity, so using machine learning techniques to identify the mapping from properties to utility may be a useful approach.

3.2   Cost: How Can We Make Constraints Cheaper to Acquire?

A single pairwise constraint specifies a relationship between two data points. For a data set with n items, there are $\frac{1}{2}n(n-1)$ possible constraints. Therefore, the number of constraints needed to specify a given percentage of the relationships (say, 10%) increases quadratically with the data set size. For large data sets, the constraint specification effort can become a significant burden.

There are several ways to mitigate the cost of collecting constraints. If constraints are derived from a set of labeled items, we obtain $L(L-1)$ constraints for the cost of labeling only L items. If the constraints arise independently (not from labels), most constrained clustering algorithms can leverage constraint properties such as transitivity and entailment to deduce additional constraints automatically. A more efficient way to obtain the most useful constraints for the least effort is to permit the algorithm to actively solicit only the constraints it needs. Klein et al. [9] suggested an active constraint acquisition method in which a hierarchical clustering algorithm can identify the m best queries to issue to the oracle. Recent work has also explored constraint acquisition methods for partitional clustering based on a farthest-first traversal scheme [16] or identifying points that are most likely to lie on cluster boundaries [17]. When constraints are derived from data labels, it is also possible to use an unsupervised support vector machine (SVM) to identify "pivot points" that are most useful to label [18].

A natural next step would be to combine methods for active constraint acquisition with methods for quantifying constraint set utility. In an ideal world, we would like to request the constraint(s) which will result in the largest increase in utility for the existing constraint set. Davidson et al. [15] showed that when restricting evaluation to the most coherent constraint sets, the average performance increased for most of the data sets studied. This early result suggests that coherence, and other utility measures, could be used to guide active constraint acquisition.

Challenges in this area are: 1) to incorporate measures of constraint set utility into an active constraint selection heuristic, akin to the MaxMin heuristic for classification [19], so that the best constraint can be identified and queried prior to knowing its designation (must/cannot), and 2) to identify efficient ways to query the user for constraint information at a higher level, such as a cluster description or heuristic rule that can be propagated down to individual items to produce a batch of constraints from a single user statement.

3.3   Sharing: When and How Should Constraints Be Propagated to Neighboring Points?

Another way to get the most out of a set of constraints is to determine how they can be propagated to other nearby points. Existing methods that learn distance metrics use the constraints to "warp" the original distance metric to bring must-linked points closer together and to push cannot-linked points farther apart [9,10,8,3]. They implicitly rely on the assumption that it is "safe" to propagate constraints locally, in feature space. For example, if a must be linked to b, and the distance $dist(a, c)$ is small, then when the distance metric is warped to bring a closer to b, it is also likely that the distance $dist(b, c)$ will shrink and the algorithm will cluster b and c together as well. The performance gains that have been achieved when adapting the distance metric to the constraints are a testament to the common reliability of this assumption.

However, the assumption that proximity can be used to propagate constraints is not always a valid one. It is only reasonable if the distance in feature space is

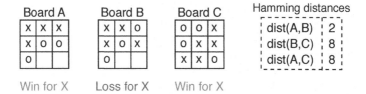

Fig. 1. Three items (endgame boards) from the `tic-tac-toe` data set. For clarity, blanks are represented as blanks, rather than spaces marked 'b'. The Hamming distances between each pair of boards are shown on the right.

consistent with the distances that are implied by the constraint set. This often holds true, since the features that are chosen to describe the data points are consistent with the data labels, which are commonly the source of the constraints. One exception is the `tic-tac-toe` data set from the UCI archive [5]. In this data set, each item is a 3x3 tic-tac-toe board that represents an end state for the game, assuming that the 'x' player played first. The boards are represented with nine features, one for each position on the board, and each one can take on a value of 'x', 'o', or 'b' (for blank). The goal is to separate the boards into two clusters: one with boards that show a win for 'x' and one with all other boards (losses and draws).

This data set is challenging because proximity in the feature space does not correlate well with similarity in terms of assigned labels. Consider the examples shown in Figure 1. Hamming distance is used with this data set, since the features have symbolic values. Boards A and B are very similar (Hamming distance of 2), but they should be joined by a cannot-link constraint. In contrast, boards A and C are very different (Hamming distance of of 8), but they should be joined by a must-link constraint. In this situation, propagating constraints to nearby (similar) items will not help improve performance (and may even degrade it).

Clustering performance on this data set is typically poor, unless a large number of constraints are available. The basic k-means algorithm achieves a Rand Index of 51%; COP-KMEANS requires 500 randomly selected constraints to increase performance to 92% [2]. COP-COBWEB is unable to increase its performance above the baseline of 49% performance, regardless of the number of constraints provided [1]. In fact, when we examine performance on a held-out subset of the data[1], it only increases to 55% for COP-KMEANS, far lower than the 92% performance on the rest of the data set. For most data sets, the held-out performance is much higher [2]. The low held-out performance indicates that the algorithm is unable to generalize the constraint information beyond the exact items that participate in constraints. This is a sign that the constraints and the features are not consistent, and that propagating constraints may be dangerous. The results of applying metric learning methods to this data set have not yet

---

[1] The data subset is "held-out" in the sense that no constraints were generated on the subset, although it was clustered along with all of the other items once the constraints were introduced.

been published, probably because the feature values are symbolic rather than real-valued. However, we expect that metric learning would be ineffective, or even damaging, in this case.

Challenges to be addressed in this area are: 1) to characterize data sets in terms of whether or not constraints should be propagated (when is it "safe" and when should the data overrule the constraints?), and 2) to determine the degree to which the constraints should be propagated (e.g., how far should the local neighborhood extend, for each constraint?). It is possible that constraint set coherence [15] could be used to help estimate the relevant neighborhood for each point.

4 Conclusions

This paper outlines several important unanswered questions that relate to the practice of constrained clustering. To use constrained clustering methods effectively, it is important that we have tools for estimating the *value* of a given constraint set prior to clustering. We also seek to minimize the *cost* of acquiring constraints. Finally, we require guidance in determining when and how to *share* or propagate constraints to their local neighborhoods. In addressing each of these subjects, we will make it possible to confidently apply constrained clustering methods to very large data sets in an efficient, principled fashion.

Acknowledgments. I would like to thank Sugato Basu and Ian Davidson for ongoing discussions on constrained clustering issues and their excellent tutorial, "Clustering with Constraints: Theory and Practice," presented at KDD 2006. The research described in this paper was funded by the NSF ITR Program (award #0325329) and was carried out at the Jet Propulsion Laboratory, California Institute of Technology, under a contract with the National Aeronautics and Space Administration.

References

1. Wagstaff, K., Cardie, C.: Clustering with instance-level constraints. In: Proceedings of the Seventeenth International Conference on Machine Learning, pp. 1103–1110 (2000)
2. Wagstaff, K., Cardie, C., Rogers, S., Schroedl, S.: Constrained k-means clustering with background knowledge. In: Proceedings of the Eighteenth International Conference on Machine Learning, pp. 577–584 (2001)
3. Bilenko, M., Basu, S., Mooney, R.J.: Integrating constraints and metric learning in semi-supervised clustering. In: Proceedings of the Twenty-First International Conference on Machine Learning, pp. 11–18 (2004)
4. Selman, B., Mitchell, D.G., Levesque, H.J.: Generating hard satisfiability problems. Artificial Intelligence 81, 17–29 (1996)
5. Blake, C.L., Merz, C.J.: UCI repository of machine learning databases (1998), http://www.ics.uci.edu/~mlearn/MLRepository.html

6. Shental, N., Bar-Hillel, A., Hertz, T., Weinshall, D.: Computing Gaussian mixture models with EM using equivalence constraints. In: Advances in Neural Information Processing Systems 16 (2004)
7. Wagstaff, K.L.: Intelligent Clustering with Instance-Level Constraints. PhD thesis, Cornell University (2002)
8. Bar-Hillel, A., Hertz, T., Shental, N., Weinshall, D.: Learning a Mahalanobis metric from equivalence constraints. Journal of Machine Learning Research 6, 937–965 (2005)
9. Klein, D., Kamvar, S.D., Manning, C.D.: From instance-level constraints to space-level constraints: Making the most of prior knowledge in data clustering. In: Proceedings of the Nineteenth International Conference on Machine Learning, pp. 307–313 (2002)
10. Xing, E.P., Ng, A.Y., Jordan, M.I., Russell, S.: Distance metric learning, with application to clustering with side-information. In: Advances in Neural Information Processing Systems 15 (2003)
11. Bradley, P.S., Bennett, K.P., Demiriz, A.: Constrained k-means clustering. Technical Report MSR-TR-2000-65, Microsoft Research, Redmond, WA (2000)
12. Tung, A.K.H., Ng, R.T., Lakshmanan, L.V.S., Han, J.: Constraint-based clustering in large databases. In: Van den Bussche, J., Vianu, V. (eds.) ICDT 2001. LNCS, vol. 1973, pp. 405–419. Springer, Heidelberg (2000)
13. Murtagh, F.: A survey of algorithms for contiguity-constrained clustering and related problems. The Computer Journal 28(1), 82–88 (1985)
14. Pensa, R.G., Robardet, C., Boulicaut, J.F.: Towards constrained co-clustering in ordered 0/1 data sets. In: Esposito, F., Raś, Z.W., Malerba, D., Semeraro, G. (eds.) ISMIS 2006. LNCS (LNAI), vol. 4203, pp. 425–434. Springer, Heidelberg (2006)
15. Davidson, I., Wagstaff, K.L., Basu, S.: Measuring constraint-set utility for partitional clustering algorithms. In: Fürnkranz, J., Scheffer, T., Spiliopoulou, M. (eds.) PKDD 2006. LNCS (LNAI), vol. 4213, pp. 115–126. Springer, Heidelberg (2006)
16. Basu, S., Banerjee, A., Mooney, R.J.: Active semi-supervision for pairwise constrained clustering. In: Proceedings of the SIAM International Conference on Data Mining, pp. 333–344 (2004)
17. Xu, Q., DesJardins, M., Wagstaff, K.L.: Active constrained clustering by examining spectral eigenvectors. In: Hoffmann, A., Motoda, H., Scheffer, T. (eds.) DS 2005. LNCS (LNAI), vol. 3735, pp. 294–307. Springer, Heidelberg (2005)
18. Xu, Q.: Active Querying for Semi-supervised Clustering. PhD thesis, University of Maryland, Baltimore County (2006)
19. Tong, S., Koller, D.: Support vector machine active learning with applications to text classification. Journal of Machine Learning Research 2, 45–66 (2002)

Mining Bi-sets in Numerical Data

Jérémy Besson[1,2], Céline Robardet[1],
Luc De Raedt[3], and Jean-François Boulicaut[1]

[1] LIRIS UMR 5205 CNRS/INSA Lyon
Bâtiment Blaise Pascal, F-69621 Villeurbanne, France
[2] UMR INRA/INSERM 1235
F-69372 Lyon cedex 08, France
[3] Albert-Ludwigs-Universitat Freiburg
Georges-Kohler-Allee, Gebaude 079 D-79110 Freiburg, Germany
celine.robardet@insa-lyon.fr

Abstract. Thanks to an important research effort the last few years, inductive queries on set patterns and complete solvers which can evaluate them on large 0/1 data sets have been proved extremely useful. However, for many application domains, the raw data is numerical (matrices of real numbers whose dimensions denote objects and properties). Therefore, using efficient 0/1 mining techniques needs for tedious Boolean property encoding phases. This is, e.g., the case, when considering microarray data mining and its impact for knowledge discovery in molecular biology. We consider the possibility to mine directly numerical data to extract collections of relevant bi-sets, i.e., couples of associated sets of objects and attributes which satisfy some user-defined constraints. Not only we propose a new pattern domain but also we introduce a complete solver for computing the so-called numerical bi-sets. Preliminary experimental validation is given.

1 Introduction

Popular data mining techniques concern 0/1 data analysis by means of set patterns (i.e., frequent sets, association rules, closed sets, formal concepts). The huge research effort of the last 10 years has given rise to efficient complete solvers, i.e., algorithms which can compute complete collections of the set patterns which satisfy user-defined constraints (e.g., minimal frequency, minimal confidence, closeness or maximality). It is however common that the considered raw data is available as matrices where we get numerical values for a collection of attributes describing a collection of objects. Therefore, using the efficient techniques in 0/1 data has to start by Boolean property encoding, i.e., the computation of Boolean values for new sets of attributes. For instance, raw microarray data can be considered as a matrix whose rows denote biological samples and columns denote genes. In that context, each cell of the matrix is a quantitative measure of the activity of a given gene in a given biological sample. Several researchers have considered how to encode Boolean gene expression properties like, e.g., gene over-expression [1,7,12,11]. In such papers, the computed Boolean matrix has the same number of attributes than the raw data but it encodes only one specific property. Given such datasets, efficient techniques like association rule mining (see, e.g., [1,7]) or formal concept discovery (see, e.g., [4]) have been considered.

Such a Boolean encoding phase is however tedious. For instance, we still lack a consensus on how the over-expression property of a gene can be specified or assessed. As a result, different views on over-expression will lead to different Boolean encoding and thus potentially quite different collections of patterns. To overcome these problems, we investigate the possibility to mine directly the numerical data to find interesting local patterns. Global pattern mining from numerical data, e.g., clustering and bi-clustering, has been extensively studied (see [10] for a survey). Heuristic search for local patterns has been studied as well (see, e.g., [2]). However, very few researchers have investigated the non heuristic, say complete, search of well-specified local patterns from numerical data. In this paper, we introduce the Numerical Bi-Sets as a new pattern domain (NBS). Intuitively, we specify collections of bi-sets, i.e., associated sets of rows and columns such that the specified cells (for each row-column pair) of the matrix contain similar values. This property is formalized in terms of constraints, and we provide a complete solver for computing NBS patterns. We start from a recent formalization of constraint-based bi-set mining from 0/1 data (extension of formal concepts towards fault-tolerance introduced in [3]) both for the design of the pattern domain and its associated solver. The next section concerns the formalization of the NBS pattern domain and its properties. Section 3 sketches our algorithm and Section 4 provides preliminary experimental results. Section 5 discusses related work and, finally, Section 6 concludes.

2   A New Pattern Domain for Numerical Data Analysis

Let us consider a set of objects $\mathcal{O}$ and a set of properties $\mathcal{P}$ such that $|\mathcal{O}| = n$ and $|\mathcal{P}| = m$. Let us denote by $\mathcal{M}$ a real valued matrix of dimension $n \times m$ such that $\mathcal{M}(i,j)$ denotes the value of property $j \in \mathcal{P}$ for the object $i \in \mathcal{O}$ (see Table 1 for an example). Our language of patterns is the language of bi-sets, i.e., couples made of a set of rows (objects) and a set of columns (properties). Intuitively, a bi-set (X, Y) with $X \in 2^{\mathcal{O}}$ and $Y \in 2^{\mathcal{P}}$ can be considered as a rectangle or sub-matrix within $\mathcal{M}$ modulo row and column permutations.

Definition 1 (NBS). *Numerical Bi-Sets (or NBS patterns) in a matrix are the bi-sets (X, Y) such that $|X| \geq 1$ and $|Y| \geq 1$ ($X \subseteq \mathcal{O}, Y \subseteq \mathcal{P}$) which satisfy the constraint $\mathcal{C}_{in} \wedge \mathcal{C}_{out}$:*

$$\mathcal{C}_{in}(X, Y) \equiv |\max_{i \in X,\, j \in Y} \mathcal{M}(i,j) - \min_{i \in X,\, j \in Y} \mathcal{M}(i,j)| \leq \epsilon$$

$$\mathcal{C}_{out}(X, Y) \equiv \forall y \in \mathcal{P} \setminus Y,\, |\max_{i \in X,\, j \in Y \cup \{y\}} \mathcal{M}(i,j) - \min_{i \in X,\, j \in Y \cup \{y\}} \mathcal{M}(i,j)| > \epsilon$$

$$\forall x \in \mathcal{O} \setminus X,\, |\max_{i \in X \cup \{x\},\, j \in Y} \mathcal{M}(i,j) - \min_{i \in X \cup \{x\},\, j \in Y} \mathcal{M}(i,j)| > \epsilon$$

where ϵ is a user-defined parameter.

Each NBS pattern defines a sub-matrix $\mathcal{S}$ of $\mathcal{M}$ such that the absolute value of the difference between the maximum value and the minimum value on $\mathcal{S}$ is less

Table 1. A real valued matrix; the bold rectangles indicate two NBS patterns

	p_1	p_2	p_3	p_4	p_5
o_1	1	2	2	1	6
o_2	2	1	1	0	6
o_3	2	2	1	7	6
o_4	8	9	2	6	7

or equal to ϵ (see $\mathcal{C}_{in}$). Furthermore, no object or property can be added to the bi-set without violating this constraint (see $\mathcal{C}_{out}$). This ensures the maximality of the specified bi-sets.

In Figure 1 (left), we can find the complete collection of NBS patterns which hold in the data from Table 1 when we have $\epsilon = 1$. In Table 1, the two bold rectangles are two examples of such NBS patterns (i.e., the underlined patterns of Figure 1 (left)). Figure 1 (right) is an alternative representation for them: each cross in the 3D-diagram corresponds to an element in the matrix from Table 1.

The search space for bi-sets can be ordered thanks to a specialization relation.

Definition 2 (Specialization and monotonicity). *Our specialization relation on bi-sets denoted $\preceq$ is defined as follows: $(\perp_O, \perp_P) \preceq (\top_O, \top_P)$ iff $\perp_O \subseteq \top_O$ and $\perp_P \subseteq \top_P$. We say that $(\top_O, \top_P)$ extends or is an extension of $(\perp_O, \perp_P)$. A constraint $\mathcal{C}$ is anti-monotonic w.r.t. $\preceq$ iff $\forall B$ and $D \in 2^O \times 2^P$ s.t. $B \preceq D$, $\mathcal{C}(D) \Rightarrow \mathcal{C}(B)$. Dually, $\mathcal{C}$ is monotonic w.r.t. $\preceq$ iff $\mathcal{C}(B) \Rightarrow \mathcal{C}(D)$.*

Assume $\mathcal{W}_\epsilon$ denotes the whole collection of NBS patterns for a given threshold ϵ. Let us now discuss some interesting properties of this new pattern domain:

- $\mathcal{C}_{in}$ and $\mathcal{C}_{out}$ are respectively anti-monotonic and monotonic w.r.t. $\preceq$ (see Property 1).
- Each NBS pattern (X, Y) from $\mathcal{W}_\epsilon$ is maximal w.r.t. $\preceq$ (see Property 2).
- If there exists a bi-set (X, Y) with similar values (belonging to an interval of size ϵ), then there exists a NBS (X', Y') from $\mathcal{W}_\epsilon$ such that $(X, Y) \preceq (X', Y')$ (see Property 3).
- When ϵ increases, the size of NBS pattern increases too, whereas some new NBS patterns which are not extensions of previous one can appear (see Property 4).
- The collection of numerical bi-sets is paving the dataset (see Corollary 1), i.e., any data item belongs to at least one NBS pattern.

Property 1 (Monotonicity). The constraint $\mathcal{C}_{in}$ is anti-monotonic and the constraint $\mathcal{C}_{out}$ is monotonic.

Proof. Let (X, Y) a bi-set s.t. $\mathcal{C}_{in}(X, Y)$ is true, and let (X', Y') be a bi-set s.t. $(X', Y') \preceq (X, Y)$. This implies that $\mathcal{C}_{in}(X', Y')$ is also true:

$$| \max_{i \in X', j \in Y'} \mathcal{M}(i, j) - \min_{i \in X', j \in Y'} \mathcal{M}(i, j)|$$
$$\leq | \max_{i \in X, j \in Y} \mathcal{M}(i, j) - \min_{i \in X, j \in Y} \mathcal{M}(i, j)| \leq \epsilon$$

$$((o_1, o_2, o_3, o_4), (p_5))$$
$$\frac{((o_3, o_4), (p_4, p_5))}{((o_4), (p_1, p_5))}$$
$$((o_1, o_2, o_3, o_4), (p_3))$$
$$((o_4), (p_1, p_2))$$
$$((o_2), (p_2, p_3, p_4))$$
$$((o_1, o_2), (p_4))$$
$$((o_1), (p_1, p_2, p_3, p_4))$$
$$((o_1, o_2, o_3), (p_1, p_2, p_3))$$

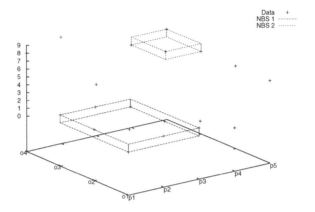

Fig. 1. Examples of NBS

If (X, Y) satisfies $\mathcal{C}_{out}$ and $(X, Y) \preceq (X', Y')$, then $\mathcal{C}_{out}(X', Y')$ is also true:

$$\forall y \in \mathcal{P} \setminus Y, \left| \max_{i \in X, \, j \in Y \cup \{y\}} \mathcal{M}(i, j) - \min_{i \in X, \, j \in Y \cup \{y\}} \mathcal{M}(i, j) \right|$$
$$> \forall y \in \mathcal{P} \setminus Y', \left| \max_{i \in X', \, j \in Y' \cup \{y\}} \mathcal{M}(i, j) - \min_{i \in X', \, j \in Y' \cup \{y\}} \mathcal{M}(i, j) \right| > \epsilon$$

Property 2 (Maximality). The NBS patterns are maximal bi-sets w.r.t. our specialization relation $\preceq$, i.e., if $(X, \bot_P)$ and $(X, \top_P)$ are two NBS patterns from $\mathcal{W}_\epsilon$, then $\bot_P \not\subseteq \top_P$ and $\top_P \not\subseteq \bot_P$.

Proof. Assume $\bot_P \subseteq \top_P$. $(X, \bot_P)$ does not satisfy Equation 2, because for $y \in \top_P \setminus \bot_P$, $|\max_{i \in X} \mathcal{M}(i, y) - \min_{i \in X} \mathcal{M}(i, y)| \leq \epsilon$.

Property 3 (NBS patterns extending bi-sets of close values). Let $I_1, I_2 \in \mathbb{R}$, $I_1 \leq I_2$, and (X, Y) be a bi-set such that $\forall i \in X$, $\forall j \in Y$, $\mathcal{M}(i, j) \in [I_1, I_2]$. Then, there exists a NBS (U, V) with $\epsilon = |I_1 - I_2|$ such that $X \subseteq U$ and $Y \subseteq V$.

Thus, if there are bi-sets of which all values are within a small range, there exists at least one NBS pattern which extends it.

Proof. V can be recursively constructed from $Y' = Y$ by adding a property y s.t. $y \in \mathcal{P} \setminus Y'$ to Y' if $|\max_{i \in X,\, j \in Y' \cup \{y\}} \mathcal{M}(i,j) - \min_{i \in X,\, j \in Y' \cup \{y\}} \mathcal{M}(i,j)| \leq \epsilon$, and then continue until no further property can be added. At the end, $Y' = V$. After that, we extend in a similar way the set X towards U. By construction, (U, V) is a NBS pattern with $\epsilon = |I_1 - I_2|$. Notice that we can have several (U, V) which extend (X, Y).

When $\epsilon = 0$, the NBS pattern collection contains all maximal bi-sets of identical values. As a result, we get a paving (with overlapping) of the whole dataset.

Property 4 (NBS pattern size is growing with ϵ). Let (X, Y) be a NBS pattern from $\mathcal{W}_\epsilon$. There exists $(X', Y') \in \mathcal{W}_{\epsilon'}$ with $\epsilon' > \epsilon$ such that $X \subseteq X'$ and $Y \subseteq Y'$.

Proof. Proof is trivial given Property 3.

Corollary 1. *As $\mathcal{W}_0$ is paving the data, then $\mathcal{W}_\epsilon$ is paving the data as well.*

3   Algorithm

The whole collection of bi-sets ordered by $\preceq$ forms a lattice whose bottom is $(\bot_O, \bot_P) = (\emptyset, \emptyset)$ and top is $(\top_O, \top_P) = (\mathcal{O}, \mathcal{P})$. Let us denote by $\mathcal{B}$ the set of sublattices[1] of $((\emptyset, \emptyset), (\mathcal{O}, \mathcal{P}))$: $\mathcal{B} = \{((\bot_O, \bot_P), (\top_O, \top_P))$ s.t. $\bot_O, \top_O \in 2^{\mathcal{O}}, \bot_P, \top_P \in 2^{\mathcal{P}}$ and $\bot_O \subseteq \top_O,\ \bot_P \subseteq \top_P\}$ where the first (resp. the second) bi-set is the bottom (resp. the top) element.

Property 5. Let $NBS_F = ((\bot_O, \bot_P), (\top_O, \top_P)) \in \mathcal{B}$, for all $(X, Y) \in NBS_F$ we have the following properties:

- $e \in \bot_O \Rightarrow e \in X$
- $e \in \bot_P \Rightarrow e \in Y$
- $e \notin \top_O \Rightarrow e \notin X$
- $e \notin \top_P \Rightarrow e \notin Y$

$NBS_F = ((\bot_O, \bot_P), (\top_O, \top_P))$ is the set of all the bi-sets (X, Y) s.t. $\bot_O \subseteq X \subseteq \top_O$ and $\bot_P \subseteq Y \subseteq \top_P$. A sublattice represents explicitly a search space for bi-sets.

Our algorithm NBS-MINER explores some of the sublattices of $\mathcal{B}$ built by means of three mechanisms: enumeration, pruning and propagation. It starts with the sublattice $((\emptyset, \emptyset), (\mathcal{O}, \mathcal{P}))$, i.e., the lattice containing all the possible bi-sets. Table 2 introduces the algorithm NBS-MINER. We now provide details about the three mecanisms.

3.1   Candidate Enumeration

The enumeration function splits recursively the current sublattice (the candidate), say NBS_F, in two new sublattices containing all the bi-sets of NBS_F.

---

[1] X is a sublattice of Y if Y is a lattice, X is a subset of Y and X is a lattice with the same join and meet operations than Y.

Property 6. Let $NBS_F = ((\bot_O, \bot_P), (\top_O, \top_P)) \in \mathcal{B}$ and $e \in \top_O \setminus \bot_O$, then $NBS_1 = ((\bot_O \cup \{e\}, \bot_P), (\top_O, \top_P))$ and $NBS_2 = ((\bot_O, \bot_P), (\top_O \setminus \{e\}, \top_P))$ is a partition of NBS_F. NBS_1 contains all the bi-sets of NBS_F which contain e and NBS_2 contains all the bi-sets of NBS_F which do not contain e. If $e \in \top_P \setminus \bot_P$, $NBS_1 = ((\bot_O, \bot_P \cup \{e\}), (\top_O, \top_P))$ and $NBS_2 = ((\bot_O, \bot_P), (\top_O, \top_P \setminus e))$ is a partition of NBS_F as well.

The enumeration function selects an element of the set $e \in \top_O \setminus \bot_P \cup \top_P \setminus \bot_P$ and its generates two new sublattices. More formally, we use the following functions *Enum* and *Choose*.

Let $Enum : \mathcal{B} \times \mathcal{O} \cup \mathcal{P} \to \mathcal{B}^2$ such that

$$Enum(((\bot_O, \bot_P), (\top_O, \top_P)), e)$$
$$= \begin{cases} (((\bot_O \cup \{e\}, \bot_P), (\top_O, \top_P)), ((\bot_O, \bot_P), (\top_O \setminus \{e\}, \top_P))) & \text{if } e \in \mathcal{O} \\ (((\bot_O, \bot_P \cup \{e\}), (\top_O, \top_P)), ((\bot_O, \bot_P), (\top_O, \top_P \setminus \{e\}))) & \text{if } e \in \mathcal{P} \end{cases}$$

where $e \in \top_O \setminus \bot_O$ or $e \in \top_P \setminus \bot_P$. *Enum* generates two new sublattices which are a partition of its input parameter.

Let $Choose : \mathcal{B} \to \mathcal{O} \cup \mathcal{P}$ be a function which returns one of the element $e \in \top_O \setminus \bot_O \cup \top_P \setminus \bot_P$.

3.2   Candidate Pruning

Obviously, we do not want to explore all the bi-sets. We want either to stop the enumeration when one can ensure that none bi-set of NBS_F is a NBS (Pruning) or to reduce the search space when a part of NBS_F can be removed witout loosing any NBS pattern (Propagation). The sublattice allows to compute bounds of any (anti-)monotonic constraints w.r.t. $\preceq$. For instance, $\mathcal{C}_{min\_area}(X, Y) \equiv \#X \times \#Y > 20$ is a monotonic constraint and $\mathcal{C}_{max\_area}(X, Y) \equiv \#X \times \#Y < 3$ is an anti-monotonic constraint, when $\#E$ denotes the size of the set E. If $NBS_F = ((\{o_1, o_3\}, \{p_1, p_2\}), (\{o_1, o_2, o_3, o_4\}, \{p_1, p_2, p_3, p_4\}))$ then none of the bi-sets of NBS_F satisfy $\mathcal{C}_{min\_area}$ and $\mathcal{C}_{max\_area}$. Actually, we have $\#\{o_1, o_3\} \times \#\{p_1, p_2\} > 3$ and $\#\{o_1, o_2, o_3, o_4\} \times \#\{p_1, p_2, p_3, p_4\} < 20$. None bi-set satisfies $\mathcal{C}_{min\_area}$ and $\mathcal{C}_{max\_area}$, whatsoever the enumeration. Intuitively, the monotonic constraints use the top of the sublattice to compute a bound whereas the anti-monotonic constraints use its bottom.

For the pruning, we use the following function:

Let $Prune_{\mathcal{C}}^m : \mathcal{B} \to \{\text{TRUE,FALSE}\}$ be a function which returns TRUE iff the monotonic constraint $\mathcal{C}^m$ (w.r.t. $\preceq$) is satisfied by the top of the sublattice.

$$Prune_{\mathcal{C}}^m((\bot_O, \bot_P), (\top_O, \top_P)) \equiv \mathcal{C}^m(\top_O, \top_P)$$

If $Prune_{\mathcal{C}}^m((\bot_O, \bot_P), (\top_O, \top_P))$ is false then none of the bi-sets contained in the sublattice satisfies $\mathcal{C}^m$.

Let $Prune_{\mathcal{C}}^{am} : \mathcal{B} \to \{\text{TRUE,FALSE}\}$ be a function which returns TRUE iff the anti-monotonic constraint $\mathcal{C}^{am}$ (w.r.t $\preceq$) is satisfied by te bottom of the sublattice:

$$Prune_{\mathcal{C}}^{am}((\bot_G, \bot_M), (\top_G, \top_M)) \equiv \mathcal{C}^{am}(\bot_G, \bot_M)$$

If $Prune_{\mathcal{C}}^{am}((\bot_O, \bot_P), (\top_O, \top_P))$ is false then none of the bi-sets contained in the sublattice satisfies $\mathcal{C}^{am}$.

Let $Prune_{\mathcal{C}_{NBS}} : \mathcal{B} \to \{\text{TRUE},\text{FALSE}\}$ be the pruning function. Due to Property 1, we have

$$Prune_{\mathcal{C}_{NBS}}((\bot_O, \bot_P), (\top_O, \top_P)) \equiv \mathcal{C}_{in}(\bot_O, \bot_P) \wedge \mathcal{C}_{out}(\top_O, \top_P)$$

When $Prune_{\mathcal{C}_{NBS}}((\bot_O, \bot_P), (\top_O, \top_P))$ is false then no NBS pattern is contained in the sublattice $((\bot_O, \bot_P), (\top_O, \top_P))$.

3.3 Propagation

The propagation plays another role. It enables to reduce the size of the search space, i.e., it does not consider the entire current sublattice NBS_F but a smaller sublattice $NBS_P \in \mathcal{B}$ such that $NBS_P \subset NBS_F$. For instance, if $((\bot_O \cup \{e_1\}, \bot_P), (\top_O, \top_P))$ and $((\bot_O, \bot_P), (\top_O, \top_P \setminus \{e_2\}))$ do not contain any NBS pattern, then we can keep going the enumeration process with $((\bot_O, \bot_P \cup \{e_2\}), (\top_O \setminus e_1, \top_P))$ instead of NBS_F. $\mathcal{C}_{in}$ and $\mathcal{C}_{out}$ can be used to reduce the size of the sublattices by moving objects of $\top_O \setminus \bot_O$ into $\bot_O$ or outside $\top_O$, and similarly on attributes. The following function is used to reduce the size of the sublattice:

The function $Prop_{in} \mathcal{B} \to \mathcal{B}$ and $Prop_{out} \mathcal{B} \to \mathcal{B}$ are used to do it as follow:

$$Prop_{in}((\bot_O, \bot_P), (\top_O, \top_P)) = \{((\bot_O^1, \bot_P^1), (\top_O, \top_P)) \in \mathcal{B} \mid$$
$$\bot_O^1 = \bot_O \cup \{x \in \top_O \setminus \bot_O \mid \mathcal{C}_{out}((\bot_O, \bot_P), (\top_O \setminus \{x\}, \top_P)) \text{ is false}\}$$
$$\bot_P^1 = \bot_P \cup \{x \in \top_P \setminus \bot_P \mid \mathcal{C}_{out}((\bot_O, \bot_P), (\top_O, \top_P \setminus \{x\})) \text{ is false}\}\}$$

$$Prop_{out}((\bot_O, \bot_P), (\top_O, \top_P)) = \{((\bot_O, \bot_P), (\top_O^1, \top_P^1)) \in \mathcal{B} \mid$$
$$\top_O^1 = \top_O \setminus \{x \in \top_O \setminus \bot_O \mid \mathcal{C}_{in}((\bot_O \cup \{x\}, \bot_P), (\top_O, \top_P)) \text{ is false}\}$$
$$\top_P^1 = \top_P \setminus \{x \in \top_P \setminus \bot_P \mid \mathcal{C}_{in}((\bot_O, \bot_P), (\top_O, \top_P \cup \{x\})) \text{ is false}\}\}$$

Let $Prop \mathcal{B} \to \mathcal{B}$ s.t. $Prop_{in}(Prop_{out}(\mathcal{L}))$ is recursively applied as long as its result changes.

We call a leaf a sublattice $\mathcal{L} = ((\bot_O, \bot_P), (\top_O, \top_P))$ which contains only one bi-set i.e., $(\bot_O, \bot_P) = (\top_O, \top_P)$. NBS are these leaves.

Example 1. Here are examples of the function $Prop$ with the data of Table 1.

- $((\bot_O, \bot_P), (\top_O, \top_P)) = ((\{o_1\}, \{p_1\}), (\{o_1, o_2, o_3, o_4\}, \{p_1, p_2, p_3, p_4, p_5\}))$
  $Prop((\bot_O, \bot_P), (\top_O, \top_P)) = ((\bot_O, \bot_P), (\top_O \setminus \{o_4\}, \top_P \setminus \{p_5\}))$
- $((\bot_O, \bot_P), (\top_O, \top_P)) = ((\{o_1, o_2\}, \{p_1\}), (\{o_1, o_2, o_3\}, \{p_1, p_2, p_3, p_4\}))$
  $Prop_{out}((\bot_O, \bot_P), (\top_O, \top_P)) = ((\bot_O, \bot_P), (\top_O, \top_P \setminus \{p_4\}))$
  $Prop_{in}((\bot_O, \bot_P), (\top_O, \top_P \setminus \{p_4\})) =$
  $((\{o_1, o_2, o_3\}, \{p_1, p_2, p_3\}), (\{o_1, o_2, o_3\}, \{p_1, p_2, p_3\}))$

Table 2. NBS-Miner pseudo-code

$\mathcal{M}$ is a real valued matrix, $\mathcal{C}$ a conjunction of monotonic
and anti-monotonic constraints on $2^{\mathcal{O}} \times 2^{\mathcal{P}}$ and ϵ is a
positive value.

NBS-Miner

  Generate$((\emptyset, \emptyset), (\mathcal{O}, \mathcal{P}))$

End NBS-Miner
Generate$(\mathcal{L})$

  Let $\mathcal{L} = ((\bot_O, \bot_P), (\top_O, \top_P))$
  $\mathcal{L} \leftarrow Prop(\mathcal{L})$
  If $Prune(\mathcal{L})$ then
    If $(\bot_O, \bot_P) \neq (\top_O, \top_P)$ then
      $(\mathcal{L}_1, \mathcal{L}_2) \leftarrow Enum(\mathcal{L}, Choose(\mathcal{L}))$
      Generate$(\mathcal{L}_1)$
      Generate$(\mathcal{L}_2)$
    Else Store $\mathcal{L}$
    End if
  End if

End Generate

4   Experiments

We report a preliminary experimental evaluation of the NBS pattern domain and
its implemented solver. We have been considering the "peaks" matrix of matlab
(30*30 matrix with values ranging between -10 and +9). We used $\epsilon = 4.5$ and we
obtained 1700 NBS patterns. On Figure 2, we plot in white one extracted NBS.
The two axes ranged from 0 to 30 correspond to the two matrix dimensions and
the third one indicates their corresponding values (row-column pairs).

In a second experiment, we enforced that the values inside the extracted
patterns to be greater than 1.95 (minimal value constraint). Figure 3 shows the
228 extracted NBS patterns when $\epsilon = 0.1$. Indeed, the white area corresponds
to the union of 228 extracted patterns.

To study the impact of ϵ parameter, we used the malaria dataset [5]. It records
the numerical gene expression value of 3 719 genes of Plasmodium falciparum
during its complete lifecycle (a time series of 46 biological situations). We used
a minimal size constraint on both dimension, i.e., looking for the NBS patterns
(X, Y) s.t. $|X| > 4$ and $|Y| > 4$. Furthermore, we have been adding a minimal
value constraint. Figure 4 provides the mean and standard deviation of the area
of the NBS patterns from this dataset w.r.t. the ϵ value.

As it was expected owed to Property 4, the mean area increases with ϵ.

Figure 5 reports on the number of NBS patterns in the malaria dataset. From
$\epsilon = 75$ to $\epsilon = 300$, this number decreases. It shows that the size of the NBS

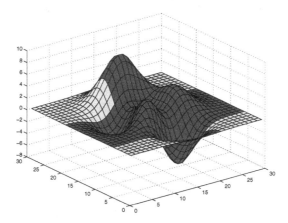

Fig. 2. An example of a NBS pattern

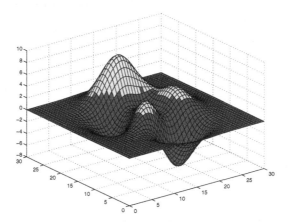

Fig. 3. Examples of extracted NBS

pattern collection tends to decrease when ϵ increases. Intuitively, many patterns are gathered when ϵ increases whereas few patterns are extended by generating more than one new pattern. Moreover, the minimal size constraint can explain the increase of the collection size. Finally, when the pattern size increases with ϵ, new NBS patterns can appear in the collection.

5   Related Work

[14,6,13] propose to extend classical frequent itemset and association rule definitions for numerical data. In [14], the authors generalize the classical notion of itemset support in 0/1 data when considering other data types, e.g., numerical ones. Support computation requires data normalization, first translating the

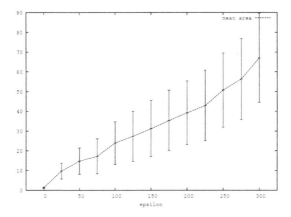

Fig. 4. Mean area of the NBS w.r.t. ϵ

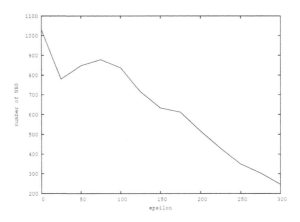

Fig. 5. Collection sizes w.r.t. ϵ

values to be positive, and then dividing each column entry by the sum of the column entries. After such a treatment, each entry is between 0 and 1, and the sum of the values for a column is equal to 1. The support of an itemset is then computed as the sum on each row of the minimum of the entries of this itemset. If the items have identical values on all the rows, then the support is equal to 1, and the more the items are different, the more the support value decreases toward 0. This support function is anti-monotonic, and thus the authors propose to adapt an APRIORI algorithm to compute the frequent itemsets according to this new support definition. [6] proposes new methods to measure the support of itemsets in numerical data and categorical data. They adapt three well-known correlation measures: KENDALL'S τ, SPEARMAN'S ρ and SPEARMAN'S FOOTRULE F. These measures are based on the rank of the values of objects for each attribute, not the values themselves. They extend these measures to sets of attributes (instead of 2 variables). Efficient algorithms are proposed. [13] uses an optimization setting for finding association rules in numerical data. The type of extracted association rules is: "if the weighted sum of some variables is greater than a threshold then a different weighted sum of variables is with high probability greater than a second threshold". They propose to use hyperplanes to represent the left-hand and the right-hand sides of such rules. Confidence and coverage measures are used. It is unclear wether it is possible to extend these approaches to bi-set computation.

Hartigan proposes a bi-clustering algorithm that can be considered as a specific collection of bi-sets [8]. He introduced a partition-based algorithm called "Block Clustering". It splits the original data matrix into bi-sets and it uses the variance of the values inside the bi-sets to evaluate the quality of each bi-set. Then, a so-called ideal constant cluster has a variance equal to zero. To avoid the partitioning of the dataset into bi-sets with only one row and one column (i.e., leading to ideal clusters), the algorithm searches for K bi-sets within the data. The quality of a collection of K bi-sets is considered as the sum of the variance of the K bi-sets. Unfortunately, this approach uses a local optimization procedure which can lead to unstable results.

In [15], the authors propose a method to isolate subspace clusters (bi-sets) containing objects varying similarly on subset of columns. They propose to compute bi-sets (X, Y) such that given $a, b \in X$ and $c, d \in Y$ the 2×2 sub-matrix entries $((a, b), (c, d))$ included in (X, Y) satisfies $|\mathcal{M}(a, c) + \mathcal{M}(b, d) - (\mathcal{M}(a, d) + \mathcal{M}(b, c))| \leq \delta$. Intuitively, this constraint enforces that the change of value on the two attributes between the two objects is confined by δ. Thus, inside the bi-sets, the values have the same profile. The algorithm first considers all pairs of objects and all pairs of attributes, and then combines them to compute all the bi-sets satisfying the anti-monotonic constraint.

Liu and Wang [9] have proposed an exhaustive bi-cluster enumeration algorithm. They are looking for order-preserving bi-sets with a minimum number of rows and a minimum number of columns. This means that for each extracted bi-set (X, Y), there exists an order on Y such that according to this order and for each element of X the values are increasing. They want to provide all the bi-clusters that, after column reordering, represent coherent evolutions of the symbols in the matrix. This is achieved by using a pattern discovery algorithm heavily inspired in sequential pattern mining algorithms. These two local pattern types are well defined and efficient solvers are proposed. Notice however that these patterns are not symmetrical: they capture similar variations on one dimension and not similar values.

Except for the bi-clustering method of [8], all these methods focus on one of the two dimensions. We have proposed to compute bi-sets with a symmetrical definition which is one of the main difficulties in bi-set mining. This is indeed one of the lessons from all the previous work on bi-set mining from 0/1 data, and, among others, the several attempts to mine fault-tolerant extensions to formal concepts instead of fault-tolerant itemsets [3].

6 Conclusion

Efficient data mining techniques tackle 0/1 data analysis by means of set patterns. It is however common, for instance in the context of gene expression data analysis, that the considered raw data is available as a collection of real numbers. Therefore, using the available algorithms needs for a beforehand Boolean property encoding. To overcome such a tedious task, we started to investigate the possibility to mine set patterns directly from the numerical data. We introduced the Numerical Bi-Sets as a new pattern domain. Some nice properties of NBS patterns have been considered. We have described our implemented solver NBS-MINER in quite generic terms, i.e., emphasizing the fundamental operations for the complete computation of NBS patterns. Notice also that other monotonic or anti-monotonic constraints can be used in conjunction with $C_{in} \wedge C_{out}$, i.e., the constraint which specifies the pattern domain. It means that search space pruning can be enhanced for mining real-life datasets provided that further user-defined constraints are given. The perspectives are obviously related to further experimental validation, especially the study of scalability issues. Furthermore, we still need for an in-depth understanding of the complementarity between NBS pattern mining and bi-set mining from 0/1 data.

Acknowledgments. This research is partially funded by the EU contract IQ FP6-516169 (FET arm of the IST programme). J. Besson is paid by INRA (ASC post-doc).

References

1. Becquet, C., Blachon, S., Jeudy, B., Boulicaut, J.-F., Gandrillon, O.: Strong-association-rule mining for large-scale gene-expression data analysis: a case study on human sage data. Genome Biology, 12 (November 2002)
2. Bergmann, S., Ihmels, J., Barkai, N.: Iterative signature algorithm for the analysis of large-scale gene expression data. Physical Review 67 (March 2003)
3. Besson, J., Pensa, R., Robardet, C., Boulicaut, J.-F.: Constraint-based mining of fault-tolerant patterns from boolean data. In: Bonchi, F., Boulicaut, J.-F. (eds.) KDID 2005. LNCS, vol. 3933, pp. 55–71. Springer, Heidelberg (2006)
4. Besson, J., Robardet, C., Boulicaut, J.-F., Rome, S.: Constraint-based concept mining and its application to microarray data analysis. Intelligent Data Analysis 9(1), 59–82 (2005)
5. Bozdech, Z., Llinás, M., Pulliam, B., Wong, E., Zhu, J., DeRisi, J.: The transcriptome of the intraerythrocytic developmental cycle of plasmodium falciparum. PLoS Biology 1(1), 1–16 (2003)
6. Calders, T., Goethals, B., Jaroszewicz, S.: Mining rank correlated sets of numerical attributes. In: Proceedings ACM SIGKDD 2006, Philadelphia, USA, August 2006, pp. 96–105 (2006)
7. Creighton, C., Hanash, S.: Mining gene expression databases for association rules. Bioinformatics 19(1), 79–86 (2002)
8. Hartigan, J.: Direct clustering of data matrix. Journal of the American Statistical Association 67(337), 123–129 (1972)

9. Liu, J., Wang, W.: Op-cluster: Clustering by tendency in high dimensional space. In: Proceedings IEEE ICDM'03, Melbourne, USA, December 2003, pp. 187–194 (2003)
10. Madeira, S.C., Oliveira, A.L.: Biclustering algorithms for biological data analysis: A survey. ACM/IEEE Trans. on computational biology and bioinformatics 1(1), 24–45 (2004)
11. Pensa, R., Boulicaut, J.-F.: Boolean property encoding for local set pattern discovery: an application to gene expression data analysis. In: Morik, K., Boulicaut, J.-F., Siebes, A. (eds.) Local Pattern Detection. LNCS (LNAI), vol. 3539, pp. 114–134. Springer, Heidelberg (2005)
12. Pensa, R.G., Leschi, C., Besson, J., Boulicaut, J.-F.: Assessment of discretization techniques for relevant pattern discovery from gene expression data. In: Proceedings ACM BIOKDD 2004, Seattle, USA, August 2004, pp. 24–30 (2004)
13. Ruckert, U., Richter, L., Kramer, S.: Quantitative association rules based on half-spaces: An optimization approach. In: Proceedings IEEE ICDM 2004, November 2004, pp. 507–510, Brighton, UK (2004)
14. Steinbach, M., Tan, P.-N., Xiong, H., Kumar, V.: Generalizing the notion of support. In: Proceedings ACM SIGKDD 2004, Seatle, USA, pp. 689–694 (2004)
15. Wang, H., Wang, W., Yang, J., Yu, P.S.: Clustering by pattern similarity in large data sets. In: Proceedings ACM SIGMOD 2002, Madison, USA, June 2002, pp. 394–405 (2002)

Extending the Soft Constraint Based Mining Paradigm

Stefano Bistarelli[1,2] and Francesco Bonchi[3]

[1] Dipartimento di Scienze, Università degli Studi "G. D'Annunzio", Pescara, Italy
[2] Istituto di Informatica e Telematica, CNR, Pisa, Italy
[3] Pisa KDD Laboratory, ISTI - C.N.R., Pisa, Italy
bista@sci.unich.it, francesco.bonchi@isti.cnr.it

Abstract. The paradigm of pattern discovery based on constraints has been recognized as a core technique in inductive querying: constraints provide to the user a tool to drive the discovery process towards potentially *interesting* patterns, with the positive side effect of achieving a more efficient computation. So far the research on this paradigm has mainly focussed on the latter aspect: the development of efficient algorithms for the evaluation of constraint-based mining queries. Due to the lack of research on methodological issues, the constraint-based pattern mining framework still suffers from many problems which limit its practical relevance. In our previous work [5], we analyzed such limitations and showed how they flow out from the same source: the fact that in the classical constraint-based mining, a constraint is a rigid boolean function which returns either *true* or *false*. To overcome such limitations we introduced the new paradigm of pattern discovery based on *Soft Constraints*, and instantiated our idea to the fuzzy soft constraints. In this paper we extend the framework to deal with probabilistic and weighted soft constraints: we provide theoretical basis and detailed experimental analysis. We also discuss a straightforward solution to deal with *top-k* queries. Finally we show how the ideas presented in this paper have been implemented in a real Inductive Database system.

1 Introduction

The paradigm of pattern discovery based on constraints was introduced with the aim of providing to the user a tool to drive the discovery process towards potentially *interesting* patterns, with the positive side effect of achieving a more efficient computation. So far the research on this paradigm has mainly focused on the latter aspect: the study of constraint properties and, on the basis of these properties, the development of efficient algorithms for the evaluation of constraint-based mining queries. Despite such algorithmic research effort, and regardless some successful applications, e.g., in medical domains [13,18], or in biological domains [4], the constraint-based pattern mining framework still suffers from many problems which limit its practical relevance. In our previous work [5], we analyzed such limitations and showed how they flow out from the

S. Džeroski and J. Struyf (Eds.): KDID 2006, LNCS 4747, pp. 24–41, 2007.

same source: the fact that in the classical constraint-based mining, a constraint is a rigid boolean function which returns either *true* or *false*. Indeed, interestingness is not a dichotomy. Following this consideration, we introduced in [5] the new paradigm of pattern discovery based on *Soft Constraints*, where constraints are no longer rigid boolean functions. In particular we adopted a definition of soft constraints based on the mathematical concept of *semiring*. Albeit based on a simple idea, our proposal has the merit of providing a rigorous theoretical framework, which is very general (having the classical paradigm as a particular instance), and which overcomes all the major methodological drawbacks of the classical constraint-based paradigm, representing a step further towards practical pattern discovery.

While in our previous paper we instantiated the framework to the *fuzzy* semiring, in this paper we extend the framework to deal with the *probabilistic* and the *weighted* semirings: these different constraints instances can be used to model different situations, depending on the application at hand. We provide the formal problem definition and the theoretical basis to develop concrete solvers for the mining problems we defined. In particular, we will show how to build a concrete *soft-constraint based pattern discovery system*, by means of a set of appropriate wrappers around a crisp constraint pattern mining system. The mining system for classical constraint-based pattern discover that we adopted is CONQUEST, a system which we have developed at Pisa KDD Laboratory [8]. Such a system is based on a mining engine which is a general Apriori-like algorithm which, by means of *data reduction* and *search space pruning*, is able to push a wide variety of constraints (practically all possible kinds of constraints which have been studied and characterized) into the frequent itemsets computation. Finally, we discuss how to answer to *top-k* queries.

2   Soft Constraint Based Pattern Mining

Classical constraint (or crisp constraints) are used to discriminate admissible and/or non-admissible values for a specific (set of) variable. However, sometimes this discrimination does not help to select a set of assignments for the variable (consider for instance overconstrained problems, or not discriminating enough constraints). In this case is preferable to use soft constraints where a specific cost/preference is assigned to each variable assignments and the best solution is selected by looking for the less expensive/more preferable complete assignment.

Several formalizations of the concept of soft constraints are currently available. In the following, we refer to the formalization based on *c-semirings* [7]. Using this framework, classical/crisp constraints are represented by using the boolean *true* and *false* representing the admissible and/or non-admissible values; when cost or preference are used, the values are instead instantiations over a partial order set (for instance, the reals, or the interval [0,1]).

Moreover the formalism must provide suitable operations for combination ($\times$) of constraints satisfaction level, and comparison ($+$) of patterns under a combination of constraints. This is why this formalization is based on the mathematical concept of semiring.

Definition 1 (c-semirings [7]). *A semiring is a tuple* $\langle A, +, \times, \mathbf{0}, \mathbf{1} \rangle$ *such that:* *A is a set and* $\mathbf{0}, \mathbf{1} \in A$; $+$ *is commutative, associative and* $\mathbf{0}$ *is its unit element;* $\times$ *is associative, distributes over* $+$, $\mathbf{1}$ *is its unit element and* $\mathbf{0}$ *is its absorbing element. A c-semiring ("c" stands for "constraint-based") is a semiring* $\langle A, +, \times, \mathbf{0}, \mathbf{1} \rangle$ *such that* $+$ *is idempotent with* $\mathbf{1}$ *as its absorbing element and* $\times$ *is commutative.*

Definition 2 (soft constraint on c-semiring [7]). *Given a c-semiring* $S = \langle A, +, \times, \mathbf{0}, \mathbf{1} \rangle$ *and an ordered set of variables* V *over a finite domain* D, *a constraint is a function which, given an assignment* $\eta : V \to D$ *of the variables, returns a value of the c-semiring. By using this notation we define* $\mathcal{C} = \eta \to A$ *as the set of all possible constraints that can be built starting from* S, D *and* V.

In the following we will always use the word semiring as standing for c-semiring.

Example 1. The following example illustrates the definition of soft constraints based on semiring, using the example mining query:

$$\mathcal{Q}: \ supp_{\mathcal{D}}(X) \geq 1500 \ \wedge \ avg(X.weight) \leq 5 \ \wedge \ sum(X.price) \geq 20$$

which requires to mine, from database $\mathcal{D}$, all patterns which are frequent (have a support at least 1500), have average weight at most 5 and a sum of prices at least 20. In this context, we have that the ordered set of variables V is $\langle supp_{\mathcal{D}}(X), avg(X.weight), sum(X.price) \rangle$; the domain D is: $D(supp_{\mathcal{D}}(X)) = \mathbb{N}$, $D(avg(X.weight)) = \mathbb{R}^+$, and $D(sum(X.price)) = \mathbb{N}$. If we consider the classical crisp framework (i.e., hard constraints) we are on the boolean semiring: $S_{Bool} = \langle \{true, false\}, \vee, \wedge, false, true \rangle$. A soft constraint C is a function $V \to D \to A$; e.g., $supp_{\mathcal{D}}(X) \to 1700 \to true$.

The $+$ operator is what we use to compare the level of constraints satisfaction for various patterns. Let us consider the relation $\leq_S$ (where S stands for the specified semiring) over A such that $a \leq_S b$ iff $a + b = b$. It is possible to prove that: $\leq_S$ is a partial order; $+$ and $\times$ are monotone on $\leq_S$; $\mathbf{0}$ is its minimum and $\mathbf{1}$ its maximum, and $\langle A, \leq_S \rangle$ is a complete lattice with least upper bound operator $+$. In the context of pattern discovery $a \leq_S b$ means that the pattern b is *more interesting* than a, where interestingness is defined by a combination of soft constraints. When using (soft) constraints it is necessary to specify, via suitable combination operators, how the level of interest of a combination of constraints is obtained from the interest level of each constraint. The combined weight (or interest) of a combination of constraints is computed by using the operator $\otimes : \mathcal{C} \times \mathcal{C} \to \mathcal{C}$ defined as $(C_1 \otimes C_2)\eta = C_1\eta \times_S C_2\eta$.

Example 2. In this example, and in the rest of the paper, we use for the patterns the notation $p : \langle v_1, v_2, v_3 \rangle$, where p is an itemset, and $\langle v_1, v_2, v_3 \rangle$ denote the three values $\langle supp_{\mathcal{D}}(p), avg(p.weight), sum(p.price) \rangle$ corresponding to the three constraints in the conjunction in the query $\mathcal{Q}$ of Example 1. Consider, for instance, the following three patterns: $p_1 : \langle 1700, 0.8, 19 \rangle$, $p_2 : \langle 1550, 4.8, 54 \rangle$, $p_3 :$

$\langle 1550, 2.2, 26 \rangle$. If we adopt the classical crisp framework, in the mining query $\mathcal{Q}$ we have to combine the three constraints using the $\wedge$ operator (which is the $\times$ in the boolean semiring S_{Bool}). Consider for instance the pattern $p_1 : \langle 1700, 0.8, 19 \rangle$ for the ordered set of variables $V = \langle supp_\mathcal{D}(X), avg(X.weight), sum(X.price) \rangle$. The first and the second constraint are satisfied leading to the semiring level *true*, while the third one is not satisfied and has associated level *false*. Combining the three values with $\wedge$ we obtain *true* $\wedge$ *true* $\wedge$ *false* $=$ *false* and we can conclude that the pattern $\langle 1700, 0.8, 19 \rangle$ is not interesting w.r.t. our purposes. Similarly, we can instead compute level *true* for pattern $p_3 : \langle 1550, 2.2, 26 \rangle$ corresponding to an interest w.r.t. our goals.

However, dividing patterns in *interesting* and *non-interesting* is sometimes not meaningful nor useful. Most of the times we want to say that each pattern is interesting with a specific level of preference. This idea is at the basis of the soft constraint based pattern mining paradigm [5].

Definition 3 (Soft Constraint Based Pattern Mining). *Let $\mathcal{P}$ denote the domain of possible patterns. A soft constraint on patterns is a function $\mathcal{C} : \mathcal{P} \to A$ where A is the carrier set of a semiring $S = \langle A, +, \times, \mathbf{0}, \mathbf{1} \rangle$. Given a combination of soft constraints $\otimes \mathcal{C}$, i.e., a description of what is considered by the user an interesting pattern, we define two different problems:*

λ-**interesting:** *given a minimum interest threshold $\lambda \in A$, it is required to mine the set of all λ-interesting patterns, i.e., $\{p \in \mathcal{P}| \otimes \mathcal{C}(p) \geq_S \lambda\}$.*

top-k: *given a threshold $k \in \mathbb{N}$, it is required to mine the top-k patterns $p \in \mathcal{P}$ w.r.t. the order $\leq_S$.*

In the rest of the paper we adopt the notation $int_S^\mathcal{P}(\lambda)$ to denote the problem of mining λ-interesting patterns (from pattern domain $\mathcal{P}$) on the semiring S, and similarly $top_S^\mathcal{P}(k)$, for the corresponding top-k mining problem. Note that the Soft Constraint Based Pattern Mining paradigm just defined, has many degrees of freedom. In particular, it can be instantiated:

1. on the domain of patterns $\mathcal{P}$ in analysis (e.g., itemsets, sequences, trees or graphs),
2. on the semiring $S = \langle A, +, \times, \mathbf{0}, \mathbf{1} \rangle$ (e.g., boolean, fuzzy, weighted or probabilistic), and
3. on one of the two possible mining problems, i.e., λ-interesting or top-k mining.

In other terms, by means of Definition 3, we have defined many different mining problems: it is worth noting that the classical constraint based frequent itemsets mining, is just a particular instance of our framework. In particular, it corresponds to the mining of λ-interesting itemsets on the boolean semiring, where $\lambda = true$, i.e., $int_b^\mathcal{I}(true)$. In our previous paper [5] we have shown how to deal with the mining problem $int_f^\mathcal{I}(\lambda)$ (i.e., λ-interesting Itemsets on the Fuzzy Semiring), in this paper we show how to extend our framework to deal with (*i*) $int_p^\mathcal{I}(\lambda)$ (i.e., λ-interesting Itemsets on the Probabilistic Semiring), (*ii*) $int_w^\mathcal{I}(\lambda)$

(i.e., λ-interesting Itemsets on the Weighted Semiring), and (iii) mining top-k itemsets on any semiring.

The methodology we adopt is based on the property that in a c-semiring $S = \langle A, +, \times, \mathbf{0}, \mathbf{1} \rangle$ the $\times$-operator is *extensive* [7], i.e, $a \times b \leq_S a$ for all $a, b \in A$. Thanks to this property, we can easily prune away some patterns from the set of possibly interesting ones. In particular this result directly applies when we want to solve a λ-interesting problem. In fact for any semiring (fuzzy, weighted, probabilistic) we have that [7]:

Proposition 1. *Given a combination of soft constraints $\otimes \mathcal{C} = C_1 \otimes \ldots \otimes C_n$ based on a semiring S, for any pattern $p \in \mathcal{P}$:*

$$\otimes \mathcal{C}(p) \geq_S \lambda \Rightarrow \forall i \in \{1, \ldots, n\} : C_i(p) \geq_S \lambda.$$

Proof. Straightforward from the extensivity of $\times$.

Therefore, computing all the λ-interesting patterns can be done by solving a crisp problem where all the constraint instances with semiring level lower than λ have been assigned level *false*, and all the instances with semiring level greater or equal to λ have been assigned level *true*. In fact, if a pattern does not satisfy such conjunction of crisp constraints, it will not be neither interesting w.r.t. the soft constraints. Using this theoretical result, and some simple arithmetic we can transform each soft constraint in a corresponding crisp constraint, push the crisp constraint in the mining computation to prune uninteresting patterns, and when needed, post-process the solution of the crisp problem, to remove uninteresting patterns from it.

3   Mining $int_p^{\mathcal{I}}(\lambda)$ (λ-Interesting Itemsets on the Probabilistic Semiring)

Probabilistic CSPs (Prob-CSPs) were introduced to model those situations where each constraint c has a certain probability $p(c)$, independent from the probability of the other constraints, to be part of the given problem (actually, the probability is not of the constraint, but of the situation which corresponds to the constraint: saying that c has probability p means that the situation corresponding to c has probability p of occurring in the real-life problem). Using the probabilistic constraints framework [14] we suppose each constraint to have an independent probability law, and combination is computed performing the product of the semiring value of each constraint instantiations. As a result, the semiring corresponding to the probabilistic framework is $S_P = \langle [0, 1], max, \times, 0, 1 \rangle$.

Consider the constraints graphical representations in Figure 1, where the semiring values between 0 and 1 are this time interpreted as probabilities. In this situation for the pattern $p_1 = \langle 1700, 0.8, 19 \rangle$ we obtain that: $C_1(p_1) = 0.83$, $C_2(p_1) = 1$ and $C_3(p_1) = 0.45$. Since in the probabilistic semiring the combination operator $\times$ is the arithmetic multiplication, we got that the interest level of p_1 is 0.37. Similarly for p_2 and p_3:

- $p_1 : C_1 \otimes C_2 \otimes C_3(1700, 0.8, 19) = \times(0.83, 1, 0.45) = 0.37$
- $p_2 : C_1 \otimes C_2 \otimes C_3(1550, 4.8, 54) = \times(0.58, 0.6, 1) = 0.35$
- $p_3 : C_1 \otimes C_2 \otimes C_3(1550, 2.2, 26) = \times(0.58, 1, 0.8) = 0.46$

Therefore, with this particular instance we got that $p_2 <_{S_P} p_1 <_{S_P} p_3$, i.e., p_3 is the most interesting pattern among the three. Dealing with the probabilistic semiring, we can readapt most of the framework developed for the fuzzy semiring. In fact the two semirings are based on the same set $[0, 1]$ and on the same $+$ operator which is *max*. The only distinguishing element is the $\times$ operator which is *min* for the fuzzy semiring, while it is the arithmetic *times* for the probabilistic semiring. This means that we can straightforwardly readapt the problem definition, the way of defining the behaviour of soft constraints, and the *crisp translation*.

Definition 4. *Let $\mathcal{I} = \{x_1, ..., x_n\}$ be a set of items, where an item is an object with some predefined attributes (e.g., price, type, etc.). A soft constraint on itemsets, based on the probabilistic semiring, is a function $\mathcal{C} : 2^{\mathcal{I}} \rightarrow [0, 1]$. Given a combination of such soft constraints $\otimes \mathcal{C} \equiv \mathcal{C}_1 \otimes ... \otimes \mathcal{C}_n$, we define the interest level of an itemset $X \in 2^{\mathcal{I}}$ as $\otimes \mathcal{C}(X) = \mathcal{C}_1(X) \times \cdots \times \mathcal{C}_n(X)$. Given a minimum interest threshold $\lambda \in]0, 1]$, the λ-interesting itemsets mining problem, requires to compute $int_p^{\mathcal{I}}(\lambda) = \{X \in 2^{\mathcal{I}} | \otimes \mathcal{C}(X) \geq \lambda\}$.*

Definition 5. *A soft constraint $\mathcal{C}$ on itemsets, based on the probabilistic semiring, is defined by a quintuple $\langle Agg, Att, \theta, t, \alpha \rangle$, where:*

- *$Agg \in \{supp, min, max, count, sum, range, avg, var, median, std, md\}$;*
- *Att is the name of the attribute on which the aggregate agg is computed (or the transaction database, in the case of the frequency constraint);*
- *$\theta \in \{\leq, \geq\}$;*
- *$t \in \mathbb{R}$ corresponds to the center of the interval and it is associated to the semiring value 0.5;*
- *$\alpha \in \mathbb{R}^+$ is the softness parameter, which defines the inclination of the preference function (and thus the width of the interval).*

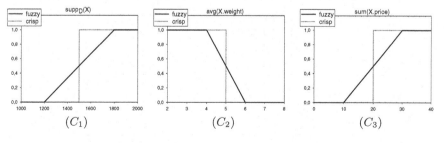

Fig. 1. Graphical representation of possible probabilistic instance of the constraints in the mining query $\mathcal{Q}$ in Example 1

In particular, if $\theta = \leq$ (as in Figure 1(C_2)) then $C(X)$ is 1 for $X \leq (t - \alpha t)$, is 0 for $X \geq (t + \alpha t)$, and is linearly decreasing from 1 to 0 within the interval $[t - \alpha t, t + \alpha t]$. The other way around if $\theta = \geq$ (as, for instance, in Figure 1(C_3)). Note that if the softness parameter α is 0, then we obtain the crisp (or hard) version of the constraint.

Example 3. Consider again the query $\mathcal{Q}$ given in Example 1, and its probabilistic instance graphically described by Figure 1. Such query can be expressed in our constraint language as:

$$\langle supp, \mathcal{D}, \geq, 1500, 0.2 \rangle, \langle avg, weight, \leq, 5, 0.2 \rangle, \langle sum, price, \geq, 20, 0.5 \rangle$$

Definition 6. *Given a probabilistic soft constraint $C \equiv \langle Agg, Att, \theta, t, \alpha \rangle$, and a minimum interest threshold λ, we define the crisp translation of C w.r.t. λ as:*

$$C_{crisp}^\lambda \equiv \begin{cases} Agg(Att) \geq t - \alpha t + 2\lambda \alpha t, & \text{if } \theta = \geq \\ Agg(Att) \leq t + \alpha t - 2\lambda \alpha t, & \text{if } \theta = \leq \end{cases}$$

In [5] we proved that, on the fuzzy semiring, given a combination of soft constraints $\otimes C \equiv C_1 \otimes \ldots \otimes C_n$, and a minimum interest threshold λ, if we consider the conjunction of crisp constraints obtained by conjoining the crisp translation of each constraint in $\otimes C$ w.r.t. λ (i.e., $C' \equiv C_{1crisp}^\lambda \wedge \ldots \wedge C_{ncrisp}^\lambda$), it holds that

$$int_f^{\mathcal{I}}(\lambda) = \{X \in 2^{\mathcal{I}} \mid \otimes C(X) \geq \lambda\} = Th(C')$$

Similarly, the following property holds:

Proposition 2. *Given the vocabulary of items $\mathcal{I}$, a combination of soft constraints $\otimes C \equiv C1 \otimes \ldots \otimes Cn$, and a minimum interest threshold λ. It holds that:*

$$int_p^{\mathcal{I}}(\lambda) \subseteq int_f^{\mathcal{I}}(\lambda)$$

Proof. Consider two real numbers x_1, x_2 in the interval $[0,1]$. It holds that $x_1 \times x_2 \leq min(x_1, x_2)$. Therefore, for a given pattern i, if in the probabilistic semiring $\otimes C(i) \geq_p \lambda$, then also in the fuzzy semiring $\otimes C(i) \geq_f \lambda$.

		$\langle supp, \mathcal{D}, \geq, t, \alpha \rangle$		$\langle avg, weight, \leq, t, \alpha \rangle$		$\langle sum, price, \geq, t, \alpha \rangle$	
	$\mathcal{D}$	t	α	t	α	t	α
$\mathcal{Q}_1$	RETAIL	20	0.8	10000	0.5	20000	0.5
$\mathcal{Q}_2$	RETAIL	20	0.5	10000	0.5	20000	0.5
$\mathcal{Q}_3$	RETAIL	20	0.2	10000	0.5	20000	0.5
$\mathcal{Q}_4$	RETAIL	20	0.8	5000	0.2	20000	0.5
$\mathcal{Q}_5$	RETAIL	20	0.8	5000	0.8	20000	0.5
$\mathcal{Q}_6$	T40I10D100K	800	0.75	15000	0.2	100000	0.5
$\mathcal{Q}_7$	T40I10D100K	800	0.75	15000	0.9	100000	0.5
$\mathcal{Q}_8$	T40I10D100K	800	0.25	15000	0.2	100000	0.2

Fig. 2. Description of queries experimented

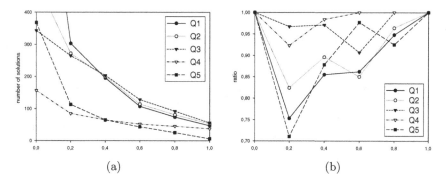

Fig. 3. Experimental results on the RETAIL dataset with λ ranging in $]0, 1]$ in the probabilistic semiring: number of solutions (a), and ratio with the number of solutions in the fuzzy semiring (b)

When dealing with the probabilistic semiring, we translate the given query to a crisp one. But afterwards, we need a post-processing step in which we select, among the solutions to the crisp query, the λ-interesting patterns. It is natural to ask ourselves how much selective is this post-processing. This could provide a measure of the kind of improvement that one could get by studying and developing ad-hoc techniques, to push probabilistic soft constraints into the pattern extraction computation.

In Figure 3, for the RETAIL dataset and the queries of Figure 2, we report: in (a), the number of λ-interesting patterns in the probabilistic semiring, while in (b) the ratio of this number with the number of solutions in the fuzzy semiring, i.e., $|int_p^{\mathcal{I}}(\lambda)| \,/\, |int_f^{\mathcal{I}}(\lambda)|$. The execution time of the post-processing is not reported in the plots, because in all the experiments conducted, it was always in the order of few milliseconds, thus negligible w.r.t. the mining time. Observing the ratio we can note that it is always equals to 1 for $\lambda = 0$ and $\lambda = 1$. In fact a pattern having at least a constraint for which it returns 0, will receive a semiring value of 0 in both the fuzzy semiring (min combination operator), and the probabilistic semiring ($\times$ combination operator). Similarly, for $\lambda = 1$, to be a solution a pattern must return a value of 1 for all the constraints in the combination, in both the semirings. Then we can observe that this ratio is quite high, always larger than 0.7 in the RETAIL dataset. This is no longer true for the queries on the T40I10D100K dataset, reported in Figure 4 (a) and (b): the ratio reach a minimum value of 0.244 for query $\mathcal{Q}_7$ when $\lambda = 0.2$.

What we can observe is that the ratio does not depend neither on the number of solutions nor on λ (apart the extreme cases 0 and 1). The ratio depends on the softness of the query: the softer the query the lower the ratio, i.e., more patterns discarded by the post-processing. This can be observed in both Figure 3(b) and 4(b): for instance, among the first three queries $\mathcal{Q}_1$ is softer than $\mathcal{Q}_2$ which in turns is softer than $\mathcal{Q}_3$, and this is reflected in the ratio

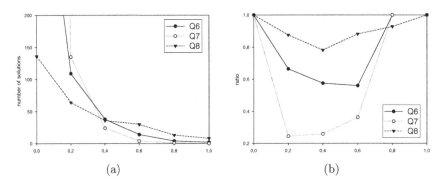

Fig. 4. Experimental results on the T40I10D100K dataset with λ ranging in $]0, 1]$ in the probabilistic semiring: number of solutions (a), and ratio with the number of solutions in the fuzzy semiring (b)

which is lower for $\mathcal{Q}_1$; similarly $\mathcal{Q}_5$ is softer than $\mathcal{Q}_4$ and its ratio is lower; in 4(b) $\mathcal{Q}_8$ is the least soft while $\mathcal{Q}_7$ is the most soft, and accordingly behaves the ratio.

4 Mining $int_w^{\mathcal{I}}(\lambda)$ (λ-Interesting Itemsets on the Weighted Semiring)

While in the fuzzy semiring each pattern has an associated level of preference (or interestingness) for each constraint, and in the probabilistic semiring a value which represents a probability, in the weighted semiring they have an associated cost. Therefore, in the weighted semiring the cost function is defined by summing up the costs of all constraints. According to the informal description given above, the weighted semiring is $S_W = \langle \mathbb{R}^+, min, sum, +\infty, 0 \rangle$.

Example 4. Consider the following weighted instance for the constraints in the query $\mathcal{Q}$ (graphically represented in Figure 5):

- $C_1(supp_{\mathcal{D}}(X)) = \begin{cases} 1750 - supp_{\mathcal{D}}(X), & \text{if } supp_{\mathcal{D}}(X) < 1750 \\ 0, & otherwise. \end{cases}$

- $C_2(avg(X.weight)) = 25 * avg(X.weight)$

- $C_3(sum(X.price)) = \begin{cases} 5 * (60 - sum(X.price)), & \text{if } sum(X.price) < 60 \\ 0, & otherwise. \end{cases}$

Note how the soft version of the constraints are defined in the weighted framework: C_1 for instance, since bigger support is better, gives a cost of 0 when the support is greater than 1750 and an increasing cost as the support decreases. Similarly for constraint C_3: we assign a cost 0 when the sum of prices is at least 60, while the cost increases linearly as the sum of prices shrinks. Constraint C_2

instead aims to have an average weight as lower as possible, and thus larger average weight will produce larger (worse) cost. In this situation we got that:

- $p_1 : C_1 \otimes C_2 \otimes C_3(1700, 0.8, 19) = sum(50, 20, 205) = 275$
- $p_2 : C_1 \otimes C_2 \otimes C_3(1550, 4.8, 54) = sum(200, 120, 30) = 350$
- $p_3 : C_1 \otimes C_2 \otimes C_3(1550, 2.2, 26) = sum(200, 55, 170) = 425$

Therefore, with this particular instance we got that $p_3 <_{S_W} p_2 <_{S_W} p_1$ (remember that the order $\leq_{S_W}$ correspond to the $\geq$ on real numbers). In other terms, p_1 is the most interesting pattern w.r.t. this constraints instance.

Since in the weighted semiring, the values correspond to costs, instead of looking for patterns with an interest level larger than λ, we seek for patterns with a cost smaller than λ.

Definition 7. *Let $\mathcal{I} = \{x_1, ..., x_n\}$ be a set of items, where an item is an object with some predefined attributes (e.g., price, type, etc.). A soft constraint on itemsets, based on the weighted semiring, is a function $\mathcal{C} : 2^\mathcal{I} \rightarrow \mathbb{R}^+$. Given a combination of such soft constraints $\otimes \mathcal{C} \equiv \mathcal{C}_1 \otimes ... \otimes \mathcal{C}_n$, we define the interest level of an itemset $X \in 2^\mathcal{I}$ as $\otimes \mathcal{C}(X) = \sum_{i=1,...,n} \mathcal{C}_i(X)$. Given a maximum cost threshold $\lambda \in \mathbb{R}^+$, the λ-interesting itemsets mining problem, requires to compute $int_w^\mathcal{I}(\lambda) = \{X \in 2^\mathcal{I} | \otimes \mathcal{C}(X) \leq \lambda\}$.*

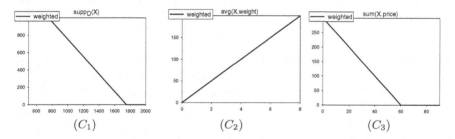

(C_1) (C_2) (C_3)

Fig. 5. Graphical representation of possible weighted instances of the constraints in in the mining query $\mathcal{Q}$ in Example 1

For sake of simplicity, we restrict to weighted constraints with a linear behavior as those ones described in Figure 5. To describe such simple behavior, we need a new parameter $\beta \in \mathbb{R}^+$ that represents the semiring value associated to the t point (playing the role of the implicitly given 0.5 value for the fuzzy and probabilistic semiring). In other words we provide two points to describe the straight line passing through them: the point (t, β) and the point $(t - \alpha t, 0)$ for $\theta =\leq$ or $(t + \alpha t, 0)$ for $\theta =\geq$. Note that α still plays the role of the softness knob.

Definition 8. *A soft constraint $\mathcal{C}$ on itemsets, based on the weighted semiring, is defined by a sextuple $\langle Agg, Att, \theta, t, \beta, \alpha \rangle$, where: Agg, Att, θ and α are defined as for the fuzzy/probabilistic case (Definition 5), t is a point in the carrier set of the weighted semiring, i.e., $t \in \mathbb{R}^+$, and β represents the semiring value associated to t.*

Example 5. Consider again the query $\mathcal{Q}$ given in Example 1, and its weighted instance graphically described by Figure 5. Such query can be expressed in our constraint language as:

$$\langle supp, \mathcal{D}, \geq, 1500, 250, \frac{1}{6} \rangle, \langle avg, weight, \leq, 5, 125, 1 \rangle, \langle sum, price, \geq, 20, 200, 1 \rangle$$

For the weighted semiring we can still rely on Proposition 1, which states that a pattern in order to be λ-interesting, must return a semiring value smaller than λ (we are dealing this time with costs; i.e., $\geq_W$ is $\leq$) for each single constraint in the query: this assures us that if a pattern does not satisfy the crisp translation of the given query, it will not be λ-interesting neither in the weighted semiring. In other words we can always use the same methodology described for the probabilistic semiring: translate the query to a crisp one, evaluate it, post-process the result to select the exact solution set.

Definition 9. *Given a weighted soft constraint $C \equiv \langle Agg, Att, \theta, t, \beta, \alpha \rangle$, and a maximum cost threshold λ, we define the crisp translation of C w.r.t. λ as:*

$$C_{crisp}^{\lambda} \equiv \begin{cases} Agg(Att) \leq t - \alpha t + \frac{1}{\beta}\lambda\alpha t, & \text{if } \theta = \leq \\ Agg(Att) \geq t + \alpha t - \frac{1}{\beta}\lambda\alpha t, & \text{if } \theta = \geq \end{cases}$$

Example 6. Given the weighted soft constraint $\langle sum, price, \geq, 20, 200, 1 \rangle$, its crisp translation is $sum(X.price) \geq 24$ for $\lambda = 180$, it is $sum(X.price) \geq 10$ for $\lambda = 250$.

Proposition 3. *Given the vocabulary of items $\mathcal{I}$, a combination of weighted soft constraints $\otimes C \equiv C_1 \otimes \ldots \otimes C_n$, and a maximum interest threshold λ. Let C' be the conjunction of crisp constraints obtained by conjoining the crisp translation of each constraint in $\otimes C$ w.r.t. λ: $C' \equiv C_{1crisp}^{\lambda} \wedge \ldots \wedge C_{ncrisp}^{\lambda}$. It holds that:*

$$int_w^{\mathcal{I}}(\lambda) \subseteq \{X \in 2^{\mathcal{I}} | \otimes C(X) \leq \lambda\} = Th(C')$$

where $Th(C')$ is the solution set for the crisp problem, according to the notation introduced in Definition 2.

In the following we report the results of some experiments that we have conducted on the same datasets used before for the fuzzy and the probabilistic semirings. We have compared 8 different instances (described in Figure 6) of the query $\mathcal{Q}$:

$$\langle supp, \mathcal{D}, \geq, t, \beta, \alpha \rangle \langle avg, weight, \leq, t, \beta, \alpha \rangle, \langle sum, price, \geq, t, \beta, \alpha \rangle$$

The results of the experiments are reported in Figure 7 and Figure 8. A first observation is that, on the contrary of what happening in the probabilistic and fuzzy semiring, here the larger is λ the larger is the number of solutions. This is trivially because the order of the weighted semiring says that smaller is better.

		$\langle supp, \mathcal{D}, \geq, t, \beta, \alpha\rangle$			$\langle avg, weight, \leq, t, \beta, \alpha\rangle$			$\langle sum, price, \geq, t, \beta, \alpha\rangle$		
	$\mathcal{D}$	t	β	α	t	β	α	t	β	α
$\mathcal{Q}_9$	RETAIL	20	600	0.8	5000	100	0.2	20000	250	0.5
$\mathcal{Q}_{10}$	RETAIL	20	600	0.2	5000	100	0.2	20000	250	0.5
$\mathcal{Q}_{11}$	RETAIL	20	600	0.8	5000	100	0.8	20000	250	0.5
$\mathcal{Q}_{12}$	RETAIL	20	600	0.8	5000	500	0.2	20000	250	0.5
$\mathcal{Q}_{13}$	RETAIL	20	600	0.8	5000	1000	0.2	20000	500	0.5
$\mathcal{Q}_{14}$	T40I10D100K	800	500	0.8	5000	200	0.5	80000	400	0.8
$\mathcal{Q}_{15}$	T40I10D100K	600	600	0.8	15000	500	0.5	80000	400	0.8
$\mathcal{Q}_{16}$	T40I10D100K	1000	500	0.5	15000	500	0.5	100000	600	0.9

Fig. 6. Description of queries experimented

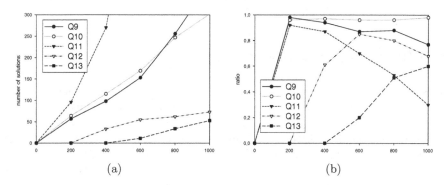

(a)   (b)

Fig. 7. Experimental results on the RETAIL dataset with λ ranging in $[0, 1000]$ in the weighted semiring: number of solutions (a), and ratio with the number of solutions of the crisp translation (b)

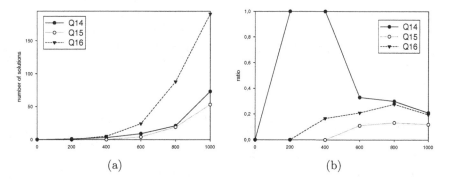

(a)   (b)

Fig. 8. Experimental results on the T40I10D100K dataset with λ ranging in $[0, 1000]$ in the weighted semiring: number of solutions (a), and ratio with the number of solutions of the crisp translation (b)

In Figure 7(a) we can observe that queries $\mathcal{Q}_{12}$ and $\mathcal{Q}_{13}$ always return a small number of solutions: this is due to the high values of β in the constraints, which means high costs, making difficult for patterns to produce a total cost smaller than λ. In Figure 7(b) and Figure 8(b) we report the ratio of the number of solution with the cardinality of the theory corresponding to the crisp translation of the queries, i.e., $|int_w^{\mathcal{I}}(\lambda)| / |Th(\mathcal{C}')|$. This gives a measure of how good is the approximation of the crisp translation, or in other terms, the amount of post-processing needed (which, however, has negligible computational cost). The approximation we obtain using our crisp solver is still quite good but, as we expected, not as good as in the probabilistic semiring. Also in this case, the softer the query the lower the ratio, i.e., the crisp approximation is better for harder constraints (closer to crisp). For instance in Figure 7(b) we can observe that $\mathcal{Q}_{10}$, which is the query with smaller values for the softness parameter α, always present a very high ratio.

5   Mining Top-k Itemsets

For sake of completeness, in this section we sketch a simple methodology to deal with *top-k* queries, according to [6]. In the following we do not distinguish between the possible semiring instances, we just describe the general methodology.

The main difficult to solve *top-k* queries is that we can know the number of solutions only after the evaluation of a query. Therefore, given k, the simple idea is to repeatedly run λ-interesting queries with different λ thresholds: we start from extremely selective λ (fast mining) decreasing in selectivity, until we do not extract a solution set which is large enough (more than k).

Considering for instance the fuzzy semiring, where the best semiring value is 1: we could start by performing a 0.95-interesting query, and if the query results in a solution set of cardinality larger than k, then we sort the solution according to their semiring value and return the best k, otherwise we slowly decrease the threshold, for instance $\lambda = 0.9$, and so on. Notice that is important to start from a very high threshold in order to perform fast mining extractions with small solution sets, and only if needed decrease the threshold to get more solutions at the cost of longer computations.

6   Soft Constraints in ConQueSt

In this section we describe how the ideas presented in this paper have been integrated within the CONQUEST inductive database system. CONQUEST is a constraint-based querying system devised with the aim of supporting the intrinsically exploratory nature of pattern discovery. It provides users with an expressive constraint-based query language (named *SPQL*) which allows the discovery process to be effectively driven toward potentially interesting patterns. The system is built around an efficient constraint-based mining engine which entails several data and search space reduction techniques, and allows new user-defined constraints to be easily added (for deeper details on the CONQUEST system, see also other paper in this volume [10]).

In order to integrate the soft constraint based pattern mining paradigm within CONQUEST, we first extended the *SPQL* query language to allow definition of soft constraints.

Example 7. In this example we show a complex *SPQL* query exploiting the soft constraint paradigm. In particular it requires to mine, in the probabilistic semi-ring, the top 5 patterns w.r.t. a given combination of 3 soft constraint: the frequency constraint, support larger than 5 with 0.4 softness, plus two aggregate soft constraints defined over the attributes product.gross_weight and product.units_per_case. This is a true mining query, defined within CON-QUEST on the famous foodmart2000 datamart.

```
1. MINE TOP 5.0 PROBABILISTIC PATTERNS
2. WITH SUPP>= 5.0 SOFT 0.4 IN
3.    SELECT product.product_name, product.gross_weight,
              product.units_per_case, sales_fact_1998.time_id,
              sales_fact_1998.customer_id, sales_fact_1998.store_id
4.    FROM [product], [sales_fact_1998]
5.    WHERE sales_fact_1998.product_id=product.product_id
6. TRANSACTION sales_fact_1998.time_id, sales_fact_1998.customer_id,
              sales_fact_1998.store_id
7. ITEM product.product_name
8. ATTRIBUTE product.gross_weight, product.units_per_case
9. CONSTRAINED BY average(product.gross_weight)<=20 SOFT 0.8 AND
              sum(product.units_per_case)>=50 SOFT 0.5
```

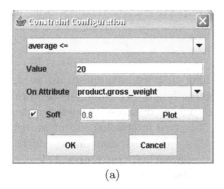
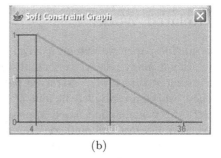

(a)   (b)

Fig. 9. CONQUEST window for the definition of a soft constraint (a), and another window with the graphical representation of the soft constraint defined (b)

In line 1. we got the soft constraint query type definition (i.e., if top-k or λ-interesting with the appropriate threshold) and the semiring in which the query must be evaluated. In line 2 a minimum frequency constraint is defined with threshold 5 and 0.4 softness level. From line 3 to 5 we got a typical SQL select-from-where statement defining the data source for the query. Lines from 6 to 8 contains the mining view definition, or in other terms, how transactions must be built from the source data (pre-processing). Line 9 contains the two other constraints with their associated softness parameters.

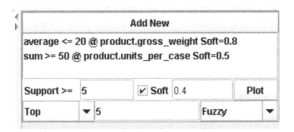

Fig. 10. CONQUEST soft constraints query definition

This query seems quite complex to be written, but CONQUEST offers simple mechanisms to facilitate the definition of a query. In figure 9 we show the window for the definition of a soft constraint, and the window with the graphical representation of the soft constraint defined.

In Figure 10 we show CONQUEST's constraint definition module, where all the three constraints of the query in Example 7 are reported. Note the dropdown menus to choose among top-k or λ-interesting, and to choose the semiring.

Finally, in Figure 11 we show CONQUEST global view with the query in Example 7 ready to be run, then the resulting top 5 patterns with two different possible views (that can be chosen from the menu): with the actual value of each pattern for each aggregate in a constraint, or with the respective interestingness value.

7   Related Work

Since in this paper we extend a novel paradigm that we introduced last year, there are not many related works in a strict sense. In a larger sense, all the work done on *interestingness* of extracted patterns can be considered related. In [22] all these works are divided in four classes: objective interestingness measures [12,3,21,15], visualization-based approaches [17], subjective domain-dependent measures of interest [20], and constraint-based approaches. Our proposal clearly collocates within the last class. As already stated in the introduction, a lot of work has been done on constraint-based pattern discovery, but almost all has been done on the development of efficient constraint-pushing algorithms. Entering in the details of these computational techniques, for which we have provided references in the introduction, is beyond the scope of this paper. The reader should refer to [11,9] for un updated state-of-the-art. What we can say here is that most of these techniques have been adopted to build CONQUEST's mining engine [8].

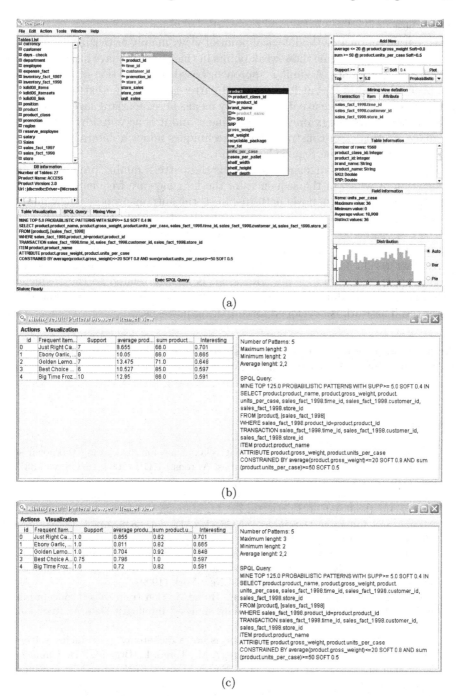

Fig. 11. CONQUEST global view with the query in Example 7 ready to be run(a); the pattern browser showing top 5 patterns (b); the pattern browser where for each pattern the interestingness level for each constraint is shown

To the best of our knowledge only few works [16,2] have studied the constraint-based paradigm by a methodological point of view, mainly criticizing some of its weak points. To overcome these weak points in this paper we have introduced the use of soft-constraints. A similar approach, based on relaxation of constraints, has been adopted in [1] but for sequential patterns. In the context of sequential patterns, constraints are usually defined by means of regular languages: a pattern is a solution to the query only if it is frequent and it is accepted by the regular language. In this case, constraint-based techniques adopt a deterministic finite automaton to define the regular language.

The use of regular languages transforms the pattern mining process into the verification of which of the sequences of the language are frequent, completely blocking the discovery of novel patterns. In [1] the authors propose a new mining methodology based on the use of constraint relaxations, which assumes that the user is responsible for choosing the strength of the restriction used to constrain the mining process. A hierarchy of constraint relaxations is developed.

Another recent work using softness in a inductive database context is [19]. In this paper the softness issue addressed, is mostly related to the frequency constraint, i.e., avoiding the exact match between candidate patterns and data instances. The work is developed for substring patterns.

Acknowledgments. The authors wish to thank Roberto Trasarti from Pisa KDD Laboratory, for the excellent work done implementing our ideas within the continuously growing CONQUEST system.

References

1. Antunes, C., Oliveira, A.L.: Constraint relaxations for discovering unknown sequential patterns. In: Goethals, B., Siebes, A. (eds.) KDID 2004. LNCS, vol. 3377, pp. 11–32. Springer, Heidelberg (2005)
2. Bayardo, R.J.: The hows, whys, and whens of constraints in itemset and rule discovery. In: Boulicaut, J.-F., De Raedt, L., Mannila, H. (eds.) Constraint-Based Mining and Inductive Databases. LNCS (LNAI), vol. 3848, pp. 1–13. Springer, Heidelberg (2006)
3. Bayardo, R.J., Agrawal, R.: Mining the most interesting rules. In: Proceedings of the Fifth ACM SIGKDD International Conference on Knowledge Discovery and Data Mining, pp. 145–154. ACM Press, New York (1999)
4. Besson, J., Robardet, C., Boulicaut, J.F., Rome, S.: Constraint-based concept mining and its application to microarray data analysis. Intelligent Data Analysis journal, 59–82 (2005)
5. Bistarelli, S., Bonchi, F.: Interestingness is not a dichotomy: Introducing softness in constrained pattern mining. In: Jorge, A.M., Torgo, L., Brazdil, P.B., Camacho, R., Gama, J. (eds.) PKDD 2005. LNCS (LNAI), vol. 3721, pp. 22–33. Springer, Heidelberg (2005)
6. Bistarelli, S., Codognet, P., Rossi, F.: Abstracting soft constraints: Framework, properties, examples. Artificial Intelligence 139(2), 175–211 (2002)
7. Bistarelli, S., Montanari, U., Rossi, F.: Semiring-based Constraint Solving and Optimization. Journal of the ACM 44(2), 201–236 (1997)

8. Bonchi, F., Giannotti, F., Lucchese, C., Orlando, S., Perego, R., Trasarti, R.: CON-QUEST: a constraint-based querying system for exploratory pattern discovery. In: Proceedings of The 22nd IEEE International Conference on Data Engineering, pp. 22–33. IEEE Computer Society Press, Los Alamitos (2006)
9. Bonchi, F., Lucchese, C.: Extending the state-of-the-art of constraint-based pattern discovery. Data and Knowledge Engineering (DKE) (to appear, 2006)
10. Bonchi, F., Giannotti, F., Lucchese, C., Orlando, S., Perego, R., Trasarti, R.: On interactive pattern mining from relational databases. In: KDID 2006. LNCS, vol. 4747, pp. 42–62. Springer, Heidelberg (2007)
11. Boulicaut, J.F., Jeudy, B.: Constraint-based data mining. In: Maimon, O., Rokach, L. (eds.) The Data Mining and Knowledge Discovery Handbook, pp. 399–416. Springer, Heidelberg (2005)
12. Brin, S., Motwani, R., Silverstein, C.: Beyond market baskets: Generalizing association rules to correlations. In: Proceedings ACM SIGMOD International Conference on Management of Data, pp. 256–276. ACM Press, New York (1997)
13. Ordonez, C., et al.: Mining constrained association rules to predict heart disease. In: Proceedings of the First IEEE International Conference on Data Mining, pp. 433–440. IEEE Computer Society Press, Los Alamitos (2001)
14. Fargier, H., Lang, J.: Uncertainty in constraint satisfaction problems: a probabilistic approach. In: Moral, S., Kruse, R., Clarke, E. (eds.) ECSQARU 1993. LNCS, vol. 747, pp. 97–104. Springer, Heidelberg (1993)
15. Hilderman, R.J., Hamilton, H.J.: Knowledge Discovery and Measures of Interest. Kluwer Academic Publishers, Boston (2002)
16. Hipp, J., Güntzer, H.: Is pushing constraints deeply into the mining algorithms really what we want?: an alternative approach for association rule mining. SIGKDD Explorations 4(1), 50–55 (2002)
17. Hofmann, H., Siebes, A., Wilhelm, A.F.X.: Visualizing association rules with interactive mosaic plots. In: Proceedings of the Sixth ACM SIGKDD International Conference on Knowledge Discovery and Data Mining, pp. 227–235. ACM Press, New York (2000)
18. Lau, A., Ong, S., Mahidadia, A., Hoffmann, A., Westbrook, J., Zrimec, T.: Mining patterns of dyspepsia symptoms across time points using constraint association rules. In: Whang, k-Y., Jeon, J., Shim, K., Srivastava, J. (eds.) PAKDD 2003. LNCS (LNAI), vol. 2637, pp. 124–135. Springer, Heidelberg (2003)
19. Mitasiunaite, I., Boulicaut, J.-F.: About softness for inductive querying on sequence databases. In: Proceedings 7th International Baltic Conference on Databases and Information Systems DB IS 2006, July 3-6 2006, Vilnius (Lithuania) (2006)
20. Silberschatz, A., Tuzhilin, A.: On subjective measures of interestingness. In: Proceedings of the First International Conference on Knowledge Discovery and Data Mining, pp. 275–281 (1995)
21. Tan, P.-N., Kumar, V., Srivastava, J.: Selecting the right interestingness measure for association patterns. In: Proc. of the Eighth ACM SIGKDD International Conference on Knowledge Discovery and Data Mining (SIGKDD'2002), ACM Press, New York (2002)
22. Tan, P.-N., Steinbach, M., Kumar, V.: Introduction to Data Mining. Addison-Wesley, Reading (2005)

On Interactive Pattern Mining
from Relational Databases

Francesco Bonchi[1], Fosca Giannotti[1], Claudio Lucchese[2,3],
Salvatore Orlando[2,3], Raffaele Perego[3], and Roberto Trasarti[1]

[1] Pisa KDD Laboratory, ISTI - CNR,
Area della Ricerca di Pisa, Via Giuseppe Moruzzi 1, Pisa, Italy
[2] Computer Science Dep., University Ca' Foscari
Via Torino 155, Venezia Mestre, Italy
[3] Pisa HPC Laboratory, ISTI - CNR,
Area della Ricerca di Pisa, Via Giuseppe Moruzzi 1, Pisa, Italy

Abstract. In this paper we present CONQUEST, a constraint based querying system devised with the aim of supporting the intrinsically exploratory (i.e., human-guided, interactive, iterative) nature of pattern discovery. Following the *inductive database* vision, our framework provides users with an expressive constraint based query language which allows the discovery process to be effectively driven toward potentially interesting patterns. Such constraints are also exploited to reduce the cost of pattern mining computation. We implemented a comprehensive mining system that can access real world relational databases from which extract data. After a preprocessing step, mining queries are answered by an efficient pattern mining engine which entails several data and search space reduction techniques. Resulting patterns are then presented to the user, and possibly stored in the database. New user-defined constraints can be easily added to the system in order to target the particular application considered.

1 Introduction

According to the *inductive database* vision [16], the task of extracting useful and interesting knowledge from data is just an *exploratory* querying process, i.e., human-guided, iterative and interactive. The analyst, exploiting an expressive query language, drives the discovery process through a sequence of complex mining queries, extracts patterns satisfying some user-defined constraints, refines the queries, materializes the extracted patterns as first-class citizens in the database, combines the patterns to produce more complex knowledge, and cross-over the data and the patterns. Therefore, an Inductive Database system should provide the following features:

Coupling with a DBMS. The analyst must be able to retrieve the portion of interesting data (for instance, by means of SQL queries). Moreover, extracted patterns should also be stored in the DBMS in order to be further queried or mined (*closure principle*).

S. Džeroski and J. Struyf (Eds.): KDID 2006, LNCS 4747, pp. 42–62, 2007.
© Springer-Verlag Berlin Heidelberg 2007

Expressiveness of the query language. The analyst must be able to interact with the pattern discovery system by specify declaratively how the desired patterns should look like and which conditions they should satisfy. The analyst is supposed to have a high-level vision of the pattern discovery system, without worrying about the details of the computational engine, in the same way as a database user has not to worry about query optimization. The task of composing all constraints and producing the most efficient mining strategy (execution plan) for a given query should be thus completely demanded to the underlying system.

Efficiency of the mining engine. Keeping query response time as small as possible is, on the one hand necessary, since our goal is to give frequent feedbacks to the user allowing realistic human-guided exploration. On the other hand, it is a very challenging task, due to the exponential complexity of pattern discovery computations. To this end, data and search space reduction properties of constraints should be effectively exploited by pushing them within the mining algorithms. Pattern discovery is usually a highly iterative task: a mining session is usually made up of a series of queries (exploration), where each new query adjusts, refines or combines the results of some previous queries. It is important that the mining engine adopts techniques for incremental mining; i.e. reusing results of previous queries, in order to give a faster response to the last query presented to the system, instead of performing again the mining from scratch.

Graphical user interface. The exploratory nature of pattern discovery imposes to the system not only to return frequent feedbacks to the user, but also to provide pattern visualization and navigation tools. These tools should help the user in visualizing the continuous feedbacks form the systems, allowing an easier and human-based identification of the fragments of interesting knowledge. Such tools should also play the role of graphical querying interface: the action of browsing pattern visualization should be tightly integrated (both by a conceptual and engineering point of view) with the action of iteratively querying.

Starting from the above requirements we designed CONQUEST, an exploratory pattern discovery system equipped with a simple, yet powerful, query language (named SPQL for *simple pattern query language*) and a user friendly interface for accessing the underlying DBMS. While designing CONQUEST query language, architecture and user interface, we have kept in mind all the tasks involved in the typical *knowledge discovery process* [11]: (*i*) source data selection, (*ii*) data preparation and pre-processing, (*iii*) pattern discovery and model building. The user supervises the whole process, not only defining the parameters of the three tasks, but also evaluating the quality of the outcome of each step and possibly re-tuning the parameters of any step. Moreover, the user is in charge of interpreting and evaluating the extracted knowledge, even if the system must provide adequate support for this task. As we will show in this paper, the three main tasks of the knowledge discovery process are represented both in the query language and in the architecture of the CONQUEST system.

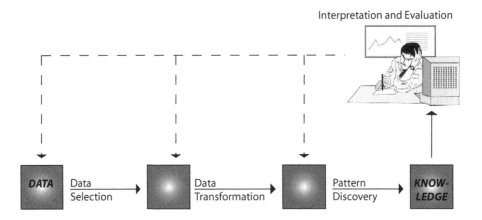

Fig. 1. CONQUEST knowledge discovery process

CONQUEST is the result of a joint work of the Pisa KDD (*Knowledge Discovery and Delivery*) and HPC (*High Performance Computing*) Laboratories: it is built around a scalable and high-performance constraint-based mining engine exploiting state-of-the-art constraint pushing techniques, as those ones developed in the last three years by our two labs [24,6,5,7,8].

1.1   Constraint Based Pattern Mining

Devising fast and scalable algorithms, able to crunch huge amount of data, has been so far one of the main goal of data mining research. Recently, researchers realized that in many practical cases it does not matter how much efficiently knowledge is extracted, since the volume of the results themselves is often embarrassing, and creates a second order mining problem for the human expert. This situation is very common in the case of association rules and frequent pattern mining [2], where the identification of the fragments of interesting knowledge, blurred within a huge quantity of mostly useless patterns, is very difficult.

The constraint-based pattern mining paradigm has been recognized as one of the fundamental techniques for inductive databases: user-defined constraints drive the mining process towards potentially interesting patterns only. Moreover, they can be pushed deep inside the mining algorithm in order to deal with the exponential search space curse, achieving better performance [28,23,15]. Constraint-based frequent pattern mining has been studied a lot as a query optimization problem, i.e., developing efficient, sound and complete evaluation strategies for constraint-based mining queries. To this aim, properties of constraints have been studied comprehensively, e.g., *anti-monotonicity*, *succinctness* [23,19], *monotonicity* [18,9,5], *convertibility* [25], *loose anti-monotonicity* [8], and on the basis of such properties efficient computational strategies have been defined. The formal problem statement follows.

Definition 1 (Constrained Frequent Itemset Mining). *Let $\mathcal{I} = \{x_1, ..., x_n\}$ be a set of distinct items, where an item is an object with some predefined attributes (e.g., price, type, etc.). An itemset X is a non-empty subset of $\mathcal{I}$. A transaction database $\mathcal{D}$ is a bag of itemsets $t \in 2^{\mathcal{I}}$, usually called transactions. A constraint on itemsets is a function $\mathcal{C} : 2^{\mathcal{I}} \rightarrow \{true, false\}$. We say that an itemset I satisfies a constraint if and only if $\mathcal{C}(I) = true$. We define the theory of a constraint as the set of itemsets which satisfy the constraint: $Th(\mathcal{C}) = \{X \in 2^{\mathcal{I}} \mid \mathcal{C}(X)\}$. The support of an itemset X in database $\mathcal{D}$, denoted $supp_{\mathcal{D}}(X)$, is the number of transactions which are superset of X. Given a user-defined minimum support, denoted σ, an itemset X is called frequent in $\mathcal{D}$ if $supp_{\mathcal{D}}(X) \geq \sigma$. This defines the minimum frequency constraint: $\mathcal{C}_{freq[\mathcal{D},\sigma]}(X) \Leftrightarrow supp_{\mathcal{D}}(X) \geq \sigma$. In general, given a conjunction of constraints $\mathcal{C}$ the constrained frequent itemsets mining problem requires to compute $Th(\mathcal{C}_{freq}) \cap Th(\mathcal{C})$.*

While developing CONQUEST we have tried to reduce as much as possible the gap existing between real-world data stored in relational DBMS, and the constraint-based pattern discovery paradigm, as defined above. In fact, the data is usually stored in relational databases, and thus in the form of relations and not of transactions. In sections 2 and 3.2 we explain how transactions are defined and constructed both at the query language and at the system level. Moreover, the constraint-based mining paradigm assumes that the constraints are defined on attributes of the items that are in functional dependency with the items. This rarely the case in real-world data: just think about the price of one item in a market over a period of one month. CONQUEST provides support to solve this cases, allowing the user to reconstruct the ideal situation of functional dependency, for instance, by choosing to take the average of prices of the item in the period as price attribute.

In this paper we provide an overview of CONQUEST's main design choices and features. The paper is organized as follows. In Section 2 we provide a brief overview of the SPQL language which is at the basis of our system. Then in Section 3 we provide an high level description of CONQUEST's architecture, we then describe the three main modules in the sections that follow. In particular, Section 3.1 describes the graphical user interface and how the interactions between the user and the system actually happens; Section 3.2 describes the query interpreter and pre-processor modules; Section 3.3 describes the mining engines and the algorithmic choices underlying it. Finally in Section 4 we discuss other existing mining systems and query languages, and in Section 5 we draw some conclusions.

2   A Simple Data Mining Query Language

According to the constraint-based mining paradigm, the data analyst must have a high-level vision of the pattern discovery system, without worrying about the details of the computational engine, in the very same way a database designer has not to worry about query optimizations. The analyst must be provided with a set of primitives to be used to communicate with the pattern discovery system, using a query language. The analyst just needs to declaratively specify in the pattern discovery query how the desired patterns should look like and which conditions they should obey (a set of constraints). Such rigorous interaction between the analyst and the pattern discovery system, can be implemented following [20], where Mannila introduces an elegant formalization for the notion of interactive mining process: the term *inductive database* refers to a relational database plus the set of all sentences from a specified class of sentences that are true w.r.t. the data. In other words, the inductive database is a database framework which integrates the raw data with the knowledge extracted from the data and materialized in the form of patterns. In this way, the knowledge discovery process consists essentially in an iterative querying process, enabled by a query language that can deal either with raw data or patterns.

Definition 2. *Given an instance* **r** *of a relation* **R***, a class* $\mathcal{L}$ *of sentences (patterns), and a selection predicate* q*, a pattern discovery task is to find a theory*

$$Th(\mathcal{L}, \mathbf{r}, q) = \{s \in \mathcal{L} | q(\mathbf{r}, s) \text{ is true}\}$$

The selection predicate q indicates whether a pattern s is considered interesting. In the constraint-based paradigm, such selection predicate q is defined by a conjunction of constraints. In this Section, going through a rigorous identification of all its basic components, we provide a definition of constraint-based frequent pattern mining query over a relational database DB [4].

The first needed component is the data source: which table must be mined for frequent patterns, and which attributed do identify transactions and items.

Definition 3 (Data Source). *Given a database* DB *any relational expression* $\mathcal{V}$ *on* preds(DB) *can be selected as* data source.

Definition 4 (Transaction id). *Given a database* DB *and a relation* $\mathcal{V}$ *derived from* preds(DB)*. Let* $\mathcal{V}$ *with attributes* sch($\mathcal{V}$) *be our data source. Any subset of attributes* $\mathcal{T} \subset$ sch($\mathcal{V}$) *can be selected as transaction identifier, and named* transaction id.

Definition 5 (Item attribute). *Given a database* DB *and a relation* $\mathcal{V}$ *derived from* preds(DB)*. Let* $\mathcal{V}$ *with attributes* sch($\mathcal{V}$) *be our data source. Given a subset of attributes* $\mathcal{T} \subset$ sch($\mathcal{V}$) *as transaction id, let* $Y = \{y | y \in$ sch($\mathcal{V}$)$\backslash \mathcal{T} \wedge \mathcal{T} \rightarrow y$ *does not hold*$\}$*; we define an attribute* $\mathcal{I} \in Y$ *an item attribute provided the functional dependency* $\mathcal{T}\mathcal{I} \rightarrow Y\backslash\mathcal{I}$ *holds in* DB.

Proposition 1. *Given a relational database* DB*, a triple* $\langle \mathcal{V}, \mathcal{T}, \mathcal{I} \rangle$ *denoting the data source* $\mathcal{V}$*, the transaction id* $\mathcal{T}$*, the item attribute* $\mathcal{I}$*, uniquely identifies a transactional database, as defined in Definition 1.*

We next distinguish between attributes which describe items (descriptive attributes), from attribute which describe transactions (circumstance attributes).

Definition 6 (Circumstance attribute). *[12] Given a database* DB *and a relation* $\mathcal{V}$ *derived from* preds(DB)*. Let* $\mathcal{V}$ *with attributes* sch($\mathcal{V}$) *be our data source. Given a subset of attributes* $\mathcal{T} \subset$ sch($\mathcal{V}$) *as transaction id, we define any attribute* $\mathcal{A} \in$ sch(R) *where* R *is a relation in* preds(DB) *circumstance attribute provided that* $\mathcal{A} \notin \mathcal{T}$ *and the functional dependency* $\mathcal{T} \rightarrow \mathcal{A}$ *holds in* DB.

Definition 7 (Descriptive attribute). *Given a database* DB *and a relation* $\mathcal{V}$ *derived from preds*(DB). *Let* $\mathcal{V}$ *with attributes sch*($\mathcal{V}$) *be our data source. Given a subset of attributes* $\mathcal{T} \subset sch(\mathcal{V})$ *as transaction id, and given* $\mathcal{I}$ *as item attribute; we define* descriptive attribute *any attribute* $\mathcal{A} \in sch(R)$ *where* R *is a relation in preds*(DB), *provided the functional dependency* $\mathcal{I} \rightarrow \mathcal{A}$ *holds in* DB.

Consider the mining view: `sales(tID, locationID, time, product, price)` where each attribute has the intended semantics of its name and with `tID` acting as the transaction id. Since the functional dependency $\{$`tID`$\} \rightarrow \{$`locationID`$\}$ holds, `locationID` is a circumstance attribute. The same is true for `time`. We also have $\{$`tID, product`$\} \rightarrow \{$`price`$\}$, and $\{$`product`$\} \rightarrow \{$`price`$\}$, thus `product` is an item attribute, while `price` is a descriptive attribute.

Constraints, as introduced in the previous Section (see Definition 1), describes properties of itemsets, i.e., a constraint $\mathcal{C}$ is a boolean function over the domain of itemsets: $\mathcal{C} : 2^{\mathcal{I}} \rightarrow \{true, false\}$. According to this view, constraints are only those ones defined on item attributes (Definition 5) or descriptive attributes (Definition 7).

Constraints defined over the *transaction id* (Definition 4) or over circumstance attributes (Definition 6) are not constraints in the strict sense. Indeed, they can be seen as selection conditions on the transactions to be mined and thus they can be satisfied in the definition of the *mining view*. Consider the relation: `sales(tID, locationID, time, product, price)` where each attribute has the intended semantics of its name and with `tID` acting as the transaction id. Since the functional dependency $\{$`tID`$\} \rightarrow \{$`locationID`$\}$ holds, `locationID` is a circumstance attribute. The constraints `locationID` $\in \{$`Florence, Milan, Rome`$\}$ is not a real constraint of the frequent pattern extraction, indeed it is a condition in the mining view definition, i.e., it is satisfied by imposing such condition in the relational expression defining the mining view (for a deeper insight on circumstance attributes and constraints defined over them see [27,12]).

We have provided all the needed components for defining a constraint-based frequent pattern query as follows.

Definition 8 (Constraint-based frequent pattern query). *Given a database* DB, *let the quintuple* $\langle \mathcal{V}, \mathcal{T}, \mathcal{I}, \sigma, \mathcal{C} \rangle$ *denotes the mining view* $\mathcal{V}$, *the transaction id* $\mathcal{T}$, *the item attribute* $\mathcal{I}$, *the minimum support threshold* σ, *and a conjunction of constraints on itemsets* $\mathcal{C}$.

The primitive for constraint-based itemset mining takes in input such quintuple and returns a binary relation recording the set of itemsets which satisfy $\mathcal{C}$ *and are frequent (w.r.t.* σ*) in the transaction database* $\langle \mathcal{V}, \mathcal{T}, \mathcal{I} \rangle$, *and their supports:*

$$freq(\mathcal{V}, \mathcal{T}, \mathcal{I}, \sigma, \mathcal{C}) = \{(I, S) \mid \mathcal{C}(I) \ \wedge \ supp_{\langle \mathcal{V}, \mathcal{T}, \mathcal{I} \rangle}(I) = S \ \wedge \ S \geq \sigma\}$$

The SPQL query language that is at the basis of CONQUEST, is essentially syntactic sugar, in SQL-like style, to express constraint-based frequent pattern queries like $freq(\mathcal{V}, \mathcal{T}, \mathcal{I}, \sigma, \mathcal{C})$. It is a superset of SQL, in a double sense: first any SPQL query contains a SQL query needed to define the data source; second, in CONQUEST we allow the user to define any SQL query, which could be useful, for instance, to pre-process the data or post-process the extracted patterns.

Table 1. An example SPQL mining query

---
1. MINE PATTERNS WITH SUPP>= 5 IN
2. SELECT product.product_name, product.gross_weight, sales_fact_1998.time_id,
   sales_fact_1998.customer_id, sales_fact_1998.store_id
3. FROM [product], [sales_fact_1998]
4. WHERE sales_fact_1998.product_id=product.product_id
5. TRANSACTION sales_fact_1998.time_id, sales_fact_1998.customer_id,
   sales_fact_1998.store_id
6. ITEM product.product_name
7. ATTRIBUTE product.gross_weight
8. CONSTRAINED BY Sum(product.gross_weight)<=30

In Table 1 we report a true SPQL mining query, defined within CONQUEST on the famous foodmart2000 datamart. A simple SPQL query consists of four parts:

1. the user-defined minimum support threshold σ in line 1;
2. the SQL style SELECT statement to specify the data source V to be extracted from the DB (lines 2–4);
3. the mining view definition by means of TRANSACTION (to identify T), ITEM (to identify I), and of ATTRIBUTE on which constraints are defined (lines 5–7);
4. the conjunction of constraints C that the extracted patterns must satisfy in line 8.

Since the data source is in relational form, a pre-processing step is needed to create a set of transactions, which are the input of any frequent pattern mining system. Transaction are created by grouping ITEM by the attributes specified in the TRANSACTION clause. For instance, in the query Table 1, transactions are built groping sales by time id, customer id and store id: this means that we consider a unique transaction when we got the same customer in the same store at the same time. It is worth noting that with this simple mechanism of defining transactions we can easily handle both the inter-attribute and the intra-attribute pattern mining cases. We have chosen a well defined set of classes of constraints. These constraints have been deeply studied and analyzed in the past few years, in order to find nice properties that can be used at mining time to reduce the computational cost. In particular the CONQUEST system is able to deal with anti-monotone, succinct [23], monotone [5], convertible [26] and loose anti-monotone [8] constraints. Such classes include all the constraints based on the aggregates listed in Table 2.

It is worth noting how all steps of the knowledge discovery process, i.e., (*i*) source data selection, (*ii*) data preparation and pre-processing and (*iii*) pattern discovery, are expressed within the typical SPQL query. In particular, the source data selection is expressed by means on the select statement, the preprocessing is expressed by means of items and transactions identification, and the mining is expressed by listing the desired constraints, including the frequency one.

Table 2. The set of available constraints

subset	subset	**supset**	superset
asubset	attributes are subset	**len**	length
asupset	attributes are superset	**acount**	attributes count
min	minimum	**max**	maximum
range	range	**sum**	sum
avg	average	**var**	variance
std	standard deviation	**spv**	sample variance
md	mean deviation	**med**	median

This is a SPQL query in its basilar form. Different kinds of SPQL query exist, since we have extended the language to accommodate the use of *soft constraints* [3], and *discretization tasks*. In CONQUEST we have introduced the possibility of defining queries according to the new paradigm of pattern discovery based on *soft constraints*[3], i.e., where constraints are no longer rigid boolean functions. This allows the user to describe what is the "shape" of the patterns of interest, and receive back those patterns that *"mostly"* exhibits such shape. The patterns are also sorted according to a measure of interestingness, i.e., how much a pattern agrees with the given description. Having this order, allows also to define top-k queries. In this paper we avoid entering in the details of these extensions. The interested reader can find an example of SPQL query using *soft constraints* in the paper [3] in this volume.

In Table 3 a portion of SPQL formal grammar definition is provided.

Table 3. A portion of SPQL formal grammar definition

```
<SpqlQuery> ::= (<SqlQuery>| <MineQuery> | <Discretize>)
<MineQuery> ::=<Header><br><SqlQuery><br><MiningDefinition><br><Constraints>
<Header> ::= MINE PATTERNS WITH SUPP >= <Number>
<MiningDefinition> ::= TRANSACTION <Transaction><br> ITEM
<Item><br>[ ATTRIBUTE <Attribute>]
<Transaction> ::= <Field>[<Separator><Transaction>]
<Item> ::= <Field>[<Separator><Item>]
<Attribute> ::= <Field>[<Separator><Attribute>]
<Field> ::= <String>.<String>
<Constraints> ::= CONSTRAINED BY <Function>
<Function> ::= (<FunctionM>(<Field>)<Op><Number> | <FunctionS>(<Field>)<Op><Set> |
               <FunctionN>()<Op><Number> ) [<Separator>(Function)]
<FunctionM> ::= (Minimum | Maximum | Range | Variance | Std_Deviation | Median | Average | Sum)
<FunctionS>::= (Subset_of | Superset_of | Attribute_Subset_of | Attribute_Superset_of )
<FunctionN>::= Length
<Op> ::= (>|<|>=|<=)
<Separator> ::= ,
<br> ::= \n
<Set> ::= <String>[<Separator><Set>]
<Discretize>::= DISCRETIZE <Field> AS <Field> <br> FROM <String> <br> IN
(<Method>| <Intervals>) BINS <br> SMOOTINGH BY <Smethod>
<Method> ::= (EQUALWIDTH | EQUALDEPTH)
<Smethod> ::= (AVERAGE | COUNT | BIN BOUNDARIES)
<Intervals>::= (<Number> <Separator> <Number>)[<Separator> <Intervals>]
<Number> ::= (0-9) [<Number>]
<String> ::= (a-z|A-Z|0-9) [<String>]
```

3   Architecture of the System

The CONQUEST architecture, as shown in Fig. 2, is composed of three main modules:

- the Graphical User Interface (GUI);
- the Query Interpreter and and Pre-processor (QIP);
- the Mining Engine (ME).

For portability reasons, the GUI and the QIP have been implemented in Java, while the ME was implemented in C++ in order to provide high performance during the most expensive task.

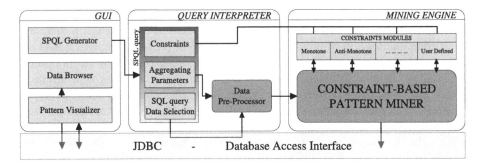

Fig. 2. CONQUEST architecture

In our vision, a mining system has to be tightly coupled with DMBS softwares, because databases are the place where data is. Our choice is to allow all the three main components to access independently a database. In fact, the GUI must show to the user the data present in the database, the QIP must retrieve the data of interested and prepare them for the mining engine, which will eventually store the discovered patterns in the database. To this end, the three components stand on a JDBC [1] abstraction layer, in order to provide independency from the particular database server software where data are stored. In fact, the JDBC API provides connectivity to a wide range of SQL databases. CONQUEST for instance, can retrieve data from PostgreSQL as well as from Microsoft Access database servers, and additional compatibility can be provided just by adding the JDBC plug-in provided by the database server software house.

The separation in these modules reflects the separation among different, well defined and independent tasks. In fact, every module could be a single software package running on a different machine. For instance, the GUI may run on the user machine, while the QIP may be located in a different site where a fast access to the database is provided, and finally the ME may be running on an high performance cluster serving many users with many different tasks. Finally, the JDBC layer allow us to ignore the physical location of the database server.

Actually, a communication protocol is established, flowing from the GUI, through the QIP and ending at the mining engine. The GUI, interactively with the user, creates a SPQL query which is then sent to the query interpreter. The latter preprocesses the data of interest and translates part of the SPQL query in an list of constraints. These constraints, and a filesystem pointer to the pre-processed data are finally sent to the ME which can now start the mining process. As long as this simple protocol is fulfilled, every single component can increase its features and improve its functionalities independently from the others.

3.1   Graphical User Interface

The user interface (see a screen-shot in Figure 3) is designed not only to stand in between the user and the mining engine, but also to stand between the user and the data. Data is assumed to be in the form of a relational database. As soon as the user connects to the database, a set of information and statistics are collected and presented in many ways. The idea is to provide a simple and high level mean to the user to define the mining task. It is simple, since the user can reach his goal just by using user friendly mouse-clicks. Moreover, many high level information and statistics are provided. Finally, the GUI is complete, meaning that any operation related to the definition of a mining query can be done just by mouse-clicks without the need of editing an SPQL query by hand.However, in the case an expert user prefers to write a query by hand, or simply to change an existing one, CONQUEST's *inverse-parser* takes care of updating the GUI's modules on-the-fly, in such a way that exists always a perfect correspondence

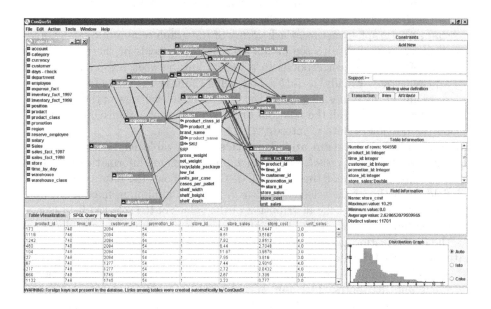

Fig. 3. CONQUEST graphical user interface

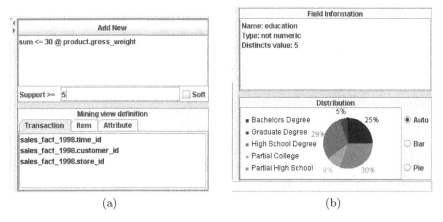

(a)   (b)

Fig. 4. CONQUEST The upper-right corner of the GUI, corresponding to the query in Table 1 (a), and the lower-right corner with the description of the education attribute of the customer table (b)

between the SPQL query textually reported in the bottom panel of the GUI, and its definition contained in the central area and in the two upper-right corner panels of the GUI. In Figure 4(a), we report the two upper-right corner panels for the query in Table 1.

Navigating the Structure of the Database. Most of the GUI is dedicated to the *Desk Area*. Here the tables present in the database are showed in a shape of a graph structure. Each vertex of the graph represents a table, and the user may choose to see or not to see all the fields of the table. Each edge of the graph corresponds to a logical link between a foreign key and a primary key. Finally, a *Tables List* helps the user to select, to hide or to show any of the tables. This gives the user an high level view of the database, allowing him grasp all the relations and connections at a glance, and to focus on the portion of data of interest.

Table-Fields Information and Statistics. Every table maybe actually visualized in the *Table Visualization* panel, but aggregated information are more useful to the user. For this reason CONQUEST shows the data type of each field, statistics of the selected field (e.g. average, minimum, maximum) and a bar or pie chart of the distribution of the values of the selected field (see a screenshot in Figure 4(b)). This information may help the user in deciding the discretization parameters and the constraints thresholds.

Interactive SPQL query definition. The first part of the SPQL query consists in the mining view definition, i.e. the set of fields defining transactions, items and attributes. The user may set the mining view simply by right-clicking directly on the *Desk Area* the table-fields of interest. Those fields will be highlighted in the *Desk Area* and reported in the *Mining View Definition* panel. Whenever a mining view definition implicitly require relational joins

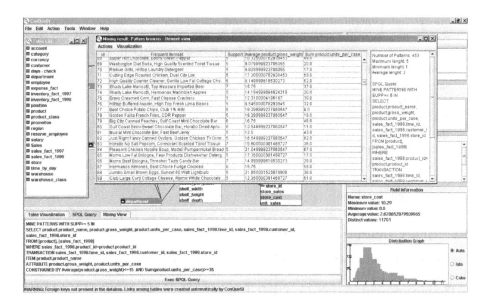

Fig. 5. The output of a mining query in the pattern browser

(e.g. transaction ids and item ids are in different table), they are automatically inserted in the final SPQL query. Constraints and respective threshold may also be set by right-clicking on the *Desk Area* or also using the *constrains* panel (in Figure 4). These facilities allows the user the fully define the mining task just by navigating the dataset graph and using mouse clicks.

Advanced SPQL query definition. At any moment, the user can edit by hand the query in the SPQL query panel. Any modification of the query will be reflected in the rest of the GUI, e.g. by updating the *Mining View Definition* panel. The possibility to edit directly the query, rather than using the GUI, does not provide any additional expressive power from a mining point of view. Anyway, since part of the SPQL query is pure SQL, we can allow the user to exploit complex SQL queries and additional constraints that are not part of the mining task, but rather they are part of the data preparation phase. Moreover, any SQL query can be submitted in place of an SPQL query, providing additional control to the analyst. Finally, before executing the mining task, a preview of the data in the transactional format, together with its items and attributes, is provided in the *Mining View* panel. This is helpful to check the output of the data preparation step before evaluating the query (or in other terms, before starting the mining).

Pattern Browser. Result of mining queries are shown to the user in a specialized interface, named *Pattern Browser* (see Figure 5. The Pattern Browser provides statistics on the query results, and various functionalities for interactive navigation the set of patterns, such as various kinds of visualizing the patterns, or sorting them. The pattern browser also shows the SPQL query that generated the patterns, and allows the user to tune the query parameters according to his needs, for instance, strengthening or relaxing some constraints on-the-fly. This allows the user to quickly make the query converge towards the desired parameters, for instance, towards a reasonably sized solution set. In the pattern browser the user can also invoke some post-processing ore require to *materialize* the extracted patterns in the underlying database. At the moment the unique kind of post-processing implemented is the extraction of *association rules* from the patterns results set, but we plan to introduce more complex post-processing which uses extracted patterns as basic bricks to build global models as clustering or classifiers. Also the set of extracted association rules can be materialized as relational tables in the underlying database.

3.2 Query Interpreter and Pre-processor

The second module takes care of interpreting the SPQL query, retrieving from the underlying DBMS the data source, and preparing it for the mining phase.

The preprocessor receives from the GUI a well-formed SPQL query, and it is in charge to accomplish the data preparation step. In fact, the Mining Engine is not able to deal with a relational dataset, it can only read data in a proper format. This format is the one traditionally used in frequent itemsets mining contexts. The input dataset is a collection of transactions, where each transaction is a set of *items*. Each of these items is stored as an integer identifier. In the relational dataset an item may be a string, or even a floating point value, but to feed the mining engine these values have to be discretized or mapped.

Thus, the query interpreter, uses the mining view definition present in the SPQL query to retrieve from the original dataset the data of interest. These data are mapped and translated in a categorical format and finally stored on disk. The rest of the query, i.e. frequency and other constraints, are forwarded to the mining engine together with a pointer the the transactional dataset.

3.3 The Mining Engine

The last module constitutes the core of the system which mines the transactional dataset and extract the patterns. The mining core guarantees the scalability and performance of the system by exploiting efficient mining algorithms and data reduction techniques coming from the constraint-based mining paradigm.

The CONQUEST mining engine is based on DCI [24], a high performance, Apriori-like, frequent itemsets mining algorithm, with has the nice feature of being resource and data aware. It is resource aware, because, unlike many other algorithms, it performs the first iterations out-of-core, reducing the dataset and rewriting it directly to the disk. When the dataset is small enough, it is converted and stored as a vertical bitmap in main memory. It is data aware because its behavior changes in presence of sparse or dense datasets. It uses a compact representation in the case of sparse datasets, and detects highly correlated items to save bitwise works in the case of dense datasets. CONQUEST by inheriting the same characteristics, is extremely robust and able to effectively mine different kinds of datasets, regardless of their size.

Although the CONQUEST mining engine adopts a level-wise Apriori-like visit of the lattice, thanks to its internal vertical bitwise representation of the dataset, and associated counting strategy, it performs better than other state-of-the-art algorithms that exploit a depth first visit. Moreover, as we have shown in our previous works [5,8], adopting a level-wise strategy has the great advantage of allowing the exploitation of different kinds of constraints all together by means of data-reduction. At each iteration of the mining process, the dataset is pruned by exploiting the independent data reductions properties of all user-specified constraints. Our framework, exploits a real synergy of all constraints that the user defines for the pattern extraction: each constraint does not only play its part in reducing the data, but this reduction in turns strengthens the pruning power of the other constraints. Moreover data-reduction induces a pruning of the search space, which in turn strengthens future data reductions. The orthogonality of the exploited constraint pushing techniques has a twofold benefit: first, all the techniques can be amalgamated together achieving a very efficient computation.

Moreover, since we have precisely identified classes of constraints which share nice properties, each class has been implemented as an independent module, which plays its role in precise points of the computation. Each module is then instantiated on the basis of the specific constraints supplied by the user. CONQUEST can be easily extended to cope with new user-defined constraints. In fact, it is not the constraint itself that performs data and search space reductions directly, but it is instead the overall framework which exploits constraints classes properties during the computation. Therefore, in order to define a novel constraint, and embed it in the computational framework, it is sufficient to communicate to the system to which classes (possibly more than one) it belongs.

4   Other Mining Query Languages

In this section we discuss other approaches to the data mining query language definition issue. For lack of space we focus only on the approaches most related to the CONQUEST proposal. We are aware that this presentation does not exhaustively cover the wide state-of-the-art of the research (and also the development) on data mining systems and query languages.

The problem of providing an effective interface between data sources and data mining tasks has been a primary concern in data mining. There are several perspectives upon which this interface is desirable, the most important ones being (i) to provide a standard formalization of the desired patterns and the constraints they should obey to; and (ii) to achieve a tighter integration between the data sources and the relational databases (which likely accommodate them). The common ground of most of the approaches can be summarized as follows:

- create and manipulate data mining models through a SQL-based interface (thus implementing a "command-driven" data mining metaphor);
- abstract away the algorithmic particulars;

– allow for mining tasks to be performed on data in the database (thus avoiding the need to export to a special-purpose environment).

Approaches differ on what kinds of models should be created (which patterns are of interest), and what operations we should be able to perform (which constraints the patterns should satisfy). The query language proposed in [21,22] extends SQL with the new operator MINE RULE, which allows the computation and coding of associations in a relational format. Let us consider the relation transaction(Date, CustID, Item, Value) that contains the transactions of a sales representative. The following rule allows the extraction of the rules with support 20% and confidence 50%:

```
MINE RULE Associations AS
    SELECT DISTINCT 1..n Item AS BODY, 1..1 Item AS HEAD,
                        SUPPORT,CONFIDENCE
    WHERE BODY.Value > 100 AND HEAD.Value > 100
    FROM transaction
    GROUP BY CustID
        HAVING COUNT(Item) > 4
    CLUSTER BY Date
        HAVING BODY.Date < HEAD.Date
  EXTRACTING RULES WITH SUPPORT: 0.2, CONFIDENCE: 0.5
```

The above expression specifies the mining of associations of purchased items such that the right part of the rule (consisting of only 1 item) has been purchased after the left part of the rule (that can consist of more than one item), and related to those customers who bought more than 4 items. Moreover, we consider only items with a value greater than 100.

The above approach reflects the following features:

– The source data is specified as a relational entity, and data preparation is accomplished by means of the usual relational operators. For example, the source table can be specified by means of usual join operations, selections and projections.
– The extended query language allows mining of unidimensional association rules. The GROUP BY keyword allows the specification of the transaction identifier, while the item description is specified in the SELECT part of the operator.
– Limited forms of background knowledge can be specified, by imposing some conditions over the admitted values of BODY and HEAD, and by using multiple source tables. Notice, however, that relying directly on SQL does not allow direct specification of more expressive constructs, such as, e.g., concept hierarchies. A limited form of data reorganization is specified by the CLUSTER keyword, that allows the specification of *topology* constraints (i.e. membership constraints of the components of rules to clusters).
– Concerning interestingness measures, the above operator allows the specification of the usual support and confidence constraints, and of further constraints over the contents of the rules (in particular, the SELECT keyword allows the specification of cardinality constraints).

– extracted knowledge is represented by means of relational tables, containing the specification of four attributes: Body, head, Support, Confidence.

Similarly to MINE RULE, the DMQL language [13,14], is designed as an extension of SQL that allows to select the primary source knowledge in SQL-like form. However, the emphasis here is on the kind of patterns to be extracted. Indeed, DMQL supports several mining tasks involving rules: characteristic, discriminant, classification and association rules. The following query:

```
use database university_database find characteristic rules
related to gpa, birth_place, address, count(*)%
from student where status = "graduate" and major = "cs"
and birth_place = "Canada"
with noise threshold = 0.05
```

specifies that the database used to extract the rules is the university database (use database university_database), that the kind of rules you are interested in are characteristic rules (find characteristic rules) w.r.t. the attributes gpa, birth place, and address (related to ...). The query specifies also that this rules are extracted on the students who are graduated in computer science, and that are born in Canada. As for MINE RULE, the specification of primary source knowledge is made explicit in the from and where clauses.

DMQL exploits follows a decoupled approach between specification and implementation, since the extraction is accomplished by external algorithms, and the specification of the query has the main objective of preparing the data and encoding them in a format suitable for the algorithms. Interestingly, DMQL allows the manipulation of a limited form of background knowledge, by allowing the direct specification of concept hierarchies.

Unfortunately, neither MINE RULE nor DMQL provide operators to further query the extracted patterns. The closure principle is marginally considered in MINE RULE (the mining result is stored into a relational table and can be further queried), but not considered at all within DMQL. By contrast, Imielinkski and others [17] propose a data mining query language (MSQL) which seeks to provide a language both to selectively generate patterns, and to separately query them. MSQL allows the extraction of association rules only, and can be seen as an extension of MINE RULE. The pattern language of MSQL is based on multidimensional propositional rules, which are specified by means of *descriptors*. A descriptor is an expression of the form: $(A_i = a_{ij})$ where A_i is an attribute, and a_{ij} is a either a value or a range of values in the domain of A_i. The rules extracted from MSQL have hence the form Body $\Rightarrow$ Consequent where Body is a conjunctset (i.e. the conjunction of an arbitrary number of descriptors such that each descriptor in the set refers to a different attribute) and Consequent is a single descriptor. Rules are generated by means of a GetRules statement which, apart from syntax issues, has similar features as MINE RULE and DMQL. In addition, MSQL allows for nested queries, that is, queries containing subqueries.

The extracted rules are stored in a *RuleBase* and then they can be further queried, by means of the SelectRules statement. It is possible to select a subset of the generated rules that verify a certain condition

```
SelectRules(R) where Body has { (Age=*), (Sex=*) } and Consequent
is { (Address=*) }
```

as well as to select the tuples of the input database that violate (satisfy) all (any of) the extracted rules:

```
Select * from Actor where VIOLATES ALL(
    GetRules(Actor)
    where Body is { (Age = *) }
    and Consequent is { (Sex = *) }
    and confidence > 0.3
        )
```

A novel and completely different perspective to inductive databases querying has been devised in [10]. The basic intuition is that, if the pattern language $\mathcal{L}$ were stored within relational tables, any constraint predicate Q could be specified by means of a relational algebra expression, and the DBMS could take care of implementing the best strategy for computing the solution space. Assume, for example, that sequences are stored within a relational engine by means of the following relations:

- Sequences(sid,item,pos), representing each sequence by means of a sequence identifier, an item and its relative position within the sequence;
- Supports(sid,supp) which specifies, for each sequence, its frequency.

Then, the following SQL query asks for the sequences holding with frequency greater than 60%, or such that item a occurs before item b within the transaction, can be expressed as follows:

```
SELECT Supports.sid
FROM Sequences S1, Sequences S2, Supports
WHERE S1.sid = Supports.sid AND S2.sid = S1.sid
  AND Supports.supp > 60
  OR (S1.item = a AND S2.item = b AND S1.pos < S2.pos)
```

Clearly, the pattern language can be extremely huge, and hence it is quite unpractical to effectively store it. Indeed, the pattern language is represented as a *virtual* table, i.e., an empty table which has to be populated. In the above example, although the Sequences and Supports tables are exploited within the query, they are assumed to be virtual tables, i.e., no materialization actually exists for them within the DBMS. The idea here is that, whenever the user queries such pattern tables, an efficient data mining algorithm is triggered by the DBMS, which materializes those tuples needed to answer the query. Afterwards, the query can be effectively executed. Thus, the core of the approach is a constraint extraction procedure, which analyzes a given SQL query and identifies the relevant constraints. The procedure builds, for each SQL query, the corresponding relational algebra tree. Since virtual tables appear in leaf nodes of the tree, a bottom-up traversal of the tree allows the detection of the necessary constraints. Finally, specific calls to a mining engine can be raised in order to populate those nodes representing virtual tables.

This approach has the merit of providing a real tight coupling between the mining and the DBMS, or in other terms, between the mining queries and the database queries. Indeed, this approach does not even require the definition of a data mining query language, since it is SQL itself to play such role. However, it is not clear how such approach could support a complex knowledge discovery process. For instance, the pre-processing step is completely overlooked by this approach: preparing the data for mining would require long and complex SQL queries. Moreover, since we got no reference to the source data, it is not clear how the mining view could be defined and/or changed within a mining session. Consider again the Sequences and Supports relations in the example above, and suppose that the support of sequences patterns are computed w.r.t. a database of sequences of events with a *weekly* timescale: what if the analyst decides to move to the *daily* timescale?

The problem of providing little support to the pre-processing and evaluation phase of the knowledge discovery process, is common to all the query languages discussed above. In CONQUEST, while we can take care of the pre-processing at the language level (e.g., easy mining view definition, attributes discretization), the evaluation phase is attacked merely at the system level by means of the pattern browser capabilities, such as the on-the-fly constraints tuning. More sophisticated post-processing of the extracted patterns, and reasoning techniques, should be studied and developed in our future work.

5 Conclusion

Many distinguishing features make CONQUEST a unique system:

Large variety of constraints handled - To the best of our knowledge, CONQUEST is the only system able to deal with so many different constraints all together, and provide the opportunity of easily defining new ones. While some prototypes for constraint-based pattern discovery exist, they are usually focused on few kinds of constraints, and their algorithmic techniques can not be easily extended to other constraints.

Usability - CONQUEST has been devised to fruitfully deal with real-world problems. The user friendly interface, the pre-processing capabilities and the simple connectivity to relational DBMS, make it easy for the user to immediately start to find nuggets of interesting knowledge in her/his data. Modularity and extensibility make the system able to adapt to changing application needs. Efficiency, robustness and scalability make possible to mine real-world huge datasets.

Robustness and resources awareness - One of the main drawbacks of the state-of-the art software for pattern discovery, is that it usually fails to mine large amounts of data due to memory lack. In this sense, CONQUESTis robust, since huge datasets are mined out-of-core until the data-reduction framework reduces the dataset size enough to move it in-core.

Efficiency - CONQUEST is a high performance mining software. As an Example consider Figure 6 where we compare execution times of CONQUEST against

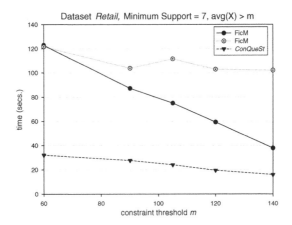

Fig. 6. Performance comparison

$\mathcal{FIC}^{\mathcal{A}}$ and $\mathcal{FIC}^{\mathcal{M}}$ [26], two depth first algorithms, ad-hoc devised to deal with the avg constraint (the one used in the comparison).

Even tough CONQUEST is already fruitfully usable on real-world problems, many direction must be explored in the next future: efficient incremental mining, advanced visualization techniques, more complex post-processing, building global models from the interesting patterns, mining patterns from complex data such as sequences and graphs. We are continuously developing new functionalities of CONQUEST.

References

1. http://java.sun.com/products/jdbc/
2. Agrawal, R., Srikant, R.: Fast Algorithms for Mining Association Rules in Large Databases. In: Proceedings of VLDB 1994 (1994)
3. Bistarelli, S., Bonchi, F.: Extending the soft constraint based mining paradigm. In: KDID 2006. LNCS, vol. 4747, pp. 24–41. Springer, Heidelberg (2007)
4. Bonchi, F.: Frequent Pattern Queries: Language and Optimizations. PhD thesis, Ph.D. thesis TD10- 03, Dipartimento di Informatica, Università di Pisa (2003)
5. Bonchi, F., Giannotti, F., Mazzanti, A., Pedreschi, D.: ExAMiner: Optimized levelwise frequent pattern mining with monotone constraints. In: Proceedings of ICDM 2003 (2003)
6. Bonchi, F., Giannotti, F., Mazzanti, A., Pedreschi, D.: ExAnte: Anticipated data reduction in constrained pattern mining. In: Lavrač, N., Gamberger, D., Todorovski, L., Blockeel, H. (eds.) PKDD 2003. LNCS (LNAI), vol. 2838, Springer, Heidelberg (2003)
7. Bonchi, F., Lucchese, C.: On closed constrained frequent pattern mining. In: Perner, P. (ed.) ICDM 2004. LNCS (LNAI), vol. 3275, Springer, Heidelberg (2004)

8. Bonchi, F., Lucchese, C.: Pushing tougher constraints in frequent pattern mining. In: Ho, T.-B., Cheung, D., Liu, H. (eds.) PAKDD 2005. LNCS (LNAI), vol. 3518, Springer, Heidelberg (2005)
9. Bucila, C., Gehrke, J., Kifer, D., White, W.: DualMiner: A dual-pruning algorithm for itemsets with constraints. In: Proceedings of ACM SIGKDD 2002, ACM Press, New York (2002)
10. Calders, T., Goetals, B., Prado, A.: Integrating pattern mining in relational databases. In: Fürnkranz, J., Scheffer, T., Spiliopoulou, M. (eds.) PKDD 2006. LNCS (LNAI), vol. 4213, pp. 454–461. Springer, Heidelberg (2006)
11. Fayyad, U.M., Piatetsky-Shapiro, G., Smyth, P.: The kdd process for extracting useful knowledge from volumes of data. Commun. ACM 39(11), 27–34 (1996)
12. Grahne, G., Lakshmanan, L.V.S., Wang, X., Xie, M.H.: On dual mining: From patterns to circumstances, and back. In: Proceedings of the 17th International Conference on Data Engineering (ICDE 2001), April 2-6, 2001, Heidelberg, Germany (2001)
13. Han, J., Fu, Y., Koperski, K., Wang, W., Zaiane, O.: DMQL: A Data Mining Query Language for Relational Databases. In: SIGMOD 1996 Workshop on Research Issues on Data Mining and Knowledge Discovery (DMKD 1996) (1996)
14. Han, J., Kamber, M.: Data Mining: Concepts and Techniques. Morgan Kaufman, San Francisco (2000)
15. Han, J., Lakshmanan, L.V.S., Ng, R.T.: Constraint-based, multidimensional data mining. Computer 32(8), 46–50 (1999)
16. Imielinski, T., Mannila, H.: A database perspective on knowledge discovery. Comm. Of The Acm 39, 58–64 (1996)
17. Imielinski, T., Virmani, A.: MSQL: A Query Language for Database Mining. Data Mining and Knowledge Discovery 3(4), 373–408 (1999)
18. Kramer, S., Raedt, L.D., Helma, C.: Molecular feature mining in hiv data. In: Proceedings of the seventh ACM SIGKDD international conference on Knowledge discovery and data mining, San Francisco, August 26-29, 2001, pp. 136–143. ACM Press, New York (2001)
19. Lakshmanan, L.V.S., Ng, R.T., Han, J., Pang, A.: Optimization of constrained frequent set queries with 2-variable constraints. SIGMOD Record 28(2) (1999)
20. Mannila, H., Toivonen, H.: Levelwise search and borders of theories in knowledge discovery. Data Mining and Knowledge Discovery 1(3), 241–258 (1997)
21. Meo, R., Psaila, G., Ceri, S.: A new SQL-like operator for mining association rules. In: Vijayaraman, T.M., Buchmann, A.P., Mohan, C., Sarda, N.L. (eds.) VLDB 1996, Proceedings of 22th International Conference on Very Large Data Bases, Mumbai (Bombay), India, 3–6 september 1996, pp. 122–133. Morgan Kaufmann, San Francisco (1996)
22. Meo, R., Psaila, G., Ceri, S.: A Tightly-Coupled Architecture for Data Mining. In: International Conference on Data Engineering (ICDE 1998), pp. 316–323 (1998)
23. Ng, R.T., Lakshmanan, L.V.S., Han, J., Pang, A.: Exploratory mining and pruning optimizations of constrained associations rules. In: Proceedings of the ACM SIGMOD 1998, ACM Press, New York (1998)
24. Orlando, S., Palmerini, P., Perego, R., Silvestri, F.: Adaptive and Resource-Aware Mining of Frequent Sets. In: Proc. of the 2002 IEEE Int. Conference on Data Mining (ICDM 2002), Maebashi City, Japan, December 2002, pp. 338–345. IEEE Computer Society Press, Los Alamitos (2002)

25. Pei, J., Han, J.: Can we push more constraints into frequent pattern mining? In: Proceedings of ACM SIGKDD 2000, ACM Press, New York (2000)
26. Pei, J., Han, J., Lakshmanan, L.V.S.: Mining frequent item sets with convertible constraints. In: Proceedings of ICDE 2001 (2001)
27. Esposito, R., Meo, R., Botta, M.: Answering constraint-based mining queries on itemsets using previous materialized results. Journal of Intelligent Information Systems (2005)
28. Srikant, R., Vu, Q., Agrawal, R.: Mining association rules with item constraints. In: Proceedings of ACM SIGKDD 1997, ACM Press, New York (1997)

Analysis of Time Series Data
with Predictive Clustering Trees

Sašo Džeroski[1], Valentin Gjorgjioski[1], Ivica Slavkov[1], and Jan Struyf[2]

[1] Dept. of Knowledge Technologies, Jožef Stefan Institute
Jamova 39, 1000 Ljubljana, Slovenia
{Saso.Dzeroski, Valentin.Gjorgjioski, Ivica.Slavkov}@ijs.si
[2] Dept. of Computer Science, Katholieke Universiteit Leuven
Celestijnenlaan 200A, 3001 Leuven, Belgium
Jan.Struyf@cs.kuleuven.be

Abstract. Predictive clustering is a general framework that unifies clustering and prediction. This paper investigates how to apply this framework to cluster time series data. The resulting system, Clus-TS, constructs predictive clustering trees (PCTs) that partition a given set of time series into homogeneous clusters. In addition, PCTs provide a symbolic description of the clusters. We evaluate Clus-TS on time series data from microarray experiments. Each data set records the change over time in the expression level of yeast genes as a response to a change in environmental conditions. Our evaluation shows that Clus-TS is able to cluster genes with similar responses, and to predict the time series based on the description of a gene. Clus-TS is part of a larger project where the goal is to investigate how global models can be combined with inductive databases.

1 Introduction

Predictive clustering is a general framework that combines clustering and prediction [1]. Predictive clustering partitions a given data set into a set of clusters such that the instances in a given cluster are similar to each other and dissimilar to the instances in other clusters. In this sense, predictive clustering is identical to regular clustering [11]. The difference is that predictive clustering associates a predictive model to each cluster. This model assigns instances to clusters and provides predictions for new instances. So far, decision trees [1,22] and rule sets [25] have been used in the context of predictive clustering.

This paper investigates how predictive clustering can be applied to cluster time series [13]. A time series is an ordered sequence of measurements of a continuous variable that changes over time. Fig. 1.a presents an example of eight time series partitioned into three clusters: cluster C_1 contains time series that increase and subsequently decrease, C_2 has mainly decreasing time series and C_3 mainly increasing ones. Fig. 1.b shows a so-called predictive clustering tree (PCT) for this set of clusters. This is the predictive model associated with the clustering.

S. Džeroski and J. Struyf (Eds.): KDID 2006, LNCS 4747, pp. 63–80, 2007.

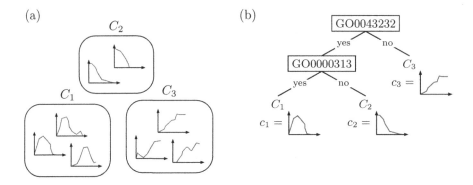

Fig. 1. (a) A set of time series clustered into three clusters. (b) A predictive clustering tree associated with this clustering. Each leaf of the tree corresponds to one cluster.

We propose a new algorithm called Clus-TS (Clustering-Time Series) that constructs trees such as the one shown in Fig. 1.b. Clus-TS instantiates the general PCT induction algorithm proposed by Blockeel et al. [1] to the task of time series clustering. This is non-trivial because the general algorithm requires computing a centroid for each cluster and for most distance measures suitable for time series clustering, no closed algebraic form centroid is known.

We evaluate Clus-TS on time series data from microarray experiments [9]. Each data set records the change over time in the expression level of yeast genes in response to a change in environmental conditions. A lot of work has been done on clustering this type of short time series gene expression data [4]. Our main motivation is to use alternative distance measures (that mainly take the shape of the time series into account) and to construct clusters that can be explained by a given set of features. Besides the time series, various other data about each gene are available. Here, we consider motifs and terms from the Gene Ontology (GO) [5]. The motifs are subsequences that occur in the amino acid sequence of many genes. The motivation for using motifs as features is due to Curk et al. [2], who use motifs in a similar analysis. The motifs or GO terms appear in the internal nodes of the PCT (Fig. 1.b) and provide a symbolic description of the clusters. C_1 includes, for example, all genes that have terms "GO:0043232" and "GO:0000313" in their description. This is related to itemset constrained clustering [20], which clusters vectors of numeric values and constrains each cluster by means of an itemset.

So far, most research on inductive databases (IDBs) [10,3] has focused on local models (i.e., models that apply to only a subset of the examples), such as frequent item sets and association rules. Clus-TS is part of a larger project [7,22,25] were the goal is to investigate how IDBs can be extended to global models, such as decision trees (for prediction) and mixture models (for clustering). Predictive clustering has been argued to provide a general framework unifying clustering and prediction, two of the most basic data mining tasks, and is therefore an excellent starting point for extending IDBs to global models [25].

In particular, we are interested in developing a system that is applicable to clustering and prediction in many application domains, including bioinformatics. Extending PCTs to time series clustering is a step in this direction.

2   Predictive Clustering Trees

2.1   Prediction, Clustering, and Predictive Clustering Trees

Predictive modeling aims at constructing models that can predict a target property of an object from a description of the object. Predictive models are learned from sets of examples, where each example has the form (D, T), with D being an object description and T a target property value. While a variety of representations ranging from propositional to first order logic have been used for D, T is almost always considered to consist of a single target attribute called the class, which is either discrete (classification problem) or continuous (regression problem).

Clustering [11], on the other hand, is concerned with grouping objects into subsets of objects (called clusters) that are similar w.r.t. their description D. There is no target property defined in clustering tasks. In conventional clustering, the notion of a distance (or conversely, similarity) is crucial: examples are considered to be points in a metric space and clusters are constructed such that examples in the same cluster are close according to a particular distance metric. A centroid (or prototypical example) may be used as a representative for a cluster. The centroid is the point with the lowest average (squared) distance to all the examples in the cluster, i.e., the mean or medoid of the examples. Hierarchical clustering and k-means clustering are the most commonly used algorithms for this type of clustering (see Section 4.4).

Predictive clustering [1] combines elements from both prediction and clustering. As in clustering, we seek clusters of examples that are similar to each other, but in general taking both the descriptive part and the target property into account (the distance measure is defined on $D \cup T$). In addition, a predictive model must be associated to each cluster. The predictive model assigns new instances to clusters based on their description D and provides a prediction for the target property T. A well-known type of model that can be used to this end is a decision tree [17]. A decision tree that is used for predictive clustering is called a predictive clustering tree (PCT, Fig. 1.b). Each node of a PCT represents a cluster. The conjunction of conditions on the path from the root to that node gives a description of the cluster. Essentially, each cluster has a symbolic description in the form of a rule (IF conjunction of conditions THEN cluster)[1], while a tree structure represents the hierarchy of clusters. Clusters that are not on the same branch of a tree do not overlap.

In Fig. 1, the description D of a gene consists of GO terms with which the gene is annotated, and the target property T is the time series recorded for the gene. In general, we could include both D and T in the distance measure. We are, however, most interested in the time series part. Therefore, we define the distance measure

---

[1] This idea was first used in conceptual clustering [15].

only on T. We consider various distance measures in Section 3.1. The resulting PCT (Fig. 1.b) represents a clustering that is homogeneous w.r.t. T and the nodes of the tree provide a symbolic description of the clusters. Note that a PCT can also be used for prediction: use the tree to assign a new instance to a leaf and take the centroid (denoted with c_i in Fig. 1.b) of the corresponding cluster as prediction.

2.2   Building Predictive Clustering Trees

Table 1 presents the generic induction algorithm for PCTs [1]. It is a variant of the standard greedy recursive top-down decision tree induction algorithm used, e.g., in C4.5 [17]. It takes as input a set of instances I (in our case genes described by motifs or GO terms and their associated time series). The procedure BestTest (Table 1, right) searches for the best acceptable test (motif or GO term) that can be put in a node. If such a test t^* can be found then the algorithm creates a new internal node labeled t^* and calls itself recursively to construct a subtree for each cluster in the partition $\mathcal{P}^*$ induced by t^* on the instances. If no acceptable test can be found, then the algorithm creates a leaf, and the recursion terminates. (The procedure Acceptable defines the stopping criterion of the algorithm, e.g., specifying maximum tree depth or a minimum number of instances in each leaf).

Table 1. The generic PCT induction algorithm Clus

procedure $\text{PCT}(I)$ **returns** tree	procedure $\text{BestTest}(I)$
1: $(t^*, h^*, \mathcal{P}^*) = \text{BestTest}(I)$	1: $(t^*, h^*, \mathcal{P}^*) = (none, 0, \emptyset)$
2: **if** $t^* \neq none$ **then**	2: **for each** possible test t **do**
3: **for each** $I_k \in \mathcal{P}^*$ **do**	3: $\mathcal{P} = $ partition induced by t on I
4: $tree_k = \text{PCT}(I_k)$	4: $h = Var(I) - \sum_{I_k \in \mathcal{P}} \frac{|I_k|}{|I|} Var(I_k)$
5: **return** node$(t^*, \bigcup_k \{tree_k\})$	5: **if** $(h > h^*) \wedge \text{Acceptable}(t, \mathcal{P})$ **then**
6: **else**	6: $(t^*, h^*, \mathcal{P}^*) = (t, h, \mathcal{P})$
7: **return** leaf(centroid(I))	7: **return** $(t^*, h^*, \mathcal{P}^*)$

Up till here, the algorithm is identical to a standard decision tree learner. The main difference is in the heuristic that is used for selecting the tests. For PCTs, this heuristic is the reduction in variance (weighted by cluster size, see line 4 of BestTest). Maximizing variance reduction maximizes cluster homogeneity. The next section discusses how cluster variance can be defined for time series.

An implementation of the PCT induction algorithm is available in the Clus system, which can be obtained at http://www.cs.kuleuven.be/~dtai/clus.

3   PCTs for Time Series Clustering

3.1   Distance Measures

In this section, we discuss a number of distance measures for time series, which will be used in the definition of cluster variance later on. Some measures require that all time series in the data set have the same length. This property holds true for the data that we consider in the experimental evaluation (Section 4).

If all time series have the same length then one can represent them as real valued vectors and use standard vector distance measures such as the Euclidean or Manhattan distance. These measures are, however, not always appropriate for time series because they assume that the time series are synchronized, and mainly capture the difference in scale and baseline. Below, we discuss three distance measures that have been proposed to alleviate these shortcomings.

Dynamic Time Warping. (DTW) [19] can capture a non-linear distortion along the time axis. It accomplishes this by assigning multiple values of one of the time series to a single value of the other. As a result, DTW is suitable if the time series are not properly synchronized, e.g., if one is delayed, or if the two time series are not of the same length. Fig. 2.a illustrates DTW and compares it to the Euclidean distance.

$d_{DTW}(X, Y)$ with $X = \alpha_1, \alpha_2, \ldots, \alpha_I$, $Y = \beta_1, \beta_2, \ldots, \beta_J$ is defined based on the notion of a warping path between X and Y. A warping path is a sequence of grid points $F = f_1, f_2, \ldots, f_K$ on the $I \times J$ plane (Fig. 2.b). Let the distance between two values α_{i_k} and β_{j_k} be $d(f_k) = |\alpha_{i_k} - \beta_{j_k}|$, then an evaluation function $\Delta(F)$ is given by $\Delta(F) = 1/(I + J) \sum_{k=1}^{K} d(f_k) w_k$. The weights w_k are as follows: $w_k = (i_k - i_{k-1}) + (j_k - j_{k-1})$, $i_0 = j_0 = 0$. The smaller the value of $\Delta(F)$, the more similar X and Y are. In order to prevent excessive distortion, we assume an adjustment window ($|i_k - j_k| \leq r$). $d_{DTW}(X, Y)$ is the minimum of $\Delta(F)$. d_{DTW} can be computed with dynamic programming in time $O(IJ)$.

Both the Euclidean distance and DTW take into account differences in scale and baseline. If a given time series is identical to a second time series, but scaled by a certain factor or offset by some constant, then the two time series will be distant. For many applications, these differences are, however, not important;

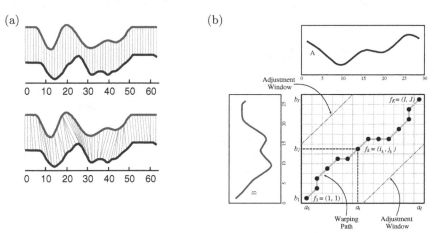

Fig. 2. (a) Euclidean distance (top) compared to DTW (bottom). (b) A warping path. (Artwork courtesy of Eamonn Keogh).

only the shape of the time series matters. The next two measures are more appropriate for such applications.

Correlation. The correlation coefficient $r(X,Y)$ between two time series X and Y is calculated as

$$r(X,Y) = \frac{E[(X - E[X]) \cdot (Y - E[Y])]}{E[(X - E[X])^2] \cdot E[(Y - E[Y])^2]}, \tag{1}$$

where $E[V]$ denotes expectation (i.e., mean value) of V. $r(X,Y)$ measures the degree of linear dependence between X and Y. It has the following intuitive meaning in terms of the shapes of X and Y: r close to 1 means that the shapes are similar. If there is a linear relation between X and Y then the time series are identical but might have a different scale or baseline. r close to -1 means that X and Y have "mirrored" shapes, and r close to 0 means that the shapes are unrelated (and consequently dissimilar). Based on this intuitive interpretation, we can define the distance between two time series as $d_r(X,Y) = \sqrt{0.5 \cdot (1 - r(X,Y))}$. d_r has, however, two drawbacks. First, it is difficult to properly estimate correlation if the number of observations is small (i.e., a short time series). Second, d_r can only capture the linear dependencies between the time series. Two time series that are non-linearly related will be distant. Fig. 3 illustrates this effect.

A Qualitative Distance. A third distance measure is the qualitative distance proposed by Todorovski et al. [23]. It is based on a qualitative comparison of the shape of the time series. Consider two time series X and Y (Fig. 3). Then choose a pair of time points i and j and observe the qualitative change of the value of X and Y at these points. There are three possibilities: increase $(X_i > X_j)$, no-change $(X_i \approx X_j)$, and decrease $(X_i < X_j)$. d_{qual} is obtained by summing the difference in qualitative change observed for X and Y for all pairs of time points, i.e.,

$$d_{\text{qual}}(X,Y) = \sum_{i=1}^{n-1} \sum_{j=i+1}^{n} \frac{2 \cdot \mathit{Diff}(q(X_i, X_j), q(Y_i, Y_j))}{N \cdot (N - 1)}, \tag{2}$$

with $\mathit{Diff}(q_1, q_2)$ a function that defines the difference between different qualitative changes (Fig. 2). Roughly speaking, d_{qual} counts the number of disagreements in change of X and Y.

d_{qual} does not have the drawbacks of the correlation based measure. First, it can be computed for very short time series, without decreasing the quality of the estimate. Second, it captures the similarity in shape of the time series, regardless

Table 2. The definition of $\mathit{Diff}(q_1, q_2)$

$\mathit{Diff}(q_1, q_2)$	increase	no-change	decrease
increase	0	0.5	1
no-change	0.5	0	0.5
decrease	1	0.5	0

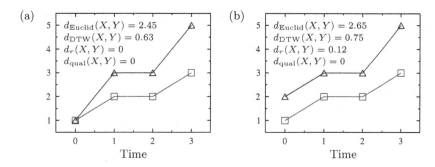

Fig. 3. Comparison of four distance measures for time series. Time series (a) are linearly related resulting in $d_r(X, Y) = 0$. Time series (b) are non-linearly related, but still have a similar shape, resulting in $d_{\text{qual}}(X, Y) = 0$.

of whether their dependence is linear or non-linear (Fig. 3). In the experimental evaluation, we will use d_{qual} (Section 4).

3.2 Computing Cluster Variance

Recall from Section 2.2 that the PCT induction algorithm requires a measure of cluster variance in its heuristics. The variance of a cluster C can be defined based on a distance measure as

$$Var(C) = \frac{1}{|C|} \sum_{X \in C} d^2(X, c), \qquad (3)$$

with c the cluster centroid of C. To cluster time series, d should be a distance measure defined on time series, such as the ones discussed in the previous section.

The centroid c can be computed as $\text{argmin}_q \sum_{X \in C} d^2(X, q)$. We consider two possible representations for c: (a) the centroid is an arbitrary time series, and (b) the centroid is one of the time series from the cluster (the cluster prototype). In representation (b), the centroid can be computed with $|C|^2$ distance computations by substituting q with each time series in the cluster. In representation (a), the space of candidate centroids is infinite. This means that either a closed algebraic form for the centroid is required or that one should resort to approximative algorithms to compute the centroid. No closed form for the centroid is known in representation (a) for the distance measure d_{qual}. To the best of our knowledge, the same holds for d_{DTW} and d_r.

An alternative way to define cluster variance is based on the sum of the squared pairwise distances (SSPD) between the cluster elements, i.e.,

$$Var(C) = \frac{1}{2|C|^2} \sum_{X \in C} \sum_{Y \in C} d^2(X, Y). \qquad (4)$$

(The factor 2 in the denominator of (4) ensures that (4) is identical to (3) for the Euclidean distance.) The advantage of this approach is that no centroid is required. It also requires $|C|^2$ distance computations. This is the same time complexity as the approach with the centroid in representation (b). Hence, using the definition based on a centroid is only more efficient if the centroid can be computed in time linear in the cluster size. This is the case for the Euclidean distance in combination with using the pointwise average of the time series as centroid. For the other distance measures, no such centroids are known. Therefore, we choose to estimate cluster variance using the SSPD.

A second advantage is that (4) can be easily approximated by means of sampling, e.g., by using,

$$Var(C) = \frac{1}{2|C|m} \sum_{X \in C} \left(\sum_{Y \in \text{sample}(C,m)} d^2(X,Y) \right), \tag{5}$$

with sample(C, m) a random sample without replacement of m elements from C, instead of (4) if $|C| \geq m$. The computational cost of (5) grows only linearly with the cluster size. In the experimental evaluation, we compare (4) to (5).

3.3 Cluster Centroids for the Tree Leaves

The PCT induction algorithm places cluster centroids in its leaves, which can be inspected by the domain expert and used as a prediction. For these centroids, we use representation (b) as discussed above.

4 Analyzing Gene Expression Time Series with PCTs

4.1 The Problem

DNA microarray analysis is an interesting application area for short time series clustering. Clustering genes by their time expression pattern makes sense because genes which are co-regulated or have a similar function, under certain conditions, will have a similar temporal profile. Instead of simply clustering the expression time series with, e.g., HAC, and later on elucidating the characteristics of the obtained clusters (as done in e.g., [4]), we perform constrained clustering with PCTs. This yields the clusters and symbolic descriptions of the clusters in one step.

We use the data from a study conducted by Gasch et al. [9]. The purpose of the study is to explore the changes in expression levels of yeast (*Saccharomyces cerevisiae*) genes under diverse environmental stresses. Various sudden changes in the environmental conditions are tested, ranging from heat shock to amino acid starvation for a prolonged period of time. The gene expression levels of around 5000 genes are measured at different time points using microarrays. The data is log-transformed and normalized based on the time-zero measurement of yeast cells under normal environmental conditions. We use three sets of experiments from Gasch et al. [9]: amino acid starvation (AAS), diauxic shift (DS), and diamide treatment (DT).

4.2   The Mining Scenario

Our mining scenario consists of two steps. In a first step, we use a local pattern mining algorithm to construct patterns based on the description of the yeast genes. In a second step, we use these local patterns as features to construct PCTs. We use two types of features: motifs and GO terms [5].

For the first set of features, we mine frequent subsequences (motifs) occurring in the DNA sequences of the yeast genes, which we obtain from the Stanford database. We use the constraint based mining algorithm FAVST [12,16]. FAVST supports three types of constraints: minimum frequency, and minimum and maximum motif length. We query FAVST for sequences that appear in 25% of the genes and consist of at least 8 nucleotides. In this way, we obtain approximately 300 motifs ranging from 8 to 10 nucleotides. These motifs are passed to Clus-TS to build PCTs with the motifs in the internal nodes.

In the second set of features, each feature is a GO term. We obtain the GO term annotations for each yeast gene from the Gene Ontology [5] (version April, 2006). Note that the GO terms are structured in a hierarchy. We use both the part_of and is_a relations to include for each gene all relevant GO terms. To limit the number of features, we set a minimum frequency threshold: each GO term must appear for at least 50 of the genes.

4.3   Predicting Time Series with PCTs

Recall that PCTs can be used both for prediction and clustering. PCTs predict values just like regular decision trees. They sort each test instance into a leaf and assign as prediction the label of that leaf. PCTs label their leaves with the training set centroids of the corresponding clusters. In this section, we evaluate PCTs in a predictive setting and in Section 4.5 we assess their clustering performance.

To evaluate predictive performance, we need an error metric. An obvious candidate is the root mean squared error (RMSE), which is defined as

$$\text{RMSE}(I, T) = \sqrt{\frac{1}{|I|} \sum_{X \in I} d^2(T(X), \text{series}(X))}, \qquad (6)$$

with I the set of test instances, T the PCT that is being tested, $T(X)$ the time series predicted by T for instance X, and $\text{series}(X)$ the actual series of X.

We compare the PCT built by Clus-TS to a default predictor DEF that always predicts the overall training set centroid. We measure predictive RMSE using 10 fold cross-validation. We set the minimum number of time series in each cluster to 10 and all other parameters of Clus-TS to their default values. Clus supports size constraints by means of the post pruning method proposed by Garofalakis et al. [8], which employs dynamic programming to find the most accurate subtree no larger than a given number of leaves. Here, accuracy is estimated as training set RMSE (see also [22]). Fig. 4 presents the results for different values of the size constraint.

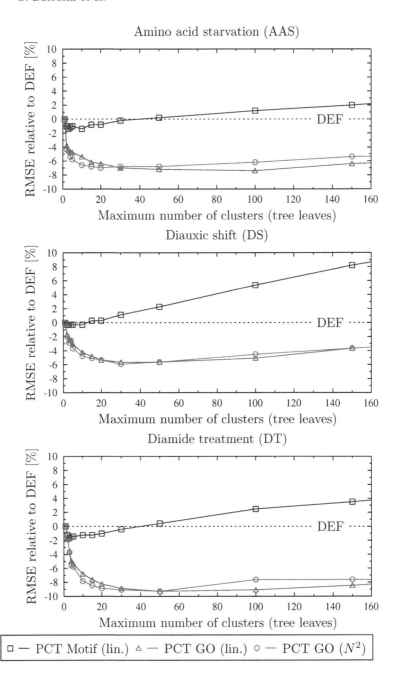

Fig. 4. RMS error versus maximum number of clusters

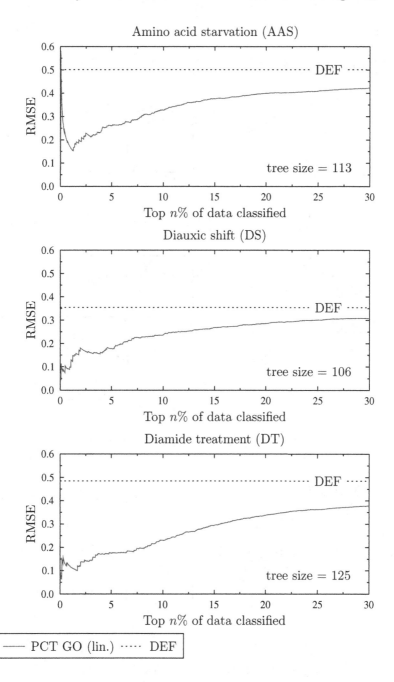

Fig. 5. RMS error versus percentage of data classified

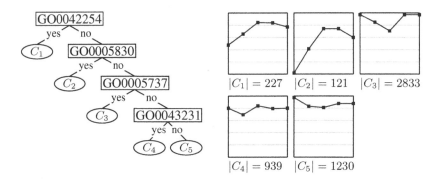

Fig. 6. Size 5 PCT for amino acid starvation (AAS)

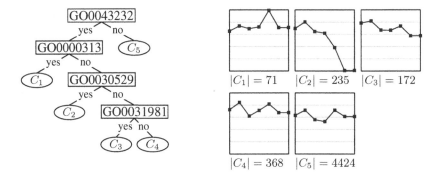

Fig. 7. Size 5 PCT for diauxic shift (DS)

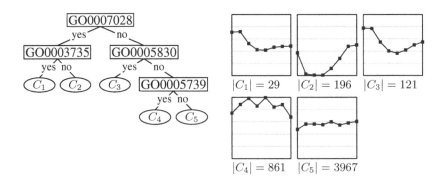

Fig. 8. Size 5 PCT for diamide treatment (DT)

The PCTs with motifs as features do not perform well (RMSE close to that of DEF) and quickly overfit for larger size trees. The optimal tree size for the PCTs with GO terms seems to be around 30 nodes. The PCTs with GO terms perform better, but still have a relatively high RMSE. Fig. 4 also compares Clus-TS with the SSPD variance estimate with quadratic time complexity (PCT N^2) to the linear approximation with sample size $m = 10$ (PCT lin.). Both estimates yield a comparable predictive performance. PCT N^2 performs slightly better for small trees, but becomes worse for larger trees. PCT N^2 is a factor 6.8 to 12.6 slower than PCT lin.

From a biological viewpoint, the PCTs cluster genes that have a similar function (GO terms) and a similar response in expression level to a certain change in environmental conditions. One problem is that, as noted by Gasch et al. [9], only a subset of the genes (about 900) have a stereotypical response to the environmental stress. That is, only a subset of the genes can be accurately clustered, whereas the other genes have an uncorrelated response. As a result, we hypothesize that the PCTs are able to more accurately predict the time series of a subset of the genes. We therefore perform the following experiment. Besides recording the predicted time series for each test set gene, we also record a confidence value for each prediction. We then sort the genes by confidence value and compute the RMSE of the top n percent most confident predictions. We use the training set RMSE of the leaf that made the prediction as confidence estimate. This is similar to the approach used for generating a ROC curve for a decision tree [6]. Fig. 5 presents the results[2]. It shows that more accurate predictions are obtained if we restrict the test set based on the confidence of the predictions. For example, if time series are predicted for the top 5%, then the RMSE decreases to about 50% of that of DEF.

Fig. 6, 7, and 8 show as an illustration the PCT for each data set obtained with the maximum size set to 5 leaves. They also show the cluster centroids for each of the leaves.

4.4   Hierarchical Agglomerative Clustering

In this section, we briefly discuss Hierarchical Agglomerative Clustering (HAC) (see, e.g., [14]). We use HAC as a baseline to compare Clus-TS to. HAC is one of the most widely used clustering approaches. It produces a nested hierarchy of groups of similar objects, based on a matrix containing the pairwise distances between all objects. HAC repeats the following three steps until all objects are in the same cluster:

1. Search the distance matrix for the two closest objects or clusters.
2. Join the two objects (clusters) to produce a new cluster.
3. Update the distance matrix to include the distances between the new cluster and all other clusters (objects).

---

[2] PCTs are obtained with the same parameters as before, except that we use validation set based pruning instead of specifying a size constraint. Clus-TS uses here 1000 genes of the original training set for pruning and the rest for the tree construction (suggested by [24]). Simply selecting a PCT from Fig. 4 is unfair; it corresponds to optimizing the size parameter on the test set.

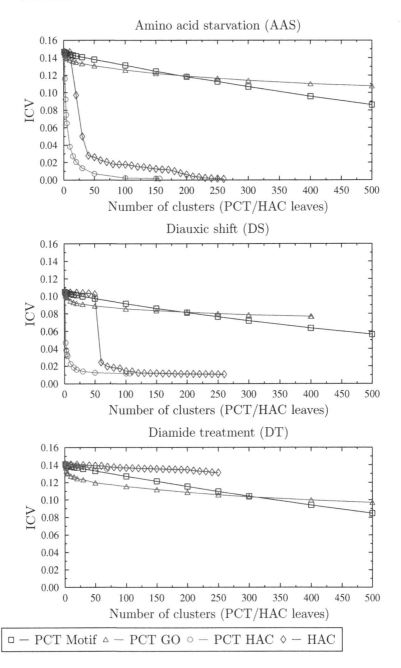

Fig. 9. ICV versus number of clusters

There are four well known HAC algorithms: single-link, complete-link, group-average, and centroid clustering, which differ in the cluster similarity measure they employ. We decided to use single-link HAC because it is usually considered to be the simplest approach and it has the lowest time complexity. Furthermore, it yields a better intra cluster variation than the PCTs. Therefore, we did not consider more elaborate approaches. Single-link HAC computes the distance between two clusters as the distance between the closest pair of objects. The HAC implementation that we use has a computational cost of $O(N^2)$, with N the number of time series, and for efficiency it uses a next-best-merge array [14].

An important drawback of single-link HAC is that it suffers from the chaining effect [14], which in some cases may result in undesirable elongated clusters. Because the merge criterion is strictly local (it only takes the two closest objects into account), a chain of points can be extended over a long distance without regard to the overall shape of the emerging cluster.

4.5   Clustering Time Series with PCTs

In this section, we compare PCTs to HAC (Section 4.4). The evaluation metric that we use is intra cluster variation (ICV) defined as

$$\text{ICV}(\mathcal{C}) = \sum_{C_i \in \mathcal{C}} \frac{|C_i|}{|C|} \text{Var}(C_i) \,, \tag{7}$$

with $\mathcal{C}$ the set of clusters (PCT or HAC leaves), $|C|$ the data set size, and $\text{Var}(C_i)$ the variance of cluster C_i (Equation 4).

We measure ICV for different values of the size constraint (Section 4.3). The minimum cluster size is set to 5. For HAC, we cut the hierarchy of clusters at different levels to obtain measurements for a varying number of clusters. Fig. 9 presents the results. For the data sets AAC and DS, HAC is able to decrease ICV much faster than PCTs. The reason is that PCTs constrain the clusters based on the given features. If the ICV-wise best split at a given point in the cluster hierarchy can not be described in terms of the features, then Clus-TS will select a suboptimal split. It is therefore important to have good descriptive features when performing predictive clustering.

To test the impact of the features, we constructed artificial data sets with the same time series, but with as features the characteristic vector of the clustering produced by HAC, that is, one Boolean feature for each cluster (internal nodes and leaves) indicating for each example if it belongs to that particular cluster or not. Fig. 9 shows that, given these features, Clus-TS even outperforms HAC.

On the DT data set, HAC performs worse compared to Clus-TS. Note that this may happen because HAC is also heuristic (e.g., because of the chaining effect, cf. Section 4.4).

5   Future Work

We plan to extend the experimental evaluation. This includes testing more data sets (e.g., all changes in environmental conditions studied in [9], or other types of short time series data), working with domain experts to interpret the clusterings, and using more types of descriptive features. Our experiments show that having appropriate features is very important for predictive clustering. It would be interesting to try experiments with more features, possibly automatically constructed using feature construction methods.

In Section 3.2, we considered two representations for the cluster centroid that are both time series. The centroid, however, does not need to be in the same domain as the objects that are being clustered. It would be interesting to investigate more expressive representations of the cluster centroid, such as a parametric representation of the distribution of the time series. The advantage of such an approach, while it can be computationally more expensive, is that it captures more information about the cluster. This is akin to classification with the Gini index or information gain heuristics [18], which summarize a set of examples by means of its class distribution instead of the majority class.

We plan to incorporate different types of constraints in our models. This is important in the context of inductive databases because the inductive queries might include various types of constraints on the resulting PCTs. Our current system already includes accuracy and size constraints [22]. In further work, we wish to investigate constraints more specific to clustering [26] and in particular clustering of time series.

Another direction of research is investigating how PCTs, and in particular PCTs for clustering time series, can be integrated tightly with inductive databases. Fromont and Blockeel [7] and Slavkov et al. [21] present ongoing work in this direction.

6   Conclusion

This paper proposes predictive clustering trees (PCTs) to cluster time series data. The main advantage of using PCTs over other clustering algorithms, such as hierarchical agglomerative clustering and k-means, is that PCTs cluster the time series and provide a description of the clusters at the same time. This allows one to relate various heterogeneous data types and to draw conclusions about their relations.

Using PCTs for time series data is non-trivial because for many appropriate distance measures (correlation based, dynamic time warping, and a qualitative distance), no closed algebraic form for the centroid is known. Therefore, we propose to compute cluster variance based on the sum of squared pairwise distances (SSPD) between the cluster elements. This method has not been used previously in predictive clustering and is one of the contributions of the paper. Our experiments show that the SSPD can be efficiently approximated by means of sampling.

Our approach combines local models (motifs of DNA) with global models (PCTs). The local models are used to describe clusters and can be used to predict cluster membership. Such a combination of models is a typical feature required from an inductive database: a first query is used to mine the local models and a second query returns global models based on these local models.

The experimental evaluation shows that PCTs can be used for predicting the expression response of yeast genes to different changes in environmental conditions. This, however, proved to be a hard task and more research is required, e.g., to find more predictive features.

Acknowledgments. This work was supported by the IQ project (IST-FET FP6-516169). Jan Struyf is a postdoctoral fellow of the Fund for Scientific Research of Flanders (FWO-Vlaanderen).

References

1. Blockeel, H., De Raedt, L., Ramon, J.: Top-down induction of clustering trees. In: 15th Int'l Conf. on Machine Learning, pp. 55–63 (1998)
2. Curk, T., Zupan, B., Petrovič, U., Shaulsky, G.: Računalniško odkrivanje mehanizmov uravnavanja istražanja genov. In: Prvo srečanje slovenskih bioinformatikov, pp. 56–58 (2005)
3. De Raedt, L.: A perspective on inductive databases. SIGKDD Explorations 4(2), 69–77 (2002)
4. Ernst, J., Nau, G.J., Bar-Joseph, Z.: Clustering short time series gene expression data. Bioinformatics 21(Suppl. 1), 159–168 (2005)
5. Ashburner, M., et al.: Gene Ontology: Tool for the unification of biology. The Gene Ontology Consortium. Nature Genet. 25(1), 25–29 (2000)
6. Ferri, C., Flach, P.A., Hernández-Orallo, J.: Learning decision trees using the area under the ROC curve. In: 19th Int'l Conf. on Machine Learning, pp. 139–146 (2002)
7. Fromont, E., Blockeel, H., Struyf, J.: Integrating decision tree learning into inductive databases. In: KDID 2006. LNCS, vol. 4747, pp. 81–96. Springer, Heidelberg (2007)
8. Garofalakis, M., Hyun, D., Rastogi, R., Shim, K.: Building decision trees with constraints. Data Mining and Knowledge Discovery 7(2), 187–214 (2003)
9. Gasch, A., Spellman, P., Kao, C., Carmel-Harel, O., Eisen, M., Storz, G., Botstein, D., Brown, P.: Genomic expression program in the response of yeast cells to environmental changes. Mol. Biol. Cell. 11, 4241–4257 (2000)
10. Imielinski, T., Mannila, H.: A database perspective on knowledge discovery. Communications of the ACM 39(11), 58–64 (1996)
11. Kaufman, L., Rousseeuw, P.J. (eds.): Finding groups in data: An introduction to cluster analysis. Wiley, Chichester (1990)
12. Lee, S.D., De Raedt, L.: An efficient algorithm for mining string data-bases under constraints. In: Goethals, B., Siebes, A. (eds.) KDID 2004. LNCS, vol. 3377, pp. 108–129. Springer, Heidelberg (2005)
13. Liao, T.W.: Clustering of time series data – a survey. Pattern Recognition 38, 1857–1874 (2005)
14. Manning, C.D., Raghavan, P., Schütze, H.: Introduction to Information Retrieval. Cambridge University Press, Cambridge (2007)
15. Michalski, R.S., Stepp, R.E.: Learning from observation: conceptual clustering. In: Machine Learning: an Artificial Intelligence Approach, vol. 1, Tioga Publishing Company (1983)
16. Mitasiunaité, I., Boulicaut, J.-F.: Looking for monotonicity properties of a similarity constraint on sequences. In: ACM Symposium of Applied Computing SAC'2006, Special Track on Data Mining, pp. 546–552. ACM Press, New York (2006)

17. Quinlan, J.R.: C4.5: Programs for Machine Learning. Morgan Kaufmann series in Machine Learning. Morgan Kaufmann, San Francisco (1993)
18. Raileanu, L.E., Stoffel, K.: Theoretical comparison between the Gini index and information gain criteria. Annals of Mathematics and Artificial Intelligence 41(1), 77–93 (2004)
19. Sakoe, H., Chiba, S.: Dynamic programming algorithm optimization for spoken-word recognition. In: IEEE Transaction on Acoustics, Speech, and Signal Processing. LNAI, vol. ASSP-26, pp. 43–49. IEEE Computer Society Press, Los Alamitos (1978)
20. Sese, J., Kurokawa, Y., Monden, M., Kato, K., Morishita, S.: Constrained clusters of gene expression profiles with pathological features. Bioinformatics 20, 3137–3145 (2004)
21. Slavkov, I., Džeroski, S., Struyf, J., Loskovska, S.: Constrained clustering of gene expression profiles. In: Conf. on Data Mining and Data Warehouses (SiKDD 2005) at the 7th Int'l Multi-Conference on Information Society 2005, pp. 212–215 (2005)
22. Struyf, J., Džeroski, S.: Constraint based induction of multi-objective regression trees. In: Bonchi, F., Boulicaut, J.-F. (eds.) KDID 2005. LNCS, vol. 3933, pp. 222–233. Springer, Heidelberg (2006)
23. Todorovski, L., Cestnik, B., Kline, M., Lavrač, N., Džeroski, S.: Qualitative clustering of short time-series: A case study of firms reputation data. In: ECML/PKDD 2002 Workshop on Integration and Collaboration Aspects of Data Mining, Decision Support and Meta-Learning, pp. 141–149 (2002)
24. Torgo, L.: A comparative study of reliable error estimators for pruning regression trees. In: Coelho, H. (ed.) IBERAMIA 1998. LNCS (LNAI), vol. 1484, Springer, Heidelberg (1998)
25. Ženko, B., Džeroski, S., Struyf, J.: Learning predictive clustering rules. In: Bonchi, F., Boulicaut, J.-F. (eds.) KDID 2005. LNCS, vol. 3933, pp. 234–250. Springer, Heidelberg (2006)
26. Wagstaff, K.L.: Value, cost, and sharing: Open issues in constrained clustering. In: KDID 2006. LNCS, vol. 4747, pp. 24–41. Springer, Heidelberg (2007)

Integrating Decision Tree Learning into Inductive Databases

Élisa Fromont, Hendrik Blockeel, and Jan Struyf

Department of Computer Science, Katholieke Universiteit Leuven,
Celestijnenlaan 200A, 3001 Leuven, Belgium
{elisa.fromont,hendrik.blockeel,jan.struyf}@cs.kuleuven.be

Abstract. In inductive databases, there is no conceptual difference between data and the models describing the data: both can be stored and queried using some query language. The approach that adheres most strictly to this philosophy is probably the one proposed by Calders et al. (2006): in this approach, models are stored in relational tables and queried using standard SQL. The approach has been described in detail for association rule discovery. In this work, we study how decision tree induction can be integrated in this approach. We propose a representation format for decision trees similar to the format proposed earlier for association rules, and queryable using standard SQL; and we present a prototype system in which part of the needed functionality is implemented. In particular, we have developed an exhaustive tree learning algorithm able to answer a wide range of constrained queries.

1 Introduction

An inductive database (IDB) [11] is a database that contains not only data, but also generalizations (patterns and models) valid in the data. In an IDB, ordinary queries can be used to access and manipulate data, while inductive queries can be used to generate (mine), manipulate, and apply patterns.

Two approaches have been studied to represent and query patterns and models in IDBs. First, depending on the models that will be stored, a special-purpose storage and query language can be created. In this context, several researchers have proposed extensions to the popular relational query language SQL. For example, Meo et al. [15] and Imielinski & Virmani [12] present extensions to SQL specifically designed for mining association rules. Kramer et al. [14] and Han et al. [10] extend this approach to other models such as classification rules, but they do not give any details about how to actually store those models in the IDB. ATLaS [24] defines new table functions and aggregates in SQL, such that writing data mining algorithms (e.g., decision tree learners) in SQL becomes convenient. This approach has the closure property due to the use of SQL in the whole data mining process, but requires a deep understanding of SQL and data mining algorithm implementation to be used in practice. De Raedt [6] proposes a query language based on first order logic, which is especially suited for relational

S. Džeroski and J. Struyf (Eds.): KDID 2006, LNCS 4747, pp. 81–96, 2007.

data. Michalski & Kaufman [16] propose to use a knowledge generation meta-language (KGL) that combines conventional database operators with operators for conducting a large number of inductive inference tasks and operators for managing knowledge.

The second approach consists of storing the patterns and models in standard relational database tables, which are provided by any relational database management system (RDBMS), and using the standard SQL language, to represent, store, and query the generalizations made on the data. This approach is being investigated by members of the ADReM group in Antwerp[1] for frequent itemset and association rule mining [4]; we will refer to it in the rest of the paper as "the ADReM approach". This approach has a number of advantages over other approaches with respect to extensibility and flexibility. In this paper, we investigate how the ADReM approach can be used for learning global models, such as decision trees, and to which extent its advantages carry over to this new setting. In particular, while *support* and *confidence* constraints are obvious when querying association rules, it is much less clear which constraints are useful for decision trees. We propose some interesting constraints for decision trees and show how they can be enforced by means of two different decision tree learning algorithms.

Section 2 presents the basic ideas behind the ADReM approach and shows how they apply in the context of association rule discovery. Section 3 extends the ADReM approach to decision tree learning. We first discuss how a standard greedy decision tree learner can be used in this context (Section 4.1). Because this approach has a number of disadvantages, we propose a new decision tree learning algorithm that employs exhaustive search (Section 4.2). The latter is more suitable for answering certain inductive queries for decision trees. Section 5 presents the perspectives of this work and Section 6 states the main conclusions.

2   The ADReM Approach to Association Rule Mining

The basic idea behind the ADReM approach is that models are stored in a relational database in the same way that other information is stored: as a collection of tuples in relational tables. While applicable to a wide range of models, this idea has primarily been studied in the context of association rules [1]. Below, we briefly review the proposed representation for association rules, the conceptual view on association rule mining that it leads to, and some implementation issues. More information can be found in [4].

2.1   The Conceptual View

Consider a set of transactions D. The set is often represented as a table with one row per transaction and one Boolean attribute per item, but conceptually it can also be represented as a binary relational table with, for each transaction, a set

---

[1] {toon.calders,bart.goethals,adriana.prado}@ua.ac.be

Sets

isid	item
i1	p3
i1	p5
i1	p6
i2	red
i3	p3
i3	p5
i3	p6
i3	red
...	...

Supports

isid	support
i1	10
i2	20
i3	8
...	...

Rules

rid	isida	isidc	isid	conf
r1	i1	i2	i3	0.8
r2	i4	i5	i6	0.4
...	...	...	...	...

Fig. 1. Storing association rules in a relational database. For example, the rule "p3,p5,p6 $\Rightarrow$ red" is represented by r1.

of tuples of the form $(tid, item)$, where tid is the transaction identifier and $item$ is an item name. The crucial difference between the first and second representation is that in the second, the item names are values instead of attributes. A query can therefore return an item name as part of its result set. Note that we are talking about the conceptual representation here; how the transaction table is really implemented is not important.

Itemsets can be represented in a similar way. Figure 1 shows the ADReM representation of frequent itemsets and association rules. The *Sets* table represents all itemsets. A unique identifier ($isid$) is associated to each itemset $IS(isid)$, and for each itemset of size n, there are n rows $(isid, item_j)_{1 \leq j \leq n}$ where $item_j$ is the jth item of $IS(isid)$. The *Supports* table stores the *support* of each itemset. The *Rules* table stores the computed association rules. For each rule $X \Rightarrow Y$, there is a row $(rid, isida, isidc, isid, conf)$ in the IDB where rid is the association rule identifier, $isida$ (resp. $isidc$) is the identifier of the itemset used in the antecedent (resp. consequent) of the rule, $IS(isid) = IS(isida) \cup IS(isidc)$ and $conf$ is the confidence of the rule.

With this representation, finding association rules subject to certain constraints can be done easily using an SQL query. For instance, the query

```
select rid
from rules r
where r.conf >= 0.8 and
      r.isidc in (select isid from sets where item = ''red'')
```

finds all association rules with a confidence of at least 0.8 that contain the item "red" in the consequent of the rule.

2.2   The Implementation

Conceptually, the database has tables that contain all itemsets and all association rules. But in practice, obviously, the large number of patterns may make it impractical to explicitly store them all in the database. This problem can be solved by making these tables virtual. As far as the user is concerned, these tables or *virtual mining views* contain all the tuples needed to answer the user query. In reality, each time such a table is queried, a efficient data mining algorithm is triggered by the DBMS to populate the views with the tuples that the DBMS needs to answer the query.

More specifically, the procedure works as follows: given a query, an execution plan is created; on the highest level this is a regular relational algebra tree with tables as leaves. Standard query optimization procedures push projection and selection conditions down this tree as far as possible, thus reducing the size of intermediate results and making the overall computation more efficient. In the ADReM approach, the leaves may be the result of a data mining process, and the projection/selection conditions may be pushed further down into the data mining algorithm. Calders et al. [4] describe this optimization process in detail.

2.3   Advantages of the Approach

The ADReM approach has several advantages over other approaches to inductive querying. The main point is that the data mining processes become much more transparent. From the user's point of view, tables with itemsets and rules etc. exist and can be queried like any other table. How these tables are filled (which data mining algorithm is run, with which parameter values, etc.) is transparent to the user. The user does not need to know about the many different implementations that exist and when to use which implementation, nor does she need to familiarize herself with new special-purpose query languages. The whole approach is also much more declarative: the user specifies conditions on the models that should result from the mining process, not on the mining process itself.

In the light of these advantages, it seems useful to try a similar approach for other data mining tasks as well. In this paper, we focus on decision tree induction.

3   Integration of Decision Tree Learning

A decision tree classifies instances by sorting them down the tree from the root to a leaf node that provides the classification of the instance [17] (Figure 2). Each internal node of the tree specifies a test on the value of one of the attributes of the instance, and each branch descending from the node corresponds to one of the possible outcomes of the test. In this paper, for simplicity reasons, we focus on decision trees with Boolean attributes. Each attribute can then be seen as an item in a transaction table and transactions are instances to classify.

In this section, we discuss the motivations for integrating decision trees into an IDB and propose a representation for decision trees that will enable the user to pose queries supporting several types of useful constraints.

3.1   Motivation

To see the motivation behind using the ADReM approach for decision tree learning, consider the current practice in decision tree induction. Given a data set, one runs a decision tree learning algorithm, e.g., C4.5 [20], and obtains one particular decision tree. It is difficult to characterize this decision tree in any other way than by describing the algorithm. The tree is generally not the most accurate tree on the training set, nor the smallest one, nor the one most likely to generalize well according to some criterion; all one can say is that the learning algorithm tends to produce relatively small trees with relatively high accuracy. The algorithm usually has a number of parameters, the meaning of which can be described quite precisely in terms of how the algorithm works, but not in terms of the results it yields. To summarize, it is difficult to describe exactly what conditions the output of a decision tree learner fulfills without referring to the algorithm.

This situation differs from the discovery of association rules, where the user imposes constraints on the rules to be found (typically constraints on the confidence and support) and the algorithm yields the set of all rules satisfying these conditions. A precise mathematical description of the result set is easy to give, whereas a similar mathematical description of the tree returned by a decision tree learner is quite difficult to give.

Are people using decision tree learners interested in having a precise specification of the properties of the tree they obtain? Aren't they only interested in finding a tree that generalizes the training instances well, without being interested in exactly how this is defined? This may often be the case, but certainly not always. Many special versions of decision tree learners have been developed: some use a cost function on attributes and try to find trees that combine a high accuracy with a low cost of the attributes they contain [22]; some take different misclassification costs into account while building the tree [7]; some do not aim for the highest accuracy but for balanced precision-recall [25]; etc. The fact that researchers have developed such learning algorithms shows that users sometimes do have more specific desiderata than just high predictive accuracy.

By integrating decision tree learning into inductive databases, we hope to arrive at an approach for decision tree learning that is just as precise as association rule learning: the user specifies what kind of trees she wants, and the system returns such trees.

Here are some queries the user might be interested in:

1. find $\{T | size(T) < 8 \wedge acc(T) > 0.8 \wedge cost(T) < 70\}$
2. find one element in $\{T | size(t) < 8 \wedge acc(t) > 0.8 \wedge cost(t) < 70\}$
3. find $\{T | size(T) < 8 \wedge (\forall T' | size(T') < 8 \Rightarrow acc(T') < acc(T))\}$
4. find $\{T | T = (t(X, t(Y, l(+), l(-)), t(Z, l(C_1), l(C_2))),$
   $X \in [A, B, C], Y \in [D, E], acc(T) > 0.8\}$

In the first query, the user asks for all decision trees T with a *size* smaller than 8 nodes, a *global accuracy* greater than 0.8 and a *cost* less than 70 (assuming that each item has a given cost). To describe the tree of interest, other criteria such as the number of misclassified examples (*error*), the *accuracy* computed for a particular class, the *precision*, the *recall*, or the area under the ROC curve (*AUC*) might also be interesting.

Since the user is interested in all the trees that fulfill the given criteria, the query cannot be answered by triggering a standard *greedy* decision tree learning algorithm. Instead, a decision tree learner is needed that can search the space of all possible trees *exhaustively* for trees that satisfy the constraints. The number of such trees might be huge and as a result executing the query might not be tractable. Note that without constraints, the number of decision trees that can be constructed from a database with d attributes and a possible values for each attribute is lower-bounded by $\prod_{i=0}^{d-1}(d-1)^{a^i}$. As in the association rule case presented in Section 2, we assume that the queries are sufficiently constrained so that a realistic number of trees is returned and stored. Which kind of constraints are adequate here is still an open question.

In the second query, the user asks for one tree that fulfills some criteria. This tree can normally be computed by a regular *greedy* tree learner. Note, however, that for greedy learners, given that at least one tree satisfying the constraints exists in the search space, there is usually no guarantee that the learner will find one.

With the third query, the user looks for the set of trees of size smaller than 8 nodes with maximal accuracy. Again, this means that the search space of trees smaller than 8 nodes must be searched exhaustively to ensure that the accuracy of the returned trees are maximal.

In the last query, the user provides *syntactic constraints* on the shape of the tree and provides some attributes that must appear in it.

More generally, we are interested in queries of the form $\{t \in T | C(t)\}$ where $C(t)$ is "any conjunction of constraints on a particular tree". This does not include the whole range of possible queries. In particular, queries that specify constraints on a *set of trees* such as "find the k best trees as different as possible that fulfill some constraints" [13] are out of the scope of this paper.

3.2   Representing Trees in a Relational Database

The virtual mining view that holds the predictive models should be precise enough to enable the user to ask SQL queries as easily as possible without having to design new keywords for the SQL language. We use the same data representation (transactions) as in Section 2, and assume that each transaction contains either the '+' item or the '-' item, which indicate the class of the transaction. We further assume that all the data-dependent measures (such as accuracy) are referring to these transactions.

Note that due to the well-known correspondence between trees and rule sets, a tree can be represented as a set of association rules: each leaf corresponds to one association rule, with as antecedent the conditions on the path from the root to that leaf and as consequent the class label of that leaf. However, while the representation with one rule per leaf is interesting for prediction purposes, the structure of the tree gives more information: e.g., the higher an attribute occurs in the tree, the more informative it is for the prediction. Such information is lost if we represent a tree as a set of association rules. We therefore choose a slightly different representation.

The decision trees generated from the data D can be stored in the same database as D and the association rules computed from D, by using the following schema (Figure 2):

1. The *Tree_sets* table is inspired by the *Sets* table used for representing association rules. We choose to represent a node of a tree by the itemset that characterizes the examples that belong to the node. For instance, if the itemset is $A\overline{B}$, the examples in this node must fulfill the criteria $A=true$ and $B=false$. In association rules, only the presence of certain items is indicated: there is no condition that specifies the absence of an item. To cope with association rules derived from trees such as the one corresponding to leaf $L2$ of the tree in Figure 2 ($A\overline{B} \Rightarrow -$), we add a *sign* attribute to the *Tree_sets* table indicating whether the presence (1) or the absence (0) of the item is required.

   As in the *Sets* table, a unique identifier ($isid$) is associated to each itemset and, for each itemset of size n, there are n rows $(isid, item_j, sign_j)_{1 \leq j \leq n}$

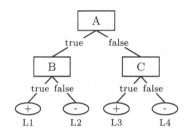

Trees_charac

treeID	size	error	accuracy	AUC	cost	...
T1	7	...	...	...	...	...
T2	...	...	...	...	...	...
...	...	...	...	...	...	...

Tree_sets

isid	item	sign
i0	∅	1
i1	A	1
i2	A	1
i2	B	1
L1	A	1
L1	B	1
L1	+	1
i3	A	1
i3	B	0
L2	A	1
L2	B	0
L2	-	1
...	...	...

All_trees

treeID	isid	leaf
T1	i1	0
T1	i2	0
T1	L1	1
...	...	...
T1	L2	1
...	...	...
T1	L3	1
...	...	...
T1	L4	1
T2	...	...
T3	...	...
...	...	...

Greedy_trees

treeID	isid	leaf
T1	i1	0
T1	i2	0
T1	L1	1
...	...	...
T1	L2	1
...	...	...
T1	L3	1
...	...	...
T1	L4	1

Fig. 2. Storing decision trees in a relational database

where $item_j$ is the jth item of the itemset identified by $isid$ and $sign_j$ is its sign. $i0$ stands for the empty itemset.

2. The *All-trees* and *Greedy-trees* tables give a precise description of each tree in terms of the itemsets from *Tree_sets*. Each tree has a unique identifier *treeID* and each itemset corresponding to one of its nodes is associated with this *treeID*. A Boolean attribute *leaf* distinguishes the internal nodes of the tree (*leaf* = 0) from its leaves (*leaf* = 1). The nodes at level k of the tree, are defined in terms of k-itemsets. The *All-trees* table holds all possible trees, whereas the *Greedy-trees* table can be queried for an implementation-dependent subset of all trees (the trees that may be found by a greedy learner under certain conditions and constraints).

3. The *Trees_charac* table lists all the tree characteristics where the user might be interested in. The table contains for each tree identified by *treeID*, a row with all characteristics *(size, error, accuracy, cost, AUC)* computed for the tree (see Section 3.1).

The *All-trees* and *Greedy-trees* tables correspond, as discussed before, to the *ideal* approach and the current and *practically feasible* approach to compute decision trees. Both tables are thus relevant in our framework.

Note that the semantics of the SELECT operator applied to the *Greedy-trees* table is different from the standard relational algebra definition of this operator. For example, querying the *Greedy-trees* table for a tree will yield a particular decision tree as result. If we subsequently add a certain constraint to the query, then the system will return a different tree (a tree satisfying this constraint). This is different from what happens when querying a regular database table because the answer set of the query with the additional constraint is not a subset of the answer to the original query. In our framework, the SELECT operator applied to the *Greedy-trees* table only outputs a single tree that fulfills the user's constraints.

3.3   Querying Decision Trees Using Virtual Views

The database schema of Section 3.2 is sufficient to be able to answer interesting queries, provided that the data mining algorithms connected to the database compute the different characteristics of the trees that hold in the IDB. We continue by presenting a number of example queries.

```
SELECT trees_charac.* FROM trees_charac, all_trees
WHERE trees_charac.treeID = all_trees.treeID AND
 accuracy >= 0.8 and size <= 8;
```

This query selects the characteristics of all trees that can be computed from the database, that have an accuracy of at least 0.80, and that contain at most 8 nodes.

```
SELECT treeID FROM trees_charac, greedy_trees
WHERE trees_charac.treeID = greedy_trees.treeID
and trees_charac.error < 10;
```

This query selects a tree constructed with a greedy algorithm that misclassifies fewer than 10 instances.

```
SELECT trees_charac.* FROM trees_charac, all_trees
WHERE trees_charac.treeID = all_trees.treeID
AND accuracy = (select max(accuracy) from trees_charac);
```

This query selects the characteristics of the most accurate tree(s).

```
SELECT treeID FROM greedy_trees, tree_sets
WHERE greedy_trees.isid = tree_sets.isid
AND (tree_sets.isid
    IN (select isid from tree_sets where item = ''A''));
```

This query selects a tree constructed with a greedy algorithm that contains the item "A".

3.4 User Defined Virtual Views

The framework is flexible enough to allow queries with constraints on metrics that were not included in the virtual view from the beginning. The user can create his own virtual mining view using information such as the support of the itemsets. We illustrate this by providing definitions for "accuracy" and "size".

The accuracy of a specific leaf in the tree can be computed from the support of the itemsets that belong to the leaf [19] as follows (for the tree in Figure 2):

$$acc(L_1) = \frac{support(+AB)}{support(AB)}, \; acc(L_2) = \frac{support(-A\overline{B})}{support(A\overline{B})}, \; \dots$$

The global accuracy of the tree is the weighted mean of the accuracies of its leaves. This can be computed without any information on the actual structure of the tree as follows:

$$acc(T) = acc(L1) \cdot \frac{support(AB)}{support(\emptyset)} + acc(L2) \cdot \frac{support(A\overline{B})}{support(\emptyset)} + \dots$$

$$= \frac{support(+AB) + support(-A\overline{B}) + \dots}{support(\emptyset)}.$$

Itemsets that include a "negative" item usually do not have their support computed. In this case, formulas based on the inclusion-exclusion principle, such as:

$$support(A\overline{B}-) = support(A-) - support(AB-)$$

can be used to compute the support of all itemsets from the support of the "positive" itemsets [3].

These formulas can be translated into the SQL language to compute all the characteristics in the *Tree_charac* table. As in Section 2, we assume that we have a *Supports* table that contains the support of all itemsets.

```
acc(T1)= SELECT SUM(Supports.support) /
                (SELECT Supports.support
                 FROM Supports WHERE Supports.isid = ''I0'')
                 as accuracy
         FROM Supports, all_trees
         WHERE Supports.isid = all_trees.isid
         AND all_trees.treeID = T1
         GROUP BY all_trees.treeID

size(T1) = SELECT COUNT(*) FROM all_trees
           WHERE all_trees.treeID = T1
```

4   Implementation

The ADReM group connected an Apriori-like algorithm for association rule mining to a standard Oracle database. The resulting system can answer inductive queries for association rules including constraints on the support of the itemsets and the confidence of the rules, and constraints requiring the presence or absence of some item in the resulting rules. We extend this system by interfacing it to a decision tree learner named CLUS[2]. CLUS is a predictive clustering tree [2] learner that uses a standard greedy recursive top-down induction algorithm to construct decision trees. CLUS can be used to answer queries with regard to the *Greedy_trees* table. To support queries on the *All_trees* table, we propose a new algorithm CLUS-EX that performs an exhaustive search for all decision trees satisfying a set of constraints. We first discuss in more detail queries on the *Greedy_trees* table (Section 4.1) and then present CLUS-EX (Section 4.2).

4.1   Greedy Tree Learning

For this task we use the standard implementation of CLUS, which is a greedy recursive top-down induction algorithm similar to C4.5 [20]. First, a large tree is built based on the training data and subsequently this tree is pruned such that the constraints in the query are satisfied. Following the precursor work by Garofalakis et al. [8], a number of constraints were implemented in CLUS [21]. It currently supports constraints on the size of the tree (i.e., an upper-bound on the number of nodes), on the error of the tree, and on the syntax of the tree. The error measure used for classification tree learning is the proportion of misclassified examples (i.e., 1.0-*accuracy*). The syntactic constraints allow the user to introduce expert knowledge in the tree. This expert knowledge takes the form of a partial tree (including the root) that must appear in the resulting tree. Essentially, this subtree specifies the important attributes in the domain. Other constraints discussed in Section 3.1 still have to be implemented in the system. Currently, queries such as the following can be used:

---

[2] http://www.cs.kuleuven.be/~dtai/clus/

```
SQL> select * from trees_charac c, greedy_trees g
where c.tree_id = g.tree_id and c.err <= 0.2 and c.sz= 9;

TREE_ID SZ ERROR ACCURACY
------- -- ----- --------
      0  9  0.02     0.98  1 rows selected.

SQL> select * from trees_charac c, greedy_trees g
where c.tree_id = g.tree_id and c.err <= 0.2 and c.sz <= 8;

TREE_ID SZ ERROR ACCURACY
------- -- ----- --------
      1  7 0.027    0.973  1 rows selected.

SQL> select * from trees_charac c, greedy_trees g
where c.tree_id = g.tree_id and c.sz< 4;

TREE_ID SZ ERROR ACCURACY
------- -- ----- --------
      2  3 0.333    0.667  1 rows selected.
```

The trees computed for the different queries can be stored in a "log" table that can be queried just as easily. After the session above, this table would contain:

TREE_ID	SZ	ERROR	ACCURACY
0	9	0.02	0.98
1	7	0.027	0.973
2	3	0.333	0.667

4.2 Exhaustive Tree Learning

This section proposes the exhaustive tree learner CLUS-EX. CLUS-EX searches the space of all possible trees of at most MaxSize (a parameter) nodes in a depth-first fashion. Basically, a queue of trees is kept; a search step consists of taking the first tree of the queue, computing refinements for it, and adding those refinements to the front of the queue. A refinement consists of splitting one leaf of the tree according to one of the available attributes. Generating all possible refinements in this way is not optimal because the same tree may be generated multiple times. To avoid identical trees from being generated, it is sufficient to restrict the refinements as follows. CLUS-EX only splits leaves that are below or to the right of the last node on the right-most path of internal nodes (or, more formally: the ones that come after the last internal node of the current tree when it is written in pre-order notation). In the example in Figure 3.a, only the dark gray leaves will be refined. The completeness and optimality of this method follow from a result by Chi et al. [5].

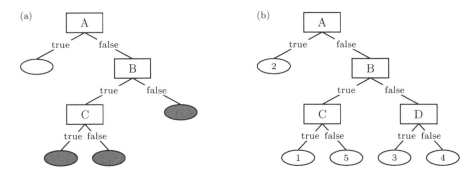

Fig. 3. (a) Example tree being refined by CLUS-EX. The right-most path of internal nodes is A, B, C. Only the leaves below or to the right of C are refined (indicated in dark gray). (b) An illustration of exploiting constraints on both the size and the error of the tree.

As discussed in Section 3.1, finding all possible trees that can be constructed on a data set is intractable in the general case. However, if the user specifies sufficiently restrictive constraints, and these constraints can be used for pruning, then the search becomes practically feasible. (This is similar to itemset mining, where a sufficiently high support threshold must be set so that the search becomes tractable.) In our case, including a size constraint in the inductive query is crucial to prune the search, that is, the search can stop as soon as the given size limit is reached. But a combination of size and error constraints can also be exploited for pruning. Assume that the constraints state that there can be at most E_{max} misclassified examples and that the size of the tree (internal nodes plus leaves) can be at most S. Take a tree of size S'. Splitting a leaf increases the size of the tree by at least 2, so at most $m = (S - S')/2$ (integer division) leaves of the current tree can be split before the maximum size is reached. Observe that the greatest error reduction occurs when the leaves with the largest number of errors (i.e., number of examples not belonging to the majority class in the leaf) are split, and all these splits yield pure leaves. Assume that the current tree has E_0 errors in leaves that cannot be split anymore by the optimal refinement operator, and k leaves L_i that still can be split (the gray leaves in Figure 3.a). Assume further that the L_i are sorted such that $e_1 \geq e_2 \geq \ldots \geq e_k$, with e_i the number of errors of L_i. Then any valid extension of this tree has a total error of at least $E_0 + \sum_{i=m+1}^{k} e_i$. If this sum is greater than E_{max}, then we can safely prune the search at this point.

Consider the example in Figure 3.b, and assume that the five leaves have (from left to right) $2, 1, 5, 3$, and 4 errors. Let MaxSize $= 11$. The current size is 9, so we can do at most one more split. Given the refinement strategy described above, we know that only the two right-most leaves can be split in the current situation (the two leaves below node D). Therefore, $E_0 = 2 + 1 + 5 = 8$ errors, and the best possible split occurs when the leaf with 4 errors is replaced by two pure leaves. The lower bound on the error is therefore $3 + 8 = 11$.

Table 1. The performance of CLUS-EX on UCI data sets. We consider for each data set different values for the MaxSize and MaxError constraints. For each constraint pair, the size of the search space (number of trees searched) without and with error based pruning is reported together with the reduction factor due to pruning (Red.). The last column is the number of trees that satisfy the constraints.

| Data set | MaxSize | MaxError | Search space (# trees searched) | | Red. | # Result |
			No pruning	Pruning		
soybean	7	0.3	177977	86821	2.0	0
soybean	9	0.3	8143901	4053299	2.0	0
soybean	7	0.6	177977	125055	1.4	848
zoo	7	0.2	13776	9218	1.5	214
zoo	7	0.3	13776	11908	1.2	2342
zoo	9	0.3	345388	276190	1.3	95299
zoo	11	0.2	7871768	4296549	1.8	708026
zoo	11	0.1	7871768	1637934	4.8	16636
audiology	7	0.3	415704	380739	1.1	0
audiology	7	0.5	415704	406290	1.0	2326

Table 1 presents the results of CLUS-EX on different symbolic UCI [18] data sets. The third and the fourth columns show the number of nodes evaluated during the search, i.e, they give an idea of the size of the search space and of the efficiency of the pruning method. The table shows that when the maximum *error* (resp. minimum *accuracy*) is sufficiently low (resp. high) compared to the size constraint, the combination of the constraints can be used to efficiently prune the search space. The table shows that restrictive constraints are crucial to restrict the search space and the number of resulting trees. The soybean and the audiology data sets contain many classes, therefore, the combination of strict error and size constraints can easily lead to an empty result set.

Currently, queries such as the following can be used with the prototype:

```
SQL> select c.tree-id,sz,accuracy,err from trees_charac c, all_trees a
where c.tree_id = a.tree_id and sz <= 7 and accuracy > 0.8');
```

TREE_ID	SZ	ERR	ACCURACY
0	7	0.125	0.875
1	7	0.125	0.875
2	7	0.125	0.875
3	7	0.125	0.875
4	7	0.125	0.875
5	7	0.125	0.875
6	7	0.125	0.875
7	7	0.125	0.875
8	5	0	1
9	5	0	1

```
SQL> select * from all_trees a, trees_sets t
where a.set_id = t.set_id and tree_id = 0;
```

TREE_ID	SET_ID	NODE	SET_ID	ITEM	SIGN
0	0	1	0	null	1
0	1	1	1	null	1
0	1	1	1	B = F	1
0	2	1	2	null	1
0	2	1	2	B = F	1
0	2	1	2	A = F	1
0	3	0	3	null	1
....	....	....	....		...

5   Perspectives

There are many open problems related to the proposed approach. For instance, for efficiency reasons, the system should be able to look at the "log" table that contains the previously computed trees to check if the answer of the current query has not already been computed, before triggering a data mining algorithm. If the user asks for all trees of size smaller than 8, and later for all trees of size smaller than 6, the results computed from the first query should be reusable for the second query. The "log" table should also contain the previous queries together with the computed trees, which raises the question of how to store the queries themselves in the database. This entire problem, called *interactive mining* because it refers to the reutilisation of queries posed within the same working session, has been investigated for association rules [9], but not for decision tree learning.

If the database is modified between two queries, then it might be interesting to reuse the previously computed predictive models to more efficiently compute new predictive models for the modified database. This problem known has *incremental learning* has already been studied for decision trees [23] when a new example is added to the database.

These functionalities have to be integrated into the prototype along with the extension of the framework to multi-valued attributes.

Because predictive models ultimately aim at predicting the class of new examples, it would be interesting to include that possibility in the IDB. This is currently non-trivial in our approach; it requires complicated queries. More generally, the limitations of our approach with respect to what can be expressed, and how difficult it is to express it, require further investigation.

Another perspective is the integration of other predictive models such as *Bayesian Networks* in the same IDB framework already designed for association rule and decision tree mining. The user might be interested in queries such as "find the Bayesian network of size 10 with maximal likelihood". Again, a structure to store Bayesian networks has to be designed and an algorithm that can build Bayesian networks under constraints has to be implemented.

6 Conclusion

In this paper we have studied how decision tree induction can be integrated in inductive databases following the ADReM approach. Considering only Boolean attributes, the representation of trees in a relational database is quite similar to that of association rules, with this difference that the conjunctions describing nodes may have negated literals whereas itemsets only contain positive literals. A more important difference is that a decision tree learner typically returns one tree that is "optimal" in some "not very precisely" defined way, whereas the IDB approach lends itself more easily to mining approaches that return all results fulfilling certain well-defined conditions. It is therefore useful to introduce both a *Greedy_trees* table and an *All_trees* table, where queries to *Greedy_trees* trigger the execution of a standard tree learner and queries to *All_trees* trigger the execution of an exhaustive tree learner. We have described a number of example queries that could be used, and proposed a new algorithm that is able to exhaustively search for decision trees under constraints. We presented a preliminary implementation of this algorithm, and discussed open questions and perspectives of this work.

The approach presented in this paper focused on the representation of the models, the querying mechanism and the constrained based mining of the models. We believe that the simplicity of this approach makes it easier to be included as a brick in a larger system able to support the whole KDD process, which is the ultimate aim of an inductive database.

Acknowledgments. Hendrik Blockeel and Jan Struyf are post-doctoral fellows of the Fund For Scientific Research of Flanders (FWO-Vlaanderen). This work is funded through the GOA project 2003/8, "Inductive Knowledge Bases", and the FWO project "Foundations for inductive databases". The authors thank Siegfried Nijssen, Sašo Džeroski, and the ADReM group for the many interesting discussions, and in particular Adriana Prado for her help with the IDB prototype implementation.

References

1. Agrawal, R., Srikant, R.: Fast algorithms for mining association rules. In: Proc. of the 20th Int. Conf. on Very Large Databases VLDB, pp. 487–499 (1994)
2. Blockeel, H., De Raedt, L., Ramon, J.: Top-down induction of clustering trees. In: 15th Int'l Conf. on Machine Learning, pp. 55–63 (1998)
3. Calders, T., Goethals, B.: Mining all non-derivable frequent itemsets. In: Elomaa, T., Mannila, H., Toivonen, H. (eds.) PKDD 2002. LNCS (LNAI), vol. 2431, pp. 74–85. Springer, Heidelberg (2002)
4. Calders, T., Goethals, B., Prado, A.: Integrating pattern mining in relational databases. In: Fürnkranz, J., Scheffer, T., Spiliopoulou, M. (eds.) PKDD 2006. LNCS (LNAI), vol. 4213, pp. 454–461. Springer, Heidelberg (2006)
5. Chi, Y., Muntz, R.R., Nijssen, S., Kok, J.N.: Frequent subtree mining - An overview. Fundamenta Informaticae 66(1-2), 161–198 (2005)
6. De Raedt, L.: A logical database mining query language. In: Cussens, J., Frisch, A.M. (eds.) ILP 2000. LNCS (LNAI), vol. 1866, pp. 78–92. Springer, Heidelberg (2000)

7. Domingos, P.: MetaCost: A general method for making classifiers cost-sensitive. In: Knowledge Discovery and Data Mining, pp. 155–164 (1999)
8. Garofalakis, M., Hyun, D., Rastogi, R., Shim, K.: Building decision trees with constraints. Data Mining and Knowledge Discovery 7(2), 187–214 (2003)
9. Goethals, B., Van den Bussche, J.: On supporting interactive association rule mining. In: Kambayashi, Y., Mohania, M.K., Tjoa, A.M. (eds.) DaWaK 2000. LNCS, vol. 1874, pp. 307–316. Springer, Heidelberg (2000)
10. Han, J., Fu, Y., Wang, W., Koperski, K., Zaiane, O.: DMQL: A data mining query language for relational databases. In: SIGMOD 1996 Workshop on Research Issues in Data Mining and Knowledge Discovery (DMKD 1996) (1996)
11. Imielinski, T., Mannila, H.: A database perspective on knowledge discovery. Comm. of the ACM 39, 58–64 (1996)
12. Imielinski, T., Virmani, A.: MSQL: A query language for database mining. Data Mining and Knowledge Discovery 3(4), 373–408 (1999)
13. Kocev, D., Džeroski, S., Struyf, J.: Similarity constraints in beam-search induction of predictive clustering trees. In: Proc. of the Conf. on Data Mining and Data Warehouses (SiKDD 2006) at the 9th Int'l Multi-conf. on Information Society (IS-2006), pp. 267–270 (2006)
14. Kramer, S., Aufschild, V., Hapfelmeier, A., Jarasch, A., Kessler, K., Reckow, S., Wicker, J., Richter, L.: Inductive databases in the relational model: The data as the bridge. In: Bonchi, F., Boulicaut, J.-F. (eds.) KDID 2005. LNCS, vol. 3933, pp. 124–138. Springer, Heidelberg (2006)
15. Meo, R., Psaila, G., Ceri, S.: An extension to SQL for mining association rules. Data Mining and Knowledge Discovery 2(2), 195–224 (1998)
16. Michalski, R.S., Kaufman, K.A.: Building knowledge scouts using KGL metalanguage. Fundamenta Informaticae 41(4), 433–447 (2000)
17. Mitchell, T.M.: Machine Learning. McGraw-Hill, New York (1997)
18. Newman, D.J., Hettich, S., Blake, C.L., Merz, C.J.: UCI repository of machine learning databases (1998)
19. Pance, P., Dzeroski, S., Blockeel, H., Loskovska, S.: Predictive data mining using itemset frequencies. In: Zbornik 8. mednarodne multikonference Informacijska druzba. Ljubljana: Institut "Jožef Stefan", pp. 224–227. Informacijska Druzba (2005)
20. Quinlan, J.R.: C4.5: Programs for Machine Learning. Morgan Kaufmann, San Francisco (1993)
21. Struyf, J., Džeroski, S.: Constraint based induction of multi-objective regression trees. In: Bonchi, F., Boulicaut, J.-F. (eds.) KDID 2005. LNCS, vol. 3933, pp. 222–233. Springer, Heidelberg (2006)
22. Turney, P.: Cost-sensitive classification: Empirical evaluation of a hybrid genetic decision tree induction algorithm. Journal of Artificial Intelligence Research 2, 369–409 (1995)
23. Utgoff, P.E.: Incremental induction of decision trees. Machine Learning 4, 161–186 (1989)
24. Wang, H., Zaniolo, C.: ATLaS: A native extension of SQL for data mining. In: SIAM Int'l Conf. Data Mining, pp. 130–144 (2003)
25. Xiaobing, W.: Knowledge representation and inductive learning with XML. In: Proc. of the IEEE/WIC/ACM Int'l Conf. on Web Intelligence (WI 2004), pp. 491–494. IEEE Computer Society Press, Los Alamitos (2004)

Using a Reinforced Concept Lattice to Incrementally Mine Association Rules from Closed Itemsets

Arianna Gallo and Rosa Meo

Dipartimento di Informatica, Università di Torino, Italy
`gallo,meo@di.unito.it`

Abstract. In the Data Mining area, discovering association rules is one of the most important task. It is well known that the number of these rules rapidly grows to be unwieldy as the frequency requirements become less strict, especially when collected data is highly correlated or dense. Since a big number of the frequent itemsets turns out to be redundant, it is sufficient to consider only the rules among *closed frequent itemsets* or *concepts*. In order to efficiently generate them, it is often essential to know the Concept Lattice, that also allows the user to better understand the relationships between the closed itemsets. We propose an *incremental* algorithm that mines all the closed itemsets, reading the data *only once*. The Concept Lattice is incrementally updated using a simple but essential structure directly connected to it. This structure allows to speed up the execution time and makes the algorithm applicable on both static and dynamic stream data and very dense datasets.

1 Introduction

In the last years, the problem of discovering association rules has been widely investigated [1,2,3,4,5]. Its aim is to find relationships between itemsets in large databases. These researches addressed both the efficiency of the extraction algorithms, and the exploitation of user preferences (constraints) about the patterns to be extracted. A frequent itemset is one that occurs in a user-specified percentage of the database, i.e. the number of its occurrences (the support value) is higher than a user-defined threshold. In general, an association rule is an expression $X \rightarrow Y$, where X and Y are sets of itemsets.

Several methods were proposed to mine frequent itemsets, most of them are a variant of Apriori [1]. The property that is at the heart of Apriori and forms the foundation of most algorithms simply states that for an itemset to be frequent all its subsets have to be frequent. This anti-monotone property reduces the candidate itemset space drastically.

Most of the well studied frequent pattern mining algorithms (such as Apriori, FP-growth, H-mine, and OP) mine the complete set of frequent itemsets. These algorithms may have good performance when the support threshold is high and the search space of the patterns is sparse. However, it is well known that when

S. Džeroski and J. Struyf (Eds.): KDID 2006, LNCS 4747, pp. 97–115, 2007.

the support threshold decreases, the number of frequent itemsets increases dramatically. Moreover, the number of association rules exponentially grows with the number of items.

The last decade witnessed a particular interest in the definition of *condensed representations*, e.g. closed itemsets [6,7,8,9,10], maximal itemsets [11,12,13], approximate itemsets [14]. Among these methods, the algorithms for *closed itemsets* (or *concepts*) mining, which mine only those frequent itemsets having no proper superset with the same support, limit the number of itemsets (patterns) produced *without information loss*. The result of such a reduction is a reasonably-sized subset of association rules that can be seen as an irreducible nucleus of association rules [15,16]. Finding only this *condensed set* is necessary and sufficient to capture *all* the information about frequent itemsets. For these reasons, mining the frequent closed itemsets instead of frequent itemsets has great advantages. For instance, when the data are dense and highly correlated, the condensed representation of frequent itemsets is greatly reduced. Then, from this set of closed itemsets, all the frequent itemsets and their frequencies can be derived *without accessing the data* [17,6,8]. In order to efficiently generate the association rules from the closed itemsets, it is often essential to know also the Concept Lattice (i.e. superset-subset relationships between the closed itemsets found) [18]. Furthermore, the *Concept Lattice* could allow the user to better understand the relationships between sets, being a condensed visualization of them.

Formal Concept Analysis (FCA) arose as a mathematical theory for the formalization of the "concept" in the early 80ies by Wille [19]. It is nowadays considered as an AI theory, and in last years became attractive also as a knowledge representation method for computer science[20]. It has been applied in many different realms like psychology, sociology, anthropology, medicine, biology, linguistics, computer science, mathematics and industrial engineering. Formal Concept Analysis allows an understanding of an important technique of graphical knowledge representation namely the line diagrams of Concept Lattices.

The Association Rules framework has first been studied in terms of Formal Concept Analysis independently in [21,22,23], and Close [21] is the first algorithm based in this approach. Relationship between FCA (concepts) and association rules (in the exact case) can be traced to the work of [24] and other works on minimal covers for functional dependencies in database systems such as [25]. In order to extract association rules from concepts, two steps must be computed. The first one builds the so called *iceberg Concept Lattice*[26]. The second step derives the *bases* [27] for association rules. In [27] the result of Duquenne and Guigues [28] and Luxenburger [29] are adopted, and *Duquenne-Guigues basis for exact association rules* (i.e., rules with 100% confidence) and *Luxenburger basis for approximate association rules* (i.e., rules with confidence≤ 100%) are introduced.

The Concept Lattice can be generated either during the closed itemsets generation steps, or in a second step, after the complete set of closeds has been mined. In the last decade, several algorithms were proposed to build the Concept Lattice [30,31,32,28,11,33,34,10]. Some of them (e.g. CHARM-L [34] and DCI-CLOSED

[10]), although their undisputed efficiency in computational time and memory consumption, turn out to be not applicable to data streams, a context in which only one access to the data is allowed.

Contributions. In this paper, we introduce a new on-line approach for the discovery of closed itemsets. Differently to most previous approaches, we make use and fully exploit the properties of the Concept Lattice [28]. Moreover, we make use of two further very useful structures, called $AMap$ and $IMap$ which allow to speed up the overall execution time. The proposed incremental algorithm builds incrementally the Lattice with *only one scan* of the dataset. It takes a database transaction at a time as input, and updates immediately the Concept Lattice, exploring simultaneously both the itemset space and the transaction space.

The incremental nature of the algorithm makes it applicable to both static and dynamic (stream) datasets. It also can take advantages to cope the problem of continuous querying during a data stream processing, one of the currently hottest topics among database researchers. The algorithm is conceived to deal with very dense datasets, where the transactions are usually longer, closed itemsets *equivalence classes* [35] are larger and the number of duplicates is higher. Dealing with dense datasets, most of the state-of-the-art mining algorithms encounter difficulties since there could be many candidates and the searches need to scan the database more than once. Instead of generating candidates in a generate and test fashion (like in level-wise algorithms), our algorithm keeps always only the closed itemsets. The algorithm outputs *all* the closed itemsets without a support threshold. This means that it is able to mine closed itemsets from very dense datasets with a threshold equal to zero, for which the performance of many mining algorithms quickly deteriorates [34].

Using our algorithm, since the updating of the Concept Lattice is incrementally made transaction by transaction, the system can always immediately display to the user the Lattice (and all the closed itemsets) representing the portion of dataset that has just been read. Hence, each time, using this such "partial" Lattice as input, all the association rules in that portion of the dataset can be computed, updated, and becomes available to the user. This allows a real time interactivity between the end-user and the whole knowledge discovery process, dealing with both static and dynamic datasets.

The proposed method is based on an intersection-based pruning strategy, already proven to be very helpful in the closed itemset selection concerning both memory consumption and run time [36,37,38,39]. The originality of our algorithm lies on the fully exploitation of both the intersection-pruning strategy and the two structures introduced above to build the Concept Lattice in an incremental fashion. In order to efficiently build the Lattice, also the closed itemset tidset (IDs of transactions in which the itemset occurs) is required. Unlike [36] which does not build the Lattice and only counts the support of each closed itemset (i.e. the cardinality of its tidset), the proposed method exploits the two structures to update the Lattice after each transaction is read (See algorithmic details in Section 5).

Motivations. In applications such as network monitoring, telecommunications data management, web personalization, manufacturing, sensor networks, ubiquitous computing, monitoring of atmospheric, astronomical, financial data, and others, data takes the form of continuous data streams rather than finite stored data sets. The Internet has scaled up the rate of transactions generating multiple streams: browser clicks, user queries, email data and traffic logs, web downloads etc. Internet also makes it easier to deploy special purpose, continuous observation points that get aggregated into vast data streams. Furthermore, wireless access networks are now in the threshold of scaling this phenomenon even more.

For the above reasons, in recent years, stream processing and in particular sensor networks has attracted much research interest. In particular, mining data streams for knowledge discovery which allows fraud detection, intrusion detection, trend learning, etc. These are of course time critical tasks and need to be completed in *near-real time* to accurately keep pace with the rate of stream updates and *accurately reflect rapidly changing* trends in the data. As a consequence, stream processing poses challenging research problems due to the large volumes of data involved and the presence of on-line processing requirements. The data is used for detecting congestion, balancing load, and signaling alarms when abnormal conditions arise. Since many applications, such as monitoring systems, are reactive in nature, data analysis algorithms are preferably *online*. In this framework, due to large data volumes (e.g. hundred Gb per hour), algorithms are preferably *one-pass*. That is, multiple scans over the dataset simply cannot be afforded. In this paper we propose an on-line, one-pass algorithm specifically designed to analyze frequent itemsets in data streams.

2   Formal Concept Analysis: Definitions and Notations

Formal Concept Analysis allows to formalize the notion of "concept" [19] as established in the international standard ISO. From a philosophical point of view, a *concept* is a unit of thoughts consisting of two parts, the *extension* and the *intension*. The extension covers all objects belonging to this concept and the intension comprises all attributes valid for all those objects. It combines objects, attributes and an incidence relation in the mathematical definition of a *formal context* and *formal concept* for a given formal context.

Let us recall from [28] some notations and the definitions of formal context and formal concept.

A formal context is a triple $\mathbb{K} := (\mathbb{G}, \mathbb{M}, R)$, where $\mathbb{G}$ is a set of objects, $\mathbb{M}$ is a set of items, and $R \subseteq \mathbb{G} \times \mathbb{M}$ is a binary relation (the *incidence* of the context) between $\mathbb{G}$ and $\mathbb{M}$. In this setting, we call *itemset* each subset of $\mathbb{M}$.

A formal concept is a pair $\mathcal{C} = (\mathbb{O}, \mathbb{I})$ where:

- $\mathbb{O} \subseteq \mathbb{G}$ is the extent of $\mathcal{C}$
    - $f(\mathbb{O}) := \{i \in \mathbb{M} | \forall o \in \mathbb{O} : (o, i) \in R\} = \mathbb{I}$
    f is a function that returns all the attributes valid for all the objects in $\mathbb{O}$
- $\mathbb{I} \subseteq \mathbb{M}$ is the intent of $\mathcal{C}$

- $g(\mathbb{I}) := \{o \in G | \forall i \in \mathbb{I} : (o,i) \in R)\} = \mathbb{O}$

g is a function that returns all the objects for which all the attributes in $\mathbb{I}$ are valid.

$\mathbb{I}$ is a *closed itemset*: $\mathbb{I} = f(g(\mathbb{I}))$.

We can note that f and g functions establish a Galois connection between the power set Lattices on G and $\mathbb{M}$. In fact, we define as $h = f \circ g : dom(\mathbb{M}) \to dom(\mathbb{M})$ the closure operator on $\mathbb{M}$. Let us note that the related closure system CS (i.e., the set of all $\mathbb{I} \in \mathbb{M}$ with $h(\mathbb{I}) = \mathbb{I}$) is the set of all intents which are common to all concepts in the context.

Let us note also that concepts are naturally ordered by the *subconcept-superconcept* relation defined by: $(\mathbb{O}_1, \mathbb{I}_1) \leq (\mathbb{O}_2, \mathbb{I}_2) \Leftrightarrow \mathbb{O}_1 \subseteq \mathbb{O}_2 \Leftrightarrow \mathbb{I}_2 \subseteq \mathbb{I}_1$.

The ordered set of all formal concepts for a given context is called Concept Lattice of the context.

3   Association Rule and Closed Itemset Mining in Formal Concept Analysis

Intuitively, while Association Rule Mining (ARM) discovers dependencies among values of an attribute grouped by some other attributes in a given relation, Formal Concept Analysis (FCA) deals with formal mathematical tools and techniques to develop and analyze relationships between concepts and to develop concept structures.

For a given context $\mathbb{K} := (G, \mathbb{M}, R)$ (i.e. the database instance D in ARM), Formal Concept Analysis starts with the same type of data as Association Rule Mining: a context consists of a set of objects G (i.e. transactions in ARM), a set of attributes $\mathbb{M}$, and a binary relation R between G and $\mathbb{M}$.

The closure operator h of the Galois connection associates with an itemset I the maximal set of items common to all the objects containing I. In other terms, the closure of I is the intersection of the sets of items of these objects. Using this closure operator, the *frequent closed itemsets* are defined.

Definition 1. *An itemset $I \subseteq \mathcal{I}$ (with I the items domain) is a closed itemset iff $h(I) = I$.*

We can easily verify that the *intent* $\mathbb{I}$ of a concept $\mathcal{C}$ is a *closed itemset* in the given context, and that the *extent* $\mathbb{O}$ is the set of transactions in which that closed occurs (i.e. the *tidset*).

As mentioned above, the frequent closed itemsets constitute, together with their support frequencies, a generating set for all frequent itemsets and their supports and thus form the basis for all association rules, their supports and their confidences.

4   The Line Diagram

A line diagram is a graphical visualization of the Concept Lattice. A line diagram consists of circles (nodes), lines (arches) and names of all objects and all attributes of the given context. It allows the investigation and interpretation of relationships between concepts, objects and attributes. This includes attribute and object hierarchies, if they exist in the given context. A line diagram contains the relationships between objects and attributes and thus is an equivalent representation of a context. As a difference to Hasse diagrams, the labeling in line diagrams is reduced: the nodes in the diagram are not annotated by their complete extent and intent, i.e. *each object and each attribute is only entered once*. This fact can be noticed in Figure 1 in which two Lattice diagrams representing the same set of concepts are represented. The diagram on the left does not contain any reduction in nodes labelling (the complete sets of attributes and objects for each concept are shown). In the diagram on the right, nodes labelling is reduced since the complete set of attributes of each node can be obtained by considering the attributes inherited from the upper nodes; conversely, the complete set of objects can be obtained by considering the objects inherited from the lower nodes. Thus, the inherited attributes and objects are not explicitly represented.

As we will see in the next sections, this property is of fundamental importance in the proposed algorithm. In fact, one of the further structures connected to the Concept Lattice is a hash map ($AMap$) on the attributes that returns for each attribute the correspondent diagram node. Since each attribute univocally identifies a node in the diagram, each entry in $AMap$ corresponds to a single node. Note that the contrary is not true, i.e. since a node in the diagram can be labelled by more than one attribute, there could exist more attribute entries in $AMap$ whose diagram node is the same.

Let us recall the main properties of each node belonging to a line diagram:

1. an object $o \in \mathbb{G}$ labels the node representing the smallest concept (most specific) with o in its extent;
2. an attribute $a \in \mathbb{M}$ labels the node representing the largest concept (most general) with a in its intent.

Let us note that higher nodes in the diagram represent more general concepts w.r.t. concepts associated the nodes in the bottom of the diagram.

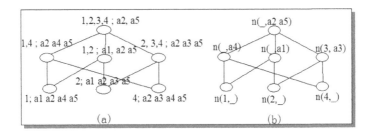

Fig. 1. Two different notations for representing nodes in a Lattice: with the complete extension and the intension sets, in the Concept Lattice (a); with the *labels*, in the Line Diagram (b)

In order to extract information of the contexts (i.e., its extension and intension), the line diagram can be read following these two simple *reading rules*:

1. An object o has an attribute a if and only if there is an upwards leading path from the diagram node labelled by object o to the node labelled by attribute a.
2. An attribute a belongs to an object o if and only if there is a downwards leading path from the diagram node labelled by attribute a to the node labelled by object o.

A more detailed description of line diagrams can be found in [40].

Let us denote with $n(labels_G, labels_M)$ a node of the diagram $\mathcal{LD}$ of the context $\mathbb{K} := (\mathbb{G}, \mathbb{M}, R)$, where $labels_G \subseteq \mathbb{G}$, and $labels_M \subseteq \mathbb{M}$. $n.labels_G$ and $n.labels_M$ define, respectively, the object and attribute labels associated to the node n. Let us recall that since a label appears in a diagram *only once*, it can *uniquely identify a node*.

A node could have no labels. As shown in Figure 1, the absence of (attributes or objects) labels is denoted by "_".

$n.intent$ and $n.extent$ denote respectively the intent and the extent of the node n. $n.parent_i$ denotes a parent of the node n in the Lattice. Using this notation, we can define two main properties of the line diagram:

Definition 2. $n.labels_G = \bigcap_{i=1}^{k}\{(n.parent_i).extent\}$ *where k is the number of parents of n.*

Definition 3. $n.labels_M = n.intent \setminus \bigcup_{i=1}^{k}\{(n.parent_i).intent\}$ *where k is the number of parents of n.*

As we will see in Section 5, the algorithm totally exploits these very useful properties.

5   The Incremental Algorithm

In this section we present a new incremental algorithm, called CLearner, aiming at "learning concepts" for a given context. The algorithm takes in each step an itemset I_k as input (i.e. the set of items in transaction k), and outputs all the closed itemsets and the Concept Lattice of the given context (i.e. the dataset). I_k represents a new information to be "pushed" into the diagram in order to "extend the knowledge" of the context by updating the Lattice in an incremental way. Indeed, during the execution of the algorithm, the Concept Lattice represents a "partial knowledge" of the context. At the end of the algorithm, the line diagram (the Concept Lattice) represents all the concepts of the given context.

In order to efficiently update the Lattice, CLearner uses two very useful and simple structures (hash maps) , $AMap$ and $IMap$. $AMap(\mathbb{M}, P)$ is an hash map on the attributes $a_j \in \mathbb{M}$, $j = \{1, .., |\mathbb{M}|\}$. To each attribute a_j in $AMap$ is associated a pointer $p_{a_j} \in P$ to a node in the Lattice. More in particular, p_{a_j} is a pointer to the node n having a_j in its set of attribute labels ($a_j \in n.labels_M$).

	a1	a2	a3	a4	a5
1	✕	✕		✕	✕
2	✕	✕	✕		✕
3		✕	✕		✕
4		✕	✕	✕	✕
5	✕	✕		✕	✕
6	✕	✕	✕	✕	✕
7	✕	✕		✕	
8	✕	✕	✕	✕	✕

Fig. 2. Example DB

The intension of this node ($n.intent$) is the *minimal closed itemset* containing a_j. We can define this such node as the "root node" of the *sub-Lattice* of all the closed itemsets containing a_j. For this reason, $AMap$ constitutes a very useful structure that allows to quickly identify the sub-Lattice of concepts in which a given attribute is present. As we can see in the sketch of CLearner below (function FindNodesToSplit), this map is used during all the execution of the algorithm. Let us recall from Section 4 that $n(a)$ is a node with the attribute a in its set of attribute labels. All the nodes are directly reachable by using $AMap$. We denote in pseudo-code a node by $n(a)$: this specifies that the node is "directly reachable by the pointer p_a associated to the attribute a in $AMap$". Note that X in the notation $n(X)$ identifies *a set* of attributes labels. However, since a node can be directly reachable by more than one pointer in $AMap$ (Section 4), searching for X in $AMap$ means searching for any one of the attributes $a \in X$. Figure 3 presents the construction of the concepts relative to the database of Figure 2 by a line diagram with a step for each database transaction read. The unique node created in the first step, representing the result of reading of the first transaction, is reachable by attributes $a1$, $a2$, $a4$ and $a5$, and we could thus denote it with $n(a1)$, $n(a2)$, $n(a4)$ or $n(a5)$.

The second hash map, $IMap(CS, P)$, is built on the closed itemsets (intensions) $\mathbb{I} \in CS$, i.e. each closed itemset in $IMap$ is associated (has a link to) a node in the Lattice. Since each node in the Lattice represents a concept, and the intent of a concept is a closed itemset, using $IMap$ each node in the Concept Lattice is directly reachable by using its intent. This structure is very useful to verify if a closed itemset was already generated from the past transactions. If so, the algorithm can directly find the respective node (concept) in the Lattice. Let us recall that such a map is very useful when the dataset is very dense, with strongly correlated data and, as a consequence, most of the closed itemsets occur frequently. Furthermore, since this map contains all the closed itemsets and it is updated transaction by transaction, it is easy for the user to quickly see the result set w.r.t. the transactions that have just been read.

Let us note that while not all the nodes in the Lattice are directly reachable by a pair (a, p_a) in $AMap$, all the nodes are directly reachable by an entry $(\mathbb{I}, p)$ in $IMap$.

○ not changed node
◎ splitted node
▧ new node from a split
● new node representing the current transaction

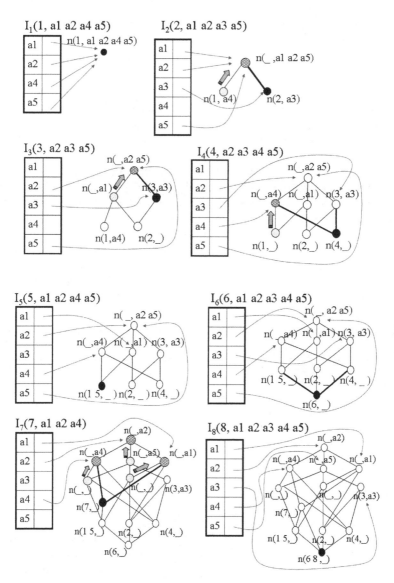

Fig. 3. Concept Lattice evolution for the context in Figure 2

The pseudo-code for CLearner algorithm appears as Algorithm 1 below.

Algorithm 1. CLearner.

```
1: for all transactions I_k ∈ dataset D do
2:      W := FindNodesToSplit(I_k)
3:      for all (a, w_a) ∈ W do
4:              Split(a, w_a, I_k)
5:      Insert(I_k, W)
```

As mentioned above, CLearner takes a transaction as input, and directly updates the Lattice. At least one node is added into the Lattice after each transaction if a node having, as its intent, exactly the attributes of that transaction does not already exist in the Lattice (i.e. as soon as the current transaction is not identical to an already read one).

The first step (Line 2 in CLearner) finds the nodes (if any) which need to be splitted in the Lattice in order to insert the node reflecting the current transaction. A node needs to be splitted if the concept that it represents does not hold for the concept represented by the current transaction. For example, let assume the Lattice is the one in step 2 of Figure 3, and the current transaction is I_3, i.e. $a2, a3, a5$. Before reading I_3, the attributes $a1$, $a2$ and $a5$ always appeared together in the past transactions. Reading I_3, the algorithm "learns" that $a2$ and $a5$ can appear without $a1$, and it splits the node $n(a1, a2, a5)$ to generate a new node $n(a2, a5)$ from $n(a1)$. The new node will be a parent of the node representing the current transaction $a2, a3, a5$.

The sketch of the FindNodesToSplit procedure is given in the following.

```
function FindNodesToSplit(I)
1: for all a ∈ I
2:         if a does not already exist in AMap then
3:                 insert a in AMap
4:         else w_a := n(a).intent \ I
5:                 if w_a ≠ ∅ ∧ ∄(a', w'_a) ∈ W|w_a = w'_a then
6:                         W := W ∪ (a, w_a)
7:                 else if a is not a label of n(a') then
8:                         W := W ∪ (a, w_a)
9: return W
```

This procedure takes transaction I as input, and uses $AMap$ to find the node that has to be splitted. For all $a \in I$, nodes $n(a)$ are those ones containing some attributes in common with I and some not. w_a corresponds to the set of items that $n(a)$ *does not share* with the current transaction. FindNodesToSplit builds the set W containing pairs (a, w_a). For each pair (a, w_a) in W the Split procedure can be executed. The pseudo-code of the Split procedure is given below.

---

procedure Split(a, w_a, I_k)
1: $X := n(a).labels_M \cap I_k$
2: **add the node** $n(X)$ **to the Lattice**
3: $n(a).labels_M := n(a).labels_M \setminus X$
4: **update** $AMap$
5: $\{n(a).parent\} := \{n(a).parent\} \cup n(X)$
6: $n(X).parents := n(a).parents.parents$
7: **add closed itemset** $\text{IMap}(n(a).intent \setminus w_a, n(X))$
8: $n(X).extent := n(a).extent \cup k$

The `Split` procedure adds a new node to the Lattice and connects it to $n(a)$. More specifically, for a given pair (a, w_a), it uses the intersection X between the intent of $n(a)$ and I (Line 1) to set the labels of a new node (Line 1). Obviously, $AMap$ has to be updated (Line 4). The new node $n(X)$ is a new parent of $n(a)$ (since $n(X).intent = n(a).intent \setminus w_a \Rightarrow n(X).intent \subset n(a).intent$). Since X is the set of attributes in common with the current transaction, each parent of $n(a)$ is also a parent of the new node (Line 5). Note that each of these $n(X)$ will be parents of the new node representing the current transaction. In this procedure also the tidsets of the involved closeds (i.e. the extent of each concept) are updated, a fundamental information to update the Lattice.

After the execution of this procedure, the Lattice is ready to be updated with the new concept representing the current transaction. The `Insert` procedure inserts this concept into the Lattice if it does not already exist in the Lattice. This check is immediately performed because one of the nodes generated in the `Split` procedure could represent the concept of the current transaction. For example, let assume the second transaction I_2 is $a1, a2, a5$ instead of $a1, a2, a3, a5$ in Figure 3. The split of node $n(a1, a2, a4, a5)$ generates node $n(a1, a2, a5)$ that already represents the current transaction. In this case, no further nodes are added to the Lattice. The pseudo-code of this procedure is presented below.

---

procedure Insert(I, W)
1: **if already exists** $\text{IMap}(I_k, n')$ **then**
2:       **add** k **to both** $n'.labels_G$ **and** $n'.extent$
3: **else add node** $n(k)$ **to the Lattice**
4:       SetParents(n, I_k)
5:       SetAsParent(n)
6: **add closed itemset** $\text{IMap}(I, n(k))$
7:       $n.labels_G := \bigcap_i \{n.parent_i.extent\} \cup k$
8:       $n.labels_M := \text{CreateLabelM}(I_k, W)$
9:       **add** k **to the extent of all nodes above** n

`Insert` procedure searches in $IMap$ if there already exists a concept (a node) with I as intent (Line 1-2). If so, it simply updates $IMap$ and the object labels of that node. Otherwise, it adds a new node and sets the parents and the children accordingly (Line 4-5). Then, it sets the object (Line 7) and the attribute labels

(Line 8, `CreateLabelM` function). To this aim, Definition 4 and 5 in Section 4 are exploited respectively. In the following, the pseudo-code of `CreateLabelM` function is given.

---

function CreateLabelM(I_k, W)
1: $S := \emptyset$
2: **for all** $(a, w_a) \in W$
3:     $S := S \cup n(a).intent$
4: $L := I \setminus S$
5: **return** L

Let us note that `SetParents` and `SetAsParent` procedures presented here are not described in their optimized version, due to space limitations. For example, as mentioned above, a set of parents of the new node representing the current transaction was already found during the `FindNodesToSplit` procedure. The pseudo-code (with capital letters because of the non-optimized version) of a non optimized version of the two procedures is given below. Let us note that in Line 2 of `SetAsParent` procedure, $n(o)$ identifies a node containing the object o as object label. No map is used for the search of $n(o)$ nodes. However, these nodes were already found in the `FindNodesToSplit` procedure.

Figure 3 shows the Concept Lattice evolution during the execution of the algorithm for the context in Figure 2. Due to lack of space, $IMap$ is not visualized in Figure 2. In each step, Figure 3 shows both $AMap$ and the Lattice with the respective links between the two structures. Different shadows are used (Figure 3) in order to better visualize the evolution of the Lattice. Note that each node is represented with the notation $n(labels_G, labels_M)$. As we can see, one node does not have object and/or attribute labels (because they are inherited by other nodes). For example, node $n(\_, a1, a2, a5)$ and node $n(2, \_)$ in the second and third step (i.e. reading I_2 and I_3 respectively) do not have object labels and attribute labels respectively. Although the two nodes $n(\_, \_)$ in the seventh step do not contain both object and attribute labels, we can easily distinguish them thanks to their intension (stored in $IMap$). Most of the incremental algorithms that build the Concept Lattice start each search from the *bottom concept*, i.e. a concept containing all the attributes in the context. Instead, unless a transaction in the context contains all the attributes in M, the Lattice built by our algorithm does not contain the bottom concept. Instead of starting from such a node, using $AMap$ we can easily *prune* the search of a node. As we can see in Figure 3, each node is reachable using $AMap$: while some of the nodes (at most $|M|$) are directly reachable (those containing an attribute label), the others can be found following (one of) the subLattice(s) of the respective root(s).

An Example. Let us describe some steps of the algorithm for the context in Figure 2. Initially, the Lattice, $AMap$ and $IMap$ are empty. CLearner takes the first transaction $I_1 = (1, a1\ a2\ a4\ a5)$ as input. Since none of these attributes hold in $AMap$, $(a1, a1\ a2\ a4\ a5)$, are inserted in $AMap$ (Lines 2-3 of

---

procedure SETPARENTS(*node*, *I*)
    Parents := ∅
    for all $n(a)$ s.t. $a \in I$
        find the set $\{n'\}$ of nodes below $n(a)$ for which $n'.intent \subset I$
        Parents := *Parents* ∪ $\{n'\}$
    $\{node.parent_i\}$:= *Parents*
end procedure
procedure SETASPARENT(*node*)
    Children := ∅
    for all $n(o)$ **s.t.** $o \in \bigcap_i \{node.parent_i.extent\}$
        if $\exists n' \in Children$ **s.t.** $n(o).extent \subset n'.extent$ **then**
            Children := *Children* \ n'
        Children := *Children* ∪ $n(o)$
    for all $n' \in Children$ **set node** *node* **as a parent**
end procedure

---

the FindNodesToSplit function). Then, a new node $n_1(1, a1\ a2\ a4\ a5)$ in the Lattice is inserted (Line 5 of Algorithm 1). Then, CLearner takes $I_2 = (1, a1\ a2\ a3\ a5)$ as input. Intuitively, this transaction suggests that the concept C_1 is not always true in the context. The algorithm adds $a3$ in $AMap$. Then it builds the set W (Lines 4-8 of FindNodesToSplit function) containing pairs of (a, w_a). Let us recall that w_a is a set of attributes that must be removed from $n(a)$ in order to build a new node (Split procedure). In Figure 3, the splitted node is shaded in grey, and the new node generated from it is striped. In the second step of the example (i.e. reading I_2) , $W = (a1, a4)$. After building the W set, the Split procedure is called to create a new node with the intersection $x := n(a).M \cap I_k = (a1, a2, a5)$. This intersection represents the portion of a closed itemset that is still always true for the given context. Finally, the node containing the new object k (the black one) is inserted (Insert procedure). For transaction I_7, before inserting $n(7, \_)$, these such steps are made three times, i.e. three nodes are splitted to generate three new nodes. For the transactions I_5 and I_8, instead, since there already exists in the Lattice (in $IMap$, actually) the respective closed itemset, the algorithm only updates both the extension (in $IMap$), and the object labels of the respective node. Note that these steps can be directly made using $IMap$ to both find the closed itemset (in order to update the extent) and reach the respective node (in order to update its object labels).

Let us emphasize that CLearner does not use any set of frequent items early mined in order to find the closed ones, i.e. it does not need any pre-preprocessing.

Furthermore, our algorithm can generate all the closed itemsets, i.e. it can be executed without a support threshold (or with this threshold equal to zero), for which the performance of the most of the algorithms quickly deteriorates. In fact, these algorithms can be applicable only in some domains, where rarely applicable rules are not of interest and may not be applicable. For example, in the market basket analysis it probably does not make sense to decide upon special advertisements based on items bought only by a very small fraction of supermarket customers. However, there are some domains in which especially rare rules are of interest for the user. For example, in the medical domain the death or severe illness of a patient may also be quite rare but obviously is nevertheless of interest [41]. As pointed out in [42], the support as a rule quality measure is commonly overestimated, and support is seen as an unavoidable means to make the complexity of the mining problem manageable for current algorithms. However, rules at very low support may be interesting. Let us consider for example two items, a and b, rather infrequent in the data. This means that also the support of the rule $a \rightarrow b$ is quite low. Nevertheless if such a rule with reasonable confidence exists, it will be of interest because the implied co-occurrence in the same transactions of two such infrequent items is probably not by accident.

The current best estimate for the above version of the algorithm's upper bound complexity to construct the Lattice L whose context has a set of objects G, each of which possesses at most $max(|m'|)$ attributes (or items) is $O(|G|(|L| + max(|m'|)))$ [43]. Indeed, the complexity depends on the number $|G|$ of transactions, on the number $|M|$ of attributes, and on the number $|L|$ of nodes in the Lattice. The procedure FindNodesToSplit takes $O(|M|)$ building the W set, considering the intent of each attribute of the current transaction. The for cycle in the algorithm 1 (Lines 3-4) is executed for each element in W. Actually, since a node to be splitted contains at least two items (otherwise we have no reason to split it), the Split procedure is executed at most $|\frac{M}{2}|$ times. Finally, the complexity of a single invocation of Insert procedure can be estimated as $O(|G||M|)$. At each call of the Insert procedure, SetParents and SetAsParent are executed once. Let us recall that the given pseudo-code of these procedures was simplified for the sake of simplicity, and does not correspond to the optimized version. The optimized versions of these procedures avoid to consider a node more than once in the Lattice. Hence, in the worst case, both SetParents and SetAsParent procedures need to reach each node in the Lattice ($|L|$). Hence, the complexity of a single step of the first for cycle in 1 (Lines 1-5) can be estimated as $O(|M| + |\frac{M}{2}| + 2|L|)$, that leads us to the total complexity of $O(|G|(|M| + |L|))$ as stated above.

The algorithm was encoded in C++. Preliminary experimental results reveal our algorithm to be competitive also with algorithms that need to pre-process the data and that do not build the Lattice (e.g., CHARM [34] and DCI-CLOSED [10]) and, certainly, the construction of the Concept Lattice requires much computation effort w.r.t. algorithms which generate only the concepts set. Of course, dealing with real dense dataset, such as connect[1], the choice to mine all the closed itemsets could be an issue. However, as showed in [33], the situation with real dataset is apparently different. A deeper comparison between our algorithm and AddIntent [33] and that in [44] has not yet been conducted. These two algorithms extract both the closed itemsets together with the Lattice, with similar methodologies. While the algorithm in [44] uses a stack and item-trie as utility data structures facilitating lookup of concepts, *AddIntent* uses a recursion and the diagram itself for the search. Moreover, in [44], the concepts are first sorted

---

[1] http://fimi.cs.helsinki.fi/data

in increasing order with respect to the corresponding intent sizes, and then *each of them* is examined. In our algorithm, instead, only supersets (to be splitted) or subsets of the current transaction are considered. Indeed, a direct comparison of our algorithm and these ones may reveal potential trade-offs between specific issues in which the algorithms differ. Detailed experiments and comparisons between our algorithms and these mining algorithms is of course a topic of further research.

6   Experimental Evaluation

We compared the performance of CLearner with existing state of the art algorithms, i.e. CHARM [9] and the algorithm proposed by T.Mielikainen in [45]. Let us note that CHARM algorithm does not build the Lattice of concepts, but just outputs the set of closed itemsets. We thus compared our algorithm also with an approach that reconstructs the Lattice in a second step, using the result of CHARM as input. We labeled this approach as Second-Step in the experiments. For testing the performances of the above algorithms, we chose two very dense datasets, i.e. mushroom and connect, both taken from the FIMI repository (http://fimi.cs.helsinki.fi/data). Mushroom dataset contains 8,124 transactions, with an average number of items per transaction equal to 23. Connect dataset contains 675,570 transactions, and each transaction has an average number of 43 items. All tests were performed on an Intel(R) Pentium(R)M with 512MB of memory, running Debian Linux 3.0. Algorithms were coded in C++.

Since running time and the usage memory of the proposed algorithm (as each closed corresponds to a node in the Lattice and viceversa) depend foremost on the total number of closeds computed, we tested how the number of closeds grows during the reading of the dataset. Figure 4 shows, for both mushroom 4(a) and connect 4(b), how the total number of closed itemsets grows as the transactions are read.

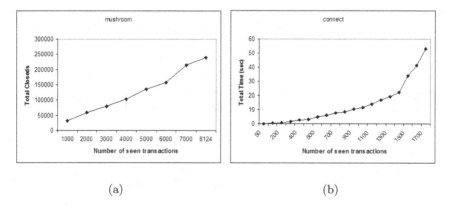

(a)   (b)

Fig. 4. Number of closed itemsets by number of seen transactions

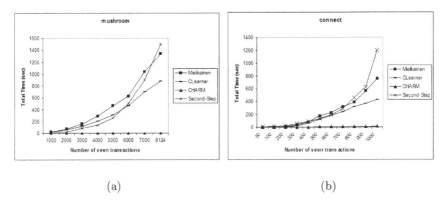

(a)   (b)

Fig. 5. CLearner performance

Figure 5 shows the performance of CLearner, CHARM, Mielikainen's algorithm and Second-Step, i.e. the approach that builds the Lattice in a second step. Let us recall that CHARM does not build the concept Lattice, but it was introduced in these experiments in order to emphasize how the constructing of the concept Lattice, though its already mentioned usefulness in the understanding of the final result, burdens the overall running time. As shown in Figure 5, CLearner outperforms both Mielikainen's algorithm, and Second-Step. As it was expected, it does not outperform CHARM, which, however, does not build the Lattice and reads the dataset more than once.

7   Conclusions and Future Work

In this paper we introduced CLearner, an incremental algorithm that generates closed itemsets together with the Concept Lattice. These closed itemsets and the Lattice allow to efficiently generate *bases* for association rules. CLearner builds the Concept Lattice for a given context (dataset) scanning it only once. Two further data structures are used to speed up the search in the Lattice, called *AMap* and *IMap*. These structures allow the algorithm to directly and automatically find a particular node. Our approach has a great advantage: it allows the user to see at each step the set of closed itemsets of the partial dataset that has just been read. Moreover, at the end of the algorithm, all the concepts together with the Lattice can be presented to the user without additional execution time.

It is well known that without any threshold on the support values, the number of closet sets becomes prohibitively large. In order to cope with very large datasets, some pruning techniques should be introduced. In Mielikainen's paper, some (although quite simplistic) efforts into this direction are being described. However, when the characteristics of the dataset are not apriori known, introducing items statistics (such as the number of remaining occurrences of each item) it is not affordable. Moreover, if all the transactions can be seen just once, they can not be reordered (for instance by cardinality).

Moreover, in order to reduce memory usage, we could decide to select nothing but frequent itemsets, choosing a threshold t1 on the support values. However, if the frequency of a non-frequent itemset is not monitored, we will never know when it becomes frequent. A naive approach is to monitor all itemsets whose support is above a reduced threshold t2, so that we will not miss itemsets whose current support is within t1 and t2 when they become frequent. However, this approach is apparently not general enough.

This work will be further extended in the following directions:

Dealing with constraints. The proposed version of the algorithm does not consider constraints (e.g. aggregate functions) over the attributes values, but we believe that most constraints can be "pushed" into the Lattice during the execution of the algorithm, thus playing a central role whether to add new nodes in the Lattice or not.

Sliding window. Especially dealing with real dense datasets, it is well known that the choice to mine all closed itemsets without a support threshold could be an issue. As the current implementation of the proposed method is still preliminary, there is plenty of room for improvements. One of topic for further improvements will be the introduction of a sliding window in our structures. Indeed, in [7], this method was already proven to be a winning choice (especially dealing with stream data). Our incremental algorithm can be easily extended with the use of a sliding window, that would be simply implemented as a threshold on the size of $IMap$. For this reason, this algorithm would turn out to be able to cope the problem of *continuous querying* over data streams [46]. Moreover, as regards memory usage, it was estimated to be linear in the number of closed itemsets in algorithm Moment. However, comparing our incremental algorithm with Moment is a topic of further research.

References

1. Agrawal, R., Mannila, H., Srikant, R., Toivonen, H., Verkamo, A.I.: Fast discovery of association rules. In: Advances in knowledge discovery and data mining, Menlo Park, CA, USA. American Association for Artificial Intelligence, pp. 307–328 (1996)
2. Srikant, R., Vu, Q., Agrawal, R.: Mining association rules with item constraints. In: Proceedings of 1997 ACM KDD, pp. 67–73. ACM Press, New York (1997)
3. Ng, R.T., Lakshmanan, L.V.S., Han, J., Pang, A.: Exploratory mining and pruning optimizations of constrained associations rules. In: Proceedings of 1998 ACM SIGMOD International Conference Management of Data, pp. 13–24. ACM Press, New York (1998)
4. Chaudhuri, S., Narasayya, V., Sarawagi, S.: Efficient evaluation of queries with mining predicates. In: Proc. of the 18th ICDE, San Jose, USA (2002)
5. Perng, C.S., Wang, H., Ma, S., Hellerstein, J.L.: Discovery in multi-attribute data with user-defined constraints. ACM SIGKDD Explorations 4(1), 56–64 (2002)
6. Pasquier, N., Bastide, Y., Taouil, R., Lakhal, L.: Efficient mining of association rules using closed itemset lattices. Information Systems 24(1), 25–46 (1999)

7. Chi, Y., Wang, H., Yu, P.S., Muntz, R.R.: Moment: Maintaining closed frequent itemsets over a stream sliding window. In: Perner, P. (ed.) ICDM 2004. LNCS (LNAI), vol. 3275, Springer, Heidelberg (2004)

8. Pei, J., Han, J., Mao, R.: CLOSET: An efficient algorithm for mining frequent closed itemsets. In: ACM SIGMOD 2000 Workshop on Research Issues in DMKD, pp. 21–30. ACM Press, New York (2000)

9. Zaki, M.J., Hsiao, C.J.: CHARM: An efficient algorithm for closed itemsets mining. In: Proceedings of the second SIAM International Conference on Data Mining, Arlington, VA, USA (2002)

10. Lucchese, C., Orlando, S., Perego, R.: Dci-closed: A fast and memory efficient mining of frequent closed itemsets. IEEE Journal Transactions on Knowledge and Data Engineering (TKDE) 18(1), 21–36 (2006)

11. Norris, E.: An algorithm for computing the maximal rectangle in a binary relation. Revue Roumaine de Mathematiques Pures et Appliquees 23, 243–250 (1978)

12. Gouda, K., Zaki, M.J.: Efficiently mining maximal frequent itemsets. In: Int. Conf. on Data Mining (ICDM), pp. 163–170 (2001)

13. Bayardo, R.: Efficiently mining long patterns from databases. In: Proceedings of the ACM-SIGMOD International Conference on the Management of Data, Seattle, Washington, USA (1998)

14. Pei, J., Dong, G., Zou, W., Han, J.: On computing condensed frequent pattern bases. In: Int. Conf. on Data Mining (ICDM), pp. 378–385 (2002)

15. Pasquier, N.: Mining association rules using formal concept analysis. In: Ganter, B., Mineau, G.W. (eds.) ICCS 2000. LNCS, vol. 1867, pp. 259–264. Springer, Heidelberg (2000)

16. Kryszkiewicz, M.: Concise representations of association rules. In: Hand, D.J., Adams, N.M., Bolton, R.J. (eds.) Pattern Detection and Discovery. LNCS (LNAI), vol. 2447, pp. 92–109. Springer, Heidelberg (2002)

17. Boulicaut, J., Bykowski, A., Rigotti, C.: Approximation of frequency queries by means of free-sets. In: Zighed, A.D.A., Komorowski, J., Żytkow, J.M. (eds.) PKDD 2000. LNCS (LNAI), vol. 1910, pp. 75–85. Springer, Heidelberg (2000)

18. Zaki, M., Phoophakdee, B.: Mirage: A framework for mining, exploring, and visualizing minimal association rules. Technical Report 03-4, Computer Science Dept. Rensselaer Polytechnic Inst. (2003)

19. Wille, R.: Restructuring lattice theory: an approaches based on hierarchies of concepts. In: Ordered Sets, pp. 445–470, Dordrecht-Boston, Reidel (1982)

20. Stumme, G.: Formal concept analysis on its way from mathematics to computer science. In: Priss, U., Corbett, D.R., Angelova, G. (eds.) ICCS 2002. LNCS (LNAI), vol. 2393, pp. 2–19. Springer, Heidelberg (2002)

21. Pasquier, N., Bastide, Y., Taouil, R., Lakhal, L.: Pruning closed itemset lattices for association rules (1998)

22. Stumme, G.: Conceptual knowledge discovery with frequent concept lattices (1999)

23. Zaki, M.J., Ogihara, M.: Theoretical foundations of association rules. In: Proceedings of 3rd SIGMOD 1998 Workshop on Research Issues in Data Mining and Knowledge Discovery (DMKD 1998), Seattle, WA (1998)

24. Guigues, J.L., Duquenne, V.: Familles minimales d'implications informatives resultant d'un tableau de donnees binaires. Math. Sci. hum. 24(95), 5–18 (1986)

25. Armstrong, W.: Dependency structure of database relationships. In: IFIP congress, pp. 580–583 (1974)

26. Stumme, G., Taouil, R., Bastide, Y., Pasquier, N., Lakhal, L.: Computing iceberg concept lattices with titanic. Data Knowledge Engineering 42, 189–222 (2002)

27. Stumme, G., Taouil, R., Bastide, Y., Pasquier, N., Lakhal, L.: Intelligent structuring and reducing of association rules with formal concept analysis. In: Baader, F., Brewka, G., Eiter, T. (eds.) KI 2001. LNCS (LNAI), vol. 2174, p. 335. Springer, Heidelberg (2001)
28. Ganter, B., Wille, R.: Formal Concept Analysis: Mathematical Foundations (Translator-C. Franzke). Springer-Verlag New York, Inc., Secaucus, NJ, USA (1997)
29. Luxenburger, M.: Implications partielles dans un contexte. Mathematiques, Informatique and Sciences Humaines 29, 35–55 (1991)
30. Lindig, C.: Fast Concept Analysis. In: Stumme, G., ed (eds.) ICCS 2000, Shaker Verlag, Aachen, Germany (2000)
31. Nourine, L., Rynaud, O.: A fast algorithm for building lattices. Information Processing Letters 71, 199–204 (1999)
32. Valtchev, P., Missaui, R., Lebrun, P.: A partition-based approach towards constructing galois (concept) lattices. Discrete Mathematics 256(3), 801–829 (2002)
33. der Merwe, D., Obiedkov, S.A., Kourie, D.G.: Addintent: A new incremental algorithm for constructing concept lattices. In: Eklund, P.W. (ed.) ICFCA 2004. LNCS (LNAI), vol. 2961, pp. 372–385. Springer, Heidelberg (2004)
34. Zaki, M.J., Hsiao, C.J.: Efficient algorithms for mining closed itemsets and their lattice structure. IEEE Transactions on Knowledge and Data Engineering 17, 4, 462–478 (2005)
35. Zaki, M.J.: Scalable algorithms for association mining. Knowledge and Data Engineering 12, 372–390 (2000)
36. Mielikainen, T.: Finding all occurring sets of interest. In: 2nd International Workshop on Knowledge Discovery in Inductive Databases, pp. 97–106 (2003)
37. Moonesinghe, H., Fodeh, S., Tan, P.N.: Frequent closed itemset mining using prefix graphs with an efficient flow-based pruning strategy. In: Perner, P. (ed.) ICDM 2006. LNCS (LNAI), vol. 4065, pp. 426–435. Springer, Heidelberg (2006)
38. Yahia, S.B., Hamrouni, T., Nguifo, E.M.: Frequent closed itemset based algorithms: a thorough structural and analytical survey. SIGKDD Explor. Newsl. 8(1), 93–104 (2006)
39. Bodon, F., Schmidt-Thieme, L.: The relation of closed itemset mining, complete pruning strategies and item ordering in apriori-based fim algorithms. In: 9th European Conference on Principles and Practice of Knowledge Discovery in Databases (PKDD) (2005)
40. Wolff, K.E.: A first course in formal concept analysis. In: Faulbaum, F. (ed.) SoftStat 1993, pp. 429–438 (1993)
41. DuMouchel, W., Pregibon, D.: Empirical bayes screening for multi-item associations. In: Proc. of ACM SIGKDD, San Francisco, USA, pp. 67–76 (2001)
42. Hipp, J., Güntzer, U.: Is pushing constraints deeply into the mining algorithms really what we want? – an alternative approach for association rule mining. SIGKDD Explorations 4, 50–55 (2002)
43. Merwe, F.V.D.: Constructing concept lattices and compressed pseudo-lattices. M.Sc. dissertation, University of Pretoria, South Africa (2003)
44. Valtchev, P., Missaoui, R., Godin, R., Meridji, M.: Generating frequent itemsets incrementally: Two novel approaches based on galois lattice theory. J. Expt. Theor. Artif. Intelligence 14, 115–142 (2002)
45. Mielikainen, T.: Intersecting data to closed sets with constarints. Goethals, B., Zaki, M. (eds.) Workshop on Frequent Itemset Mining Implementations (FIMI 2003). CEUR Workshop Preoceedings (2003)
46. Babu, S., Widom, J.: Continuous queries over data streams. In: SIGMOD 2001 Rec., pp. 109–120 (2001)

An Integrated Multi-task Inductive Database VINLEN: Initial Implementation and Early Results

Kenneth A. Kaufman, Ryszard S. Michalski,
Jarosław Pietrzykowski, and Janusz Wojtusiak

Machine Learning and Inference Laboratory, George Mason University
{kaufman,michalski,jarek,jwojt}@mli.gmu.edu

Abstract. A brief review of the current research on the development of the VINLEN multitask inductive database and decision support system is presented. The aim of this research is to integrate a wide range of knowledge generation operators in one system that given input data and relevant domain knowledge generates new knowledge according to the user's goal. The central VINLEN operator is *natural induction* that generates hypotheses from data in the form of attributional rules that resemble natural language expressions, and are easy to understand and interpret. This operator is illustrated by an application to discovering relationships between lifestyles and diseases of men age 50-65 in a large database created by the American Medical Association. The conclusion outlines plans for future research.

1 Introduction

This chapter reviews current research on the development of VINLEN, a multi-task inductive database and decision support system being developed at the GMU Machine Learning and Inference Laboratory. In VINLEN, a range of inductive as well as deductive inference capabilities are deeply integrated with a database and a knowledge base. These capabilities are realized through *knowledge generation operators* (KGOs) and combined with standard relational database management functions, implemented through an SQL client, via *Knowledge Query Language* (KQL).

KGOs operate on *knowledge segments* that link components from the knowledge base with related datasets from the database, and are used both as inputs to and outputs from VINLEN operators. This feature satisfies the closure principle required from an inductive database [9, 2].

In VINLEN, a KGO must satisfy two basic conditions: 1) that its results are in a form easy to understand and interpret by users, and (2) that they can be accepted as input to *compatible* KGOs. A compatible operator is one that can use the result from the first operator, if the result is submitted to it. This reflects the fact that the closure principle cannot be applied to all the operators from the whole spectrum of operators in VINLEN, as is similarly the case with SQL (as pointed out in [2]). For example, an evolutionary computation operator being implemented in VINLEN is incompatible with an operator that discovers attributional rules, because it can take as input only the initial population of solutions and control parameters, rather than rules.

S. Džeroski and J. Struyf (Eds.): KDID 2006, LNCS 4747, pp. 116–133, 2007.

The central knowledge generation operator in VINLEN is *natural induction* that discovers regularities in data in forms resembling simple natural language statements that are easy to interpret and understand. This is achieved by employing *attributional calculus* as a formal representation language [14]. Attributional calculus is a logic system that combines elements of propositional, predicate, and multiple-valued logics for facilitating inductive inference, and serves both as a knowledge representation formalism and an inference system.

Attributional descriptions, the primary form of knowledge representation in VINLEN, are more expressive than forms frequently used in data mining and inductive learning, such as conventional decision rules or decision trees. Conventional decision rules use only <attribute-relation-value> conditions, while attributional descriptions use conditions that may involve more than one attribute and relate them to a subset of values or to other attributes. Attributional descriptions can also be in different forms. Section 3 gives more details on this topic.

2 An Overview of VINLEN

Research on the VINLEN system grows out of our previous efforts on the development of INLEN, an early system for integrating databases with inductive learning capabilities, e.g. [16].

VINLEN represents a step beyond the approach to inductive databases taken by some authors, namely, it not only integrates a database and a knowledge base containing selected results of inductive inference (using the capabilities of the database), but is also a host for a wide range of inductive and deductive inference operators and data and knowledge management and visualization operators. It supports inferences resulting from a series of applications of its operators according to a script in *knowledge query language* KQL. This way, it can automatically conduct experiments that involve creating, storing and managing the relevant data and knowledge, laying the groundwork for a higher level of sophistication in inductive databases' functionality that employs meta-learning. Therefore, it aims at being an advanced tool for deriving knowledge from data that avoids pitfalls resulting from too limited exploration of data or the parameters of the methods.

An important concept in VINLEN is that of a *knowledge system* that consists of a specific database, which can be local or distributed, and a specific knowledge base. The knowledge system's purpose is to support data analysis, knowledge discovery, and knowledge application in a specific application area. A knowledge base contains handcrafted knowledge and results of applying knowledge generation and management operators to data in the database and/or to prior knowledge encoded in the knowledge base. All components of a knowledge system are stored in relational tables. All the entities utilized by the system, such as events (e.g., concept examples or records), datasets, attributes, attribute domains, rule conditions, rules, rulesets, and classifiers, are presented in individual tables in the database and connected via relations.

Events are stored as tuples in an *event table*. The table is populated either from external source, manually by the user, or by a VINLEN operator, for example, by selecting the most representative events from an input dataset. In addition to regular attribute values, events may contain meta-values, such as "unknown", "irrelevant" and "not-applicable" which require special handling during the learning or knowledge application processes [17]. The "unknown" values, denoted by a "?", represent cases when a regular attribute value exists, but is not known for some reason (e.g., a value was not recorded or recorded but not stored in the database). The "irrelevant" values are those considered irrelevant by an expert for a given task, and "not-applicable" values are assigned to events when a regular value does not exist for a given entity (e.g., attributes describing pregnancy do not apply to male patients).

Each event may carry additional meta-information, such as *event significance* and *event frequency*. The event significance is a value assigned to an event by the user or by the program to represent some form of importance of the event for problem at hand. It may have a different meaning for different types of problems. For example, in pattern discovery, it may represent the *typicality* of the event; in optimization, it may represent the value of the fitness function for that event. Event frequency is the number of occurrences of the given event in the training or testing data.

The prior knowledge contains definitions of the domains and types of attributes in the database, data constraints, value hierarchies of structured attributes, known relationships binding attributes, and any other background knowledge that users may have represented in the system. During the operation of an inductive database, the knowledge base is populated by newly generated data descriptions, hypothetical patterns, data classifications, statistical information, results from hypothesis testing, etc.

Both prior knowledge and VINLEN-generated knowledge are physically stored in a set of relational tables. The underlying formal representation of that knowledge are attributional descriptions that include *attributional rulesets* and *classifiers*. Attributional rulesets are sets of *attributional rules* with the same consequent (e.g., representing the same decision or class), and attributional classifiers are families of rulesets used for classifying input events into a predetermined set of classes or for recognizing instances of different patterns. An attributional rule consists of several components: a consequent, a relational symbol, a premise, an optional exception clause, and an annotation. Further details on formal representation are in Section 3.

Except for the relational symbol, these components are stored in the database in a similar way, namely, in two relational tables linked via a *1-to-n* relationship: tables of *selectors* (conditions) and *complexes* (conjunctions of conditions). A selector is described in the table by the attribute name, the operator represented by the relational symbol, a list of values, its location in the complex, and by an (optional) annotation. The annotation carries statistical information about the selector, for example, the number of positive and negative examples covered, and the number of examples covered by it and the all the previous selectors in the complex. A complex is described by its role (as a consequent, premise, exception clause, or as a precondition), its location in the ruleset, and by its own annotation that may contain such parameters as the number of positives and negatives covered by the complex, and its quality defined by special measure that reflects a tradeoff between its coverage and confidence gain [23].

All components of classifiers, such as selectors, complexes, exception clauses, single rules, rulesets, and alternative rulesets, are considered as individual entities, and as such are represented by separate tables connected by relations. Parameter sets for individual operators are stored in method-specific tables. This storage methodology facilitates an efficient access to all components of the classifiers through a standard SQL interface.

Attributional rulesets are represented in a linked table, and are described by their names, order in the classifier they belong to, and numbers of positives and negatives covered. The highest level of the knowledge segment, a classifier, is represented in another linked table, which stores the name and description of each classifier. In all these tables, entities have their unique identifiers, generated automatically by the system, which are used to link them into a hierarchy (relation). Complex and Selector tables are also used to represent conceptual clusters, with one complex describing one cluster. Clusters are grouped into clusterings by linking the Complex table with the Clustering table. Decision trees are stored using two tables: one that describes the whole tree at the general level, and the second, a linked table that keeps information about nodes of the tree, how they are organized into a hierarchy and also about splitting attributes and decisions associated with nodes.

VINLEN also implements the concept of the *experiment*, which is represented by two tables: *Experiment* and *ExperimentPart*. Each invocation of an operator leaves its trace with a timestamp in both of these tables. Since some experiments may involve a number of operators (methods), the information about utilizing a particular method is described as a part of a bigger experiment. This allows for further automation of the inference process using additional constraints; for example, it is possible to have a script that runs on a daily basis and performs tests of selected knowledge on a new testing data.

A *Target Knowledge Specification* is a generalization of a database query; specifically, it is a user's request for a knowledge segment to be created by the system, based on the data and knowledge already present. The core of VINLEN consists of *Knowledge Generation Operators*, which call upon various programs for knowledge generation (e.g., rule learning, conceptual clustering, target data generation, optimization, etc.), as well as knowledge application and data management. These operators can be invoked by a user directly, or through KQL. To provide a general overview and easy access to all VINLEN operators, we have developed a visual interface that consists of VINLEN views at different abstraction levels. Fig. 1 presents the most abstract view of the main panel of VINLEN.

The central part contains icons for managing database (DB), knowledge base (KB), and knowledge systems (KS). By clicking on DB, KB, or KS, the user can select and access a specific database, a knowledge base, or a knowledge system that is stored in VINLEN. Each of the rectangular buttons allows the user to access a family of knowledge generation operators of a given type. For example, the button "Learn Rules" allows one to access operators that learn different attributional rules, basis rules, rules with an exception clause, *multi-head rules*, and *rule-trees* (see Section 3). Other buttons have similar multi-function roles, such as "Access Attributes", "Improve Rules", "Learn Trees", "Create Clusters", "Access Scout", "Define Dataset", etc.

Appropriate matching between the operand and the operator takes place at the user interface level. When the user selects an operand – a dataset or knowledge segment – only relevant operators (methods) are enabled. This works also conversely – for a chosen operator, only appropriate operands become selectable. If a method requires more than one operand, they can be selected later in the method-specific form that appears after the corresponding operator is invoked. Such forms provide additional information about the selected knowledge or data, and allow the user to specify the parameters for the method, and to actually run the method. When the method's window is displayed, the graphical control on the form representing the selected operand is already set to the corresponding dataset or knowledge segment that was chosen as an operand when the operator was invoked. Of course, the user can always change his/her mind and choose another dataset or knowledge segment.

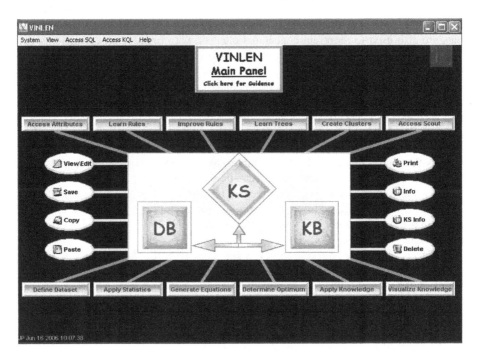

Fig. 1. The front panel of VINLEN (this is a black and white version of the actual screen)

In order to invoke a method for testing knowledge on data, the user selects the item representing this method from the menu, and the knowledge segment to be tested (in either order). On the form, two controls are shown, one representing the chosen knowledge segment, and the other one representing the dataset, which is by default set to the training data that was used to create the knowledge. Both choices can be changed at any time before running the method. Such capabilities of the system allow the user a capability for data-knowledge cross-querying (e.g. [2]).

Most operators are used in the context of a knowledge system, which means that the knowledge system needs to be opened first. Fig. 2 shows how the screen appears when a knowledge system has been opened: available datasets are listed on the left side of the central area, and existing knowledge components, of different types, are presented on the opposite side. There are some operators that do not require opening an existing Knowledge System, for example the menu allowing access to and creation of knowledge scouts, which can possibly be used to create a new knowledge system.

All operators are integrated through Knowledge Query Language (KQL), an extension of the SQL database query language. In addition to conventional data management operators, KQL includes operators for conducting inductive and deductive inference, statistical analysis, application and visualization of learned knowledge, and various support functions. KQL allows a user to define *knowledge scouts* that are KQL scripts for automatically executing a series of knowledge generation operators in search for knowledge of interest to the user.

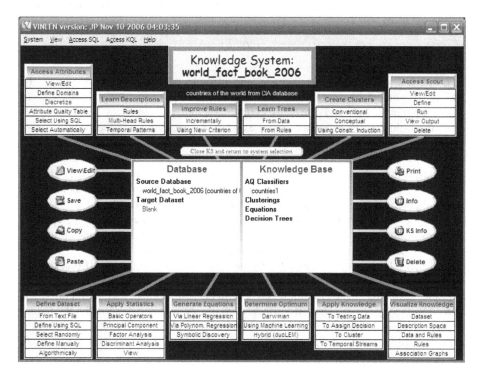

Fig. 2. An opened Knowledge System (a black and white version of the actual screen)

3   Knowledge Representation and VINLEN Operators

As mentioned earlier, VINLEN aims at providing users with an extensive set of knowledge generation and data management operators, and with a language, KQL, used to develop scouts for executing sequences of these operators. Such scouts can thus automatically perform knowledge discovery experiments.

The basic functionality of VINLEN allows the user to browse, edit, copy, delete, print, define, import and export data and knowledge. More advanced functions support data selection, attribute evaluation and selection, attribute discretization, and estimation of parameter settings for operators to achieve a desired result, and a range of learning and knowledge discovery functions. The rule learning module is based on the AQ21 program for natural induction [23].

As mentioned earlier, VINLEN's knowledge representation is based on attribu-tional calculus [14]. The basic unit of knowledge representation is an attributional rule in the form:

$$Consequent <= Premise \ |\_ \ Exception$$

where *Consequent, Premise,* and *Exception* are *conjunctive descriptions,* or *com-plexes,* which are conjunctions of *attributional conditions.* An attributional condition (a.k.a. *selector*) can be viewed as equivalent to a simple natural language statement. Its general form is:

$$[L \ rel \ R]$$

where:

L (the left side or referent) contains one attribute, or several attributes joined by "&" or "v", called internal conjunction and disjunction, respectively. L can also be one of the standard *derived attributes:* count, max, min, and avg.

R (the right side or reference) is an expression specifying a value or a subset of values from the domain of the attribute(s) in L. If the subset contains values of a nominal (unordered) attribute, they are joined by the symbol "v" (called internal dis-junction); if the subset contains consecutive values of a linear attribute[1], they are rep-resented by joining the extreme values by operator "..", called range. R can also be a single attribute of the same type as the attribute or attributes in L.

rel is a relational symbol from the set: ||. The relational operators $\{=, \neq\}$ apply to all types of attributes. Relations $\{>, \geq, <, \leq\}$ apply only to linear attributes (rank, in-terval, ratio and absolute).

Brackets [ ], may be omitted if their omission causes no confusion. If brackets are used, the conjunction of two selectors is usually written as their concatenation. If an attribute, x, is binary, the condition $[x = 1]$ can be written simply as the literal x, and $[x = 0]$ as the literal ~x. Thus, if attributes are binary, attributional conditions reduce to propositional literals. An attributional condition is called *basic,* if its left side, L, is a single attribute, its relational symbol is one of $\{ =, >, \geq, <, \leq \}$, and its right side, R, is a single value; otherwise, it is called *extended.*

Examples of basic conditions and their natural language interpretation:

$[x1 = 1]$, alternatively, x1   (The value x1 is 1)
$[x1 = 0]$, alternatively, $\sim x1$ (The value x1 is 0, the alternative is used when x1 is binary)
[color = red]   (The color is red)
[length < 5"]   (The length is smaller than 5 inches)
[temperature $\geq 32°$ C]   (The temperature is greater than or equal to $32°$ C)
[tools={mallet, knife}]   (The tools are the pair, mallet and knife)
[blood_type = ?}   (The blood type is unknown)

Examples of extended conditions:

[color = red v blue v green] (The color is red, blue or green)
[blood-type $\neq$ A]   (The blood type is not A)

---

[1] The linear attributes are these with ordered domains, namely rank, interval, and ratio.

[length= 4..12]	(The length is between 4 and 12, inclusive)
[color ≠ green v red]	(The color is not green, nor red)
[height > width]	(The height is greater than the width)
[height v width < 3 m]	(The height or the width is smaller than 3 m)
[height & width ≥ 7 cm]	(The height and width are both at least 7 cm)
[height & width < length]	(Both the height and the width are smaller than the length)

Operators "v" and "&", when applied to non-binary attributes or to their values, are called *internal disjunction* and *internal conjunction*, respectively. As mentioned earlier, a set of attributional rules with the same consequent is called an attributional ruleset. A set of attributional rulesets whose consequents span all values of an output (dependent) variable is called an attributional classifie*r* (a.k.a. *ruleset family*).

The VINLEN system integrates operators for performing the following learning and inference functions:

- Learning complete and consistent attributional classifiers;
- Optimizing attributional classifiers;
- Discovering patterns in data (attributional rules that represent strong regularities but may be partially inconsistent with the data);
- Generation of multi-head attributional rules (with more than one attribute in the consequent of a rule), see [5];
- Creating attributional rule-tree (ART) classifiers, that combine tree-like and ruleset representations, and improve learning efficiency [15];
- Deriving optimized decision trees from attributional classifiers (Rule To Trees method, RTT), e.g. [20];
- Applying attributional classifiers to data, and evaluating the results in the case of testing data [21];
- Discovering conceptual clusters in data e.g. [18];
- Determining the optimum of a given function using non-Darwinian evolutionary computation [22].

To facilitate the interpretability and understandability of learned knowledge, VINLEN includes operators that visualize knowledge in the form of *concept association graphs* (e.g. [10]) and *generalized logic diagrams* (e.g. [19]).

An interesting operator, being a step towards extending the capabilities of the system by meta-learning, is the Data and Parameter Selection (DPS) operator. This method optimizes the process of rule learning and pattern discovery with respect to execution time and the quality of the results by selecting the most relevant attributes, most representative examples and the most appropriate parameters for the given task. The results are stored in the database, and can later be used for current or further experiments, and to support decision making.

VINLEN also offers a set of methods for manipulation of the representation space, that allow the user to manually remove attributes from a dataset, create new ones using SQL or a discretization method, or keep only these satisfying one of the evaluation criteria (e.g. PROMISE [21], GainRatio). Attributes can also take on new types, or become a hierarchy, as specified manually (using graphical controls) by the user.

Additionally, a *cost* can be set for each attribute, the aggregation of which is used during rule evaluation as another constraint. Users can also freely view and edit datasets defined in the system by adding, removing or modifying individual events.

4 Knowledge Scouts

VINLEN operators (learning and inference operators, as well as data and knowledge management operators) can be used in developing knowledge scouts. A knowledge scout is a KQL script that can automatically apply various operators in search of *target knowledge* in the database. The target knowledge is defined abstractly by specifying properties of pieces of knowledge that are of interest to the given user (or specified group of users). Simple examples of target knowledge specification are "Determine an attributional classifier AC from the dataset DS that maximizes a given ruleset quality criterion", or "Determine a conceptual clustering CC of the dataset DS that optimizes the clustering quality criterion."

After describing a general KQL syntax, this section presents simple examples illustrating knowledge scouts for a sequence of steps in a data / knowledge mining process. The examples follow the basic KQL syntax that is sketched below, but do not include all details and possible parameters, which are beyond the scope of this paper.

The only mandatory part of a KQL scout's knowledge generation instruction is the CREATE keyword followed by the specification of the output type. Other parts are optional and with default values determined automatically, e.g. the name of the resulting knowledge or data unit, its location, method used, etc. The clause IN specifies the location of the result, for example, when creating a new attribute, it defines which dataset it will belong to. The clause AS is used to specify how the results affect the existing knowledge or data unit with the same name: e.g., it can be replaced, modified (for example the domain of the attribute can be extended, or a rule can be added to a ruleset) or given a new name provided interactively by the user. The keyword ASKED specifies that this decision should be made subsequently by the user, during the execution of the script. The FROM clause specifies the input(s) to the KQL operators. It can followed by the WITH / WITHOUT modifier that allows for selection from only certain input set, for example, only a selection of attributes from a given dataset. USING specifies the name of the method to be used, which may be followed by the WHERE clause which describes the parameters of the method. Clause HAVING allows for constraining the results according to some criteria.

The following is a sample of the syntax of knowledge scouts.

```
CREATE <output_type> [ <output_name> [IN <target_name>
[ AS NEW | MODIFICATION | REPLACEMENT | ASKED ] ] ]

[ FROM [ <source_name> [ AND <source_name> [...] ] ] ]

[ WITHOUT | WITH [<source_name>.]<element_name> ]

[ USING [ <method_name> [ AND <method_name> [...] ] ] ]

[ WHERE [ [ <method_name>.]<parameter_name> IS | IS NOT
| ARE | ARE NOT | HAS | HAS NOT <parameter_value> [ AND
[...] ] ] ]

[ HAVING [ACCURACY HIGHEST | ... ] [COMPLEXITY ... ]
```

The following sections describe examples of knowledge scouts.

Creating a new knowledge system: As a result of the shown example command, a new knowledge system *Countries* (user-entered data is in italics in the following examples) is created with automatically determined attribute types, roles of the attributes as input or output and name based on the user specified input text file.

```
CREATE KNOWLEDGE SYSTEM Countries

FROM FILE worldfactbook2006.txt
```

Creating a discretized version of an attribute: The target type is linear (values are ordered), and by default the target dataset is the same as the source dataset. The automatic discretization method based on the ChiMerge algorithm is used here with the parameter NUMBER OF INTERVALS set to 5. The second parameter provides an ordered list of names, a subset of which is used as the set of values of the created attribute. If there are 5 intervals created, then all the names are used, if there are 4 intervals then the middle name is not used; finally, if there are only 3 intervals then peripheral names are not used.

```
CREATE ORDINAL ATTRIBUTE BirthRate

FROM Birth_rate

USING CHIMERGE

WHERE NUMBER OF INTERVALS IS 5

AND NAMES ARE VeryLow, Low, Medium, High, VeryHigh
```

Creating a structured (hierarchical) version of the attribute Country based on geography: At the bottom level are names of the countries; higher levels describe continents and oceans. The keyword ATTRIBUTE is implied in the keyword STRUCTURED describing the type of the attribute. The ellipsis in the end of the WHERE clause indicates that the user needs to provide the actual entire list of selected countries.

```
CREATE STRUCTURED HierarchyOfCountries

FROM Countries

USING USER INPUT

WHERE NorthAmerica INCLUDES UnitedStates, Canada, Mexico AND

CentralAmerica INCLUDES Panama, Nicaragua, Honduras, … AND

SouthAmerica INCLUDES Colombia, Brazil, Argentina, … AND

America INCLUDES NorthAmerica, CentralAmerica, SouthAmerica AND

Europe INCLUDES Spain, France, Ukraine, … AND … AND

World INCLUDES America, Europe, Australia, …
```

Selecting a subset of data using simple selection: A dataset is selected from the whole database describing the countries in North America and Europe using the previously created hierarchy. The hierarchical information is preserved, but the hierarchy is only a subset of the source hierarchy.

```
CREATE DATASET NorthAmericaAndEurope

WITHOUT ATTRIBUTE Countries

USING SIMPLE SELECT

WHERE HierarchyOfCountries IS NorthAmerica, Europe
```

Selecting a subset of data for training: A new dataset is being created through random selection of 60% of the events from the default dataset in the current knowledge system.

```
CREATE DATASET NAEtraining1

FROM NorthAmericaAndEurope

USING RANDOM SELECTION

WHERE DISTRIBUTION IS UNIFORM AND TRAINING VS TESTING
EVENTS RATIO IS 60%
```

Learning a classifier: This operation invokes a learning operator, indicated by the <method_name> to hypothesize a complete and consistent classifier, named GDP-NAE, for the output attribute GDP (using its all values), with search process limited by the parameter. In the example below, the learning method is AQ21.

```
CREATE COMPLETE AND CONSISTENT CLASSIFIER GDP-NAE

FROM NAEtraining1

USING AQ21

WHERE CONSEQUENT IS GDP = * AND SEARCH SCOPE IS 3
```

Testing an attributional classifier: Here the ATEST method is used to evaluate the performance of the *GDP-NAE* model with the *NAEtesting1* dataset, using strict evaluation of selectors. The results are stored in the database under the name *TestGDPInNorthAmericaAndEurope*.

```
CREATE TEST TestGDPInNorthAmericaAndEurope

FROM GDP-NAE AND NAEtesting1

USING ATEST

WHERE SELECTOR EVALUATION IS STRICT
```

Visualizing knowledge: This script invokes the CAG visualization module with its default parameter values to present the classifier in a computer window.

```
CREATE VISUALIZATION CAGOfGDPInNorthAmericaAndEurope

FROM GDPInNorthAmericaAndEurope

USING CAG
```

Creating an attributional rule-tree classifier: Such a classifier represents knowledge as a shallow (1-2 levels) tree with classes or rulesets as leaves. This method is especially useful for problems with many (>7) classes, as it provides a more easily comprehended representation, and also improves the learning efficiency by reducing the number of negative examples. Let us assume that *OilConsumption* is a discretized attribute with many classes.

```
CREATE CLASSIFIER OilConsumption

FROM NorthAmericaAndEurope

USING ART

WHERE GROUPING IS PARTITIONING
```

Finding the optimum of a fitness function for a certain design: The script finds an optimal design using the learnable evolution model (LEM), the EVAP simulator to evaluate the fitness function, and a randomly generated initial population.

```
CREATE OPTIMAL DESIGN HeatExchanger1

USING LEM

WHERE FITNESS IS Evap AND INITIALPOPULATION IS RANDOM
```

In order to synthesize target knowledge, a knowledge scout may consist of many lines of KQL code that request an execution of a sequence of KQL operators involving data, intermediate results, previously learned knowledge and background knowledge. The latter may include the types of attributes, their domains (including hierarchies of structured attributes), problem constraints, and rules for constructing derived attributes. At every step of running the knowledge scout, an application of one operator may depend on the results of previous operators, due to the inclusion of tests of properties of data and knowledge components, of the results of their application to data, and the use of a branching operator in KQL. For example, a condition for repeating a learning operator may be:

"If the average consistency of attributional rules in the classifier is smaller than .95, or the number of rules in the classifier is greater than 10, the accuracy of the classifier on the testing data is smaller than .93, and the number of learning runs is smaller than 50, repeat the run with the *search scope* 15; otherwise, return the results."

The ultimate goal of the development of KQL is to be able to use language constructs in a highly declarative form that leaves the details of how the goals are to be achieved to the program, including selection and experimentation with a number of different methods, based on the meta-learning capabilities, as in the example below.

```
CREATE CLASSIFIER WorldFactbookPatterns
FROM WorldFactBook
USING DPS, AQ21 AND ART AND RTT, ATEST, CAG
WHERE TRAINING VS TESTING EVENTS RATIO IS 50%
HAVING ACCURACY HIGHEST AND COMPLEXITY LOWEST AND
EXECUTION TIME < 1.5 HRS
```

The above code defines a knowledge scout that is asked to apply three different learning operators (AQ21, ART and RTT) to the dataset *WorldFactBook1* (describing the countries of the world) and to determine three best classifiers that can be obtain by AQ21, ART and RTT operators within 1.5 hour total (each operator is allocated the same amount of time). The input dataset for the operators is to be created by the operator DPS that selects the most relevant attributes and the most representative examples from *WorldFactBook1*. This obtained set is split 50%-50% (overriding default ratio) into a training and a testing set. The classifier quality criterion first maximizes the accuracy and then minimizes the complexity of the classifier.

Operator AQ21 will create a standard attributional classifier, ART (Attributional Rule-Tree) will seek an attributional rule-tree, and RTT (Rule-To-Trees) will take the learned attributional classifier and create from it the "best" decision tree according to the default optimality measure. All operators are to be applied with default parameters. The results from each method are evaluated by the ATEST method, and graphically illustrated by the.CAG operator that presents them in the form of a concept association graph.

5 An Example of Application to a Medical Domain

This section illustrates an application of the VINLEN's knowledge generation operator to a problem of determining relationships between lifestyles and diseases of non-smoking males, aged 50-65, and displaying results in the form of a concept association graph. The study employed a database from the American Cancer Society that contained 73,553 records of responses of patients to questions regarding their lifestyles and diseases. Each patient was described in terms of 32 attributes: 7 lifestyle attributes (2 Boolean, 2 numeric, and 3 rank), and 25 Boolean attributes denoting diseases. The learning operator determined patterns (approximate attributional rules) characterizing the relationships between the 25 diseases and the lifestyles and other diseases. Fig. 3 shows a slightly simplified example of the discovered patterns (*HBP* stands for High Blood Pressure, and *Rotundity* is a discretized ratio of the patient's weight and height.

[Arthritis = Present] <=
      [HBP = present: 432, 1765] &
      [Education <= college_graduate: 940, 4529] &
      [Rotundity >= low: 1070, 5578]
      p = 325, n = 1156; P = 1171, N = 6240

Fig. 3. A pattern for Arthritis discovered from the medical database

The two numbers listed within each condition after the colon denote the numbers of positive and negative examples in the training set covered by that condition, respectively; p and n, are the numbers of positive and negative examples in the training set covered by the entire rule, respectively; and P and N are the numbers of positive and negative examples in the training data for that class (here, Arthritis), respectively.

The pattern in Fig. 3 defines a set of conditions under which patients had arthritis relatively frequently. These conditions include the presence of high blood pressure, no education beyond college, and more than "very low" rotundity. In the training data, about 16% of the patients had arthritis (P / (P + N)), but among patients satisfying the pattern, the percentage grows to 22% (p / (p + n)). The most significant factor in the pattern is high blood pressure, which by itself has confidence of about 19%.

The discovered attributional patterns are visualized using a *concept association graph* (CAG). Fig. 4 presents one such graph that was automatically generated using the CAG visualization operator.

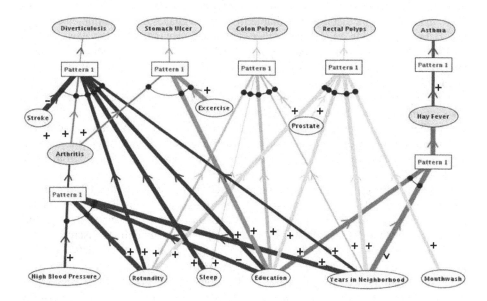

Fig. 4. Concept Association Graph representing seven patterns in the medical database

A CAG should not be confused with a Bayesian network, an entirely different concept. In CAG, links connected by an arch indicate a logical conjunction of the conditions pointing to the consequent node. The strength of each condition measured by a user-selected parameter, e.g., condition confidence or coverage, is indicated by the link thicknesses. For example, in Fig. 4, the thicknesses of links are proportional to the condition confidences. In addition, to indicate the general type of the relationship between the condition and the consequent, links are annotated by a symbol "+", "–", "v", or "^". Symbols "+" and "-" indicate that higher attribute values in the condition correspond to higher and lower values of the condition, respectively; "v" and "^" indicate that extreme attribute values correspond to higher or lower values of the consequent attribute, respectively. A CAG is thus an abstract visualization of a set of attributional rules.

While no claim is made as to the medical validity and significance of the presented relationships, this result indicates that the developed methodology is potentially capable of discovering important patterns in the data, and representing them in an understandable way, either as qualitative relationships in the form of attributional rules, or graphically via a concept association graph.

6 Relation to Other Work

VINLEN aims at integrating a wide range of capabilities and types of operators, many of which are unique. The knowledge query language, KQL, that provides a mechanism for invoking these operators automatically, is significantly different from other high-level languages developed for data exploration and knowledge discovery. It employs many operators that are unavailable in other languages, and it is implemented in C^{++}, rather than Prolog, as are many other knowledge management languages.

Among the non-Prolog-based languages, MINE RULE [11], which was used to analyze users' internet activity [13], is syntactically similar to KQL, as it also builds upon the SQL data query language. In contrast to VINLEN, which implements a wide range of operators, it integrates, however, only one inductive operator, which creates association rules from the data stored in the transactional format.

Another related language, KQML [3], allows the user to query for specific pieces of knowledge, but it does not support multiple discovery operators and the abstract templates available in KQL. The discovery operators are quite different from those used in VINLEN.

MSQL is a language for data mining proposed in [8]. Similarly to KQL it satisfies the closure principle, allowing results from one method to be used as inputs for another one; and it allows constraint of resulting rules based on their support, confidence or complexity (length in this case); as well as allowing defined discretizations. Although VINLEN's script language does not currsently include constructs for specifying lists of alternative attributes, or for query nesting, or for selecting data confirming / contradicting given hypotheses as MSQL does, it offers richer knowledge representation (e.g. selectors with internal disjunction, multi-head rules, counting attributes, compound attributes, explicitly defined hierarchies) and a broader set of available operators (e.g. for clustering, or different types of attributional classifiers).

DMQL [6] provides quite a broad scope of knowledge types and knowledge manipulation operations, including data selection and knowledge visualization. It also allows for explicit specification of hierarchies, attribute discretization, definition of rule constraints in terms of syntax templates or rule interestingness measures based on "novelty" (usually in relation to the user's beliefs). Currently KQL lacks the latter two features; nevertheless, it provides different kinds of knowledge generation operators, constraining rules based on their evaluation rankings as opposed to thresholds.

A query language that is somewhat related to KQL is described in [2]. It has the capability for specifying the type of knowledge to search for, e.g., rules with confidence levels above a given threshold. Being a Prolog-based language, it has the capability for directly expressing relational descriptions, but does not involve such a wide range and versatile operators that VINLEN does. While VINLEN can also search for rules with confidence levels above a certain threshold, it can also seek rules with maximum confidence values.

The WEKA system (available at http://www.cs.waikato.ac.nz/ml/weka/) also uses GUI, and offers a number of operators that can be expanded by independent developers, as well as graphical tools to design the learning / testing process. It includes different operators than VINLEN. In particular, it does not have the ability to discover patterns with the expression power of attributional rules. It also lacks a dedicated script language like KQL, and outputs results into separate files for each experiment, which is a less flexible method than storing both the data and the resulting knowledge in the system's database and knowledge base, respectively.

VINLEN is still under development, and at present our primary stress is on developing and implementing new capabilities, rather than on the system efficiency. Therefore, we have not yet addressed many important aspects described in [2, 9, 12], such as the query optimization and evaluation, caching intermediate results, keeping track of dataset and knowledge segment relations, or updating datasets and knowledge segments with respect to changes to other data and knowledge (data and knowledge integrity constraints). These issues are topics are on the agenda for the future research.

7 Summary and Future Work

This paper reviewed current research on the development of VINLEN, a system that aims at integrating a wide range of operators for data management, data analysis, knowledge discovery and visualization, knowledge testing and its application to decision support, classification, and optimization. The advantages of such integration and of inductive databases are now being widely recognized, as evidenced by the recent international workshop on Inductive Databases that led to this book, and earlier efforts e.g. [2, 4, 7, 9, 12]. The underlying knowledge representation used in VINLEN is based on attributional calculus, a logic and representation system that combines aspects of propositional, predicate, and multi-valued logic for the purpose of facilitating knowledge discovery.

Individual operators can be invoked by the user via the graphical user interface, or automatically, via a knowledge scout, a script in knowledge query language KQL. KQL is an extension of SQL that adds to it operators for knowledge generation, management, visualization, and application.

While the system is still under development, most of the operators planned for inclusion have already been developed and implemented as separate programs, and some have been already integrated in it. This chapter focused on two central operators, already implemented in VINLEN, namely, learning attributional classifiers, and visualizing the classifiers using concept association graphs. These operators have been illustrated by an example in a medical domain.

Other operators, such as conceptual clustering, intelligent target data generation and parameter setting, optimization of functions or systems via Learnable Evolution, and database management through an SQL client have been developed and implemented, and are in the process of being integrated in VINLEN. Various statistical operators, modules for applying knowledge to data for generating decisions, and a mechanism for creating knowledge query language scripts to guide data exploration tasks are still under development.

After gathering experience with the inter-operation of many methods integrated via KQL, we plan to address the remaining challenges of VINLEN development, such as KQL query evaluation and optimization, caching/reusing results of reasoning during the user's interaction with the system, and meta-learning. We also plan to address the issues of efficiency and scalability of the system with very complex problems.

Summarizing, the major contributions of the current VINLEN project are the development of a general methodology for a tight integration of a database, knowledge base, data management operators, a range of knowledge generation operators, an initial knowledge query language, a user-oriented visual interface implementation, and an experimental demonstration of the effectiveness of the implemented operators for natural induction and visualization of attributional classifiers via concept association graphs.

Acknowledgments. Research described here has been conducted in the Machine Learning and Inference Laboratory at George Mason University, and has been supported in part by the National Science Foundation under Grants No. IIS-9906858 and IIS-0097476, and in part by the UMBC/LUCITE #32 grant. In a few cases, presented results have been obtained under earlier grants from the National Science Foundation, the Office of Naval Research, or the Defense Advanced Research Projects Agency. The findings and opinions expressed here are those of the authors, and do not necessarily reflect those of the above sponsoring organizations.

References

1. Blockeel, H.: Experiment Databases: A Novel Methodology for Experimental Research. In: Bonchi, F., Boulicaut, J.-F. (eds.) KDID 2005. LNCS, vol. 3933, pp. 72–85. Springer, Heidelberg (2006)
2. De Raedt, L.: A Perspective on Inductive Databases. ACM SIGKDD Explorations Newsletter 4(2), 69–77 (2002)
3. Finin, T., Fritzson, R., McKay, D., McEntire, R.: KQML as an Agent Communication Language. In: Proceedings of the Third International Conference on Information and Knowledge Management, CIKM 1994, pp. 456–463. ACM Press, New York (1994)
4. Flach, P., Dzeroski, S.: Editorial: Inductive Logic Programming is Coming of Age. Machine Learning 44(3), 207–209 (2001)
5. Głowiński, C., Michalski, R.S.: Discovering Multi-head Attributional Rules in Large Databases. In: Tenth International Symposium on Intelligent Information Systems, Zakopane, Poland (2001)
6. Han, J., Kamber, M.: Data Mining – Concepts and Techniques. Morgan Kaufmann, San Francisco (2001)
7. Hätönen, K., Mika Klemettinen, M., Miettinen, M.: Remarks on the Industrial Application of Inductive Database Technologies. In: Boulicaut, J.-F., De Raedt, L., Mannila, H. (eds.) Constraint-Based Mining and Inductive Databases. LNCS (LNAI), vol. 3848, pp. 196–215. Springer, Heidelberg (2006)
8. Imieliński, T., Virmani, A.: MSQL: A query language for database mining. Data Mining and Knowledge Discovery 3(4), 373–408 (1999)
9. Imieliński, T., Mannila, H.: A Database Perspective on Knowledge Discovery. Communications of the ACM 39, 58–64 (1996)

10. Kaufman, K., Michalski, R.S.: A Knowledge Scout for Discovering Medical Patterns: Methodology and System SCAMP. In: Proceedings of the Fourth International Conference on Flexible Query Answering Systems, FQAS'2000, Warsaw, Poland, pp. 485–496 (2000)
11. Meo, R., Giuseppe, P., Stefano, C.: An Extension to SQL for Mining Association Rules. Data Mining and Knowledge Discovery V2(2), 195–224 (1998)
12. Meo, R., Lanzi, P.L., Klemettinen, M. (eds.): Database Support for Data Mining Applications. LNCS (LNAI), vol. 2682. Springer, Heidelberg (2004)
13. Meo, R., Vernier, F., Barreri, R., Matera, M., Carregio, D.: Applying a Data Mining Query Language to the Discovery of Interesting Patterns in WEB Logs. In: Workshop on Inductive Databases and Constraint Based Mining, Hinterzarten, Germany (2004)
14. Michalski, R.S.: ATTRIBUTIONAL CALCULUS: A Logic and Representation Language for Natural Induction. Reports of the Machine Learning and Inference Laboratory, MLI 04-2, George Mason University, Fairfax, VA (2004)
15. Michalski, R.S.: Attributional Ruletrees: A New Representation for AQ Learning. Reports of the Machine Learning and Inference Laboratory, MLI 02-1, George Mason University, Fairfax, VA (October 2002) (slightly updated in May 2004)
16. Michalski, R.S., Kerschberg, L., Kaufman, K., Ribeiro, J.: Mining For Knowledge in Databases: The INLEN Architecture, Initial Implementation and First Results. Intelligent Information Systems: Integrating Artificial Intelligence and Database Technologies 1(1), 85–113 (1992)
17. Michalski, R.S., Wojtusiak, J.: Reasoning with Meta-values in AQ Learning. Reports of the Machine Learning and Inference Laboratory, George Mason University, Fairfax, VA (2006)
18. Seeman, W.D., Michalski, R.S.: The CLUSTER3 System for Goal-oriented Conceptual Clustering: Method and Preliminary Results. In: Proceedings of the Data Mining and Information Engineering Conference, Prague, Czech Republic (2006)
19. Śnieżyński, B., Szymacha, R., Michalski, R.S.: Knowledge Visualization Using Optimized General Logic Diagrams. In: Proceedings of the Intelligent Information Processing and Web Mining Conference, Gdansk, Poland (2005)
20. Szydło, T., Śnieżyński, B., Michalski, R.S.: A Rules-to-Trees Conversion in the Inductive Database System VINLEN. In: Proceedings of the Intelligent Information Processing and Web Mining Conference, Gdansk, Poland (2005)
21. Wojtusiak, J.: AQ21 User's Guide. Reports of the Machine Learning and Inference Laboratory, MLI 04-3, George Mason University, Fairfax, VA (2004) (updated in September 2005)
22. Wojtusiak, J., Michalski, R.S.: The LEM3 Implementation of Learnable Evolution Model and Its Testing on Complex Function Optimization Problems. In: Proceedings of Genetic and Evolutionary Computation Conference, Seattle, WA (2006)
23. Wojtusiak, J., Michalski, R.S., Kaufman, K., Pietrzykowski, J.: The AQ21 Natural Induction Program for Pattern Discovery: Initial Version and its Novel Features. In: Proceedings of the 18th IEEE International Conference on Tools with Artificial Intelligence, Washington D.C., IEEE Computer Society Press, Los Alamitos (2006)

Beam Search Induction and Similarity Constraints for Predictive Clustering Trees

Dragi Kocev[1], Jan Struyf[2], and Sašo Džeroski[1]

[1] Dept. of Knowledge Technologies, Jožef Stefan Institute
Jamova 39, 1000 Ljubljana, Slovenia
`Dragi.Kocev@ijs.si`, `Saso.Dzeroski@ijs.si`
[2] Dept. of Computer Science, Katholieke Universiteit Leuven
Celestijnenlaan 200A, 3001 Leuven, Belgium
`Jan.Struyf@cs.kuleuven.be`

Abstract. Much research on inductive databases (IDBs) focuses on local models, such as item sets and association rules. In this work, we investigate how IDBs can support global models, such as decision trees. Our focus is on predictive clustering trees (PCTs). PCTs generalize decision trees and can be used for prediction and clustering, two of the most common data mining tasks. Regular PCT induction builds PCTs top-down, using a greedy algorithm, similar to that of C4.5. We propose a new induction algorithm for PCTs based on beam search. This has three advantages over the regular method: (a) it returns a set of PCTs satisfying the user constraints instead of just one PCT; (b) it better allows for pushing of user constraints into the induction algorithm; and (c) it is less susceptible to myopia. In addition, we propose similarity constraints for PCTs, which improve the diversity of the resulting PCT set.

1   Introduction

Inductive databases (IDBs) [9,5] represent a database view on data mining and knowledge discovery. IDBs contain not only data, but also models. In an IDB, ordinary queries can be used to access and manipulate data, while inductive queries can be used to generate, manipulate, and apply models. For example, "find a set of accurate decision trees that have at most ten nodes" is an inductive query.

IDBs are closely related to constraint-based mining [3]. Because the inductive queries can include particular constraints, the IDB needs constraint-based mining algorithms that can be called to construct the models that satisfy these constraints. The above example query includes, for instance, the constraint that the trees can contain at most ten nodes.

Much research on IDBs focuses on local models, i.e., models that apply to only a subset of the examples, such as item sets and association rules. We investigate how IDBs can support global models. In particular, we consider predictive clustering trees (PCTs) [1]. PCTs generalize decision trees and can be used for both prediction and clustering tasks. We define PCTs in Section 2.

S. Džeroski and J. Struyf (Eds.): KDID 2006, LNCS 4747, pp. 134–151, 2007.

Regular PCT induction builds PCTs top-down using a greedy algorithm similar to that of C4.5 [12] or CART [4]. This approach has three main disadvantages w.r.t. inductive databases: (a) it returns only one PCT. This is incompatible with the IDB view that inductive queries should (if possible) return the set of all models satisfying the constraints in the query; (b) many useful constraints are not easy to push into the induction algorithm. Size constraints, such as the one in our example query, must be handled mostly during post-pruning [7]; and (c) because the algorithm is greedy, it is susceptible to myopia: It may not find any tree satisfying the constraints, even though several exist in the hypothesis space.

In this paper, we propose a new induction algorithm for PCTs that addresses these three problems to a certain extent, while maintaining an acceptable computational cost. The algorithm employs beam search. Beam search considers at each step of the search the k best models according to a particular evaluation score. Therefore, it returns a set of models instead of just one model. Beam search also supports pushing of size constraints into the induction algorithm, as we will show in Section 4. Finally, beam search is known to be less susceptible to myopia than regular greedy search.

Preliminary experiments have revealed a disadvantage of using beam search for constructing PCTs. Namely, the beam tends to fill up with small variations of the same PCT, such as trees that differ only in one node. To alleviate this, we propose similarity constraints for PCTs. We show that these constraints improve beam diversity.

The remainder of this paper is organized as follows. In Section 2 we present PCTs. The beam search algorithm is explained in Section 3. In Sections 4 and 5 we discuss anti-monotonic and similarity constraints that can be pushed in the beam search induction process. Section 6 presents the experimental setup, and Section 7 discusses the experimental results. We conclude and discuss further work in Section 8.

2   Predictive Clustering Trees

PCTs [1] generalize classification and regression trees and can be used for a variety of learning tasks including different types of prediction and clustering. The PCT framework views a decision tree as a hierarchy of clusters (Fig. 1): the top-node of a PCT corresponds to one cluster containing all data, which is recursively partitioned into smaller clusters while moving down the tree. The leaves represent the clusters at the lowest level of the hierarchy and each leaf is labeled with its cluster's centroid. PCTs are constructed such that each split maximally improves average cluster homogeneity.

PCTs can be built with a greedy recursive top-down induction algorithm (PCT-TDI, Table 1), similar to that of C4.5 [12] or CART [4]. The algorithm takes as input a set of training instances I. The main loop searches for the best acceptable attribute-value test that can be put in a node (BestTest, Table 1). If such a test t^* can be found then the algorithm creates a new internal node labeled

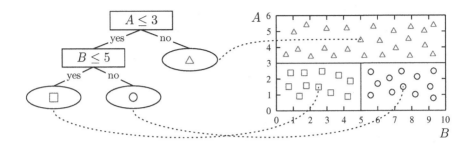

Fig. 1. A classification tree (left) is a special case of a PCT. It hierarchically partitions the instances into homogeneous clusters (right).

Table 1. The top-down induction (TDI) algorithm for PCTs

procedure PCT-TDI(I)	**procedure** BestTest(I)
1: $(t^*, h^*, \mathcal{P}^*) = \text{BestTest}(I)$	1: $(t^*, h^*, \mathcal{P}^*) = (none, 0, \emptyset)$
2: **if** $t^* \neq none$ **then**	2: **for each** possible test t **do**
3: **for each** $I_k \in \mathcal{P}^*$ **do**	3: $\mathcal{P} = \text{Partition}(t, I)$
4: $tree_k = \text{PCT}(I_k)$	4: $h = Var(I) - \sum_{I_k \in \mathcal{P}} \frac{|I_k|}{|I|} Var(I_k)$
5: **return** $\text{node}(t^*, \bigcup_k \{tree_k\})$	5: **if** $(h > h^*) \wedge \text{Acceptable}(t, \mathcal{P})$ **then**
6: **else**	6: $(t^*, h^*, \mathcal{P}^*) = (t, h, \mathcal{P})$
7: **return** $\text{leaf}(\text{centroid}(I))$	7: **return** $(t^*, h^*, \mathcal{P}^*)$

t^* and calls itself recursively to construct a subtree for each subset in the partition $\mathcal{P}^*$ induced by t^* on the training instances. If no acceptable test can be found, then the algorithm creates a leaf. (A test is unacceptable if $\min_{I \in \mathcal{P}} |I| < m$, with m a parameter that lower-bounds the number of instances in a leaf.) The heuristic that ranks the tests is computed as the reduction in variance caused by partitioning the instances (Line 4 of BestTest).

The difference with standard decision tree learners is that PCTs treat the variance function and the centroid function that computes a label for each leaf as parameters that can be instantiated for a given learning task. For a clustering task, the variance function takes all the attributes into account, while for a prediction task it focuses on the target attribute that is to be predicted. The same holds for the centroid function.

PCTs include classification and regression trees [4] as a special case. To construct a regression tree, for example, the regular definition of variance is used and the centroid is computed as the mean of the target values in the node. To construct a classification tree, the variance is computed either as the entropy of the class attribute (then the heuristic is equivalent to information gain [12]), or by converting the target attribute to a set of binary attributes (one for each class) and using the regular definition of variance over the resulting 0/1 vectors

Table 2. The beam search algorithm CLUS-BS

procedure CLUS-BS(I,k)	procedure Refine(T, I)
1: $i = 0$	1: $R = \emptyset$
2: $T_{\text{leaf}} = \text{leaf}(\text{centroid}(I))$	2: **for each** leaf $l \in T$ **do**
3: $h = \text{Heuristic}(T_{\text{leaf}}, I)$	3: $I_l = \text{Instances}(I,l)$
4: $\text{beam}_0 = \{(h, T_{\text{leaf}})\}$	4: **for each** attribute a **do**
5: **repeat**	5: $t = $ best test on a
6: $i = i + 1$	6: $\{I_1, I_2\} = \text{Partition}(t, I_l)$
7: $\text{beam}_i = \text{beam}_{i-1}$	7: $l_1 = \text{leaf}(\text{centroid}(I_1))$
8: **for each** $T \in \text{beam}_{i-1}$ **do**	8: $l_2 = \text{leaf}(\text{centroid}(I_2))$
9: $R = \text{Refine}(T, I)$	9: $n = \text{node}(t, \{l_1, l_2\})$
10: **for each** $T_{\text{cand}} \in R$ **do**	10: $T_r = $ replace l by n in T
11: $h = \text{Heuristic}(T_{\text{cand}}, I)$	11: $R = R \cup \{T_r\}$
12: $h_{\text{worst}} = \max_{T \in \text{beam}_i} \text{Heuristic}(T, I)$	12: **return** R
13: $T_{\text{worst}} = \text{argmax}_{T \in \text{beam}_i} \text{Heuristic}(T, I)$	
14: **if** $h < h_{\text{worst}}$ **or** $\|\text{beam}_i\| < k$ **then**	
15: $\text{beam}_i = \text{beam}_i \cup \{(h, T_{\text{cand}})\}$	
16: **if** $\|\text{beam}_i\| > k$ **then**	
17: $\text{beam}_i = \text{beam}_i \setminus \{(h_{\text{worst}}, T_{\text{worst}})\}$	
18: **until** $\text{beam}_i = \text{beam}_{i-1}$	
19: **return** beam_i	

(then the heuristic reduces to the Gini index [4]). The centroid function labels a leaf with the majority class of the examples. These definitions can be trivially extended to the multi-objective case (more than one target attribute) and to less trivial learning tasks, such as multi-label and hierarchical classification [2], or clustering of time series [6].

PCTs are implemented in the CLUS system. CLUS implements syntactic constraints and constraints on the size and/or accuracy of the trees [13]. It also implements various pruning methods, which are commonly used by decision tree learners to avoid over-fitting. More information about PCTs and CLUS can be found at http://www.cs.kuleuven.be/~dtai/clus and in reference [1].

3   Beam Search

We propose the beam search algorithm CLUS-BS, shown in Table 2. The beam is a set of PCTs ordered by their heuristic value. The algorithm starts with a beam that contains precisely one PCT: a leaf covering all the training data I.

Each iteration of the main loop creates a new beam by refining the PCTs in the current beam. That is, the algorithm iterates over the trees in the current beam and computes for each PCT its set of refinements (Fig. 2). A refinement is a copy of the given PCT in which one particular leaf is replaced by a depth one sub-tree (i.e., an internal node with a particular attribute-value test and two leaves). Note that a PCT can have many refinements: a PCT with L leaves yields $L \cdot M$ refined trees, with M the number of possible tests that can be put in a new node. In CLUS-BS, M is equal to the number of attributes. That is, CLUS-BS considers for each attribute only the test with the best heuristic value. Note that the number of possible tests on a numeric attribute A is typically huge: one test $A < a_i$, for each possible split point a_i. CLUS-BS only constructs one refined tree for the split that yields the best heuristic value. This approach limits the number of refinements of a given PCT and increases the diversity of the trees in the beam.

CLUS-BS computes for each generated refinement its heuristic value. The heuristic function differs from the heuristic used in the top-down induction algorithm (TDI) from Section 2. The heuristic in the latter is local, i.e., it only depends on the instances local to the node that is being constructed. In CLUS-BS, the heuristic is global and measures the quality of the entire tree. The reason is that beam search needs to compare different trees, whereas TDI only needs to rank different tests for the same tree node. The heuristic that we propose to use is:

$$h(T, I) = \left(\sum_{\text{leaf} \in T} \frac{|I_{\text{leaf}}|}{|I|} \, Var(I_{\text{leaf}}) \right) + \alpha \cdot \text{size}(T) \,, \tag{1}$$

with I all training data and I_{leaf} the examples sorted into leaf. It has two components: the first one is the average variance of the leaves of the PCT weighted by size, and the second one is a size penalty. The latter biases the search to smaller trees and can be seen as a soft version of a size constraint. The size function that we use throughout the paper counts the total number of nodes in the PCT (internal nodes + leaves).

After the heuristic value of a tree is computed, CLUS-BS compares it to the value of the worst tree in the beam. If the new tree is better, or if there are fewer than k trees (k is the beam width), then CLUS-BS adds the new PCT to the beam, and if this exceeds the beam width, then it removes the worst tree from the beam. The algorithm ends when the beam no longer changes. This either occurs if none of the refinements of a tree in the beam is better than the current worst tree, or if none of the trees in the beam yields any valid refinements. This is the point in the algorithm where the user constraints from the inductive query can be used to prune the search: a refinement is valid in CLUS-BS if it does not violate any of these constraints. Section 4 discusses this in detail.

Note that (1) is similar to the heuristic used in the TDI algorithm from Section 2. Assume that there are no constraints, $\alpha = 0$ and $k = 1$. In this case, the tree computed by CLUS-BS will be identical to the tree constructed with TDI. The only difference with TDI is the order in which the leaves are refined: TDI refines depth-first, whereas CLUS-BS with a beam width of one refines best-first.

The computational cost of CLUS-BS is as follows. Computing the best test for one attribute for the instances in a given leaf costs $O(|I_{\text{leaf}}| \log |I_{\text{leaf}}|)$ (to find

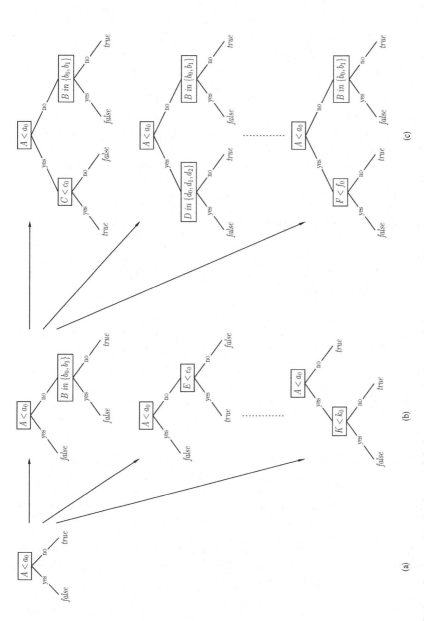

Fig. 2. Refining the trees in the beam. (a) A tree in the beam; (b) the refinements of the tree in (a); (c) the refinements of the top-most tree in (b). Note that the refinements (c) are only computed in a subsequent iteration of the search after the top-most tree of (b) has entered the beam.

the best split point for a numeric attribute, the instances must be sorted; after sorting, finding the best split can be done in $O(|I_{\text{leaf}}|)$ time [12]). If the score of the best test is better than that of the worst tree in the beam, then the refined tree must be constructed $O(\text{size}(T))$ and inserted into the beam $O(\log k)$ (if the beam is implemented as a balanced binary search tree). Repeating this for all attributes and all leaves yields $O(|A|\cdot|I|\log|I|+|A|\cdot|\text{leaves}(T)|\cdot(\text{size}(T)+\log k))$ because each instance occurs in at most one leaf. If s upper-bounds the size of the trees in the beam, then the cost of refining the entire beam is $O(k \cdot |A| \cdot |I|\log|I| + s^2k \cdot |A| + s \cdot |A| \cdot k\log k)$. Finally, the cost of running n iterations of CLUS-BS is $O(nk \cdot |A| \cdot |I|\log|I| + ns^2k \cdot |A| + ns \cdot |A| \cdot k\log k)$. For comparison, the computational cost of TDI is $O(D \cdot |A| \cdot |I|\log|I|)$, with D the depth of the tree. Assuming that the first term dominates the complexity of CLUS-BS, it follows that CLUS-BS is $O(kn/D)$ times slower. Note that n is in the best case equal to the number of leaves in the largest tree because each iteration can add at most one leaf.

4   Anti-monotonic Constraints

CLUS-BS supports any conjunction or disjunction of constraints that are anti-monotonic with regard to the refinement order. We define this more precisely with the following definitions.

Definition 1 (Refinement set). *The refinement set $\rho^*(T)$ of a tree T given a refinement operator ρ is the set that is obtained by recursively applying ρ, that is, $\lim_{n\to\infty}\rho^n(T)$, with $\rho^0(T) = \{T\}$ and $\rho^i(T) = \rho^{i-1}(T) \cup \left(\bigcup_{T_r \in \rho^{i-1}(T)} \rho(T_r)\right)$ if $i > 0$.*

In CLUS-BS, $\rho(T)$ is implemented by the Refine procedure in Table 2. Consider again Fig. 2. All trees shown in this figure are part of $\rho^*(T)$, with T the tree in Fig. 2.a.

Definition 2 (Refinement order). *The refinement order $\geq_{\text{ref}}$ is a partial order defined on trees as $T_1 \geq_{\text{ref}} T_2$ if and only if $T_1 \in \rho^*(T_2)$.*

Note that $T_1 \geq_{\text{ref}} T_2$ can be thought of as "T_2 is a subtree of T_1 sharing the same root".

Definition 3 (Anti-monotonic constraint). *A constraint is a Boolean function over trees. A constraint c is anti-monotonic with respect to $\geq_{\text{ref}}$ if and only if $\forall T_1, T_2 : (T_1 \geq_{\text{ref}} T_2 \wedge c(T_1)) \to c(T_2)$.*

If one considers an increasing sequence of trees according to the refinement order (E.g., going from (a) to (c) in Fig. 2) then the value of an anti-monotonic constraint can only decrease along the sequence, that is, change from true to false. This observation is exploited by CLUS-BS. If a given refinement violates one of the anti-monotonic constraints, then the search can be pruned (by not adding the refinement to the beam) because any subsequent refinement will also violate the constraint (because of its anti-monotonicity).

We list a number of useful anti-monotonic constraints for trees.

1. The maximum size constraint $c_s(T) = (\text{size}(T) \leq s)$ upper-bounds the size of the tree. This constraint is useful for decision trees because domain experts are typically interested in small trees for interpretability reasons.
2. The minimum cluster size constraint $c_m(T) = (\min_{\text{leaf} \in T} |I_{\text{leaf}}| \geq m)$ lower-bounds the number of instances in each leaf of the tree. This constraint is implemented by most decision tree learners.
3. The maximum depth constraint upper-bounds the maximum depth of the tree. Sometimes it is useful to constrain tree depth, for example, because the resulting tree will be more balanced.
4. The maximum prediction cost constraint. This is an extension of the maximum depth constraint, where each test is weighted by its prediction cost. Prediction cost constraints are useful in medical applications where the attributes correspond to expensive lab tests. In such applications, it is useful to upper-bound the prediction cost of the tree.

All the above constraints are anti-monotonic and can be handled efficiently by CLUS-BS. In the experimental evaluation, we investigate the effect of using maximum size constraints (Section 6).

So far, we assumed that the user is interested in obtaining trees that are as accurate as possible. For decision trees, this is accomplished algorithmically by using a heuristic function that is known to yield accurate trees. Another possibility is that the user explicitly provides a constraint on the accuracy of the tree, e.g., $\text{acc}(T, I) \geq 85\%$. (Note that this constraint is not anti-monotonic.) The goal is then to find, e.g., the smallest tree that satisfies this constraint. To this end, the algorithm is run repeatedly with increasing values for the size constraint until the accuracy constraint is satisfied [13].

5   Similarity Constraints

The heuristic value defined in Section 3 only takes the variance and the size of the PCT into account. In this section, we define a soft similarity constraint, which can be included in the heuristic computation and biases the search towards a diverse set of trees (which are dissimilar to each other, as much as possible). We will call CLUS-BS with these (dis)similarity constraints included CLUS-BS-S.

To quantify the (dis)similarity of two trees, CLUS-BS-S requires a distance function between trees. Two obvious approaches are: (a) define the distance based on the syntactic representation of the trees, or (b) define the distance based on the predictions that the trees make on the training instances. One problem with (a) is that many syntactically different trees can represent the same concept, for example, the trees in Fig. 3 both represent the concept $A \wedge B$. If our goal is to find trees that are semantically different, then (b) is to be preferred and we therefore focus on this approach here.

Fig. 3. Syntactically different trees representing the concept $A \wedge B$

We propose to compute the distance between two trees (T_1 and T_2) as the normalized root mean squared distance between their predictions on the data set at hand, that is

$$d(T_1, T_2, I) = \frac{1}{\eta} \cdot \sqrt{\frac{\sum_{t \in I} d_p(p(T_1, t), p(T_2, t))^2}{|I|}} \,, \qquad (2)$$

with η a normalization factor, $|I|$ the number of training instances, $p(T_j, t)$ the prediction of tree T_j for instance t, and d_p a distance function between predictions. In (2), η and d_p depend on the learning task. For regression tasks, d_p is the absolute difference between the predictions, and $\eta = M - m$, with $M = \max_{t \in I, j \in \{1,2\}} p(T_j, t)$ and $m = \min_{t \in I, j \in \{1,2\}} p(T_j, t)$. This choice of η ensures that $d(T_1, T_2, I)$ is in the interval $(0, 1)$. For classification tasks, $d_p = \delta$ with

$$\delta(a, b) = \begin{cases} 1 \text{ if } a \neq b \\ 0 \text{ if } a = b \end{cases}, \qquad (3)$$

and η is 1. These distance functions can be easily adapted to the more general PCT types mentioned in Section 2 (e.g., for multi-target prediction, multi-label and hierarchical classification and clustering of time series).

The heuristic value of a tree can now be modified by adding a term that penalizes trees that are similar to the other trees in the beam.

$$h(T, \text{beam}, I) = \left(\sum_{\text{leaf} \in T} \frac{|I_{\text{leaf}}|}{|I|} Var(I_{\text{leaf}}) \right) + \alpha \cdot \text{size}(T) + \beta \cdot \text{sim}(T, \text{beam}, I) \quad (4)$$

Because the heuristic value of a tree now also depends on the other trees in the beam, it changes when a new tree is added. Therefore, each time that CLUS-BS-S considers a new candidate tree, it recomputes the heuristic value of all trees already in the beam using (4), which incorporates the similarity to the new candidate tree (T_{cand}) by using (5).

$$\text{sim}(T, \text{beam}, I) = 1 - \frac{d(T, T_{cand}, I) + \sum_{T_i \in \text{beam}} d(T, T_i, I)}{|\text{beam}|} \qquad (5)$$

Note that (5) is in the interval $(0, 1)$ because the numerator has $|\text{beam}|$ non-zero terms that are in $(0, 1)$. CLUS-BS-S computes the heuristic value of T_{cand}

Table 3. The data sets and their p roperties: number of instances ($|I|$), number of discrete/continuous input attributes (D/C), number of classes (Cls), probability of majority class (Maj), entropy of the class distribution (Ent), mean value of the target ($Mean$), and standard deviation of the target ($St.dev.$)

(a) Classification data sets.

Data set	$|I|$	D/C	Cls	Maj	Ent
car	1728	6/0	4	0.70	1.21
mushroom	8124	22/0	2	0.52	1.00
segment	2310	0/19	7	0.14	2.81
vowel	990	3/10	11	0.09	3.46
vehicle	846	0/19	4	0.26	2.00
iris	150	0/4	3	0.33	1.58
ionosphere	351	0/34	2	0.64	0.94
chess	3196	36/0	2	0.52	1.00

(b) Regression data sets.

Data set	$|I|$	D/C	$Mean$	$St.dev.$
autoPrice	159	0/15	11445.73	5877.86
bodyfat	252	0/14	19.15	8.37
cpu	209	1/6	99.33	154.76
housing	506	1/12	22.53	9.20
pollution	60	0/15	940.36	62.21
servo	167	4/0	1.39	1.56
pyrim	74	0/27	0.66	0.13
machine_cpu	209	0/6	105.62	160.83

using (4). If the heuristic value of the candidate tree is better than that of the worst tree in the beam, the candidate tree enters the beam and the worst tree is removed.

6 Experiments

6.1 Aims

We compare CLUS with the regular recursive top-down induction algorithm (TDI, Table 1) to CLUS with beam search (BS, Table 2), and beam search with similarity constraints (BS-S). Our aim is to test the following hypotheses.

1. Hill-climbing search, which is used by TDI, suffers from shortsightedness. TDI may return a suboptimal model due to its limited exploration of the hypothesis space. Beam search is known to be less susceptible to this problem. We therefore expect that on average BS will yield models that are more accurate or at least as accurate as the models built by TDI.
2. Similarity constraints improve the diversity of the beam, possibly at the cost of some predictive accuracy. Diversity is important for the domain expert, who is typically interested in looking at different models, for example because one PCT is easier to interpret than the other PCTs. Note that if we consider all models in the beam to make up the answer to the inductive query, then all these PCTs should be reasonably accurate.

6.2 Setup

We perform experiments on 8 regression and 8 classification data sets from the UCI machine learning repository [10]. Table 3 lists the properties of the data sets. We set the parameters of the beam search algorithms ad-hoc to the following values: $k = 10$, $\alpha = 10^{-5}$, and $\beta = 1$, where k is the beam width, α is the size penalty and β is the influence of the similarity constraint (Equations (1) and (4)). For the classification data sets, we use the version of the heuristic that employs class entropy to estimate the variance of the target attribute. All experiments are performed with the CLUS system (Section 2), in which the algorithms BS and BS-S have been implemented.

We measure the predictive performance of each algorithm using 10 fold cross-validation. For the classification data sets, we report accuracy and for the regression data sets the Pearson correlation coefficient. Because the beam search algorithms yield not one but k trees, we have to select one of these k trees to compare to TDI. We decided to use the tree that performs best on the training data (T_{train}) for this purpose.

To test if all trees in the beam are sufficiently accurate, we measure their average predictive accuracy (or correlation coefficient). We also measure the minimum and maximum accuracy (or correlation coefficient) of the trees in the beam and use these to calculate the difference in performance between the worst tree and T_{train} and the best tree and T_{train}. That is, we compute $D_{\text{worst}} = A_t - A_w$ and $D_{\text{best}} = A_b - A_t$, with A_t the test set performance of T_{train}, and A_w the minimum and A_b the maximum test set performance of the trees in the beam. If $D_{\text{worst}} = 0$, then T_{train} is the worst tree in the beam, and if $D_{\text{best}} = 0$, then it is the best tree in the beam. We report the average of D_{worst} and D_{best} over the 10 cross-validation folds.

To quantify the effect of the similarity constraints, we calculate for the two beam search algorithms beam similarity, which we define as the average similarity of the trees in the beam. Similarity(beam, I) = $\frac{1}{|\text{beam}|} \sum_{T \in \text{beam}} \text{sim}(T, \text{beam}, I)$, with $\text{sim}(T, \text{beam}, I) = 1 - \frac{1}{|\text{beam}|} \sum_{T_i \in \text{beam}} d(T, T_i, I)$, the similarity of tree T w.r.t. the other trees in the beam, and $d(T, T_i, I)$ the distance between trees T and T_i as defined in Section 5. We report beam similarity on the test set averaged over the 10 cross-validation folds.

We perform experiments for different values of the size constraint. Recall that in the beam search algorithm, this type of constraints can be enforced during the search (Section 4). For TDI this is not possible and therefore we use a two step approach that first builds one large tree and subsequently prunes it back to satisfy the size constraint [7]. We also report results without any size constraint. For these results we use, both for TDI and BS, the same pruning algorithm that is also used in C4.5 [12] (for classification data sets) and in M5 [11] (for regression data sets).

7   Results and Discussion

7.1   Predictive Performance

Table 4 compares the cross-validated accuracy of TDI, BS, and BS-S on the classification data and Table 5 the cross-validated correlation coefficient for the regression data. The tables contain results for different values of the size constraint: maximum size ranging from 5 (SC5) to 51 (SC51) nodes, and no size constraint (NoSC). Each column includes the number of statistically significant wins ($p \leq 0.05$), which are obtained by a 10 fold cross-validated paired t-test and indicated in bold face.

The results confirm our first hypothesis. BS yields models of comparable accuracy to TDI. BS wins on 5 classification and 3 regression tasks. TDI wins on 2 classification and no regression tasks. This confirms that BS yields more accurate models, which can be explained because it is less susceptible to myopia. There is no clear correlation between the number of wins and the value of the size constraint.

BS-S wins on 6 classification and 4 regression tasks and loses on 13 classification and 1 regression tasks. BS-S performs, when compared to BS, worse on classification data than on regression data. This is because the heuristic (used in BS-S) trades off accuracy for diversity. If a given tree in the beam is accurate, then new trees will be biased to be less accurate because the similarity score favors trees with different predictions. For classification problems this effect is more pronounced because a 0/1 distance between predictions is used, whereas in the regression case a continuous distance function is used. The latter makes it "easier" to have different predictions that are still reasonably accurate. Also, this effect is stronger for bigger size constraints (the majority of the losses of BS-S are for SC31, SC51 and NoSC) because the relative contribution of the similarity score to the heuristic is greater for bigger size constraints. Note that the losses are in the range of 1-2% accuracy, so for the majority of domains this is not a serious problem.

Our second hypothesis was that BS-S trades off accuracy for beam diversity. Table 6 lists the beam similarity for BS and BS-S for the classification data and SC7. The beam similarity of BS-S is always smaller than that of BS. Fig. 4 shows the trees in the final beam for the "vehicle" data for BS and BS-S. The trees of BS all have the same test in the top node and include tests on 5 attributes. The BS-S trees have tests on 3 different attributes in the top node and include tests on 6 attributes in total. This shows that the trees produced by BS-S not only produce different predictions, but are also syntactically different from the trees constructed with BS.

Table 6 lists the average accuracy of the trees in the beam and shows how much worse (better) the worst (best) tree is compared to the result reported in Table 4. Consider first the results for BS. For the data sets "mushroom", "segment", and "vehicle", all trees are of comparable accuracy. For "car", "vowel", "iris", "ionosphere", and "chess", the differences in accuracy become larger. For most of these, T_{train} is on average among the best trees. This is most obvious for "chess" where $D_{best} = 0$. Only for 2 out of 8 data sets ("car" and "ionosphere") $D_{best} > D_{worst}$. Note that the differences are larger for BS-S than for BS. This shows that the variance in accuracy increases with the beam diversity.

7.2   Induction Time

Table 7 compares the running times of all algorithms and the number of models evaluated by BS and BS-S. Observe that BS-S is (much) slower than BS and

Table 4. Comparison of beam search (BS) and BS with similarity constraints (BS-S) to top-down induction (TDI) on classification data (accuracy)

Data set	TDI	BS	TDI	BS	TDI	BS	TDI	BS
	SC5		SC7		SC11		SC17	
car	77.8	77.8	**79.2**	77.1	82.2	81.8	87.0	85.6
mushroom	99.4	99.4	99.4	**99.6**	99.9	**100.0**	100.0	100.0
segment	40.0	40.7	55.6	55.6	80.9	81.1	90.2	90.4
vowel	20.6	20.7	25.2	27.3	31.6	33.6	38.9	**42.3**
vehicle	48.7	51.2	51.2	**60.2**	64.5	64.5	68.9	66.4
iris	92.0	92.0	94.0	96.0	93.3	93.3	93.3	92.7
ionosphere	89.5	89.2	88.6	88.3	88.9	90.6	88.6	88.9
chess	75.5	76.9	90.4	90.4	94.1	93.8	96.5	96.9
Wins	0	0	1	2	0	1	0	1
	SC31		SC51		NoSC (Acc)		NoSC (Size)	
car	92.8	92.6	**95.0**	94.0	97.5	97.6	113	117
mushroom	100.0	100.0	100.0	100.0	100.0	100.0	15	11
segment	94.9	94.2	96.2	96.0	96.7	96.8	85	85
vowel	49.2	51.8	55.7	**61.2**	79.2	80.8	191	179
vehicle	70.0	72.5	71.7	72.7	73.9	72.0	167	179
iris	93.3	92.7	93.3	92.7	92.7	92.7	9	11
ionosphere	88.9	88.9	88.9	88.9	88.6	89.5	29	27
chess	97.8	97.7	99.3	99.4	99.4	99.5	53	53
Wins	0	0	1	1	0	0		

Data set	TDI	BS-S	TDI	BS-S	TDI	BS-S	TDI	BS-S
	SC5		SC7		SC11		SC17	
car	77.8	77.8	**79.2**	77.1	82.2	81.1	87.0	86.0
mushroom	99.4	99.4	99.4	**99.6**	99.9	**100.0**	100.0	99.6
segment	40.0	39.6	55.6	55.1	80.9	81.0	90.2	**91.6**
vowel	20.6	20.7	25.2	27.3	31.6	**36.0**	38.9	**42.0**
vehicle	48.7	51.2	51.2	**60.2**	64.5	64.3	68.9	68.7
iris	92.0	92.0	94.0	96.0	93.3	93.3	93.3	92.7
ionosphere	89.5	89.2	88.6	88.6	88.9	92.0	88.6	91.5
chess	75.5	76.9	90.4	90.4	94.1	93.8	**96.5**	95.6
Wins	0	0	1	2	0	2	2	2
	SC31		SC51		NoSC (Acc)		NoSC (Size)	
car	**92.8**	90.9	**95.0**	93.3	97.5	97.2	113	95
mushroom	**100.0**	99.6	**100.0**	99.6	**100.0**	99.6	15	11
segment	**94.9**	94.3	**96.2**	94.8	**96.7**	95.4	85	81
vowel	49.2	50.3	55.7	57.9	79.2	81.7	191	187
vehicle	70.0	67.4	71.7	71.4	73.9	71.6	167	189
iris	93.3	92.7	93.3	92.7	92.7	94.7	9	13
ionosphere	88.9	90.6	88.9	90.3	88.6	92.0	29	25
chess	97.8	97.6	**99.3**	98.3	**99.4**	98.3	53	43
Wins	3	0	4	0	3	0		

Table 5. Comparison of beam search (BS) and BS with similarity constraints (BS-S) to top-down induction (TDI) on regression data (correlation coefficient)

Data set	TDI	BS	TDI	BS	TDI	BS	TDI	BS
		SC5		SC7		SC11		SC17
autoPrice	0.86	0.88	0.88	0.90	0.87	0.89	0.88	0.89
bodyfat	0.87	0.87	0.94	0.94	0.95	0.95	0.97	0.96
cpu	0.92	0.92	0.92	0.92	0.93	0.94	0.95	0.95
housing	0.76	0.76	0.80	0.78	0.86	0.85	0.89	0.88
pollution	0.44	0.44	0.50	0.53	0.48	0.41	0.55	0.51
servo	0.82	0.82	0.89	0.91	0.90	**0.94**	0.91	0.93
pyrim	0.64	0.49	0.68	0.54	0.72	0.65	0.73	0.74
machine_cpu	0.80	0.79	0.84	0.83	0.87	0.86	0.88	0.87
Wins	0	0	0	0	0	1	0	0
		SC31		SC51		NoSC (Acc)		NoSC (Size)
autoPrice	0.88	0.90	0.88	0.91	0.88	0.91	17	17
bodyfat	0.98	0.97	0.97	0.97	0.96	0.97	65	77
cpu	0.95	0.95	0.95	0.95	0.94	0.94	23	51
housing	0.91	0.90	0.90	0.89	0.90	0.89	63	55
pollution	0.52	**0.62**	0.53	0.59	0.49	0.52	13	13
servo	0.92	0.95	0.92	**0.95**	0.91	0.91	21	17
pyrim	0.73	0.74	0.73	0.68	0.58	0.56	11	11
machine_cpu	0.89	0.89	0.90	0.89	0.89	0.87	33	27
Wins	0	1	0	1	0	0		

Data set	TDI	BS-S	TDI	BS-S	TDI	BS-S	TDI	BS-S
		SC5		SC7		SC11		SC17
autoPrice	0.86	0.88	0.88	0.90	0.87	0.86	0.88	0.91
bodyfat	0.87	0.87	0.94	0.94	0.95	0.95	0.97	0.97
cpu	0.92	0.92	0.92	0.92	0.93	0.93	0.95	0.95
housing	0.76	0.76	0.80	0.78	0.86	0.85	0.89	0.89
pollution	0.44	0.44	0.50	0.50	0.48	0.47	0.55	0.60
servo	0.82	0.82	0.89	0.91	0.90	**0.94**	0.91	0.93
pyrim	0.64	0.34	0.68	0.63	0.72	0.53	0.73	0.68
machine_cpu	0.80	0.79	0.84	0.83	0.87	0.85	0.88	0.88
Wins	0	0	0	0	0	1	0	0
		SC31		SC51		NoSC (Acc)		NoSC (Size)
autoPrice	0.88	**0.90**	0.88	**0.91**	0.88	0.90	17	29
bodyfat	0.98	0.97	0.97	0.97	0.96	0.98	65	71
cpu	0.95	0.95	0.95	0.95	0.94	0.95	23	41
housing	0.91	0.90	**0.90**	0.89	0.90	0.90	63	75
pollution	0.52	0.62	0.53	0.51	0.49	0.52	13	13
servo	0.92	0.95	0.92	**0.96**	0.91	0.91	21	19
pyrim	0.73	0.65	0.73	0.64	0.58	0.54	11	13
machine_cpu	0.89	0.90	0.90	0.90	0.89	0.88	33	25
Wins	0	1	1	2	0	0		

(a) Without similarity constraint (BS):

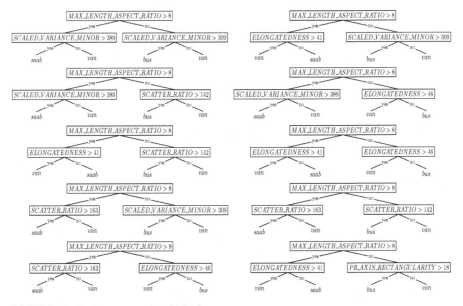

(b) With similarity constraint (BS-S):

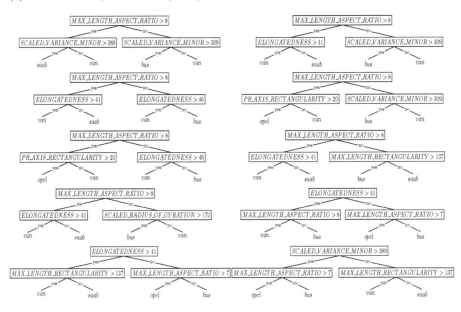

Fig. 4. Trees in the final beam for the "vehicle" data (BS and BS-S), SC7

Table 6. Average cross-validated accuracy of all trees in the beam, comparison of the worst tree in the beam to the reported result of T_{train} (D_{worst}), comparison of the best tree in the beam to T_{train} (D_{best}), and beam similarity. Results for trees constrained to have at most 7 nodes (SC7).

Data set	Avg. test perf.		D_{worst}		D_{best}		Beam similarity	
	BS	BS-S	BS	BS-S	BS	BS-S	BS	BS-S
car	78.8	77.4	1.1	8.5	4.3	4.3	0.67	0.61
mushroom	99.4	98.8	0.2	3.6	0.0	0.0	0.99	0.90
segment	55.6	55.1	1.0	4.2	0.2	2.6	0.82	0.38
vowel	25.1	25.3	7.2	7.9	2.5	3.8	0.43	0.27
vehicle	59.6	55.8	1.5	13.2	0.1	1.2	0.89	0.47
iris	93.0	93.3	5.3	10.7	1.3	2.0	0.91	0.86
ionosphere	88.6	88.1	2.0	8.6	4.0	5.4	0.86	0.72
chess	82.4	81.3	13.8	17.3	0.0	0.0	0.67	0.55

Table 7. Run times and number of evaluated models. (The experiments were run on an AMD Opteron Processor 250 2.4GHz system with 8GB of RAM running Linux).

Classification data set	Run time [s]			Evaluated models	
	TDI	BS	BS-S	BS	BS-S
car	0.06	0.80	31.25	2638	57879
mushroom	0.08	1.38	20.17	217	4761
segment	0.28	10.17	168.05	2168	151868
vowel	0.34	9.52	249.62	6567	483294
vehicle	0.14	6.18	264.18	6723	590628
iris	0.04	0.04	0.09	198	809
ionosphere	0.10	1.01	5.35	779	29926
chess	0.08	2.35	111.55	1800	92256
Regression data set					
autoPrice	0.06	0.37	40.03	2856	69158
bodyfat	0.06	0.48	84.05	2471	94185
cpu	0.08	0.21	9.67	1333	12415
housing	0.09	3.30	1009.27	10821	549292
pollution	0.04	0.09	3.09	1288	13049
servo	0.06	0.16	6.67	2114	11239
pyrim	0.03	0.16	2.65	1195	9357
machine_cpu	0.06	0.25	21.44	2178	28131

TDI. The longer running time of BS-S is due to two reasons. First, it evaluates more PCTs because of the similarity measure that is included in the heuristic score. In BS, the score of the "worst" tree in the beam monotonically improves with the iteration number. In BS-S, this is no longer the case because the score of the trees in the beam needs to be recomputed when a new tree enters the beam (because of the similarity component). As a result, it becomes harder for BS-S to satisfy the stopping criterion (the beam no longer changes). Second, in

BS-S, evaluating a single model takes a factor $O(k^2 \cdot |I|)$ longer than in BS, with k the beam width and $|I|$ the number of instances. (We exploit properties of the distance measure ($d(T_a, T_b, I) = d(T_b, T_a, I)$ and $d(T_a, T_a, I) = 0$) to make the evaluation of the similarity component efficient).

8   Conclusion and Further Work

We propose a new algorithm for inducing predictive clustering trees (PCTs) that uses beam search. The main advantages of this algorithm are that: it induces a set of PCTs instead of just one PCT; it supports pushing of anti-monotonic user constraints, such as maximum tree size, into the induction algorithm; and it is less susceptible to myopia. In order to improve beam diversity, we introduce soft similarity constraints based on the predictions of the PCTs.

Our current set of experiments takes into account fixed values for the parameters k (the beam width), and α and β (the contribution of tree size and similarity score to the heuristic value). In future work, we plan to perform experiments for different values of β to gain more insight in the trade-off between predictive performance and beam similarity. Also, the influence of the beam width will be investigated.

We plan to investigate the use of alternative distance functions for the similarity score. Recall that we hypothesized that the reason for having less accurate trees in the classification case is that the distance function is less "continuous" than in the regression case. We plan to investigate smoother distance functions for classification. Such functions could, for example, take the predicted class distribution into account instead of just the predicted majority class.

Model diversity, which can be controlled by means of the heuristic proposed in Section 5, has been shown to increase the predictive performance of classifier ensembles [8]. Therefore, we plan to investigate if beam search with similarity constraints can be used to construct an accurate ensemble of PCTs. That is, instead of selecting from the beam the one PCT that performs best on the training data, the PCT ensemble will combine all PCTs in the beam by means of a combination function, such as majority voting. We also plan to investigate other alternatives for introducing diversity in the beam.

The experimental evaluation of this paper focuses on classification and regression trees. In future work, we plan to test beam search for more general PCT types. Note that this is, from an algorithmic point of view, trivial: the only component that changes is the definition of the variance and distance functions. In this context, we plan to investigate the use of beam search for multi-target prediction tasks [1], where non-trivial interactions between the target attributes may exist.

Acknowledgments. This work was supported by the IQ project (IST-FET FP6-516169). Jan Struyf is a postdoctoral fellow of the Fund for Scientific Research of Flanders (FWO-Vlaanderen).

References

1. Blockeel, H., De Raedt, L., Ramon, J.: Top-down induction of clustering trees. In: 15th Int'l Conf. on Machine Learning, pp. 55–63 (1998)
2. Blockeel, H., Schietgat, L., Struyf, J., Džeroski, S., Clare, A.: Decision trees for hierarchical multilabel classification: A case study in functional genomics. In: Fürnkranz, J., Scheffer, T., Spiliopoulou, M. (eds.) PKDD 2006. LNCS (LNAI), vol. 4213, pp. 18–29. Springer, Heidelberg (2006)
3. Boulicaut, J.-F., Jeudy, B.: Constraint-based data mining. In: Maimon, O., Rokach, L. (eds.) The Data Mining and Knowledge Discovery Handbook, pp. 399–416. Springer, Heidelberg (2005)
4. Breiman, L., Friedman, J.H., Olshen, R.A., Stone, C.J.: Classification and regression trees, Wadsworth, Belmont (1984)
5. De Raedt, L.: A perspective on inductive databases. SIGKDD Explorations 4(2), 69–77 (2002)
6. Džeroski, S., Slavkov, I., Gjorgjioski, V., Struyf, J.: Analysis of time series data with predictive clustering trees. In: KDID 2006. LNCS, vol. 4747, pp. 63–80. Springer, Heidelberg (2007)
7. Garofalakis, M., Hyun, D., Rastogi, R., Shim, K.: Building decision trees with constraints. Data Mining and Knowledge Discovery 7(2), 187–214 (2003)
8. Hansen, L.K., Salamon, P.: Neural network ensembles. IEEE Transactions on Pattern Analysis and Machine Intelligence 12, 993–1001 (1990)
9. Imielinski, T., Mannila, H.: A database perspective on knowledge discovery. Communications of the ACM 39(11), 58–64 (1996)
10. Merz, C.J., Murphy, P.M.: UCI repository of machine learning databases. University of California, Department of Information and Computer Science, Irvine, CA (1996), http://www.ics.uci.edu/~mlearn/mlrepository.html
11. Quinlan, J.R.: Learning with continuous classes. In: 5th Australian Joint Conference on Artificial Intelligence, pp. 343–348. World Scientific, Singapore (1992)
12. Quinlan, J.R.: C4.5: Programs for Machine Learning. Morgan Kaufmann series in Machine Learning. Morgan Kaufmann, San Francisco (1993)
13. Struyf, J., Džeroski, S.: Constraint based induction of multi-objective regression trees. In: Bonchi, F., Boulicaut, J-F. (eds.) KDID 2005. LNCS, vol. 3933, pp. 222–233. Springer, Heidelberg (2006)

Frequent Pattern Mining and Knowledge Indexing Based on Zero-Suppressed BDDs

Shin-ichi Minato and Hiroki Arimura

Graduate School of Information Science and Technology,
Hokkaido University, Sapporo, 060-0814 Japan

Abstract. Frequent pattern mining is one of the fundamental techniques for knowledge discovery and data mining. During the last decade, several efficient algorithms for frequent pattern mining have been presented, but most algorithms have focused on enumerating the patterns that satisfy the given conditions, considering the storage and indexing of the pattern results for efficient inductive analysis to be a separate issue. In this paper, we propose a fast algorithm for extracting all/maximal frequent patterns from transaction databases and simultaneously indexing a huge number of patterns using Zero-suppressed Binary Decision Diagrams (ZBDDs). Our method is comparably fast as existing state-of-the-art algorithms and not only enumerates/lists the patterns but also compactly indexes the output data in main memory. After mining, the pattern results can be analyzed efficiently by using algebraic operations. BDD-based data structures have previously been used successfully in VLSI logic design, but our method is the first practical application of BDD-based techniques in the data mining area.

1 Introduction

Frequent pattern mining is one of the fundamental techniques for knowledge discovery and data mining. Since their introduction by Agrawal et al. [1], frequent pattern mining and association rule analysis have received much attention from researchers, and many papers have been published about new algorithms and improvements for solving such mining problems [10,12,24]. However, most of these pattern-mining algorithms have focused on enumerating or listing the patterns that satisfy the given conditions, considering the storage and indexing of the pattern results for efficient inductive analysis to be a separate issue.

In this paper, we propose a fast algorithm for extracting all/maximal frequent patterns from transaction databases and simultaneously indexing a huge number of result patterns in computer memory using Zero-suppressed Binary Decision Diagrams (ZBDDs). Our method not only enumerates/lists the patterns but also indexes the output data compactly in main memory. After mining, the pattern results can be analyzed efficiently by using algebraic operations.

The key to our method is the use of data structures based on Binary Decision Diagrams (BDDs) to represent sets of patterns. BDDs [5] are graph-based representations of Boolean functions and are now widely used in the VLSI logic design and verification area. For data mining applications, it is important to use the ZBDD

S. Džeroski and J. Struyf (Eds.): KDID 2006, LNCS 4747, pp. 152–169, 2007.

[16], a special type of BDD, which is suited to handling large-scale sets of combinations. Using ZBDDs, we can implicitly enumerate combinatorial itemset data and efficiently compute set operations over the ZBDDs. The preliminary idea of using ZBDDs was presented in our previous workshop paper [19]. In this paper, we propose a fast pattern mining algorithm based on this data structure. Our work is the first practical application of the BDD-based technique to the data mining area.

In related work, the *FP-tree* [12] receives a great deal of attention because it supports fast manipulation of large-scale itemset data using a compact tree structure in main memory. Our method uses a similar approach to handling sets of combinations in main memory but is more efficient in these respects:

- A ZBDD is a kind of Directed Acyclic Graph (DAG) for representing itemsets, while the FP-tree is a tree representation. In general, DAGs can be more compact than trees.
- Our method uses ZBDDs not only as the internal data structure but also as the output data structure. This provides an efficient knowledge index for subsequent inductive analysis.

Our mining algorithm is based on a recursive depth-first search of the database represented by ZBDDs. We show two versions of the algorithm, generating all frequent patterns and generating maximal frequent patterns. Experimental results show that our method is comparably fast as existing state-of-the-art algorithms, such as those based on FP-trees. Especially for cases where the ZBDD nodes are well shared, exponential speed-up is observed compared with existing algorithms based on explicit table/tree representations.

Recently, data mining methods have often been discussed in the context of Inductive Databases [3,14], the integrated processes of knowledge discovery. In this paper, we also show a number of examples of postprocessing following frequent pattern mining. We place the ZBDD-based method at the core of integrated discovery processes that efficiently execute various operations to find interest patterns and analyze the information included in large-scale combinatorial itemset databases.

2 BDDs and Zero-Suppressed BDDs

Here we briefly describe the basic techniques of BDDs and Zero-suppressed BDDs for representing sets of combinations efficiently.

2.1 BDDs

A BDD is a directed graph representation of a Boolean function, as illustrated in Fig. 1(a). It is derived by reducing a binary tree graph representing the recursive *Shannon's expansion*, shown in Fig. 1(b). The following reduction rules yield a *Reduced Ordered BDD (ROBDD)*, which can efficiently represent the Boolean function (see [5] for details).

- Delete all redundant nodes whose two edges point to the same node. (Fig. 2(a))
- Share all equivalent subgraphs. (Fig. 2(b))

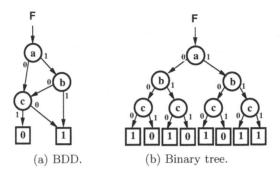

Fig. 1. BDD and binary tree: $F = (a \wedge b) \vee \bar{c}$

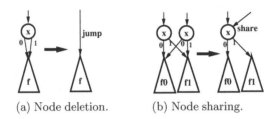

Fig. 2. Reduction rules of ordinary BDDs

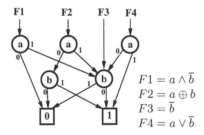

$F1 = a \wedge \bar{b}$
$F2 = a \oplus b$
$F3 = \bar{b}$
$F4 = a \vee \bar{b}$

Fig. 3. Shared multiple BDDs

ROBDDs provide canonical forms for Boolean functions when the variable order is fixed. Most research on BDDs is based on the reduction rules above. In the following sections, ROBDDs will be referred to as BDDs (or ordinary BDDs) for the sake of simplicity.

As shown in Fig. 3, a set of multiple BDDs can share their subgraphs with each other under the same fixed variable ordering. In this way, we can handle a number of Boolean functions simultaneously in a monolithic memory space.

Using BDDs, we can uniquely and compactly represent many practical Boolean functions including AND, OR, parity, and arithmetic adder functions. Using Bryant's algorithm [5], we can efficiently construct a BDD for the result of a binary logic operation (e.g. AND, OR, XOR) on a given pair of operand BDDs. This

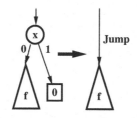

Fig. 4. ZBDD reduction rule

algorithm is based on hash table techniques, and the computation time is almost linearly related to the data size unless there is data overflow in main memory (see [5] or [17] for details).

Based on these techniques, several BDD packages were developed in the 1990s and are widely used for large-scale Boolean function manipulation, especially in the VLSI CAD area.

2.2   Sets of Combinations and ZBDDs

BDDs were originally developed for handling Boolean function data. However, they can also be used for the implicit representation of sets of combinations. Here we use the term "sets of combinations" for a set of elements each of which is a combination of n items. This data model often appears in real-life problems, such as combinations of switching devices (ON/OFF), fault combinations, and sets of paths in networks.

A combination of n items can be represented by an n-bit binary vector, $(x_1 x_2 \ldots x_n)$, where each bit, $x_k \in \{1, 0\}$, expresses whether the item is included in the combination or not. A set of combinations can be represented by a list of the combination vectors. In other words, a set of combinations is a subset of the power set of n items.

A set of combinations can be mapped into Boolean space by using n-input variables for each bit of the combination vector. If we choose any particular combination vector, a Boolean function determines whether the combination is included in the set of combinations. Such Boolean functions are called *characteristic functions*. For example, the left side of Fig. 5 shows a truth table representing a Boolean function $(ab\bar{c}) \vee (\bar{b}c)$ but also represents a set of combinations $\{ab, ac, c\}$. Using BDDs for characteristic functions, we can implicitly and compactly represent sets of combinations. The logic operations AND/OR for Boolean functions correspond to the set operations intersection/union for sets of combinations. By using BDDs for characteristic functions, we can manipulate sets of combinations efficiently. They can be generated and manipulated within a time roughly proportional to the BDD size. When we handle combinations that include many similar patterns (subcombinations), the BDDs are greatly reduced by the node-sharing effect, and sometimes an exponential reduction in processing time and space can be obtained.

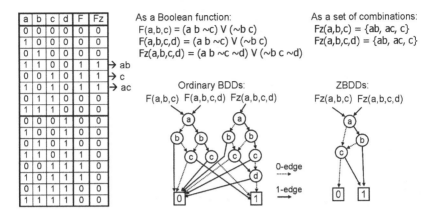

Fig. 5. Effect of ZBDD reduction rule

The **ZBDD** [16,18] is a special type of BDD, used for the efficient manipulation of sets of combinations. ZBDDs are based on the following special reduction rules.

- Delete all nodes whose 1-edge directly points to the 0-terminal node, and jump through to the 0-edge's destination, as shown in Fig. 4.
- Share equivalent nodes, similarly to ordinary BDDs.

Note that we do not delete the nodes whose two edges point to the same node, which would have been deleted by the original rule. The zero-suppressed deletion rule is asymmetric for the two edges, as we do not delete the nodes whose 0-edge points to a terminal node. It is proved that ZBDDs also give canonical forms as do ordinary BDDs under a fixed variable ordering.

Here we summarize the features of ZBDDs:

- In ZBDDs, the nodes of irrelevant items (i.e. never chosen in any combination) are automatically deleted by the ZBDD reduction rule. In ordinary BDDs, irrelevant nodes remain and may compromise the reduction available by sharing nodes. An example is shown in Fig. 5. In this case, the item d is irrelevant, but the ordinary BDDs for characteristic functions $Fz(a, b, c)$ and $Fz(a, b, c, d)$ have different forms. On the other hand, ZBDDs for $Fz(a, b, c)$ and $Fz(a, b, c, d)$ have identical forms and are therefore completely shared.
- Each path from the root node to the 1-terminal node corresponds to each combination in the set. That is, the number of such paths in the ZBDD equals the number of combinations in the set. In ordinary BDDs, this property does not always hold.
- When no equivalent nodes exist in a ZBDD, i.e. the worst case, the ZBDD structure explicitly stores all items in all combinations while also using an explicit linear linked list data structure. That is, (the order of) the ZBDD size never exceeds that of the explicit representation. If more nodes are shared, the ZBDD is more compact than the linear list.

Table 1. Primitive ZBDD operations

"∅"	Returns the empty set. (0-terminal node)
"**1**"	Returns a null-combination. (1-terminal node)
P.top	Returns the item-ID at the root node of P.
P.offset(v)	Subset of combinations not including item v.
P.onset(v)	Gets $P - P$.offset(v) and then deletes v from each combination.
P.change(v)	Inverts existence of v (add / delete) on each combination.
$P \cup Q$	Returns union set.
$P \cap Q$	Returns intersection set.
$P - Q$	Returns difference set. (in P but not in Q.)
P.count	Counts number of combinations.

Table 1 shows most of the primitive operations for ZBDDs. In these operations, The execution time for $\emptyset$, **1**, and $P.top$ is a constant, and those for the remainder are almost linearly to the size of the graph. We can describe a variety of processing operations on sets of combinations by compositions of these primitive operations.

2.3   ZBDD-Based Database Analysis

In this paper, we discuss a method for manipulating large-scale transaction databases using ZBDDs. Here we consider binary transaction databases, each record of which holds a combination of items chosen from a given item list. Such a combination is called a *itemset*.

For analyzing these large-scale transaction databases, frequent pattern mining [2] and *maximum frequent pattern mining* [6] are especially important and have been discussed actively during the last decade. Since their introduction by Agrawal et al. [1], many papers have been published about new algorithms and improvements for solving such mining problems [10,12,24]. Recently, graph-based methods, such as FP-growth [12], have received a great deal of attention, because they can quickly manipulate large-scale itemset data by constructing compact graph structures in main memory.

The ZBDD-based method is a similar approach to handling sets of combinations in main memory but is more efficient because ZBDD is a kind of DAG for representing itemsets, while FP-growth uses a tree representation for the same objects. In general, DAGs can be more compact than trees.

Another important point is that our method uses ZBDDs not only as the internal data structure but also as the output data structure. Most of the existing state-of-the-art pattern mining algorithms focus on enumerating or listing the patterns that satisfy the given conditions, and they consider the storage and indexing of the pattern results for efficient data analysis to be a separate issue. In this paper, we present a fast algorithm for pattern mining and simultaneously indexing a huge number of patterns compactly in main memory for subsequent analysis. The results can be analyzed flexibly by using algebraic operations implemented via ZBDDs.

In addition, we will now explain why we use ZBDDs instead of ordinary BDDs for this application. Table 2 lists the basic statistics of a typical data mining

Table 2. Statistics of typical benchmark data

Data name	$\#I$	$\#T$	$total|T|$	$avg|T|$	$avg|T|/\#I$
T10I4D100K	870	100,000	1,010,228	10.1	1.16%
mushroom	119	8,124	186,852	23.0	19.32%
pumsb	2,113	49,046	3,629,404	74.0	3.50%
BMS-WebView-1	497	59,602	149,639	2.5	0.51%
accidents	468	340,183	11,500,870	33.8	7.22%

Fig. 6. Example of itemset-histogram   **Fig. 7.** ZBDD vector for itemset-histogram

benchmark data [10]. $\#I$ shows the number of items used in the data, $\#T$ is the number of itemsets included in the data, $avg|T|$ is the average number of items per itemset, and $avg|T|/\#I$ is the average appearance ratio of each item. From this table, we can observe that the item's appearance ratio is very small in many cases. This observation means that we often handle very sparse combinations in many practical data mining/analysis problems, and in such cases, the ZBDD reduction rule is extremely effective. If the average appearance ratio of each item is 1%, ZBDDs are potentially more compact than ordinary BDDs by a factor of up to 100. In the literature, there is an early report by Jiang et al. [13] applying BDDs to data mining problems, but the results seem less than excellent because of the overhead of using ordinary BDDs. Therefore, we should use ZBDDs instead of ordinary BDDs for success in many practical data mining/analysis problems.

3   A ZBDD-Based Pattern-Mining Algorithm

In this section, we first introduce the data structure of the itemset-histogram and ZBDD vectors [19], and then present our new algorithm, ZBDD-growth, which extracts all frequent patterns from a given transaction database using a ZBDD-based data structure.

3.1   Itemset-Histograms and ZBDD Vectors

An *Itemset-histogram* is a table that lists the number of appearances of each itemset in the given database. An example of itemset-histogram is shown in

Fig. 6. This is essentially a compressed table for the database that combines the itemsets appearing more than once into one line, together with the frequency of occurrence.

Our pattern mining algorithm uses a ZBDD-based itemset-histogram representation as the internal data structure, as presented in our previous paper [19]. Here we describe how to represent itemset-histograms using ZBDDs. Because ZBDDs are representations of sets of combinations, a simple ZBDD distinguishes only the existence of each itemset in the database. In order to represent the number of appearances of itemsets, we decompose the number into the m digits of a ZBDD vector $\{F_0, F_1, \ldots, F_{m-1}\}$ to represent integers up to $(2^m - 1)$, as shown in Fig. 7. That is, we encode the appearance numbers into binary digital code, with F_0 representing the itemsets appearing an odd number of times (LSB = 1), F_1 representing the itemsets whose appearance number's second lowest bit is 1, and similarly for each digit up to F_{m-1}.

In the example of Fig. 7, the frequencies of itemsets are decomposed as: $F_0 = \{abc, ab, c\}$, $F_1 = \{ab, bc\}$, $F_2 = \{abc\}$, following which each digit can be represented by a simple ZBDD. The three ZBDDs share their subgraphs with each other.

Now we explain the procedure for constructing a ZBDD-based itemset-histogram from an original database. We read the itemset data one by one from the database and accumulate the single itemset data into the histogram. More precisely, we generate a ZBDD of T for a single itemset picked up from the database and accumulate it into the ZBDD vector. The ZBDD of T can be obtained by starting from "1" (a null combination), and applying "Change" operations several times to join the items in the itemset. Next, we compare T and F_0, and if they have no common parts, we just add T to F_0. If F_0 already contains T, we eliminate T from F_0 and carry T up to F_1. This ripple-carry procedure continues until T and F_k have no common part. After finishing accumulations for all data records, the itemset-histogram is complete.

Using the notation $F.\text{add}(T)$ for the addition of an itemset T to the ZBDD vector F, we can describe the procedure for generating the itemset-histogram H for a given database D.

$H = \mathbf{0}$
forall $T \in D$ **do**
$H = H.\text{add}(T)$
return H

When we construct a ZBDD vector for an itemset-histogram, the number of ZBDD nodes in each digit is bounded by the total appearance of items in all itemsets. If there are many partially similar itemsets in the database, the subgraphs of ZBDDs will be well shared, and a compact representation is obtained. The bit-width of the ZBDD vector is bounded by $\log S_{max}$, where S_{max} is the appearance of the most frequent items.

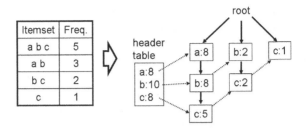

Fig. 8. Example of FP-tree

Once we have generated a ZBDD vector for the itemset-histogram, various operations can be executed efficiently. These are instances of operations used in our pattern mining algorithm:

- H.factor0(v): Extracts sub-histogram of itemsets without item v.
- H.factor1(v): Extracts sub-histogram of itemsets including item v and then deletes v from the itemsets (also considered as the quotient of H/v).
- $v \cdot H$: Attaches an item v to each itemset in the histogram F.
- $H_1 + H_2$: Generates a new itemset-histogram with the sum of the frequencies of corresponding itemsets.
- H.count: The number of itemsets appearing at least once.

These operations can be composed as a sequence of ZBDD operations. The result is also compactly represented by a ZBDD vector. The computation time bound is approximately linearly related to the total ZBDD size.

3.2   ZBDD Vectors and FP-Trees

FP-growth [12], one of the state-of-the-art algorithms, constructs an "FP-tree" for a given transaction database and then searches frequent patterns using this data structure. An example of an FP-tree is shown in Fig. 8. We can see that the FP-tree is a trie [9] of itemsets with their frequencies. In other words, **FP-growth is based on the tree representation of itemset-histograms.** That is, ZBDD-growth is logically based on the same internal data structure as FP-growth. This is the reason for calling this algorithm ZBDD-growth. However, the ZBDD-based method will be more efficient because ZBDDs can share equivalent subgraphs and the computation time is bounded by the ZBDD size. The benefit of ZBDDs is especially noticeable when large numbers of patterns are produced.

3.3   A Frequent Pattern Mining Algorithm

Our new algorithm, ZBDD-growth, is based on a recursive depth-first search over the ZBDD-based itemset-histogram representation. The basic algorithm is shown in Fig. 9.

```
ZBDDgrowth(H, α)
{
    if(H has only one item v)
        if(v appears more than α )
            return v ;
        else return "0" ;
    F ← Cache(H) ;
    if(F exists) return F ;
    v ← H.top ; /* Top item in H */
    H₁ ← H.factor1(v) ;
    H₀ ← H.factor0(v) ;
    F₁ ←ZBDDgrowth(H₁, α) ;
    F₀ ←ZBDDgrowth(H₀ + H₁, α) ;
    F ← (v · F₁) ∪ F₀ ;
    Cache(H) ← F ;
    return F ;
}
```

```
ZBDDgrowthMax(H, α)
{
    if(H has only one item v)
        if(v appears more than α )
            return v ;
        else return "0" ;
    F ← Cache(H) ;
    if(F exists) return F ;
    v ← H.top ; /* Top item in H */
    H₁ ← H.factor1(v) ;
    H₀ ← H.factor0(v) ;
    F₁ ←ZBDDgrowthMax(H₁, α) ;
    F₀ ←ZBDDgrowthMax(H₀ + H₁, α) ;
    ┌─────────────────────────────────────┐
    │ F ← (v · F₁) ∪ (F₀ − F₀.permit(F₁)) ; │
    └─────────────────────────────────────┘
    Cache(H) ← F ;
    return F ;
}
```

Fig. 9. ZBDD-growth algorithm   **Fig. 10.** ZBDD-growth-max algorithm

In this algorithm, we choose an item v used in the itemset-histogram H and compute the two sub-histograms H_1 and H_0 (i.e. $H = (v \cdot H_1) \cup H_0$). As v is the top item in the ZBDD vector, H_1 and H_0 can be obtained simply by referring to the 1-edge and 0-edge of the highest ZBDD-node, so the computation time is constant for each digit of ZBDD.

The algorithm consists of the two recursive calls, one of which computes the subset of patterns including v, while the other computes the patterns excluding v. The two subsets of patterns can be obtained as a pair of pointers to ZBDDs, and then the final ZBDD is computed. This procedure may theoretically require an exponential number of recursive calls. However, we can prepare a hash-based cache to store the result of each recursive call. Each entry in the cache is formed as pair (H, F), where H is the pointer to the ZBDD vector for a given itemset-histogram, and F is the pointer to the result of the ZBDD. On each recursive call, we check the cache to see if the same histogram H has already appeared, and if so, we can avoid duplicate processing and return the pointer to F directly. By using this technique, the computation time becomes almost linearly related to the total ZBDD size.

In our implementation, we include some simple techniques for pruning the search space. For example, if H_1 and H_0 are equivalent, we may skip the computation of F_0. In other cases, we can halt the recursive calls when the total of frequencies in H is no more than α. Other more elaborate pruning techniques exist, but they need additional computation cost for checking conditions, so they are sometimes but not always effective.

3.4   Extension for Maximal Pattern Mining

We can extend the ZBDD-growth algorithm to extract only the maximal frequent patterns [6], each of which is not included in any other frequent patterns. The algorithm is shown in Fig. 10.

```
P.permit(Q)
{
    if(P = "0" or Q = "0") return "0" ;
    if(P = Q) return F ;
    if(P = "1") return "1" ;
    if(Q = "1")
        if(P include "1" ) return "1" ;
        else return "0" ;
    R ← Cache(P, Q) ;
    if(R exists) return R ;
    v ← TopItem(P, Q) ; /* Top item in P, Q */
    (P_0, P_1) ← factors of P by v ;
    (Q_0, Q_1) ← factors of Q by v ;
    R ← (v · P_1.permit(Q_1)) ∪ (P_0.permit(Q_0 ∪ Q_1)) ;
    Cache(P, Q) ← R ;
    return R ;
}
```

Fig. 11. Permit operation

The difference from the original algorithm is in only one line, shown in the frame box. Here, we check each pattern in F_0 and delete it if the pattern is included in one of the patterns of F_1. In this way, we generate only maximal frequent patterns. This is a similar approach to that used in MAFIA [6].

The process of deleting non-maximal patterns is a very time-consuming task. However, we found that one ZBDD-based operation, called the *permit* operation by Okuno et al. [21], can be used to solve this problem[1]. P.permit(Q) returns a set of combinations in P each of which is a subset of some combination in Q. For example, when $P = \{ab, abc, bcd\}$ and $Q = \{abc, bc\}$, then P.permit(Q) returns $\{ab, abc\}$. The permit operation is efficiently implemented as a recursive procedure of ZBDD manipulation, as shown in Fig. 3.4. The computation time of the permit operation is almost linearly related to the ZBDD size.

4   Experimental Results

Here we show the experimental results for evaluating our new method. We used a Pentium-4 PC, 800MHz, 1.5GB of main memory, with SuSE Linux 9. We can deal with up to 20,000,000 ZBDD nodes in this machine. In these experiments, our implementation of the ZBDD-growth algorithm does not print out the pattern list but constructs the ZBDD results in main memory and counts the number of patterns included in the ZBDD. Counting patterns requires only a time linearly related to the ZBDD size, even if an exponential number of patterns are contained.

For comparison, we also executed the FP-growth algorithm [12], using an implementation by Goethals [11]. This implementation also does not print out the pattern list, only counts the number of patterns.

---

[1] The Permit operation is similar to the *SubSet* operation of Coudert et al. [8], defined for ordinary BDDs.

Table 3. "One-pair-missing"

$a_2b_2a_3b_3\cdots a_{n-1}b_{n-1}a_nb_n$
$a_1b_1 \qquad a_3b_3\cdots a_{n-1}b_{n-1}a_nb_n$
$a_1b_1a_2b_2 \qquad \cdots a_{n-1}b_{n-1}a_nb_n$
$\vdots \qquad \ddots \qquad \vdots$
$a_1b_1a_2b_2a_3b_3\cdots \qquad a_nb_n$
$a_1b_1a_2b_2a_3b_3\cdots a_{n-1}b_{n-1}$

Table 4. Results for "one-pair-missing"

n	#Patterns	(output) |ZBDD|	ZBDD-growth Time(sec)	FP-growth [12] Time(sec)
8	58,974	35	0.01	0.11
10	989,526	45	0.01	1.93
12	16,245,774	55	0.01	32.20
14	263,652,486	65	0.02	518.90
15	1,059,392,916	70	0.02	1966.53
16	4,251,920,574	75	0.02	(timeout)

Table 5. Generation of itemset-histograms [19]

Data name	$\#T$	$total\|T\|$	|ZBDD| Vector	Time(s)
T10I4D100K	100,000	1,010,228	552,429	43.2
mushroom	8,124	186,852	8,006	1.2
pumsb	49,046	3,629,404	1,750,883	188.5
BMS-WebView-1	59,602	149,639	46,148	18.3
accidents	340,183	11,500,870	3,877,333	107.0

4.1 Experiment with a Mathematical Example

First, we present an experiment for a set of artificial examples where ZBDD-growth is extremely effective. The database, named "one-pair-missing," has the form shown in Table 3. That is, this database has n records, each of which contains $(n - 1)$ pairs of items with only one pair missing. It may produce an exponentially increasing number of frequent patterns.

The experimental results with frequency threshold $\alpha = 1$ are shown in Table 4. We observe the exponential explosion of the number of patterns, compared with the linearly increasing sizes of the ZBDDs needed to represent such a large number of patterns. In such cases, ZBDD-growth runs extremely fast, while FP-growth requires a time exponentially related to the output data size.

4.2 Experiments for Benchmark Examples

Next, we show the results for the benchmark examples [11]. Table 5 shows the time and space required to generate ZBDD vectors of itemset-histograms [19] as the preprocessing of the ZBDD-growth algorithm. In this table, $\#T$ shows the number of itemsets, $total\|T\|$ is the total of itemset sizes (total appearances of items), and $\|ZBDD\|$ is the number of ZBDD nodes for the itemset-histograms. We see that itemset-histograms can be constructed for all cases within a feasible time and space. The ZBDD sizes are similar to or less than $total\|T\|$.

After generating ZBDD vectors for the itemset-histograms, we applied the ZBDD-growth algorithm to generate frequent patterns. Table 6 shows the results for the selected benchmark examples, "mushroom", "T10I4D100K", and "BMS-WebView-1". The execution time includes the time for generating the initial ZBDD vectors for itemset-histograms. The results show that ZBDD-growth is much faster than FP-growth for "mushroom" but is not as effective for "T10I4D100K". This is a reasonable result because "T10I4D100K" is known to

Table 6. Results for benchmark examples

Data name: Min. freq. α	#Frequent patterns	(output) |ZBDD|	ZBDD-growth Time(s)	FP-growth [11] Time(s)
mushroom: 5,000	41	11	1.2	0.1
1,000	123,277	1,417	3.7	0.3
200	18,094,821	12,340	9.7	5.4
16	1,176,182,553	53,804	7.7	244.1
4	3,786,792,695	59,970	4.3	891.3
1	5,574,930,437	40,557	1.8	1,322.5
T10I4D100K: 5,000	10	10	81.3	0.7
1,000	385	382	135.5	3.1
200	13,255	4,288	279.4	4.5
16	175,915	89,423	543.3	13.7
4	3,159,067	1,108,723	646.0	38.8
1	2,217,324,767	(mem.out)	−	317.1
BMS-WebView1: 1,000	31	31	27.8	0.2
200	372	309	31.3	0.4
50	8,191	3,753	49.0	0.8
34	4,849,465	64,601	120.8	8.3
32	1,531,980,297	97,692	133.7	345.3
31	8,796,564,756,112	117,101	138.1	(timeout)
30	35,349,566,550,691	152,431	143.9	(timeout)

be an artificial database comprising completely random combinations, so there are very few relationships between the itemsets. In such cases, the compression of ZBDDs is not effective, and only the overhead factor is revealed. For "BMS-WebView-1", ZBDD-growth is slower than FP-growth when the output size is small. However, an exponential factor of reduction is observed in cases that generate many patterns. Especially for $\alpha = 31$ and 30, more than one trillion patterns are generated and compactly stored in memory, which has not been possible when using conventional data structures.

4.3   Maximal Frequent Pattern Mining

We also show the experimental results for maximal frequent pattern mining using the ZBDD-growth-max algorithm. In Table 7, we show the results for the same examples used in the original ZBDD-growth experiment. The last column $Time_{(max)}/Time_{(all)}$ shows the ratio of computation time between ZBDD-growth-max and the original ZBDD-growth algorithm. We observe that the computation time is almost the same (within a factor of two) for the two algorithms. In other words, the additional computation cost for ZBDD-growth-max is almost the same order as the original algorithm. Our ZBDD-based "permit" operation can efficiently filter the maximal patterns within a time that depends on the ZBDD size, which is almost the same cost as manipulating ZBDD vectors of itemset-histograms.

In many conventional methods, maximal pattern mining is less time consuming than generating all patterns because there are many fewer maximal patterns than all patterns. However, the complexity of ZBDD-growth does not directly depend on the number of patterns. We observe that ZBDD size is not significantly different between the maximal and all-pattern cases, so the computation time is also not significantly different.

Table 7. Results of maximal pattern mining

Data name: Min. freq. α	#Maximal freq. patterns	(output) |ZBDD|	ZBDD-growth-max Time(s)	$Time_{(max)}$ /$Time_{(all)}$
mushroom: 5,000	3	10	1.2	1.00
1,000	467	744	4.1	1.10
200	3,111	4,173	10.7	1.10
16	24,060	13,121	8.1	1.06
4	39,456	14,051	4.2	0.98
1	8,124	8,006	1.2	0.70
T10I4D100K: 5,000	10	10	107.1	1.32
1,000	370	376	203.1	1.50
200	1,938	2,609	462.8	1.66
16	68,096	66,274	922.4	1.70
4	400,730	372,993	1141.2	1.77
1	77,443	532,061	140.5	–
BMS-WebView1: 1,000	29	30	34.9	1.25
200	264	289	41.2	1.32
50	3,546	3,064	71.2	1.45
34	15,877	16,854	173.1	1.43
32	15,252	17,680	196.6	1.47
31	13,639	17,383	208.7	1.51
30	11,371	16,323	219.7	1.53

5   Postprocessing for Generated Frequent Patterns

Our ZBDD-based method features an algorithm that uses ZBDDs not only as the internal data structure but also as the output data structure, indexing a large number of patterns compactly in main memory. The results can be analyzed flexibly, by using algebraic operations implemented in ZBDDs. Here we show several examples of postprocessing operations on the output data.

(**Subpattern matching for the frequent patterns**):   From the frequent-pattern results F, we can efficiently filter a subset S, such that each pattern in S contains a given sub-pattern P.

$S = F$
forall $v \in P$ **do:**
$S = S.\text{onset}(v).\text{change}(v)$
return S

Conversely, we can extract a subset of patterns not satisfying the given conditions. This is easily done by computing $F - S$. The computation time for the sub-pattern matching is much smaller than the time for frequent pattern mining.

The above operations are sometimes called constraint pattern mining. In conventional methods, it is too time consuming to generate all frequent patterns before filtering. Therefore, many researchers consider direct methods of constraint pattern mining without generating all patterns. However, using the ZBDD-based method, a large number of patterns can be stored and indexed compactly in main memory. In many cases, therefore, it is possible to generate all frequent patterns and then process them using algebraic ZBDD operations.

(**Extracting Long/Short Patterns**):   Sometimes we are interested in the long/short patterns, comprising a large/small number of items. Using ZBDDs, all combinations of less than k out of n items are efficiently represented in polynomial size, bounded by $O(k \cdot n)$. This ZBDD represents a length constraint on patterns. We then apply an intersection (or difference) operation to the frequent patterns that meet the length constraint of the ZBDD. In this way, we can easily extract a set of long/short frequent patterns.

(**Comparison between Two Sets of Frequent Patterns**):   Our ZBDD manipulation environment can efficiently store more than one set of results of frequent pattern mining. Therefore, we can compare two sets of frequent patterns generated under different conditions. For example, if a database gradually changes over time, the itemset-histograms and frequent patterns do not stay the same. Our ZBDD-based method can store and index a number of snapshots of pattern sets and easily show the intersection, union, and difference between any pair of snapshots. When many similar ZBDDs are generated, their ZBDD nodes are effectively shared within a monolithic multi-rooted graph, requiring much less memory than that required to store each ZBDD separately.

(**Calculating Statistical Data**):   After generating a ZBDD for a set of patterns, we can quickly count the number of patterns by using a primitive ZBDD operation S.count. The computation time is linearly bounded by the ZBDD size, not depending on the pattern count. We can also efficiently calculate other statistical measures, such as *Support* and *Confidence*, which are often used in probabilistic analysis and machine learning.

(**Finding Disjoint Decompositions in Frequent Patterns**):   In a recent paper [20], we presented an efficient ZBDD-based method for finding all possible *simple disjoint decompositions* in a set of combinations. If a given set of patterns f can be decomposed as $f(X, Y) = g(h(X), Y)$, with X and Y having no common items, then we call it a simple disjoint decomposition. The decomposition method can be applied to the result of our ZBDD-growth algorithm, and we can extract other aspects of hidden structures from the complex itemset data. This will be a powerful tool for database analysis.

6   Related Works

A ZBDD can be regarded as a compressed representation of a *trie* [9] for a set of patterns, by sharing subgraphs of the tree structure. From this viewpoint, it can be compared with the existing state-of-the-art condensed representations, such as closed sets [22], free sets [4], and non-derivable itemsets [7].

Recently, Mielikäinen et al. [15] reported a fast method of answering itemset support query for frequent itemsets using a condensed representation. Their data structure is based on a trie with a frequency number on each node. Using this data structure, they represent a histogram of the frequent patterns occurring more than α times. In this way, counting the occurrence number for a given pattern can extremely be accelerated. In addition, they also proposed some techniques not to store all frequent patterns in the trie, by only storing a

Table 8. Comparison with a condensed representation [15]

Data name (min. freq.)	#freq. patterns	condensed rep. [15] (in KB)		ZBDD (in KB)	
		all-freq-hist	closed-freq-hist	all-freq-set	all-freq-hist
mushroom (α: 500)	1,442,503	56,348	420	160	1,513
pumsb (α: 35,000)	1,897,479	74,120	10,416	250	16,293
BMS-WebView-1 (α: 35)	1,177,607	46,000	3,308	1,898	10,014

part of patterns (e.g. closed patterns) to save the memory requirement without information loss.

Here we show an experiment to compare our ZBDD-based method with Mielikäinen's results. In the Table 8, the first column shows the data name with the minimum frequency α. The second column shows the total amount of all frequent patterns for α. In the columns of condensed representations, "all-freq-hist" shows the memory requirement in KByte to represent a histogram of all frequent patterns in the trie, and "closed-freq-hist" shows the results only storing closed patterns in the trie. In the columns of our ZBDD-based representation, "all-freq-set" shows the ZBDD size in KByte to represent a set of all frequent patterns (without counting frequency number for each patterns), and "all-freq-hist" shows the size of a ZBDD vector to represent the histogram of frequent patterns. Here we assume that one ZBDD node consumes 40 Byte in average.

In general, ZBDD-based "all-freq-set" is much more compact than using a trie, since the equivalent subgraphs are shared in a ZBDD. Notice that a simple ZBDD represents just a set of frequent patterns, but not representing a histogram. To store the occurrence numbers exactly, we have to use ZBDD vectors, shown as "all-freq-hist" in the table. This is still more compact than trie-based "all-freq-hist".

The condensed representation "closed-freq-hist" would be more powerful than using ZBDDs in terms of memory reduction. They use a domain-specific property of frequent itemsets, i.e. monotonous relation. However, if we consider more various inductive queries after generating frequent patterns, it would not work well because such a beautiful property of itemsets may be broken. ZBDDs can be used more robustly as they are based on more general data compression principles. The results may depend on what kind of operations are performed after generating patterns. Analysis of those data efficiencies will be an interesting future work.

7   Conclusion

In this paper, we have presented a new ZBDD-based frequent pattern-mining algorithm. Our method generates a ZBDD for a set of frequent patterns from the ZBDD vector for the itemset-histogram of a given transaction database. Our experimental results show that our ZBDD-growth algorithm is comparably fast as existing state-of-the-art algorithms such as FP-growth. Especially for the cases where the ZBDD nodes are well shared, an exponential speed-up is observed, compared with existing algorithms based on explicit table/tree representation.

On the other hand, for the cases where ZBDD nodes are not well shared, or the number of patterns is very small, the ZBDD-growth method is not effective and the overhead factors dominate. However, we do not have to use the ZBDD-growth algorithm in all cases. We may use existing methods for cases where they are more effective than ZBDD-growth. In addition, we could develop a hybrid program that uses an FP-tree or a simple array for the internal data structure but with the output constructed as a ZBDD.

The ZBDD-based method will be useful as a fundamental technique for database analysis and knowledge indexing, and will be utilized for various applications in inductive data analysis.

Acknowledgments. This research was partially supported by Grant-in-Aid for Specially Promoted Research on "Semi- Structured Data Mining," 17002008, Ministry of Education, Culture, Sports, Science and Technology of Japan.

References

1. Agrawal, R., Imielinski, T., Swami, A.N.: Mining Association Rules between Sets of Items in Large Databases. In: Buneman, P., Jajodia, S. (eds.) Proc. of the 1993 ACM SIGMOD International Conference on Management (Data of SIGMOD Record), vol. 22(2), pp. 207–216. ACM Press, New York (1993)
2. Agrawal, R., Mannila, H., Srikant, R., Toivonen, H., Verkamo, A.I.: Fast Discovery of Association Rules. In: Advances in Knowledge Discovery and Data Mining, pp. 307–328. MIT Press, Cambridge (1996)
3. Boulicaut, J.-F.: Proc. 2nd International Workshop on Knowledge Discovery in Inductive Databases (KDID'03), Cavtat-Dubrovnik (2003)
4. Boulicaut, J.-F., Bykowski, A., Rigotti, C.: Free-sets: A Condensed Representation of Boolean Data for the Approximation of Frequency Queries. Journal of Data Mining and Knowledge Discovery (DMKD) 7(1), 5–22 (2003)
5. Bryant, R.E.: Graph-based Algorithms for Boolean Function Manipulation. IEEE Trans. Computers 35(8), 677–691 (1986)
6. Burdick, D., Calimlim, M., Gehrke, J.: MAFIA: A Maximal Frequent Itemset Algorithm for Transactional Databases. In: Proc. ICDE 2001, pp. 443–452 (2001)
7. Calders, T., Goethals, B.: Mining All Non-derivable Frequent Itemsets. In: Elomaa, T., Mannila, H., Toivonen, H. (eds.) PKDD 2002. LNCS (LNAI), vol. 2431, pp. 74–85. Springer, Heidelberg (2002)
8. Coudert, O., Madre, J.C., Fraisse, H.: A New Viewpoint on Two-level Logic Minimization. In: Proc. of 30th ACM/IEEE Design Automation Conference, pp. 625–630 (1993)
9. Fredkin, E.: Trie Memory. CACM 3(9), 490–499 (1960)
10. Goethals, B.: Survey on Frequent Pattern Mining, Manuscript (2003), http://www.cs.helsinki.fi/u/goethals/publications/survey.ps
11. Goethals, B., Javeed Zaki, M. (eds.): Frequent Itemset Mining Dataset Repository, Frequent Itemset Mining Implementations (FIMI'03) (2003), http://fimi.cs.helsinki.fi/data/

12. Han, J., Pei, J., Yin, Y., Mao, R.: Mining Frequent Patterns without Candidate Generation: A Frequent-Pattern Tree Approach. Data Mining and Knowledge Discovery 8(1), 53–87 (2004)

13. Jiang, L., Inaba, M., Imai, H.: A BDD-based Method for Mining Association Rules. In: Proceedings of 55th National Convention of IPSJ, IPSJ, September 1997, vol. 3, pp. 397–398 (1997)

14. Mannila, H., Toivonen, H.: Multiple Uses of Frequent Sets and Condensed Representations. In: Proc. KDD, pp. 189–194 (1996)

15. Mielikäinen, T., Panov, P., Dzeroski, S.: Itemset Support Queries using Frequent Itemsets and Their Condensed Representations. In: Todorovski, L., Lavrač, N., Jantke, K.P. (eds.) DS 2006. LNCS (LNAI), vol. 4265, pp. 161–172. Springer, Heidelberg (2006)

16. Minato, S.: Zero-suppressed BDDs for Set Manipulation in Combinatorial Problems. In: Proc. 30th ACM/IEEE Design Automation Conf (DAC-93), pp. 272–277 (1993)

17. Minato, S.: Binary Decision Diagrams and Applications for VLSI CAD. Kluwer Academic Publishers, Dordrecht (1996)

18. Minato, S.: Zero-suppressed BDDs and Their Applications. International Journal on Software Tools for Technology Transfer (STTT) 3(2), 156–170 (2001)

19. Minato, S., Arimura, H.: Efficient Combinatorial Itemset Analysis Based on Zero-Suppressed BDDs. In: Proc. of IEEE/IEICE/IPSJ International Workshop on Challenges in Web Information Retrieval and Integration (WIRI-2005), pp. 3–10 (2005)

20. Minato, S.: Finding Simple Disjoint Decompositions in Frequent Itemset Data Using Zero-suppressed BDD. In: Proc. of IEEE ICDM 2005 workshop on Computational Intelligence in Data Mining, November 2005, pp. 3–11. IEEE Computer Society Press, Los Alamitos (2005)

21. Okuno, H., Minato, S., Isozaki, H.: On the Properties of Combination Set Operations. Information Processing Letters 66, 195–199 (1998)

22. Pasquier, N., Bastide, Y., Taouil, R., Lakhal, L.: Efficient Mining of Association Rules Using Closed Itemset Lattices. Journal of Information Systems 24(1), 25–46 (1999)

23. Baeza-Yates, R., Ribiero-Neto, B.: Modern Information Retrieval. Addison Wesley, Reading (1999)

24. Zaki, M.J.: Scalable Algorithms for Association Mining. IEEE Trans. Knowl. Data Eng. 12(2), 372–390 (2000)

Extracting Trees of Quantitative Serial Episodes

Mirco Nanni[1] and Christophe Rigotti[1,2]

[1] KDD Laboratory, University of Pisa and ISTI-CNR Pisa, Italy
[2] INSA-LIRIS UMR 5205 CNRS, Lyon, France

Abstract. Among the family of the local patterns, episodes are commonly used when mining a single or multiple sequences of discrete events. An episode reflects a qualitative relation *is-followed-by* over event types, and the refinement of episodes to incorporate quantitative temporal information is still an on going research, with many application opportunities. In this paper, focusing on serial episodes, we design such a refinement called *quantitative episodes* and give a corresponding extraction algorithm. The three most salient features of these quantitative episodes are: (1) their ability to characterize main groups of homogeneous behaviors among the occurrences, according to the duration of the *is-followed-by* steps, and providing quantitative bounds of these durations organized in a tree structure; (2) the possibility to extract them in a complete way; and (3) to perform such extractions at the cost of a limited overhead with respect to the extraction of standard episodes.

1   Introduction

Sequential data is a common form of information available in several application contexts, thus naturally inducing a strong interest for them among data analysts. A decade-long attention has been paid by researchers in data mining to study forms of patterns appropriated to this kind of data, such as sequential patterns [1] and episodes [9,7]. In particular, in this paper we will focus on *serial episodes*, that are sequences of event types extracted from single or multiple input sequences, and that reflect a qualitative relation *is-followed-by* between the event types.

Episodes have natural applications into several domains, including for instance the analysis of business time series [2], medical data [10], geophysical data [11] and also alarm log analysis for network monitoring (especially in telecommunications) [5]. However, in many applications episodes clearly show some limitations, due to the fact that the information provided by the *is-followed-by* relation is not always enough to properly characterize the phenomena at hand. This, in particular, pulls our research toward the refinement of episodes to incorporate quantitative temporal information, able to describe the time intervals observed for the *is-followed-by* relation.

In this paper, we propose a refinement of episodes called *quantitative episodes*, that provides quantitative temporal information in a readable, tree-based graphically representable form. These quantitative episodes describe the main groups

S. Džeroski and J. Struyf (Eds.): KDID 2006, LNCS 4747, pp. 170–188, 2007.
© Springer-Verlag Berlin Heidelberg 2007

of homogeneous behaviors within the occurrences of each episode, according to the elapsed times between the consecutive event types of the episode. Moreover, they are not provided in an isolated way, but in trees giving a global view of how the occurrences of the corresponding episode differentiate in homogeneous groups along the elements of the pattern. From a computational point of view, the main interest of the quantitative episodes is that they can be mined in a sound and complete way without increasing the cost of extractions significantly when compared to extractions of episodes alone. This is achieved through an extraction algorithm that tightly integrates episode extraction with a computationally reasonable analysis of temporal quantitative information.

This paper is organized as follows: in Section 2 some preliminary definitions needed concerning episodes are recalled from the literature; Section 3, then, introduces quantitative episodes; Section 4 presents the principle of an algorithm for efficiently extracting quantitative episodes, which is evaluated experimentally in Section 5; finally, in Section 6 we briefly review the related literature and conclude with a summary in Section 7.

2 Preliminary Definitions

We briefly introduce standard notions [8], or give equivalent definitions when more appropriated to our presentation.

Definition 1 (*event, event sequence, operator* $\sqsubseteq$). Let E be a set of *event types* and $\prec$ a total order on E. An *event* is a pair denoted (e, t) where $e \in E$ and $t \in \mathbb{N}$. The value t denotes the time stamp at which the event occurs. An *event sequence* S is a tuple of events $S = \langle (e_1, t_1), (e_2, t_2), \ldots, (e_l, t_l) \rangle$ such that $\forall i \in \{1, \ldots, l-1\}$, $t_i < t_{i+1} \vee (t_i = t_{i+1} \wedge e_i \prec e_{i+1})$. Given two sequences of events S and S', S' is a *subsequence* of S, denoted $S' \sqsubseteq S$, if S' is equal to S or if S' can be obtained by removing some elements in S.

Definition 2 (*episode, occurrence, minimal occurrence, support*). An *episode* is a non empty tuple α of the form $\alpha = \langle e_1, e_2, \ldots, e_k \rangle$ with $e_i \in E$ for all $i \in \{1, \ldots, k\}$. In this paper, we will use the notation $e_1 \to e_2 \to \ldots \to e_k$ to denote the episode $\langle e_1, e_2, \ldots, e_k \rangle$ where '$\to$' may be read as 'is followed by'. The *size* of α is denoted $|\alpha|$ and is equal to the number of elements of the tuple α, i.e., $|\alpha| = k$. The *prefix* of α is the episode $\langle e_1, e_2, \ldots, e_{k-1} \rangle$. We denote it as $prefix(\alpha)$. An episode $\alpha = \langle e_1, e_2, \ldots, e_k \rangle$ *occurs* in an event sequence S if there exists at least one sequence of events $S' = \langle (e_1, t_1), (e_2, t_2), \ldots, (e_k, t_k) \rangle$ such that $\forall i \in \{1, \ldots, k-1\}, t_i < t_{i+1}$ and $S' \sqsubseteq S$. The pair $\langle t_1, t_k \rangle$ is called an *occurrence* of α in S. Moreover, if there is no other occurrence $\langle t'_1, t'_k \rangle$ such that $[t'_1, t'_k] \subset [t_1, t_k]$, then the pair $\langle t_1, t_k \rangle$ is called a *minimal occurrence* of α. The support of α in S, denoted $support(\alpha, S)$, is the number of minimal occurrences of α in S.

Intuitively, a minimal occurrence is simply an occurrence that does not strictly contain another occurrence of the same episode. These episodes and their occurrences correspond to the *serial* episodes of [8]. For instance, let $S = \langle (a, 0), (b, 1), $

$\langle c, 1 \rangle, (b, 2) \rangle$ be an event sequence and $\alpha = a \rightarrow b$ be an episode. Then, α has two occurrences in S: $\langle 0, 1 \rangle$ and $\langle 0, 2 \rangle$. The former is a minimal occurrence, while the latter is not, since $[0, 1] \subset [0, 2]$. Notice that there is no occurrence of episode $\alpha' = b \rightarrow c$.

These definitions, and the ones introduced in the rest of the paper, are given for a single sequence S, but they extend trivially to multiple sequences. In that case the support is the sum of the number of occurrences in all sequences[1].

3   Quantitative Episodes

In this section we introduce an extension of episodes that includes quantitative information. The precise definitions will be preceded by an intuitive, informal presentation of the key ideas.

3.1   Informal Presentation

The idea of quantitative episodes essentially consists in dividing the set of occurrences of an episode into homogeneous, significantly populated groups. Homogeneity, in particular, is obtained when on each step, made of two consecutive elements of the episode, the occurrences in the same group show similar transition times (i.e., similar times elapsed between an element and the next one within the episode). The result can be graphically summarized through a tree-like structure, as the one depicted in Figure 1 that represents homogeneous groups of occurrences of an episode $\alpha = A \rightarrow B \rightarrow C \rightarrow D$. The figure can be read in the following way:

- The episode has 1000 occurrences in the sequence of events, and this value is written under the first event of the episode.
- Among these 1000 occurrences, there are 2 subgroups that show homogeneous duration for step $A \rightarrow B$: one (the upper branch of the split) corresponds to transition times between 2 and 10, and covers 500 occurrences; the other (lower branch) corresponds to transition times in interval $[15, 20]$ and covers 400 occurrences. Notice that 100 occurrences of $A \rightarrow B \rightarrow C \rightarrow D$ are lost, meaning that they exhibit a rather isolated duration for step $A \rightarrow B$ and cannot be associated with other occurrences to form a significantly populated group.
- In the largest group obtained above, all occurrences present similar step durations for steps $B \rightarrow C$ and $C \rightarrow D$, and are kept together in a single group. The other group, containing 400 occurrences, is split further into homogeneous groups w.r.t. duration of step $B \rightarrow C$. Notice that the resulting homogeneous groups overlap, sharing a subset of occurrences and resulting in non-disjoint time intervals. Indeed, we can observe that the total count of

---

[1] Notice that here, the support is not the number of sequences containing at least one occurrence of the pattern, as in the case of sequential patterns over a base of sequences [1].

occurrences in the two groups (205+202) is greater than the original total amount (400), since some occurrences are counted twice.
- One of these two groups is further split into two (disjoint) groups while the other is not.
- Each path from the root to a leaf in the tree corresponds to a group of occurrences that shows an homogeneous behavior along all the steps of the episode, and covers a sufficient number of occurrences (in this example, at least 90). This homogeneous behavior can be represented by the sequence of time intervals on the path, and can be added to the episode as a *quantitative feature* to form a *main grouping quantitative episode*. The tree in Figure 1 depicts four such patterns (one for each path from the root to a leaf). The tree relates these patterns together, showing how the occurrences can be differentiated into groups along the steps of the episode.

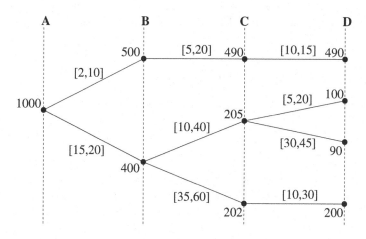

Fig. 1. Tree of quantitative episodes for episode $\alpha = A \rightarrow B \rightarrow C \rightarrow D$

Example 1. In a medical context, we can assume to have recorded the sequences of symptoms, diseases and therapies of all patients in a hospital. Then, mining frequent quantitative episodes can yield a set of common patterns in the history of patients in terms of sequences of symptoms, etc., together with the common timings between pairs of consecutive events, that can help to characterize, e.g., the course of diseases, reactions to therapies, etc. As a fictional example, we can consider the tree of Figure 1 with A = *benign disease*, B = *symptom 1*, C = *symptom 2*, D = *severe disease*, and using days as time unit. In this case, beside the interesting evolution of a disease, the tree points out the existence of different groups of patients, each following the same evolution but with different timings. The first differentiation occurs between the appearance of the benign disease and the first symptom, in one case taking no more than 10 days, and in the other case taking approximately between two and three weeks. Then, the second group of patients further differentiate in the timings between the two symptoms (10 to 40 days in one case and 35 to 60 in the second one) and one subgroup shows differences also on the last step (5 to 20 days in one case and 30 to 45 in the second one). This kind of information could be useful to domain experts, both as ready-to-use knowledge for the daily care of patients, and as insight for the a more general study and understanding of the diseases involved.

Some sample quantitative episode trees, obtained on real data involving the logs of a web site, are provided in Section 5.2, Figure 10.

We notice that our approach essentially produces trees rooted on the first event of each episode, from which all the differentiations in time develop. While this choice looks very natural, since it follows the order of events in the episode, other choices could be useful in specific contexts as, for example, rooting the tree on the last event of the episode. However, such variants of the quantitative episodes studied in this paper follow the same principles, and in some cases they can be obtained by simply preprocessing the input data, e.g., moving the root of the tree on the last event of episodes can be obtained by essentially reversing the order of the input sequences.

3.2   Quantitative Episode Definition

Definition 3 (*quantitative episode*). A *quantitative episode* (*q-episode*) is a pair $P = \langle \alpha, IT \rangle$ where α is an episode of size $k > 1$, and $IT = \langle it_1, \ldots, it_{k-1} \rangle$, with $\forall i \in \{1, \ldots, k-1\}, it_i = [a_i, b_i] \subset \mathbb{N}^+$ (i.e., it_i is an interval in $\mathbb{N}^+$). The size of P, denoted $|P|$ is defined as $|P| = |\alpha|$.

The it_i intervals are intended to represent values of elapsed time between the occurrences of two consecutive event types of the episode α. For instance $\langle A \rightarrow B \rightarrow C \rightarrow D, \langle [15, 20], [10, 40], [5, 20] \rangle \rangle$ is one of the q-episodes depicted in Figure 1.

To handle the time stamps of the events corresponding to all event types within an episode the definition of occurrence needs to be modified as follows.

Definition 4 (*occurrence*). An *occurrence* of an episode $\alpha = \langle e_1, e_2, \ldots, e_k \rangle$ in an event sequence S is a tuple $\langle t_1, t_2, \ldots, t_k \rangle$ such that there exists $S' = \langle (e_1, t_1), (e_2, t_2), \ldots, (e_k, t_k) \rangle$ satisfying $\forall i \in \{1, \ldots, k-1\}, t_i < t_{i+1}$ and $S' \sqsubseteq S$.

Notice that subsequence S' in the definition above can be formed by non-contiguous elements of sequence S.

Let us now consider the notion of minimality of occurrences. Let $S = \langle (a, 1), (b, 3), (b, 6), (c, 9) \rangle$ be an event sequence and $\alpha = a \rightarrow b \rightarrow c$ be an episode. Then $\langle 1, 3, 9 \rangle$ and $\langle 1, 6, 9 \rangle$ are two occurrences of α. If we consider a notion of minimal occurrence based only on the starting date and the ending date of the occurrences, then both are minimal. This does not fit with the intuition behind the original notion of minimal occurrence, according to which in such a situation there is only one minimal occurrence, i.e., the occurrence $\langle 1, 9 \rangle$ (only the starting and ending dates are used to identify occurrences in the original framework).

Thus, using occurrences that account for the intermediate time stamps as in Definition 4, the notion of minimal occurrence has to be redefined, and must not be based only on the starting and ending dates of the occurrences. Moreover, this extension has to be made by carefully avoiding counterintuitive situations. For instance, in the previous example, if we choose as minimal occurrences those containing only minimal occurrences of the different parts of the episode, then $\langle 1, 3, 9 \rangle$ is no longer a minimal occurrence of α, since $\langle 3, 9 \rangle$ is not a minimal occurrence of $b \rightarrow c$ (the minimal occurrence of this part of the episode α is $\langle 6, 9 \rangle$). The same arises for $\langle 1, 6, 9 \rangle$ because $\langle 1, 6 \rangle$ is not minimal for the part $a \rightarrow b$ (the minimal occurrence of this part of the episode α is $\langle 1, 3 \rangle$). Whence, α would have no minimal occurrence in S.

In the definition we retain (given as Definition 5), we use two criteria: (1) minimality based on the starting and ending dates, and (2) when several occurrences start and end at the same dates we choose the occurrence containing the earliest possible intermediate time stamps. This second condition is expressed simply through a minimality requirement with respect to the prefix of the episode. Intuitively this means that the minimal occurrence among several occurences having the same starting and ending dates is the one formed as soon as possible, e.g., in the previous example the minimal occurrence of α is $\langle 1, 3, 9 \rangle$.

Definition 5 (*minimal occurrence*). An occurrence $\langle t_1, \ldots, t_k \rangle$ of an episode α in event sequence S is a *minimal occurrence* if (1) there is no other occurrence $\langle t'_1, \ldots, t'_k \rangle$ of α such that $[t'_1, t'_k] \subset [t_1, t_k]$, and (2) if $k > 2$ then $\langle t_1, \ldots, t_{k-1} \rangle$ is a minimal occurrence of $prefix(\alpha)$.

As we will consider only minimal occurrences of episodes, we will simply use the term *occurrence*, when there is no ambiguity.

For a step $e_i \rightarrow e_{i+1}$ in an episode α, and its durations among a set of occurrences of α, now we define how these duration values are grouped. Informally, groups correspond to maximal sets of duration values that form *dense* intervals, where dense means that any sub-interval of significant size w_s contains a significant number of values n_s. More precisely, $w_s \in \mathbb{R}, w_s \geq 1$ and $n_s \in \mathbb{N}^+$ are termed the *density parameters* and characterize the groups in the following definition.

Definition 6 (*occurrence groups*). *Let $\mathcal{O}$ be a set of occurrences of episode α and i be an integer parameter such that $1 \leq i < |\alpha|$ (i identifies a step $e_i \rightarrow e_{i+1}$). Let $\Delta_i(x) = t_{i+1} - t_i$ for any occurrence $x = \langle t_1, \ldots, t_{|\alpha|} \rangle$ (i.e., the duration of step $e_i \rightarrow e_{i+1}$ for occurrence x). Then, the occurrence groups of $\mathcal{O}$ at level i, denoted as $group(\mathcal{O}, i)$, are defined as follows:*

$$group(\mathcal{O}, i) = \{ \; g \mid g \text{ is a maximal subset of } \mathcal{O} \text{ s.t.:}$$
$$\forall a, b \in [\min_{x \in g} \Delta_i(x), \max_{x \in g} \Delta_i(x)],$$
$$b - a \geq w_s \; \Rightarrow \; |\{x \in g \mid \Delta_i(x) \in [a, b]\}| \geq n_s \}$$

For example, consider the set of occurrences $\mathcal{O} = \{x_1, \ldots, x_8\}$ having the respective durations 3,4,6,6,8,9,15,16,16 for step $e_i \rightarrow e_{i+1}$ (i.e., the values of Δ_i).

Let the density parameters be $w_s = 3$ and $n_s = 2$ (i.e., at least two elements in any sub-interval of size 3). Then $group(\mathcal{O}, i) = \{\{x_1, \ldots, x_5\}, \{x_6, x_7, x_8\}\}$ (corresponding respectively to the durations $3, 4, 6, 6, 8, 9$ and $15, 16, 16$).

The next definition specifies the tree structure of the occurrence groups.

Definition 7 (*occurrence group tree*). *Let $\mathcal{O}$ be the set of occurrences of episode α. Then, the* occurrence group tree *(group tree for short) of α is a rooted tree with labelled edges such that:*

- *the tree has $|\alpha|$ levels, numbered from 1 (the root) to $|\alpha|$ (the deepest leaves);*
- *each node v is associated with a set $v.g$ of occurrences of α;*
- *the root is associated with $root.g = \mathcal{O}$, i.e., with all the occurrences of α;*
- *if a node v at level i, $1 \le i < |\alpha|$, is such that $group(v.g, i) = \{g_1, \ldots, g_k\}$, then it has k children $v_1, \ldots, v_k$, with $v_j.g = g_j, i \in \{1, \ldots, k\}$.*
- *each edge connecting node v at level i with its child v_j is labelled with the interval $[\min_{x \in v_j.g} \Delta_i(x), \max_{x \in v_j.g} \Delta_i(x)]$;*

Notice that such tree is unique, up to permutations in the order of the children of each node. Then, the main grouping q-episodes correspond simply to the sets of occurrences that have not been separated from the root to a leaf and that have a significant size.

Definition 8 (*main grouping q-episode*). *A q-episode $P = \langle \alpha, IT \rangle$ is said to be a* main grouping q-episode *if the group tree of α contains a path from the root to a leaf v such that:*

- *the labels of the edges met along the path correspond to the intervals in IT;*
- *and $|v.g|$, called the support of P, is greater or equal to σ_g, a user defined minimum group size.*

For instance, Figure 1 depicts a tree of main grouping q-episodes for $\alpha = A \rightarrow B \rightarrow C \rightarrow D$ and $\sigma_g = 90$ (a group tree restricted to paths forming main grouping q-episodes).

Since a minimal occurrence of α can be obtained only by extending a minimal occurrence of $prefix(\alpha)$, we have the following simple property that is used as a safe pruning criterion in the extraction principle.

Theorem 1. *Let α be an episode such that $|\alpha| > 1$. If there exists a main grouping q-episode $\langle \alpha, IT \rangle$, then there exists a main grouping q-episode $\langle prefix(\alpha), IT' \rangle$.*

4   Extracting q-Episodes

In this section, we present an algorithm to extract all main grouping q-episodes, based on the computation of the group trees. Even though the notion of group tree is rather intuitive, the difficulties lay in the fact that we have to compute such a tree for every episode. We describe the overall principle of the approach and then give the corresponding abstract algorithm.

4.1   Principle

A simple preliminary remark is that the tree computation can be limited to episodes occurring at least σ_g times, since σ_g is the minimal support of a main grouping q-episode and a q-episode cannot be more frequent than its corresponding episode. However, in practice we are still facing a large number of frequent episodes. So, we propose the algorithm *Q-epiMiner* that interleaves frequent episode extraction and group tree computation in a tight efficient way.

Let $\alpha = \langle e_1, \ldots, e_n \rangle$ be an episode. For each event type e_i in α, $i > 1$, we consider a list D_i that collects the durations between e_{i-1} and e_i, i.e., the values $\Delta_{i-1}(x)$ for all occurrences x of α, and we suppose that each D_i is sorted by increasing duration value. By convention, for the sake of uniformity, D_1 contains a duration of 0 for all occurrences (there is no element before e_1).

In the following, we describe how these lists $D_1, \ldots, D_n$ can be used to compute the group tree of pattern α, and then how they can be updated when expanding α with an event type e_{n+1}.

Splitting one node. Splitting the group of occurrences of α associated to one node of the tree at level i (to obtain its children at level $i+1$) can be done simply by a single scan of the elements in the group if these elements are ordered by the duration between e_i and e_{i+1}. For instance, consider a node associated to the occurrences introduced in the previous example on page 175, corresponding to durations $[3, 4, 6, 6, 8, 9, 15, 16, 16]$, and consider the same density parameters $w_s = 3$ and $n_s = 2$. Then a single scan through the list allows to find the low density areas, as for example $[10, 13]$ that is a sub-interval of size 3 without any element of list $[3, 4, 6, 6, 8, 9, 15, 16, 16]$ in it, and thus the scan leads to obtain the two maximal sublists satisfying the density criterion: $[3, 4, 6, 6, 8, 9]$ and $[15, 16, 16]$. The same principle can be applied even when the maximal sublists are overlapping. For instance, if the list of durations is $[3, 4, 6, 6, 8, 9, 12, 15, 16, 16]$, a single scan allows to determine that for example only one element is in interval $[10, 13]$, while at least two are in the intervals (of size 3) $[9, 12]$ and $[12, 15]$. Whence we have the two maximal sublists satisfying the density criterion: $[3, 4, 6, 6, 8, 9, 12]$ and $[12, 15, 16, 16]$.

In the following, we use a function named *splitGroup* performing this simple treatment. We suppose that it takes as input a list of occurrences in a group, sorted by duration of $e_i \rightarrow e_{i+1}$, and gives as output a collection of all maximal sublists satisfying the density criterion.

Computing the whole tree. Suppose that we have already computed the groups of occurrences denoted $g_1, \ldots, g_k$ that are associated respectively to the nodes $v_1, \ldots, v_k$ of a level i of the tree. These groups are split in the following way to obtain the nodes of the next level. Firstly, we create for each node v_j an empty list denoted $v_j.sortedGroup$. Then we scan D_{i+1} from first to last element, and for each occurrence found in D_{i+1} if the occurrence is in a group g_j then we insert the occurrence at the end of $v_j.sortedGroup$. Now, we have at hand for each v_j its group of occurrences sorted by increasing duration between e_i and e_{i+1}. Then, we can apply on each $v_j.sortedGroup$ the $splitGroup$ function to compute the children of v_j and their associated groups of occurrences and thus obtain the next level of the group tree. Repeating this process allows to build the group tree in a levelwise way, taking advantage of the sorted lists[2] $D_1, \ldots, D_n$. In the following, we assume that such a tree is computed by a function $computeTree$, applied on a tuple $\langle D_1, \ldots, D_n \rangle$.

Obtaining the information needed to compute the tree. The other key operation is the efficient computation of the sorted lists $D'_1, \ldots, D'_n, D'_{n+1}$ of a pattern $\alpha \to e$. Suppose that we know the list L_e of occurrences of $\alpha \to e$, and the sorted lists $D_1, \ldots, D_n$ of durations corresponding to the occurrences of α. Then, the main property used is that $D'_1, \ldots, D'_n$ are sublists of, respectively, $D_1, \ldots, D_n$, since each occurrence of $\alpha \to e$ comes from the expansion of an occurrence of α. So a list D'_i can be obtained simply by scanning D_i from the first to the last element and picking (in order) the elements in D_i corresponding to occurrences of α that have been extended to form an occurrence of $\alpha \to e$. The result is a list D'_i sorted by increasing duration between e_{i-1} and e_i. The case of the list D'_{n+1} is different since it does not correspond to durations already computed. This list is constructed by scanning L_e to obtain the durations between e_n and e_{n+1}, and then by sorting these durations in increasing order. It should be noticed that while all other operations made on lists in the algorithm are reduced to simple scans, this sort is the only operation with a non linear complexity with respect to the size of the list. Having at hand the sorted lists $D'_1, \ldots, D'_n, D'_{n+1}$ we can then compute the group tree of $\alpha \to e$ by calling $computeTree(\langle D'_1, \ldots, D'_n, D'_{n+1} \rangle)$.

Integration with the extraction of episodes. One remaining problem to be solved is to build the occurrence list of the episode under consideration (as the list L_e for $\alpha \to e$). Fortunately, several approaches to extract episodes, or closely related patterns like *sequential patterns*, are based on the use of such occurrence lists (e.g., [8,11,14]), providing the information needed to update the duration lists D_i. The basic idea is that if we store in a list L the locations (positions in the data sequence) of the occurrences of a pattern α, then for an event type e, we can use[3] L to build the list L_e of occurrences of $\alpha \to e$. Notice that the expansion is made using occurrences of e that are not necessarily contiguous to the last elements of the occurrences of α. In our case, for the occurrences of an episode $\alpha = \langle e_1, \ldots, e_n \rangle$ the location information stored in L are simply the time stamps of the last element e_n of α, sorted by increasing value. In the following, we use a function $expand$ that takes the input sequence S and L, and that returns a set $\mathcal{L}_{exp}$ of tuples $\langle e, L_e \rangle$. The set $\mathcal{L}_{exp}$ contains for each event type e, the list L_e of locations of occurrences of $\alpha \to e$. As for L, the location information in L_e

---

[2] It should be noticed that the construction starts using D_2 to obtain $root.sortedGroup$, and that D_1 (containing only durations set to zero by convention) is not really used, but is only mentioned for the sake of the uniformity of the notation.

[3] Together with other information, like the data sequence itself, or the location of the occurrences of e.

are the time stamps of the last element of $\alpha \to e$ and L_e is sorted by increasing location value. It should be noticed that since L is ordered by occurrence time stamp, computing $\mathcal{L}_{exp}$ under the minimal occurrence semantics is linear with respect to $|S|$.

The last important aspect is the enumeration strategy of the episodes. The key remark is that a standard depth-first prefix-based strategy fits both with the episode extraction and with the use of the sorted lists D_i to derive the sorted lists D_i' to compute the group trees. A depth-first approach is particularly interesting here, since it allows to limit the amount of memory needed. So, we adopt such a strategy, that can simply be sketched as follows: when an episode α is considered we use it as a *prefix* to expand it and to obtain new episodes of the form $\alpha \to e$, and then, one after the other, we consider and expand each of these $\alpha \to e$.

It should be noticed that these choices made for the part that extracts the episodes (i.e., using occurrence lists together with a depth-first strategy) correspond to a typical approach used to mine serial episodes under the minimal occurrence semantics, similar for instance to the one used in [11].

Algorithm 1 (*Q-epiMiner*)

Extracts the main grouping q-episodes in event sequence S according to minimum group size σ_g, and density parameters w_s and n_s.

begin
    Scan S to compute the set T_{freq} of event types occurring at least σ_g times.
    for all $e \in T_{freq}$
        $L_e :=$ *empty list*
    for all $(e, t) \in S$ *from first to last, and such that $e \in T_{freq}$*
        Generate occid a new occurrence identifier.
        Append $\langle occid, t, 0 \rangle$ to the end of L_e.
    for all $e \in T_{freq}$
        $D_1 := L_e$
        $explore(S, \langle e \rangle, L_e, \langle D_1 \rangle)$
end

Fig. 2. Algorithm *Q-epiMiner*

Pruning strategy and correctness. As mentioned at the beginning of the section, if an episode α has a support strictly less than σ_g it cannot be used to form any main grouping q-episode. The same holds for any expansion of α since it cannot have a greater support. So, the expansion of α can be safely avoided. Furthermore, consider an episode α such that all leaves at level $|\alpha|$ are associated to groups of size strictly less than σ_g (α has no corresponding main grouping q-episode, but α itself can have a support greater or equal to σ_g). By Theorem 1, we can also safely avoid the expansion of α, since this expansion cannot correspond

Algorithm 2 (explore)

Input: $(S, \alpha, L, \langle D_1, D_2, \ldots, D_n \rangle)$
where S is the event sequence, α the episode considered,
L the list of occurrences of the last element of α and
$\langle D_1, D_2, \ldots, D_n \rangle$ the duration lists associated to α with $n = |\alpha|$.

begin
  $\mathcal{L}_{exp} := expand(S, L)$
  for all $\langle e, L_e \rangle \in \mathcal{L}_{exp}$ *such that* $|L_e| \geq \sigma_g$
    for all $\langle occid, t, dt \rangle \in L$
      $occid.isExtended := (\exists \langle occid', t', dt' \rangle \in L_e, occid' = occid)$
    for i **from** *1* **to** n
      $D_i' := empty\ list$
      for all $\langle occid, t, dt \rangle \in D_i$ *from first to last*
        if $occid.isExtended = $ **true then**
          Append $\langle occid, t, dt \rangle$ *to the end of* D_i'.
    $D_{n+1}' := L_e$ *sorted by increasing value of dt (third element in the tuples)*
    $T := computeTree(\langle D_1', D_2', \ldots, D_{n+1}' \rangle)$
    if T *has at least one node at level $n+1$ associated to a group of size*
    at least σ_g **then**
      Output all paths in T from the root to the nodes at level $n+1$
      that are associated to groups of size at least σ_g.
      $explore(S, \alpha \to e, L_e, \langle D_1', D_2', \ldots, D_{n+1}' \rangle))$
end

Fig. 3. Function *explore*

to any main grouping q-episode. The exhaustive enumeration strategy of the episodes and the safety of the pruning strategy ensure the correctness of the general extraction principle.

4.2   Abstract Algorithm

For the sake of simplicity of the presentation we use a common data structure for all the lists L, L_e, D_i, D_i'. Each of them is represented by a list of tuples $\langle occid, t, dt \rangle$ where $occid$ is a unique occurrence identifier, t is a time of occurrence, and dt is a duration between two elements in a pattern.

The extraction is performed by the Algorithm Q-epiMiner, given as Algorithm 1 (Figure 2). It first considers the patterns of size 1 and constructs the lists L_e of occurrences of each event type e (the unique occurrence identifiers are generated in any order). Then it calls *explore* (Algorithm 2 in Figure 3) to expand each of these patterns of size 1.

The function *explore* first expands the occurrences of episode α with respect to all event types, using *expand*. We required that *expand* preserves the *occid*

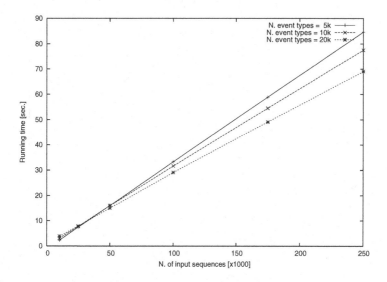

Fig. 4. Scalability w.r.t. number of input sequences

values[4] and computes the new durations (between the two last elements of the episode). For instance, if $\langle \#999, 42, 5 \rangle$ is in L and this occurrence can be extended by event (e,50) then $\langle \#999, 50, 8 \rangle$ is in L_e (where 8 is the duration, $8 = 50 - 42$). Next, *explore* takes each extension that is frequent enough (first pruning criterion), computes the lists D'_i from the lists D_i ($1 < i \leq n$) and then D'_{n+1} by sorting L_e. After having computed the group tree T of the current extension (calling function *computeTree*), it applies the second pruning criterion and if needed makes the new pattern grow in a recursive way.

Notes on implementation. To reduce drastically the memory needed by function *explore*, the copy in lists $D'_1, \ldots, D'_n$ of the elements of lists $D_1, \ldots, D_n$ (for *occid* corresponding to occurrences that have been extended) is not really performed. Instead we implement a virtual deletion in the lists D_i by hiding the elements with an *occid* that has not been extended (*occid.isExtended* = *false*), and use these lists in place of the lists D'_i when calling *computeTree*. The hidden elements are then restored in the lists D_i before picking the next extension in $\mathcal{L}_{exp}$.

5   Experiments

In this section we present the results of a set of experiments, on synthetic and real datasets, mainly aimed at studying how the size of the input data and the value

---

[4] Preserving the *occid* is possible because under the minimal occurrence semantics, for a given event type e, an occurrence of α can be extended to form at most one occurrence of $\alpha \to e$.

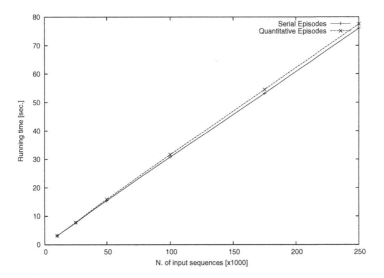

Fig. 5. Scalability comparison w.r.t. serial episode extraction

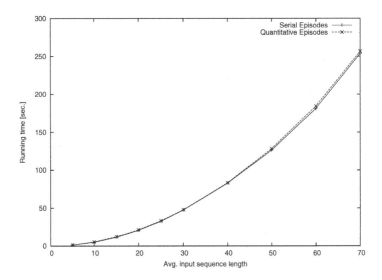

Fig. 6. Scalability w.r.t. input sequence length, with 100K sequences

of some input parameters impact on the performances of the *Q-epiMiner* algorithm described in this paper. The experiments presented are made on datasets containing several sequences. As mentioned previously, the definitions extended trivially to that case (the support is simply the sum of the support in all sequences). The only change in the abstract algorithm is that the occurrence locations are not simply time stamps, but sequence identifiers together with time

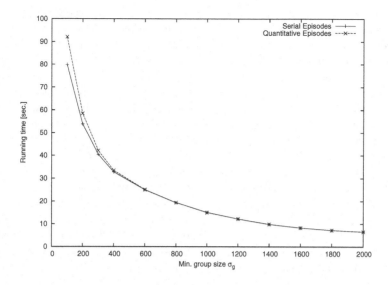

Fig. 7. Scalability w.r.t. min. group size σ_g, with 100K sequences

stamps in the sequences. The algorithm was implemented in C, and all experiments were performed on a Intel Xeon 2Ghz processor with 1Gb of RAM over a Linux 2.6.14 platform.

5.1 Performance Analysis on Synthetic Datasets

In order to collect large datasets having controlled characteristics, we randomly generated them by means of the Quest Synthetic Data Generator from IBM[5], by varying the number of input sequences generated (from 10K to 250K), the sequence length[6] (from 5 to 70) and the number of different event types used (from 5K to 20K). Where not specified hereafter, the following default parameter values were adopted: 100K input sequences, sequence length equal to 25, 5K event types, $w_s = 8$ and $n_s = 4$.

The curves in Figure 4 show the execution times of the prototype over datasets of increasing size and for three different numbers of event types used in the data. The σ_g parameter was set to 40 for 10K sequences and then was increased proportionally, up to 1000 for 250K sequences. As we can see, the execution time always grows almost linearly, having a higher slope when fewer event types are in the data[7]. A similar scalability analysis is provided in Figure 5, where *Q-epiMiner* is compared against the extraction of serial episodes having at least a support of

---

[5] http://www.almaden.ibm.com/software/projects/iis/hdb/Projects/
data_mining/mining.shtml

[6] The parameter of the generator controlling the number of events per time stamp was set to 1.

[7] Fewer event types with the same number of sequences leads to higher supports for the remaining event types and more frequent patterns of large size.

σ_g. This extraction is performed using the frequent serial episodes mining technique embedded in *Q-epiMiner*, (i.e., without computing the durations, groups and trees, and implemented with the same low level optimizations). As explained in Section 4.1, this technique corresponds to a typical approach used to extract serial episodes under the minimal occurrence semantics. The values of σ_g were the same as in the previous experiment. The two curves are very close, meaning that the overhead introduced by the computation of main grouping q-episodes is well balanced by the pruning it allows. Finally, similar results are obtained by varying the length of the input sequences (see Figure 6), where both curves have an apparently-quadratic growth (σ_g was set to 80 for length 5 and then was increased proportionally, up to 1120 for length 70). Obviously, for very long sequences usual episode constraints, like maximum window size, might be used [8].

Figure 7 reports the behaviour of the prototype when the minimum size of the groups is varied from 100 to 2000, and again its comparison to the mining of frequent serial episodes at minimum support σ_g. Here also, the two algorithms behave very similarly, this time showing a fast drop in the execution time as σ_g grows – as usual for frequent pattern mining algorithms.

5.2   Experiments on a Real Dataset

In this set of experiments we used real world data consisting of the July 2000 weblog from the web server of the Department of Electrical Engineering and Computer Sciences, University of California at Berkeley[8]. In a preprocessing step, all non-HTML pages where removed and user sessions were extracted, resulting in 90295 user sessions (used as input sequences) of average length of 13.0 with 72014 distinct pages.

The figure 8 describes the performances of the *Q-epiMiner* prototype on the Berkeley dataset for different minimum group sizes with $w_s = 120$ (time in sec.) and $n_s = 15$. It confirms the results obtained on synthetic data, i.e., execution times drop very quickly as σ_g increases. Moreover, an additional curve is plotted that represents a version of *Q-epiMiner* that does not apply any pruning based on the absence of a main grouping q-episode, but only applies a pruning based on the support of the episodes (an episode is not expanded only when its support is strictly less than σ_g). This curve shows the effectiveness of the full pruning made by *Q-epiMiner*. It should also be noticed that in these experiments, *Q-epiMiner* performs even better than the serial episode miner (with minimum support set to σ_g), confirming the fact that the pruning capabilities of the prototype are able to balance its potential overhead.

Finally, Figure 9 presents the effect of varying the density parameters (with $\sigma_g = 200$). It shows that, quite reasonably, the execution time decreases with larger minimum density parameter n_s (since they allow a stronger pruning), and increases with larger window sizes w_s (which acts in the opposite direction).

We conclude this section by providing in Figure 10 two sample outputs obtained from the Berkeley dataset. The first one describes a navigation pattern

---

[8] http://www.cs.berkeley.edu/logs/http

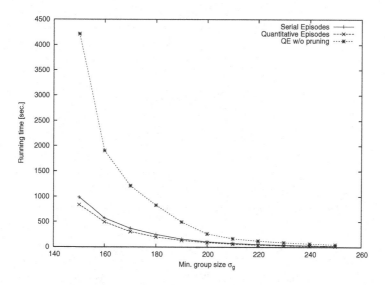

Fig. 8. Berkely dataset: Scalability w.r.t. min. group size σ_g

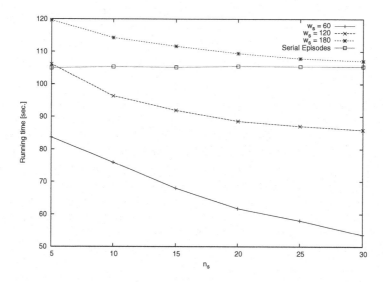

Fig. 9. Berkely dataset: effects of the density parameters

that starts from the web site root, visits a page about classes for students, and ends on the general alphabetically-sorted directory of people. In particular, we notice that the tree contains two groups that split at the first step, showing well separated intervals of times: $[1, 549]$ against $[993, 1850]$ (time in sec.). Furthermore, while the first group (which was faster in performing the first step of the episode) takes from a few seconds up to 10 minutes to move to the third page,

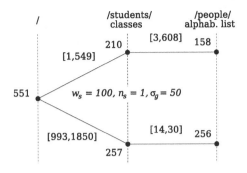

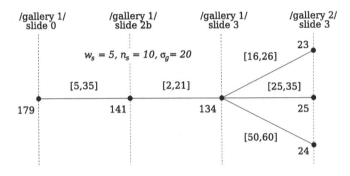

Fig. 10. Examples of trees of main grouping q-episodes

the second group has a very compact behaviour, only taking between 14 and 30 seconds. The second output concerns the visit of a sequence of four pages in some photo galleries. The tree starts with a single branch for the first two steps, which take respectively up to 35 and up to 21 seconds, and splits only at the third step, where three groups are formed. The first two overlap ($[16, 26]$ and $[25, 35]$), therefore showing only a weak differentiation, and represent *fast* visitors, while the third one is separated from them, and corresponds to *slow* visitors that take from 50 seconds up to one minute. In both the examples, each time a group splits some of the occurrences it contains are lost, i.e., they are not part of any subgroup (of size at least σ_g) created by the split.

6   Related Work

The need of quantitative temporal information in patterns over event sequences has been pointed in recent works in the data mining literature [13,3,12,4,6,11].

An important difference between these approaches and the q-episodes introduced here, is that the former provide patterns in isolation, while q-episodes are related in tree structures. Such trees give a global view of how the occurrences of a pattern differentiate in homogeneous groups along the sequence of event types (from the first to the last element of the pattern).

Different notions of intervals are also considered. In [6] the intervals are not determined by the data but are fixed by the user; only the interval between the beginning and the end of a pattern is considered in [11]; and in [3] intervals are derived from intervals of occurrences of patterns of size two only.

The other approaches [13,12,4] compute the intervals from the data and for all pattern lengths, as in the case of the q-episodes. However, among these approaches, only [4] considers an exhaustive extraction (at the cost of intrinsically expensive algorithmic solutions), while the others compute only *some* of the patterns using heuristics and/or non-deterministic choices.

Finally, it should be noticed that the overhead of computing the quantitative temporal information was not assessed in these previous works.

7   Conclusion

In this paper we introduced *quantitative episodes*, an extension of serial episodes that refines standard episodes by integrating quantitative temporal information. A tight integration of episode extraction and occurrence group tree computation allowed to obtain a complete and efficient algorithm that adds a negligible overhead to the extraction of serial episodes, as assessed by the experimental results on performances. These features, and the possibility of an easy-to-grasp representation of the output into a graphical tree-like structure, make the approach suitable for many applications. Future evolutions of this work will include its use in place of standard episode extraction in concrete application domains, as well as its extension to deal with quantitative aspects other than time. In particular, we aim to treat the spatial information contained in spatio-temporal sequences describing the trajectory of moving objects, such GPS traces and similar forms of data.

Acknowledgments. This research is partly funded by EU contracts IQ IST-FP6-516169, and GeoPKDD IST-FP6-014915.

References

1. Agrawal, R., Srikant, R.: Mining sequential patterns. In: Yu, P.S., Chen, A.S.P. (eds.) Proc. of the 11th International Conference on Data Engineering (ICDE'95), Taipei, Taiwan, pp. 3–14. IEEE Computer Society Press, Los Alamitos (1995)
2. Das, G., Lin, K., Mannila, H., Renganathan, G., Padhraic Smyth, P.: Rule discovery from time series. In: Proc. of the 4th International Conference on Knowledge Discovery and Data Mining (KDD'98), August 1998, pp. 16–22. AAAI Press, New York (USA) (1998)
3. Dousson, C., Duong, T.V.: Discovering chronicles with numerical time constraints from alarm logs for monitoring dynamic systems. In: Proc. of the 16th Int. Joint Conference on Artificial Intelligence (IJCAI'99), San Francisco, CA, USA, pp. 620–626 (1999)
4. Giannotti, F., Nanni, M., Pedreschi, D.: Efficient mining of temporally annotated sequences. In: Jonker, W., Petković, M. (eds.) SDM 2006. LNCS, vol. 4165, Springer, Heidelberg (2006)

5. Hatonen, K., Klemettinen, M., Mannila, H., Ronkainen, P., Toivonen, H.: TASA: Telecomunications alarm sequence analyzer or: How to enjoy faults in your network. In: 1996 IEEE Network Operations and Management Symposium (NOMS'96), Kyoto, Japan, April 1996, pp. 520–529 (1996)
6. Hirate, Y., Yamana, H.: Sequential pattern mining with time intervals. In: Ng, W.-K., Kitsuregawa, M., Li, J., Chang, K. (eds.) PAKDD 2006. LNCS (LNAI), vol. 3918, Springer, Heidelberg (2006)
7. Mannila, H., Toivonen, H.: Discovery of generalized episodes using minimal occurrences. In: Proc. of the 2nd International Conference on Knowledge Discovery and Data Mining (KDD'96), August 1996, Portland, Oregon, pp. 146–151 (1996)
8. Mannila, H., Toivonen, H., Verkamo, A.: Discovery of frequent episodes in event sequences. Data Mining and Knowledge Discovery 1(3), 259–298 (1997)
9. Mannila, H., Toivonen, H., Verkamo, I.: Discovering frequent episodes in sequences. In: Proc. of the 1st International Conference on Knowledge Discovery and Data Mining (KDD'95), Montreal, Canada, August 1995, pp. 210–215. AAAI Press, Montreal (1995)
10. Meger, N., Leschi, C., Lucas, N., Rigotti, C.: Mining episode rules in STULONG dataset. In: Proc. of the ECML/PKDD Discovery Challenge, September 2004, Pisa, Italy (2004)
11. Meger, N., Rigotti, C.: Constraint-based mining of episode rules and optimal window sizes. In: Boulicaut, J.-F., Esposito, F., Giannotti, F., Pedreschi, D. (eds.) PKDD 2004. LNCS (LNAI), vol. 3202, pp. 313–324. Springer, Heidelberg (2004)
12. Vautier, A., Cordier, M.-O., Quiniou, R.: An inductive database for mining temporal patterns in event sequences. In: ECML/PKDD Workshop on Mining Spatial and Temporal Data (2005)
13. Yoshida, M., et al.: Mining sequential patterns including time intervals. In: Data Mining and Knowledge Discovery: Theory, Tools and Technology II. SPIE Conference (2000)
14. Zaki, M.: Spade: an efficient algorithm for mining frequent sequences. Machine Learning, Special issue on Unsupervised Learning 42(1/2), 31–60 (2001)

IQL: A Proposal for an Inductive Query Language

Siegfried Nijssen and Luc De Raedt

Institut für Informatik, Albert-Ludwigs-Universität,
Georges-Köhler-Allee, Gebäude 097, D-79110, Freiburg im Breisgau, Germany
Departement Computerwetenschappen, Katholieke Universiteit Leuven,
Celestijnenlaan 200A, B-3001, Leuven, Belgium
`siegfried.nijssen@cs.kuleuven.be`

Abstract. The overall goal of this paper is to devise a flexible and declarative query language for specifying or describing particular knowledge discovery scenarios. We introduce one such language, called IQL. IQL is intended as a general, descriptive, declarative, extendable and implementable language for inductive querying that supports the mining of both local and global patterns, reasoning about inductive queries and query processing using logic, as well as the flexible incorporation of new primitives and solvers. IQL is an extension of the tuple relational calculus that includes functions as primitives. The language integrates ideas from several other declarative programming languages, such as pattern matching and function typing. We hope that it will be useful as an overall specification language for integrating data mining systems and principles.

1 Introduction

The area of inductive databases [8], inductive query languages, and constraint-based mining [1] has promised a unifying theory and framework for reasoning about data mining principles and processes, which should also result in powerful inductive query languages for supporting complex data mining tasks and scenarios. The key idea is to treat patterns and models as first-class citizens that can be queried and manipulated. The slogan: "From the user point of view, there is no such thing as real discovery, just a matter of the expressive power of the available query language" has been advocated.

There has been a lot of progress in the past few years witnessed by the introduction of several inductive query languages, such as MINE RULE [12], MSQL [9], DMQL [7] and XMine [3]; Microsoft's Data Mining Extensions (DMX) of SQL Server [16]; the algebra of the 3W model [10]; the query language of the SINDBAD project [11]; the logic based query languages of MolFEA [13] and LDL-Mine [6], which all have contributed new insights: MINE RULE, MSQL, DMQL and XMine focus on the derivation of either frequent itemsets or association rules; notation wise, these languages are extensions of the industry standard SQL language. Microsoft's SQL server includes a larger set of algorithms, and

S. Džeroski and J. Struyf (Eds.): KDID 2006, LNCS 4747, pp. 189–207, 2007.

provides an interface for learning, clustering and applying a wider range of data mining algorithms, including association rules, decision trees and Bayesian networks; however, it does not provide a framework for reusing frequent itemsets, or for specifying additional constraints. Similar to Microsoft's SQL server, also SINDBAD provides an extension of SQL, in which data mining algorithms are included as functions that transform relations into relations, but only little attention is devoted to the use of constraints. The approach of Calders et al. [4], on the other hand, concentrates mainly on the specification of constraints. The algebra of the 3W model supports association rule discovery as well as learning rule based classifiers, but focuses more on postprocessing than on the specification of constraints. The language of MolFEA allows for the discovery of patterns under constraints, and is more abstract, but does not integrate classification or clustering algorithms. LDL-Mine is similar in spirit to our proposal, but takes Datalog as its starting point and is less focused on the representation of constraints. The data mining algebra and the Datalog++ foundations of LDL-Mine are sufficiently complete to represent data mining algorithms themselves. Relevant is finally also the study of Siebes [15] concerned with upgrading relational algebra operators, such as selection and projection, to data mining models.

Despite this plethora of languages, there is still no comprehensive theory of inductive querying or a unifying query language that is powerful yet simple. In this paper, we propose the inductive query language IQL, which addresses some of the limitations of existing approaches, and integrates many of the ideas that have been proposed in the aforementioned papers, such as the use of *data as a bridge* [11], the conception of domains as *virtual relations* [4], and the use of *logic* as a query language [13]. In contrast to earlier work, the overall goal of this research is to devise a flexible and declarative query language for specifying KDD scenarios.

We designed IQL with the following goals with in mind:

- to provoke discussion on inductive query languages;
- to encompass a rich variety of data mining tasks, including: local pattern mining over different domains, clustering, classification, regression as well as probabilistic modeling;
- to integrate models as first-class citizens of the database;
- to support reasoning about queries, their execution and their optimization;
- to integrate data mining primitives in a database language; as database language we employ an extension of the tuple relational calculus rather than SQL because this allows us to focus more on the principles of the language than on the syntax, but our ideas extend to many other languages;
- to design an extendable language, in which other researchers can describe and possibly implement their constraints, primitives and approaches; if this succeeds, IQL might become a unifying description or specification language for data mining;
- to design an implementable language, even though we wish to stress that –at this point– we are not concerned with the efficiency of the resulting system but rather with the underlying principles.

The final language that we have in mind is very general, and includes for instance existentially and universally quantified formulas. At this point it is an open question if this very general language is implementable. For restrictions that we will point out throughout the paper, we will show that it can indeed be implemented. IQL under these restrictions will be referred to as *simplified* IQL (sIQL).

The paper is organized as follows: Section 2 provides an intuitive introduction to our query language; Section 3 introduces IQL in more detail. We discuss how IQL can be implemented in Section 4. Within IQL we believe that certain primitives should be supported. These are provided in Section 5. We sketch what kind of reasoning is supported by IQL in Section 6. A scenario is described in Section 7. A brief investigation of the possibilities to integrate IQL in other query languages is provided in Section 8. Finally we conclude in Section 9.

Given that IQL is a query language, there are many similarities between IQL and other languages for writing programs or queries. We choose to point out these relations throughout the whole paper, instead of including an additional section for related work.

2 Some Example Queries

The best way to introduce the ingredients of a language, and hence also those of IQL, is by providing some examples. IQL is derived from and extends the query language we introduced earlier [13]. An example inspired on that language, but rewritten in IQL is:

create table R **as**
$$\{< pattern : S, \; freq1 : freq(S, D_1), \; freq2 : freq(S, D_2) > \; | \; S \in Sequence \; \wedge$$
$$S \preceq \text{``}C - H - 0 - n\text{''} \; \wedge \; freq(S, D_1) = 0 \; \wedge \; freq(S, D_2) \geq 1 \; \}.$$

This query generates a relation in which the tuples consist of sequential patterns and their frequency in datasets D_1 and D_2. Furthermore, all patterns must occur at least once in dataset D_2, must not occur in D_1 and must be more general than (i.e., a substring of) "$C - H - O - n$" . This query thus corresponds to a typical local pattern mining step. By convention, we write variables and relations with capitals.

As a second example, consider

create view R' **as** $\{ T + < target : apply(D, T) > \; |$
$$D \in DecisionTree[< A : integer, B : integer >, < C : string >] \; \wedge$$
$$C4.5(D, R) \wedge T \in R \; \}.$$

This query creates a view R', which extends the relation R with the attribute *target*. The value of *target* is the prediction made by a decision tree generated by C4.5 on the projection of R on the attributes A, B and C (as the class attribute). So, this query does not only generate a decision tree but also applies it to a data set, which corresponds – in part – to a cross-over operation.

These two examples illustrate the following key ingredients of IQL:

- queries are generating relations of the form { tuple | condition (tuple) };
- IQL is an extension of the relational tuple calculus;
- the result of a query is a relation, hence, the closure property is satisfied;
- the values of the tuples can be complex, e.g. sequences, functions, etc.; we also allow for operations such as "+" and "-" on tuples, which add, respectively remove attributes from tuples;
- the logical connectives $\land, \lor, \neg$ are permitted; (in sIQL, we do not allow $\lor$;)
- IQL is able to employ functions; for instance, $freq(P, D)$, which computes the frequency of the pattern P in the dataset D;
- IQL employs a typing system; for instance, the decision tree D maps tuples with attributes A and B onto their classes C;
- as in [4] a virtual relation represents a domain, for instance, $DecisionTree$;
- as in the language by [13], there are some built-in predicates such as $\preceq$, which denotes generality, and $freq(P, D)$;
- calls to specific algorithms, such as C4.5, can be integrated; this may be realized using pattern matching, cf. Section 5.

Let us now define these ingredients in a more formal manner.

3   Manipulation of Data

To manipulate data as well as pattern and functions, we shall employ an extension of the tuple relational calculus. The tuple relational calculus is a standard theoretical query language for relational databases [5,14]. By using the relational calculus, we keep the desirable closure property: the result of each query is a relation. Furthermore, the relational calculus is based on logic and is therefore declarative.

Essential in the relational model is that data is stored in relations, each of which consists of a set of tuples. A tuple is an expression of the form $< n_1 : v_1, \ldots, n_k : v_k >$ where n_i is an attribute, and v_i a value out of the domain D_i of the attribute n_i, e.g. the tuple $< a : 0, b : 1 >$. For reasons of convenience, we allow tuples to be joined or subtracted using the $+$ and $-$ symbols [1]. The schema of a tuple is denoted by $< n_1 : D_1, \ldots, n_k : D_k >$. For instance, in the above example, this is $< a : boolean, b : boolean >$. A relation is then a set of tuples over a particular schema, e.g. $R = \{ < a : 0, b : 1 >, < a : 1, b : 0 > \}$. We will also say that the type of a relation is $\{< n_1 : D_1, \ldots, n_k : D_k >\}$. In tuple relational calculus, variables range over tuples in relations.

The *syntax* of the tuple relational calculus is then defined as follows. A query is an expression of the form $\{T|q\}$, where T is a tuple and q is a formula.

---

[1] For simplicity we shall assume that no clashes occurs (as e.g. in $< temp : 5 > + < temp : 6 >$).

A *formula* is usually built from the traditional connectives $\wedge$, $\vee$ and $\neg$, and contains variables that can be quantified using the $\exists$ and $\forall$ quantifiers. In sIQL, we restrict ourselves to formulas without the $\forall$ quantifier and $\vee$ connective. The following atoms are allowed:

- atoms of the form $e_1 \theta e_2$, where $\theta \in \{\geq, \leq, >, <, =, \neq\}$ and e_i is a term. Constants, attributes a of tuples T (denoted by $T.a$) and tuples with one attribute can be used as terms;
- $T \in R$, where T is a tuple variable, and R is a relation.

From a data mining perspective, a dataset is conceived as a set of tuples, each of which contains information about an example. One crucial aspect of IQL is that we allow for arbitrary domains. For instance, we shall consider the domain of graphs, sequences, ... For such domains, there will typically be special built-in operators such as for instance the generality or covers relation $\preceq$ stressed by [13]. Similarly, we can conceive a pattern set as a set of tuples, each of which contains a pattern.

Even though we assume that the inductive database conceptually deals with domains such as graphs or sequences, this does not mean that we claim that an inductive database should be able to store such structures entirely in an attribute. For instance, an attribute in the graph domain could also be implemented as an identifier pointing to another relation storing the real graphs. At this point, we abstract from implementation details, such as how objects are incorporated or implemented, and essentially only assume that they can be manipulated and passed on using IQL calculus.

A crucial extension is that we allow for functions. To achieve this, we propose the use of a typing system which includes the following types:

- basic types;
  Examples: *integer, float, boolean*
- complex types;
  Examples: *decisionTree, itemset*
- a tuple type $<>$, which is taken on by every tuple. We can specialize this type; if $\tau_1, \ldots, \tau_n$ are types, and $\lambda_1, \ldots \lambda_n$ are identifiers,

$$< \lambda_1 : \tau_1, \ldots, \lambda_n : \tau_n >$$

specifies tuples that contain at least the given attributes; so, we constrain tuples to a certain *schema*;
  Examples: $< $ *pattern:itemset,support:integer* $ >$, $< $ *tree:decisiontree, acc : float* $ >$
- if τ is the type of a tuple, then

$$\{\tau\}$$

is the type of a relation of tuples of this type;
  Examples: $\{<>\}$, $\{< $ *pattern:itemset,support:integer* $ >\}$
- a schema type, which allows one to pass on a list of attribute identifiers to a function; so, the expression $< A : integer, B : integer >$ is of type *schema*.
  Example: *schema*

- if τ is a complex type and $\theta_1, \ldots, \theta_n$ are tuple types, then

$$\tau[\theta_1, \ldots, \theta_n]$$

  is a parameterized type; in contrast to functional programming languages, the parameter types are not intended to allow for generic programming; $\theta_1, \ldots, \theta_n$ are intended to associate to a model the schema of the data it was learned from, which could be used later on to constrain the applications of the model;
  Example: *decision Tree[< A:integer,B:integer >, < C:string >]*
  In this example, $<$ *A:integer,B:integer* $>$ is the set of attributes that are used to perform predictions by the decision tree, and $<$ *C:string* $>$ is the attribute that is predicted by the tree.

Using these types, we can now specify what the signature of a function is:

$$(\sigma_1, \ldots, \sigma_n) \rightarrow \theta,$$

where σ_i is an input parameter type and θ is a return value type. In addition to the $<>$ type, we will also allow variables in signatures, denoted by α, β, $\ldots$. These variables represent the type $<>$, but take on the schema of the tuple or relation that is passed to the function. The idea is that they can be used to express further constraints on the schemas of relations that are passed on to a function.

Examples

- *apply* : $(decisionTree[\alpha, \beta], \gamma) \rightarrow integer$ $(\alpha \subseteq \gamma)$
  This signature defines a function that applies a decision tree to a tuple in a relation. The variables α, β and γ in this signature, which are used in stead of the general $<>$ type, can be used to express additional constraints. In this case, it is required that the input attributes of the decision tree should occur in the relation to which it is applied.
- *join* : $(\{\alpha\}, \{\beta\}, schema[\gamma]) \rightarrow \{\alpha + \beta\}$ $(\gamma \subseteq \alpha, \gamma \subseteq \beta)$
  This signature defines a function that takes two relations as input, and a set of attribute identifiers that are common to both relations, and produces a relation in which tuples are joined on these common attributes. In this notation, γ takes on the tuple schema that is passed as parameter to the function.

As we allow for functions, we can also easily deal with predicates, by conceiving predicates as functions with boolean return type. Functions and predicates are incorporated in IQL by allowing expressions of the form $f(e_1, \ldots, e_n)$ where f is a function and the e_i are expressions with types that should satisfy the constraints specified in the signature of the function. These expressions can occur in atoms, as well as in tuples, as they denote particular values.

As illustrated by the *join* function, the inclusion of functions in IQL means that many common operations of the relational algebra can be implemented. IQL is however more powerful than the traditional relational algebra to which additional operators are added. A query which can be expressed in IQL is

$$\{D + T | D \in R \wedge T \in f(D)\},$$

for some relation R and function f that returns a relation. In this query, we iterate over one relation, and apply an operator on each tuple in the relation, resulting in a relation for that particular tuple.

The final elements of IQL are:

– in addition to types, we also allow for the definition of *type classes*, which are similar to those found, for instance, in the functional programming language Haskell. Concretely, a type class specifies a set of function headers in which the class is a parameter. A type can only be an instance of a class iff all these functions are implemented for the type.
Examples: For the class *classifier*, we can require that the function *apply* :
$(classifier[\alpha, \beta], \gamma) \rightarrow integer$
exists. The *classifier* type can be used for instance for relations containing multiple types of classifiers; still, we can apply the common operation *apply* to all of them.

– we introduce a *virtual relation* of schema $\{< element{:}\tau >\}$ for every complex type τ (similar to [4]). These relations are necessary to define the pattern type or model type of interest;
Example: $\{T | T \in Itemset \wedge freq(T, D) \geq 10\}$
Here, the schema of *Itemset* is $\{< element{:}itemset >\}$. Observe that we capitalize the first letter of the type name when used as a relation.

– we allow new relations to be created that contain the result of a query, and we allow for the definition of functions; views are special functions without arguments.
Examples
create function $f(id : Int)$ **as** $\{ t - < id > | t \in D \wedge t.id = id \}$
create table F **as** $\{ < pattern : S, id : V.id, freq : freq(S, f(V.id)) > |$
$\qquad\qquad V \in ID \wedge S \in Sequence \wedge freq(S, f(V.id)) \geq 10 \};$
Here ID and D are relations in the database.

4 Evaluation of Queries

Given that our language supports statements such as 'create table' that modify the state of the inductive database, our language can be considered imperative. Still, the queries themselves are more declarative in nature, and the question rises as to how we can evaluate them. An important property of our language is that it supports both declarative and procedural mechanisms for specifying queries. Assume that we have an algorithm for learning decision trees[2], then we can represent this using a function

$$dtLearner : (\{\alpha\}, schema[\beta], schema[\gamma]) \rightarrow \{< tree : decisionTree[\beta, \gamma] >\}$$
$$(\beta \subseteq \alpha, \gamma \subseteq \alpha);$$

the decision tree learner takes as input the relation for which a decision tree is to be learned, and furthermore, the identifiers of attributes that are used as inputs and class attribute, respectively. It produces a relation containing decision trees (in most cases, only one decision tree). This function can be used in a query such as

create table T **as** $dtLearner(R, < A : integer >, < B : string >)$

Alternatively, we could also define a function

$$isLearnedTree : (\{\alpha\}, decisionTree[\beta, \gamma]) \rightarrow boolean \qquad (\beta \subseteq \alpha, \gamma \subseteq \alpha),$$

which succeeds if a decision tree has been learned from certain data by an algorithm. This function can be used to allow for the query

create table T **as**
$$\{T | T \in DecisionTree[< A : integer >, < B : string >] \wedge isLearnedTree(D, T)\}.$$

The main idea behind the evaluation of our query language is to rewrite the declarative query into its procedural form, not unlike the way that relational calculus is rewritten in relational algebra. We can achieve this through the *pattern matching* principle that is common in many declarative programming languages, such as Prolog and Haskell, but clearly, the pattern matching system of IQL must be more powerful than the systems used in these languages. It is an open question as to how powerful the pattern matching system for (full) IQL should be, but to illustrate that evaluation by pattern matching is possible, we will show this for the simplified IQL in the remainder of this section.

In sIQL, we propose to drive the pattern matching system by declarations of the following form:

$$\{T_1 + \cdots + T_n | \phi\} \equiv f,$$

where ϕ is a conjunctive formula of the form $\phi = \{T_1 \in R_1 \wedge \ldots \wedge T_n \in R_n \wedge a_1 \wedge \ldots \wedge a_m\}$; $R_1, \ldots, R_n$ are relations and $a_1, \ldots, a_m$ are atoms; on the righthand side of the declaration a function call f is given. As an example, we can have the following declaration:

$$\{\underline{T} | \underline{T} \in decisionTree[\underline{B}, \underline{G}], isLearnedTree(\underline{D}, \underline{T})\} \equiv dtLearner(\underline{D}, \underline{B}, \underline{G}), \quad (1)$$

In this declaration, some variables are underlined. These variables are *substitutable*. A substitution for a pattern is a set $\theta = \{V_1/T'_1, \ldots, V_n/T'_n\}$; when the substitution

---

[2] For reasons of simplicity, we assume that this algorithm does not have additional parameters.

is applied to the pattern, all substitutable variables V_i are simultaneously replaced with corresponding new terms T_i' as defined in the substitution set θ.

The declarations are used to guide the rewriting of queries. If the formula ϕ of a pattern equals part of a query after a substitution, the matched atoms in the query are replaced with the righthand side of the declaration that matched.

For instance, for the query:

$$\{C|C \in decisionTree[< a : integer >, < b : integer >] \wedge$$
$$isLearnedTree(R, C) \wedge acc(C, R) \geq 10\},$$

we can apply substitution $\theta = \{T/C, B/ < a : integer >, G/ < b : integer >, D/R\}$ to the formula of Equation 1 to obtain a match.

The rewriting proceeds as follows. First, we compute the atoms that were not matched with the pattern, $q - \phi\theta$, to make sure that they reoccur in the rewritten query. Then, we add a new atom $(T \in f\theta)$ to this set of atoms, which ranges over the result of a function call as defined by the righthand side of the matched declaration (we abort the pattern matching if we detect a type mismatch). Finally, we have to make sure that all variables that ranged over relations that disappeared in the new query, range over the result of the function call. This can be achieved by applying a final substitution[3].

In our example, after applying substitution θ, we can rewrite the query into

$$\{T|T \in dtLearner(R, < a : integer >, < b : integer >) \wedge acc(T, R) \geq 10\}.$$

For a query that does not contain virtual relations, and for which all functions are implemented, we can use a straightforward evaluation method, similar to the evaluation of *list comprehensions* in programming languages such as Haskell or Python: first, the atoms are ordered. Then, for every atom $T \in R$ ('generator expressions'), if R is function call, it is evaluated; for every possible value in the resulting relation, the remainder of the atoms is evaluated. Other atoms ('guard expressions') are evaluated by performing the necessary function calls first, and testing the results of the function calls. The lefthand side of the query is evaluated for every combination of tuples that survives all guards.

5   Primitives and Extensions

In this section, we study a list of possible queries, and investigate how they can be represented in our language. In this discussion, we will point out whether the queries are already supported by the sIQL or if the full IQL is required.

Condensed representations. We have seen already that frequent pattern miners in general can be represented by introducing a type class *pattern*. Algorithms

---

[3] For reasons of simplicity, we assume there are no name clashes between the attributes of relations; we assume that the function that is called, returns a tuple that contains all attributes of the matched relations.

for mining using condensed representations, such as closed itemsets, can be represented by including functions

$$isClosed : (itemset, \{itemset\}) \rightarrow boolean,$$

which checks if an itemset is closed within a certain database, and

$$closedMiner : (\{itemset\}, integer) \rightarrow \{itemset\},$$

which returns the set of frequent closed itemsets for a given database and support threshold. These functions are used in the declaration

$$\{\underline{I}|\underline{I} \in Itemset, freq(\underline{I}, \underline{R}) \geq \underline{T}, isClosed(\underline{I}, \underline{R})\} \equiv closedMiner(\underline{R}, \underline{T}).$$

This procedure can be repeated for every kind of condensed representation and type of pattern. Observe that if the *isClosed* function is implemented separately, we have two different ways to evaluate a closed itemset mining query: one option is to call a closed itemset miner; another option is to call a frequent itemset miner, and to postprocess the results. It is a matter of optimization which of these two options is chosen.

A useful feature of IQL could be to introduce templates. It can then be specified that for a condensed representation, the above mentioned set of two functions types and one declaration should be provided.

Miners under multiple constraints. Some data mining algorithms are able to deal with conjunctions of constraints of arbitrary size, for instance, the MolFEA algorithm [13]. It is obvious that such algorithms are straightforwardly represented in IQL. Evaluation within the sIQL setting is however difficult, as every pattern in the pattern matching system has a fixed size. Both a more complicated pattern matching system and a more complicated typing system are required to pass variable numbers of constraints to an algorithm.

Top-k pattern miners. A recent branch of research involves that of mining top k patterns, where the top k patterns are determined according to some convex measure, such as the χ^2 test. One way that a user could specify such a query is

create view $V = \{< itemset : I, value : \chi^2(I, D) > |I \in Itemset\}$

$$\{I|I \in Itemset \wedge rank(I, V) \leq 10\}.$$

Here, χ^2 is a function with signature

$$\chi^2 : (itemset, \{< itemset : itemset, class : string >\}) \rightarrow float;$$

this function computes the correlation of an itemset in a dataset that contains at least an itemset attribute and a class attribute. The *rank* function has signature

$$rank : (itemset, \{< itemset : itemset, value : float >\}) \rightarrow integer$$

and returns the position of an itemset in a set of itemsets that is sorted according to associated floating point values.

The link between a top k pattern miner and a declarative query is formalized by the declaration

$$\{\underline{I}|\underline{I} \in \textit{Itemset}, \textit{rank}(\underline{I}, \underline{V}) \leq \underline{T}\} \equiv \textit{TopKChi2Miner}(\underline{D}, \underline{T})$$

under the constraint that $\underline{V}$ is a view of the form $\{< \textit{itemset} : \underline{I}, \textit{value} : \chi^2(\underline{I}, \underline{D}) > |\underline{I} \in \textit{Itemset}\}$.

A variation of this approach, which allows us to deal with a larger number of convex measures, is to replace the χ^2 function with a general function

$$\textit{applyconvex} : (\textit{measure}, \textit{itemset}, \{< \textit{itemset} : \textit{itemset}, \textit{class} : \textit{string} >\}) \rightarrow \textit{float}.$$

A benefit of using views, is that it is easy to incorporate additional constraints on top k patterns. For instance, if we are interested in the top k free itemsets, this can be expressed by modifying the view into

create view $V =$
$\quad \{< \textit{itemset} : I, \textit{value} : \chi^2(I, D) > |I \in \textit{Itemset} \wedge \textit{isFree}(I, D)\}$

As soon as the user introduces a minimum frequency constraint in the view,

create view $V =$
$\quad \{< \textit{itemset} : I, \textit{value} : \chi^2(I, D) > |I \in \textit{Itemset} \wedge \textit{freq}(I, D) \geq 10\},$

a different query evaluation plan can emerge in which the view is first materialized; the end result can be obtained by postprocessing the materialized view.

Classification algorithms. We have already seen how a decision tree can be integrated in IQL. It is easy deal to with further constraints on decision trees. For instance, if we define the function $size : \textit{decisiontree}[\alpha, \beta] \rightarrow \textit{integer}$, this function can be used in a declaration:

$$\{\underline{T}|\underline{T} \in \textit{DecisionTree}[\underline{B}, \underline{G}], \textit{isLearnedTree}(\underline{D}, \underline{T}), \textit{size}(\underline{T}) \leq \underline{M}\} \equiv$$
$$\textit{dtMaxLearner}(\underline{D}, \underline{B}, \underline{G}, \underline{M})\},$$

for an appropriate decision tree learner *dtMaxLearner*.

Observe that if we have two decision tree learners, this query may be evaluated in two ways:

– the specialized decision tree learner can be used;
– a general decision tree learner can be used, whose output is postprocessed.

In the second approach, the result of the query may be empty if by default a heuristic decision tree learner is used, and this algorithm finds a tree that is too large. It is an essential property of many data mining algorithms that their output is not defined otherwise than through the implementation of the algorithm itself, while in ordinary databases, the outcome of a query does not depend on the evaluation strategy (see, for instance, also [15] about this issue). If one believes that deterministic behavior is also desirable in inductive databases, there are several possible solutions:

- we can disallow predicates and declarations that could lead to alternative query execution plans for heuristic algorithms; for instance, in the case of decision trees, we could forbid the use of predicates such as *isLearnedTree* in favor of predicates such as *C4.5*;
- if multiple query evaluation plans exist within the database, we execute them all; the result of the query is the union of all executions.

Our query language also shows that for several kinds of queries on classification models currently no solvers exist, for instance:

create view $V = \{< model : T, value : accuracy(T, D), value2 : size(T) > |$
$$T \in DecisionTree[< A : integer, B : integer >] \wedge leafsup(T, D) \geq 2\}$$

$$\{T | T \in V \wedge rank(T, V) \leq 2\}.$$

This query asks for all decision trees for which the accuracy is maximal and ties are cut by taking the smallest possible tree. The search space is restricted to those trees in which each leaf contains at least two examples of the training data. Similar queries can also be posed for other types of models.

Probabilistic Models. In contrast to classifiers, probabilistic models do not output a single class, but a probability distribution over a set of target attributes. The type of the *apply* function is

$$apply : (probmodel[\alpha, \beta], \gamma) \rightarrow \{< string, float >\} \quad (\alpha \subseteq \gamma, \beta \subseteq \gamma >),$$

and reflects that for every example, a distribution over the class attributes is returned. The approach for learning probabilistic models is similar to that for classification models.

Clustering. Clustering algorithm do not target a specific class attribute, but rather try to find meaningful groups within the data, and can easily be integrated in IQL. For instance, assume that we have a k-means clustering algorithm that puts examples into multiple clusters and assigns a degree of membership for each cluster (for example, according to the distance to the cluster centre). Then the following declaration formalizes such an algorithm:

$$\{\underline{T} + \underline{L} + \underline{C} \mid \underline{C} \in KMeansClustering[\underline{X}],$$
$$isClustering(\underline{C}, \underline{R}), size(\underline{C}) = \underline{N}, \underline{T} \in \underline{R}, \underline{L} \in apply(\underline{C}, \underline{T})\} \equiv$$
$$kMeansLearner(\underline{T}, \underline{N}, \underline{X}),$$

where we assume the following function types:

$$isClustering : (kMeansClustering[\alpha], \{\beta\}) \rightarrow boolean \quad (\alpha \subseteq \beta)$$
$$size : (kMeansClustering[\alpha]) \rightarrow integer$$
$$apply : (kMeansClustering[\alpha], \beta) \rightarrow$$
$$\beta \cup < cluster : integer, membership : float > \quad (\alpha \subseteq \beta)$$

This query attaches to every example the clusters that it is part of, and the degree of this membership. Observe that in this pattern, learning and prediction are combined. For many clustering algorithms, it is difficult to separate these operations. However, if a clustering algorithm generates a model for assigning clusters to unseen examples, then it can be handled as a classifier or a probabilistic model.

Feature Construction. Once a set of local patterns has been mined, a common operation is to use the patterns for creating new features for a set of examples. For instance, for a frequent itemset $\{A, B\}$ in a relation R, one could add an attribute AB to R which is *true* for every tuple that contains $\{A, B\}$, and *false* otherwise.

To support this operation, we require that two types of functions are supported by the inductive database. First, a function

$$name : (type) \rightarrow string,$$

is required for every *type*, which assigns names to data mining objects. We leave it unspecified whether this name should be interpretable; important is that it if two objects are not equivalent, they should never be given the same name.

Then, a function

$$transpose : (\{\alpha\}, boolean) \rightarrow \{\alpha - \beta\} \quad (\beta =< name : string, value : boolean >, \beta \subseteq \alpha)$$

is required. This function groups all tuples in the input relation according to all attributes other than *name* and *value*, and creates a new relation in which new attributes are added for every *name*, of which the values are obtained from the *value* fields; if no value is available, the default value is used that is a parameter of the function. An example of the application of the *transpose* function is given below.

Id	Name	Value
1	A	*true*
1	B	*true*
2	A	*true*
2	B	*false*

$\Rightarrow$

Id	A	B
1	*true*	*true*
2	*true*	*false*

Only after a table is created using this function, and the query is finished, its schema is known.

To be able to create a binary value from a pattern, we assume that a function

$$covers : (pattern, pattern) \rightarrow boolean$$

is provided for patterns. Alternatively, the "$\subseteq$" symbol can be used in an infix notation.

6   Reasoning

IQL allows one to reason about queries, as [13]. For instance, consider the sequence:

create table R **as** { $< pattern : S, freq : freq(S, union(D_1, D_2)) > |$

$$S \in Sequence \wedge freq(S, union(D_1, D_2)) \geq 5 \};$$

create table R' **as** $\{< pattern : S, freq : freq(S, D_1) > |$

$$S \in Sequence \wedge freq(S, D_1) \geq 5\};$$

and assume that the queries are posed sequentially. If the inductive querying system has the following background knowledge,

$$D_1 \subseteq union(D_1, D_2)$$
$$D_2 \subseteq union(D_1, D_2)$$
$$D_1 \subseteq D_2 \implies \forall T : freq(T, D_1) \leq freq(T, D_2)$$

Then one can actually see that the answer to the first query is a superset of that of the second one. Therefore, rather than calling the frequent pattern miner again for the second query, one might simply go through the result of the first one to verify which patterns satisfy the second frequency constraint. Examples of this kind of reasoning, and a deeper discussion of these issues, is provided in [13]. Observe, however, that the frequencies of all frequent sequences have to be computed to finally answer the second query, as the frequencies in the second query may be smaller than in the first.

In IQL, this type of reasoning can be extended to constraints on other domains. For instance, a decision tree with minimum accuracy 0.9 on a dataset R is also a decision tree with minimum accuracy 0.8 on the same dataset.

Due to its close connection to relational calculus, there are similar optimization possibilities in IQL as in relational calculus. For instance, consider this query:

$$\{T+ < prediction : apply(C, T) > |$$
$$T \in R \wedge C \in DecisionTree[< A : Int >, < B : Int >] \wedge isLearnedTree(C, R)\};$$

to evaluate this query, the query optimizer should first construct the decision tree, and then apply it to all examples; it should not choose to construct the decision tree repeatedly for every example again.

We already pointed out that there can be multiple execution plans if multiple matching patterns and algorithms are provided. It is possible to perform query optimization by comparing execution plans.

7   Scenario

IQL should support the description of scenarios [2]. In this section we will demonstrate a typical scenario, in which a pattern miner is used to find frequent patterns, these frequent patterns are then used to create features, and finally a classification model is learned.

The first step in this scenario is easily described. Assume that we have a database of molecules *HIV*, and we are looking for subgraphs with a high support in *active* molecules, but a low support in the *inactive* molecules:

create function *hiv*(*d* : *string*) **as**
{ *T*− < *activity* > | *T* ∈ *HIV* ∧ *T.activity* = *d* }

create table *R* **as**
{ *S* | *S* ∈ *Graph* ∧ *freq*(*S*, *hiv*(*"active"*)) ≥ 10 ∧ *freq*(*S*, *hiv*(*"inactive"*)) ≤ 10 }

Next, we use the local patterns to create features.

create function *f*(*Data* : {< *id* : *integer*, *graph* : *graph*, *activity* : *string* >}) **as**
transpose(
{< *id* : *T.id*, *activity* : *T.activity*, *name* : *name*(*G*), *value* : *covers*(*G*, *T.graph*) > |
$$T \in Data \wedge G \in R\}, false)$$

create table *Features* **as** *f*(*HIV*)

The result of this query is a relation in which columns denote whether a graph contains a certain subgraph or not. We can build a decision tree for this relation.

create table *R′* **as**
{*D*|*D* ∈ *DecisionTree*[*schema*(*Features*)−< *id*, *activity* >, < *activity* : *boolean* >]
∧ *isLearnedTree*(*D*, *Features*)}.

Here, *schema* returns the schema of relation *Features*; the classifier should use the features in this relation, excluding the *id* and *activity* attributes. Finally, we can use this decision tree to predict the activity of molecules in a dataset *HIV′*.

create table *HIVPredictions* **as**
{*T′*+ < *pred* : *apply*(*D*, *T*) > |*T* ∈ *f*(*HIV′*) ∧ *D* ∈ *R′* ∧ *T′* ∈ *HIV′* ∧ *T.id* = *T′.id*}.

This query shows how using traditional data manipulation operations, we can associate the prediction of a molecule to its original representation, instead of its binary feature representation.

8   Extensions of Other Query Languages

In this paper we concentrated on an extension of the tuple relational calculus. The tuple relational calculus has the advantage that, when writing queries, we do not need to be concerned with the exact schema of relations. An open question is to what extent the principles of the IQL can be integrated in other query languages. In this section, we preliminarily investigate the issues that rise if we extend other query languages to obtain the same expressive power as the simplified version of the IQL.

Domain Relational Calculus. In domain relational calculus, the variables do not range over tuples in relations, but over values of attributes. Furthermore, it is common that attributes are identified by their position in tuples, and not by their names. Our example query for learning a decision tree would be formulated in domain relational calculus as follows:

create view R' **as** $\{\ < X_1, X_2, X_3, apply(D, < X_1, X_1, X_3 >) >\ |$
$$< D > \in DecisionTree[\{1, 2\}, \{3\}] \land$$
$$C4.5(< D >, R) \land < X_1, X_2, X_3 > \in R\ \}.$$

We do not expect many problems to extend sIQL towards domain relational calculus. More complications can be expected when additional quantifiers and negations are allowed.

Datalog and Prolog. Datalog differs from domain relational calculus in several aspects. First, notation wise, the infix predicate $\in$ is not used. Second, more importantly, queries can define new relations recursively. Datalog is therefore more expressive than either tuple or domain relational calculus.

Our most important extension of the tuple relational calculus consists of adding functions. One might therefore think that our query language is very similar to Prolog. Our functions play however a slightly different role than the functions in Prolog. The functions in our language act as predicates in Prolog, and transform input into output. Furthermore, our functions can take relations as input and produce new relations as output. The main point of our pattern matching mechanism is to rewrite queries such that they use functions that are implemented in an arbitrary language. In Prolog, this behavior can only be achieved through the use of meta-predicates (such as *call*) that can be used to emulate higher order logics. To illustrate this issue, consider the query which creates a new table through a function:

create function $f(id : Int)$ **as** $\{\ t - < id >\ |\ t \in D \land t.id = id\ \}$
create table F **as** $\{\ < pattern : S, id : V.id, freq : freq(S, f(V.id)) >\ |$
$$V \in ID \land S \in Sequence \land freq(S, f(V.id)) \geq 10\ \};$$

This function repeatedly creates a temporary relation that is passed to another predicate. A Prolog *freq* predicate would have to take a formula (query) as argument and materialize this formula in order to compute the frequency.

Overall, it is already feasible to integrate principles of sIQL in Datalog, but additional research is required to make this integration smoother.

Algebra. To give relational algebra the same expressive power as sIQL, we face similar problems as with Datalog. The most obvious way to integrate functions into the algebra, is to conceive functions as additional operators in the algebra; after all, we have already pointed out that queries expressed in relational algebra can be conceived as repeated applications of functions in sIQL. Still, we need additional formalisms to deal with functions that do not act on relations, or functions that are repeatedly applied to relations created by another function.

One way to address this problem is to add a *loop operator* ι to the relational algebra. Given a function $f(\sigma_1, \sigma_2, \ldots, \sigma_n)$, we can define that

operator $\iota_f(R_0, R_1, \ldots, R_n)$:
Let $< \lambda_1 : \tau_1, \ldots, \lambda_m : \tau_m >$ be the schema of R_0
$R' = \emptyset$
for each $T \in R_0$ **do**
  for $1 \leq i \leq n$ **do**
    select tuples from R_i such that $R_i.\lambda_1 = T.\lambda_1 \wedge \ldots \wedge R_i.\lambda_m = T.\lambda_m$,
      for those attributes of T that also occur in R_i
    project $\lambda_1, \ldots, \lambda_m$ away from the selected tuples
    store the resulting relation in x_i
  Let $x' = f(x_1, \ldots, x_n)$
  $R' = R' \cup (T \times x')$
return R'

The main idea behind this loop operator is that R_0 contains the values of an iterator, and the relations R_i $(i \geq 1)$ contain the parameters with which the function is called for each value of the iterator. For each value of the iterator a call is performed; the result is stored. If a relation R_i contains multiple rows for the same iterator value, a relation with multiple tuples is passed to the function.

Given the function f which selects tuples based on their class attribute, we can now formulate the following query:

$$\sigma_{freq \geq 10}(\iota_{freq}(Sequence \times ID, I(Sequence), \iota_f(ID, V))),$$

In this query $\iota_f(ID, V)$ creates a relation which for every identifier in ID, stores the selected part of the dataset V. Relation $I(Sequence)$ is the relation that associates every sequence with itself. Next ι_{freq} associates to every combination of a sequence and an identifier the corresponding frequency. Only those sequences with a frequency greater than 10 end up in the resulting relation. As this relation cannot be evaluated due to the infinity of $Sequence$, it would have to be rewritten into

$$\iota_{frequentSequenceMiner}(ID, 10, \iota_f(ID, V)).$$

How such rewriting can be achieved, and if there is an automatic way of rewriting sIQL in a well-specified relational algebera, is an open question which we will not address further in this paper.

9   Conclusions

We presented a relational calculus for data mining. A key ingredient was the inclusion of functions. This allowed us to integrate a large set of algorithms into IQL, including classification algorithms and clustering algorithms.

The inclusion of functions in the calculus has major other consequences. Common operators in relational algebra, such as *join* and *project*, can also be conceived as functions. We have seen that our language is more powerful than a relational algebra to which functions are added.

To evaluate queries, we proposed the use of *pattern matching*, which is common in many other declarative programming languages. We investigated how several common data mining operations can be expressed as queries in our calculus, and found that most algorithms can be integrated by making the pattern matching language more powerful. One could argue that the power of the declarative languages is determined by the power of its pattern matching language. We provided a concrete evaluation strategy for a simplified version of the IQL.

Even though IQL was presented in a rather informal way, we believe that IQL can already be used as a description language and interface to a wide variety of data mining algorithms and techniques in a uniform and theoretically appealing way. The authors would also like to herewith invite other groups interested in the development of inductive query languages to describe their favorite constraint based mining tools within IQL.

Acknowledgments. This work was supported by the EU FET IST project IQ ("Inductive Querying"), contract number FP6-516169. The authors would like to thank John Lloyd for interesting discussions, and visitors of the workshop for their comments.

References

1. Bonchi, F., Boulicaut, J.-F. (eds.) KDID 2005. LNCS, vol. 3933, Springer, Heidelberg (2006)
2. Boulicaut, J.-F., De Raedt, L., Mannila, H. (eds.): Constraint-Based Mining and Inductive Databases. LNCS (LNAI), vol. 3848. Springer, Heidelberg (2006)
3. Braga, D., Campi, A., Ceri, A., Lanzi, S., Klemetinen, M.: Mining association rules from XML data. In: Kambayashi, Y., Winiwarter, W., Arikawa, M. (eds.) DaWaK 2002. LNCS, vol. 2454, Springer, Heidelberg (2002)
4. Calders, T., Goethals, B., Prado, A.: Integrating pattern mining in relational databases. In: Fürnkranz, J., Scheffer, T., Spiliopoulou, M. (eds.) PKDD 2006. LNCS (LNAI), vol. 4213, Springer, Heidelberg (2006)
5. Date, C.J.: An introduction to database systems. Addison-Wesley, Reading (2000)
6. Giannotti, F., Manco, G., Turini, F.: Specifying mining algorithms with iterative user-defined aggregates. IEEE Transactions Knowledge and Data Engineering , 1232–1246 (2004)
7. Han, J., Fu, Y., Koperski, K., Wang, W., Zaiane, O.: DMQL: A data mining query language for relational databases. In: Proceedings of the ACM SIGMOD Workshop on research issues on data mining and knowledge discovery, ACM Press, New York (1996)
8. Imielinski, T., Mannila, H.: A database perspective on knowledge discovery. Communications of the ACM 39(11), 58–64 (1996)
9. Imielinski, T., Virmani, A.: MSQL: A query language for database mining. Data Mining and Knowledge Discovery 2(4), 373–408 (1999)
10. Johnson, T., Lakshmanan, L.V., Ng, R.: The 3w model and algebra for unified data mining. In: Proc. VLDB Int. Conf. Very Large Data Bases, pp. 21–32 (2000)

11. Kramer, S., Aufschild, V., Hapfelmeier, A., Jarasch, A., Kessler, K., Reckow, S., Wicker, J., Richter, L.: Inductive databases in the relational model: The data as the bridge. In: Bonchi, F., Boulicaut, J-F. (eds.) KDID 2005. LNCS, vol. 3933, pp. 124–138. Springer, Heidelberg (2006)
12. Meo, R., Psaila, G., Ceri, S.: An extension to SQL for mining association rules. Data Mining and Knowledge Discovery 2(2), 195–224 (1998)
13. De Raedt, L.: A perspective on inductive databases. SIGKDD Explorations 4(2), 69–77 (2003)
14. Ramakrishnan, R., Gehrke, J.: Database Management Systems. McGraw-Hill, New York (2004)
15. Siebes, A.: Data mining in inductive databases. In: Bonchi, F., Boulicaut, J-F. (eds.) KDID 2005. LNCS, vol. 3933, Springer, Heidelberg (2006)
16. Tang, Z., MacLennan, J.: Data Mining with SQL Server 2005. Wiley, Chichester (2005)

Mining Correct Properties in Incomplete Databases

François Rioult and Bruno Crémilleux

GREYC, CNRS - UMR 6072, Université de Caen
F-14032 Caen Cédex France
{Francois.Rioult,Bruno.Cremilleux}@info.unicaen.fr

Abstract. Missing values issue in databases is an important problem because missing values bias the information provided by the usual data mining methods. In this paper, we are searching for mining patterns satisfying correct properties in presence of missing values (it means that these patterns must satisfy the properties in the corresponding complete database). We focus on k-free patterns. Thanks to a new definition of this property suitable for incomplete data and compatible with the usual one, we certify that the extracted k-free patterns in an incomplete database also satisfy this property in the corresponding complete database. Moreover, this approach enables to provide an anti-monotone criterion with respect to the pattern inclusion and thus design an efficient level-wise algorithm which extracts correct k-free patterns in presence of missing values.

1 Introduction

Missing values in databases is a problem as old as the origin of these storage structures. It is an important issue because information extracted by usual data mining or statistics methods in incomplete data are biased and do not reflect the sound knowledge on the domain. We show in Section 3.1 the damages due to missing values in the pattern mining area. The popular uses of (frequent) patterns (e.g., rules, classification, clustering) are no longer reliable. The basic idea of elementary techniques to cope with missing values is to guess them (e.g., use of the mean, the most common value, default value) and complete them. Unfortunately, these techniques are not satisfactory because they exaggerate correlations [1] and missing values completion remains a hard track.

On the contrary, in this paper, we are searching for mining patterns satisfying properties in presence of missing values which are also satisfied in the corresponding complete database. Our key idea is to highlight properties from an incomplete database, these properties must be consistent in the real database without missing values. We say that these properties are *correct*. This can be achieved because some characteristics are not removed by missing values. For instance, if a pattern is frequent in a database with missing values, it must be frequent in the corresponding complete database. In Section 4.1, we propose

S. Džeroski and J. Struyf (Eds.): KDID 2006, LNCS 4747, pp. 208–222, 2007.

an operator to define the relation between an incomplete database and every possible completion.

In this paper, we focus on the property of k-freeness [2]. This property is at the core of frequent pattern mining, association rules building, and more generally *condensed representations* of frequent patterns [3] which enable multiple uses of frequent patterns. Our main contribution is to propose a new definition of the k-freeness property in incomplete data which is fully compatible with the usual one in a database without missing values. This new definition certifies that the extracted patterns satisfying this definition in an incomplete database are k-free in the corresponding complete database and, in fact, in every completion of the incomplete database. Moreover, this approach leads to an anti-monotone criterion with respect to the pattern inclusion and thus allows to design an efficient level-wise algorithm which extracts k-free patterns in presence of missing values. This work is a first step towards classification in incomplete databases with generalized associations and its application to missing values imputation.

The presentation is organized as follows: Section 2 gives the background about the k-freeness of patterns and the generalized association rules. Section 3 briefly shows the damages caused by the missing values and presents our position statement. We define in Section 4 the computation of k-free patterns in presence of missing values and demonstrate that these patterns are correct in the corresponding complete database. Experiments on benchmark data confirm the effectiveness of our method (Section 5).

2 k-Free Patterns and Generalized Association Rules

In this section, we introduce the k-free patterns and the generalized association rules which stem from these patterns.

2.1   Preliminaries

Let us consider a database which gathers *objects* depicted by quantitative or qualitative *attributes* in an *attribute/values* format (see Table 1). Eight objects are described by three attributes X_1, X_2 and X_3. In the field of boolean pattern mining, qualitative attributes need to be discretized in order to get boolean contexts (this article does not discuss this stage).

Let r be a database and $(\mathcal{A}, \mathcal{O}, R)$ a *boolean context* where $\mathcal{O}$ is the set of objects, $\mathcal{A}$ is the set of attributes and R is a binary relation. An object is a subset of $\mathcal{A}$ (for example, $o_1 = \{a_1, a_3, a_5\}$) and it will be denoted as a string (i.e., $a_1 a_3 a_5$). $|r|$ is the number of objects in r, *i.e.* $|r| = |\mathcal{O}|$. Table 2 indicates the boolean context where X_3 is coded by the attributes a_5 to a_7.

A *pattern* X is a subset of $\mathcal{A}$, its *support* is the set of objects containing X (we denote $supp(X) = r_X = \{o \in \mathcal{O} \mid X \subseteq o\}$) and its *frequency* $\mathcal{F}(X) = |supp(X)|$ is the number of objects in the support. A *classical* association rule [4] is an expression $X \rightarrow Y$, where X and Y are two patterns. It is quantified by its frequency (i.e., $\mathcal{F}(X \cup Y)$) and its confidence: $conf(X \rightarrow Y) = \mathcal{F}(X \cup Y)/\mathcal{F}(X)$.

Table 1. Attribute/value format database

objects	attributes		
	X_1	X_2	X_3
o_1	+	→	0.2
o_2	−	→	0
o_3	+	→	0.1
o_4	+	←	0.4
o_5	−	→	0.6
o_6	−	→	0.5
o_7	+	←	1
o_8	−	←	0.8

Table 2. Boolean context r

objects	attributes						
	a_1	a_2	a_3	a_4	a_5	a_6	a_7
o_1	×		×		×		
o_2		×	×		×		
o_3	×		×		×		
o_4	×			×		×	
o_5		×	×			×	
o_6		×	×			×	
o_7	×			×			×
o_8		×		×			×

2.2 Generalized Association Rules and k-Freeness

We start by recalling generalized patterns [2] because they are at the core of the generalized association rules. A *generalized pattern* is made of boolean attributes and negations of boolean attributes. For example, the generalized pattern $Z = a_1\overline{a_2}a_3$ can be written as the union of a *positive* part $X = a_1a_3$ and a *negative* one $\overline{Y}$ where $Y = a_2$. An object o supports $Z = X \cup \overline{Y}$ if $X \subseteq o$ and $Y \cap o = \emptyset$. To alleviate the notations, we omit the union sign in the following and write $X\overline{Y}$ instead of $X \cup \overline{Y}$. $\mathcal{F}(X\overline{Y})$ is central: if it is null, one element of Y is always present with X and ensures a generalized association between X et Y. These associations lead to the *generalized association rules* introduced in [2] which are a generalized form of association rules. The originality of these rules (also called *disjunctive rules*) is to conclude on a disjunction of attributes as indicated by Definition 1, which comes from [2].

Definition 1. *A generalized association rule based on $Z = X \cup Y$ is an expression $X \to \vee Y$ where X and Y are two classical patterns. It is exact in a database r if every object of r containing the premise X also contains one attribute of the conclusion Y. We denote $\models_r X \to \vee Y \iff \mathcal{F}(X\overline{Y}, r) = 0$.*

We define the frequency of a generalized association rule as follows (this definition diverges from that of the classical association rules).

Definition 2. *The frequency $\mathcal{F}(X \to \vee Y)$ of $X \to \vee Y$ is the number of objects containing X and at least one attribute of Y. We get $\mathcal{F}(X \to \vee Y) = \mathcal{F}(X) - \mathcal{F}(X\overline{Y})$.*

Let us move now to k-free patterns. They have been proposed[1] by Calders and Goethals [2], and they are very useful to compute the generalized association rules. A k-free pattern expresses the absence of correlation between its attributes:

Definition 3 (k-free pattern). *A pattern Z is k-free in a complete database r (without missing values) and we denote $kFree(Z, r)$ if it does not exist any*

---

[1] With $k = 2$, these patterns have been introduced by [5] with the term of *disjunction-free sets*.

generalized association rules based on Z in r, or: $\forall X \cup Y = Z$, $|Y| \leq k \Rightarrow$ $\mathcal{F}(X\overline{Y}) \neq 0$.

The k-free patterns have excellent properties to sum up the collections of frequent patterns. For example, in the `mushroom` dataset [6], there are $2.7 \cdot 10^9$ present patterns, but $426,134$ 1-free and $224,154$ 2-free patterns. With k higher than 5, the number of k-free patterns keeps under $214,530$, and they are mined in two minutes. Until now, k-free patterns have mostly been employed to compute condensed representations of frequent patterns [3] but they get meaningful properties to produce rules. In particular, 1-free patterns are used to compute the non redundant classical association rules [7,8]. The premise of such a rule is a 1-free X and its conclusion is the GALOIS closure $h(X)$.

2.3 Generalized Association Rules Mining

The exhibition of non redundant generalized association rules is more complex. We indicate two techniques. The first one mines the 1-free patterns and then computes their *generalized closure* [9]. It gathers all minimal patterns Y sharing one attribute with every object containing X, it is obtained by computing the minimal transversals [10] of these objects [9]. The second technique takes benefit from the anti-monotonicity of the k-freeness and the border theory of this property [11]. The rules are built from the minimal non k-free patterns, which constitute the *negative border of the k-free patterns*. Generalized association rules stem from non k-free patterns (such a rule $X \rightarrow \vee Z \backslash X$ is built from a non k-free pattern Z where X is the smallest subset of Z such that $\mathcal{F}(X\overline{Z\backslash X}) = 0$).

Generalized association rules convey correlations with a richer formalism than the classical ones. They enable new uses such as supervised classification [12] based on positive and negative rules [13] (i.e., rules concluding on an attribute or its negation). For example, the rule $a_1 \rightarrow a_4 \vee a_5$ is exact in the Table 2 data and leads to the positive rule $a_1\overline{a_4} \rightarrow a_5$ and the negative one $\overline{a_4a_5} \rightarrow \overline{a_1}$.

From the computation point of view, k-freeness is an anti-monotone property and these patterns can be efficiently mined thanks to the level-wise framework [11]. In order to check if a candidate pattern is k-free during the scan stage, the frequency of $X\overline{Y}$ is computed with the inclusion-exclusion principle [14], by using the frequencies of the subsets of XY: $\mathcal{F}(X\overline{Y}) = \sum_{\emptyset \subseteq J \subseteq Y}(-1)^{|J|}\mathcal{F}(XJ)$. As we have seen that in practice k remains low, the difficulty of computing the supports with the inclusion-exclusion principle is bearable.

3 Missing Values

We show here the damages due to the missing values and we give our position statement to solve this pattern mining problem.

3.1 Damages of Missing Values on k-Free Patterns

Assuming that some attributes of the dataset given in Table 1 are unknown, then missing values appear. We use the character '?' to denote that a value is neither

Table 3. Incomplete DB r'

objects	a_1	a_2	a_3	a_4	a_5	a_6	a_7
o_1	×		×			×	
o_2		×	×			×	
o_3	×		×		?	?	?
o_4	×			×		×	
o_5		×	×			×	
o_6	?	?	×			×	
o_7	×			×			×
o_8		×	?	?			×

Table 4. 1-free 2-frequent patterns and their closures

Complete DB r				Incomplete DB r'			
X	$h(X)$	X	$h(X)$	X	$h(X)$	X	$h(X)$
a_1		a_1a_3	a_5	a_1		a_1a_3	
a_2		a_1a_4		a_2		a_1a_5	
a_3		a_1a_5	a_3	a_3		a_2a_3	
a_4		a_2a_3		a_4	a_1	a_2a_5	a_3
a_5	a_3	a_2a_6	a_3	a_5	a_3	a_2a_6	a_3
a_6		a_3a_6	a_2	a_6		a_3a_6	
a_7	a_4			a_7		a_4a_7	

present nor absent for *every* boolean attribute coming from the corresponding attribute in the original database. We have introduced three missing values in our running example and the database r' resulting from this operation is indicated in Table 3.

The usual support computation for a pattern X in an incomplete database is realized as follows: an object belongs to the support of X if all of its attributes are present in X. If one of its attributes is missing or absent, the object does not belong to the support. How to compute the supports for generalized patterns in presence of missing values? Definition 3 does not plan this situation and the problem is particularly accurate for computing the frequency of $X\overline{Y}$. Without any recommendation, computations are performed by ignoring the missing values (i.e, they are not taken into account).

Table 4 depicts this problem. This table gives the 1-free patterns with a minimum support of two objects. The left part relates the results in the complete database, the right part in the incomplete one. For each pattern, the closure is indicated. The right part lists the 1-free patterns of r': a_1a_4 is 1-free in r and no longer in r'. Furthermore, the right part includes patterns, such as a_2a_5 and a_4a_7, which are not in r: we qualify them as *incorrect*.

Missing values lead to damages both on free patterns and their closures. Assuming that an attribute a belongs to X's closure in the complete database: it means that a is always present with X. If missing values appear on a, this association may break broken for some objects: a goes out from the closure (damage on the closure) and Xa can become free (damage on the free pattern). In our example, a_4 is in a_7's closure in r, while it goes out from this closure in r' because of the missing value in the object o_8. Thus, a_4a_7 is incorrectly declared 1-free.

Experiments on benchmarks from the UCI [6] emphasize these damages as well. Starting from a complete database, we artificially introduce missing values according to a uniform probability. Then we mine the 3-free patterns and measure the number of incorrect patterns relatively to the number of correct patterns in the original context (cf. Figure 1). The number of incorrect patterns differs according to the databases. It is less than 10% for the datasets pima, wine, liver-disorders, servo and tic-tac-toe (the corresponding chart is not reported). For the datasets given on the left part of the figure, the number of incorrect patterns is between 10 and 90% of the number of exact patterns. In the right part, this quantity rises 300%, which means that for four computed patterns, three are incorrect.

In real conditions where the complete database is not known, it is impossible to differentiate good and bad patterns, and to foresee if a small or a big proportion of incorrect patterns will appear. Our work aims at avoiding the damages by correctly computing the k-free patterns in incomplete contexts.

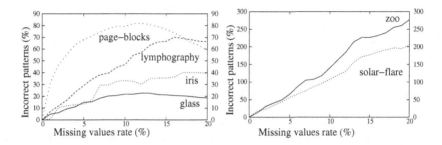

Fig. 1. Incorrect 3-free patterns in UCI datasets

3.2   Position of Our Work

There are several works which address the missing values issue in databases [15,16] but contributions in the field of data mining are few. Arnaud RAGEL [17] studied association rules mining in presence of missing values by redefining the support and the confidence, these rules may be used to a *completion* (or *imputation*) goal. We will clearly state the differences with our work in Section 4.3). More recently, [18] gives a basic completion method, founded on the probability of the different attributes. The support of a pattern for an object is no longer boolean but probabilistic. [19] computes prediction rules in the complete part of a database. These rules provide intervals for continuous attributes.

Our work stems from the following principles:

- we do not want to impute the missing values before the knowledge discovery stage, because it is a difficult operation without any specific knowledge.
- we wish to mine the whole incomplete database without reducing it to its complete part. It means that we do not want to remove objects or attributes.

We do not assume any statistical hypothesis about the probability model of the missing values. In order to deal with missing values, the next section defines a *modeling operator mv()*. We will see that this formalization is useful because it allows to define an incomplete database as the result of an operation removing some values from the complete database. Then computations performed in an incomplete database can characterize properties which are common to every corresponding complete database.

The following shows that it is possible to discover valid knowledge for the complete database under these hypothesizes. As stated in introduction, this principle is not surprising: if we consider that missing values hide the true values of the data, the frequencies of some patterns will only decrease (we do not know for some objects if they are present). A frequent pattern in an incomplete database only can be *a fortiori* frequent in the complete dataset. We will use the same principle to compute correct k-free patterns in presence of missing values.

4   Mining k-Free Patterns in Incomplete Databases

We propose here a definition of the k-freeness property in an incomplete database. We show that it enables to compute patterns ensuring the property of freeness in every completion.

4.1   Missing Values Modeling Operator

As previously explained, our position for the missing value problem requires a modeling operator. It defines the relation between an incomplete database and every possible completion.

Definition 4 (Missing values modeling operator). *Let $r = (\mathcal{A}, \mathcal{O}, R)$ be a boolean context. An operator $mv()$ is named a missing values modeling operator if it transforms a complete database r in $mv(r) = (\mathcal{A}, \mathcal{O}, mv(R))$. The new binary relation $mv(R)$ takes its values in $\{present, absent, missing\}$ and satisfies the following properties, for every attribute a in $\mathcal{A}$, every object o in $\mathcal{O}$, and value $\in \{present, absent\}$:*

1. *$mv(R)(a, o) = value \Rightarrow R(a, o) = value$;*
2. *$R(a, o) = value \Rightarrow mv(R)(a, o) \in \{value, absent\}$;*

Section 3.1 showed that computing the k-free patterns without precaution leads to incorrect patterns. In our work, we *correctly* define the computation of the k-freeness property:

Definition 5 (k-correct pattern). *Let r' be an incomplete database and $mv()$ a modeling operator for the missing values. A pattern Z is k-correct in r' if for every complete database r, $(mv(r) = r') \Rightarrow kFree(Z, r)$.*

4.2   Temporarily Deactivating Objects

We introduce here the *deactivation* of objects in an incomplete database. It differentiates on the one hand the objects which support or not a given pattern, and on the other hand the incomplete objects where the decision of support can not be taken. The deactivation enables to quantify the frequency gap between the complete and the incomplete database. In presence of missing values, the frequencies can indeed only decrease. In our example (Table 2), $\mathcal{F}(a_3a_5, r) = 3$

but $\mathcal{F}(a_3a_5, mv(r)) = 2$ (Table 3 with $r' = mv(r)$). In order to correctly compute the frequency of a pattern X in $mv(r)$, it is necessary to differentiate the objects of $mv(r)$ having a missing value among the attributes of X. These objects will be temporarily deactivated in order to compute an estimation of $supp(X, r)$ with the help of $supp(X, mv(r))$, because it is impossible to decide if they do contain X or not.

Definition 6 (Deactivated object). *For a classical pattern $X \subseteq \mathcal{A}$, an object $o \in \mathcal{O}$ is deactivated if $\forall a \in X, mv(R)(a, o) \neq absent$ and $\exists a \in X$ s.t. $mv(R)(a, o) = missing$. We denote $\mathcal{DES}(X, mv(r))$ for the objects of $mv(r)$ deactivated for X.*

Figure 2 exemplifies the notion of deactivation, by simultaneously presenting the complete database r (on the left) and the incomplete one $mv(r)$ (on the right). We suppose that each object of the top part contains X and this part is named r_X. The down part is named $r_{\overline{X}}$.

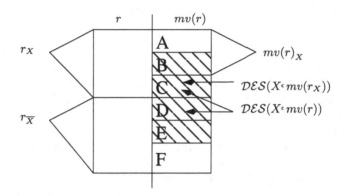

Fig. 2. Database $mv(r)$ and deactivated objects for X

On the right, the hatched zone shows the objects of $mv(r)$ which contain missing values. It is composed of six sets of objects, which are described below (their composition is indicated for our example of Table 3, with $X = a_2a_3$):

Region A: (o_2, o_5) the objects without missing value, containing X;
Region B: (no object in our example) the objects initially containing X, whose missing values do not obscure the presence of X. These objects belong to $mv(r)_X$;
Region C: (o_6) the objects initially containing X, whose missing values hide the presence of X and constitute $\mathcal{DES}(X, mv(r_X))$;
Region D: (o_8) the objects not containing X in the complete database, but which could contain it with a suitable imputation of the missing values. The object o_8 does not contain the pattern a_2a_3 in the complete database of our example, and it is preventively deactivated;

Region E: (o_3) the incomplete objects not containing X in the original dataset
     nor after any imputation of the missing values;
Region F: (o_1, o_4, o_7) the complete objects which do not contain X.

In the incomplete database $mv(r)$, each object is assigned in three different
groups for deciding the support of X:

Regions A and B: $mv(r)_X$ the objects supporting X, in spite of the missing
     values of B;
Regions C and D: $\mathcal{DES}(X, mv(r))$ the objects where the support of X is un-
     decidable;
Regions E and F: the objects not supporting X.

The deactivation allows to precisely characterize the support difference between the incomplete database and the complete one:

Proposition 1. *Let X be a classical pattern, r a database and mv a modeling
operator. $\mathcal{DES}(X, mv(r_X)) = r_X \setminus mv(r)_X$ and $|\mathcal{DES}(X, mv(r_X))| = \mathcal{F}(X, r) - \mathcal{F}(X, mv(r))$.*

Let us detail this principle for our example and the pattern a_2a_3: $r_{a_2a_3} = \{o_2, o_5, o_6\}$ and its frequency is 3. In the incomplete database, its frequency is 2
and $\mathcal{DES}(a_2a_3, mv(r_{a_2a_3})) = \{o_6\}$: we have the equality of Proposition 1. If the
complete dataset r is not known, r_X is neither known, nor $|\mathcal{DES}(X, mv(r_X))|$.
But the support can be bounded with considering the deactivated objects in
$mv(r)$ instead of $mv(r_X)$, because this database contains more objects than
$mv(r_X)$. In our example $\mathcal{DES}(a_2a_3, mv(r)) = \{o_6, o_8\}$ because of the confusion
induced in o_8 by the missing value on a_3 and a_4. $\mathcal{F}(a_2a_3, r)$ is then between
$\mathcal{F}(a_2a_3, mv(r))$ and $\mathcal{F}(a_2a_3, mv(r)) + |\mathcal{DES}(a_2a_3, mv(r))|$, i.e. between 2 and 4.

In the following, it is necessary to define the deactivation for the generalized
patterns. For that purpose, we use the inclusion-exclusion principle:

Definition 7 (Generalized deactivation)
$des(X\overline{Y}, mv(r_{X\overline{Y}})) = \sum_{\emptyset \subseteq J \subseteq Y} (-1)^{|J|} |\mathcal{DES}(XJ, mv(r_{XJ}))|$.

The set $\mathcal{DES}(X\overline{Y}, mv(r_{X\overline{Y}}))$ is not defined, so we denote the generalized deactivation with lower cases: $des(X\overline{Y}, mv(r_{X\overline{Y}}))$. It allows nevertheless to quantify
the frequency difference between the complete and the incomplete database.

Proposition 2. $des(X\overline{Y}, mv(r_{X\overline{Y}})) = \mathcal{F}(X\overline{Y}, r) - \mathcal{F}(X\overline{Y}, mv(r))$.

This frequency gap can be negative. When the association between X and Y
exists in the complete database ($\mathcal{F}(X\overline{Y}, r) = 0$), one missing value can delete
it in the incomplete one ($\mathcal{F}(X\overline{Y}, mv(r)) > 0$). In this case, the difference is
negative. In our example, $des(a_7\overline{a_4}) = 0 - 1 = -1$.

For the deactivated objects regarding an association $X \rightarrow \vee Y$, we define
$|\mathcal{DES}(X \rightarrow \vee Y, mv(r_{X \rightarrow \vee Y}))| = |\mathcal{DES}(X, mv(r_X))| - des(X\overline{Y}, mv(r_{X\overline{Y}}))$. We
then have a similar behavior as emphasized in Propositions 1 and 2:
$|\mathcal{DES}(X \rightarrow \vee Y, mv(r_{X \rightarrow \vee Y}))| = \mathcal{F}(X \rightarrow \vee Y, r) - \mathcal{F}(X \rightarrow \vee Y, mv(r))$.

Moreover, an object is deactivated for an association $X \rightarrow \vee Y$ if it is deactivated for X, or if it contains X but every attribute of Y is missing. Denoting $\mathcal{DES}(\wedge Y, mv(r_{X \rightarrow \vee Y})_X)$ for these objects, we have $|\mathcal{DES}(X \rightarrow \vee Y, mv(r_{X \rightarrow \vee Y}))| = |\mathcal{DES}(X, mv(r_{X \rightarrow \vee Y}))| + |\mathcal{DES}(\wedge Y, mv(r_{X \rightarrow \vee Y})_X)|$.

4.3   Differences with Ragel's Approach

In this section, we set our deactivation principle with respect to A. RAGEL's work [17,20]. To compute $\mathcal{F}(X, mv(r))$, A. RAGEL deactivates all objects containing a missing value in X without regarding whether an object may support X. In our example, o_6 would be deactivated for $a_2 a_4$ because a_2 is missing. Nevertheless, o_6 cannot support $a_2 a_4$ because o_6 does not contain a_4. It means that there is no complete database where o_6 can support $a_2 a_4$. This observation led M. KRYSZKIEWICZ to propose a new definition [21]. In our paper, we use this definition (cf. Definition 6).

4.4 k-Freeness Definition and Correction in Incomplete Databases

With the help of the deactivation of the incomplete objects, the frequency of $X\overline{Y}$ in r can be bounded by two quantities which are computed in $mv(r)$:

Property 1. $\mathcal{F}(X\overline{Y}, mv(r)) - |\mathcal{DES}(\wedge Y, (mv(r))_X)| \leq \mathcal{F}(X\overline{Y}, r) \leq \mathcal{F}(X\overline{Y}, mv(r)) + |\mathcal{DES}(X, mv(r))|$.

Proof. Proposition 2 says that $\mathcal{F}(X\overline{Y}, r) = \mathcal{F}(X\overline{Y}, mv(r)) + des(X\overline{Y}, mv(r_{X\overline{Y}}))$. The deactivation of an association allows to write $des(X\overline{Y}, mv(r_{X\overline{Y}})) = |\mathcal{DES}(X, mv(r_X))| - |\mathcal{DES}(X \rightarrow \vee Y, mv(r_{X \rightarrow \vee Y}))|$. On one hand, we have the upper bound $des(X\overline{Y}, mv(r_{X\overline{Y}})) \leq |\mathcal{DES}(X, mv(r_X))|$, and when avoiding the restriction on the deactivation database, $des(X\overline{Y}, mv(r_{X\overline{Y}})) \leq |\mathcal{DES}(X, mv(r))|$. On the other hand, we break up $des(X\overline{Y}, mv(r_{X\overline{Y}})) = |\mathcal{DES}(X, mv(r_X))| - (|\mathcal{DES}(X, mv(r_{X \rightarrow \vee Y}))| + |\mathcal{DES}(\wedge Y, mv(r_{X \rightarrow \vee Y})_X)|) = (|\mathcal{DES}(X, mv(r_X))| - |\mathcal{DES}(X, mv(r_{X \rightarrow \vee Y}))|) - |\mathcal{DES}(\wedge Y, mv(r_{X \rightarrow \vee Y})_X)|$. The difference $|\mathcal{DES}(X, mv(r_X))| - |\mathcal{DES}(X, mv(r_{X \rightarrow \vee Y}))|$ is positive so we have the lower bound $des(X\overline{Y}, mv(r_{X\overline{Y}})) \geq |\mathcal{DES}(\wedge Y, mv(r_{X \rightarrow \vee Y})_X)|$. Without the restriction on the deactivation database, $des(X\overline{Y}, mv(r_{X\overline{Y}})) \geq |\mathcal{DES}(\wedge Y, mv(r)_X)|$.

The k-freeness property can be defined in incomplete databases with the bounds for the frequency of $X\overline{Y}$.

Definition 8 (k-freeness in incomplete databases)

- *A pattern Z is k-free in $mv(r)$ and we denote $kFree(Z, mv(r))$ if and only if $\forall XY = Z$, $|Y| \leq k$, $\mathcal{F}(X\overline{Y}, mv(r)) - |\mathcal{DES}(\wedge Y, (mv(r))_X)| > 0$.*
- *A pattern Z is k-dependent in $mv(r)$ and we denote $kDepdt(Z, r)$ if and only if $\exists XY = Z$, $|Y| \leq k$, $\mathcal{F}(X\overline{Y}, mv(r)) + |\mathcal{DES}(X, mv(r))| = 0$.*

k-freeness and k-dependence are independently introduced. Section 4.5 will justify this distinction because these definitions are not reverse, due to the missing values.

Let us first note that, in a complete database, our definition of the k-freeness is *compatible* with the classical Definition 3. In this case, the set of deactivated objects is empty when there is no missing values. It is an important point in order to design algorithms which work indifferently on complete or incomplete contexts.

The k-freeness in an incomplete database is linked to this in a complete database with the important following theorem:

Theorem 1 (k-freeness correction). *Let r' be an incomplete database and $mv()$ a missing values modeling operator. For every complete database r such that $mv(r) = r'$ and every pattern Z,*
- $kFree(Z, r') \Longrightarrow kFree(Z, r)$;
- $kDepdt(Z, r') \Longrightarrow \neg kFree(Z, r)$.
The k-free patterns of r' are k-correct.

Proof. Property 1 shows that $\mathcal{F}(X\overline{Y}, r)$ is bounded by $\mathcal{F}(X\overline{Y}, r') - |\mathcal{DES}(\wedge Y, r'_X)|$ and $\mathcal{F}(X\overline{Y}, r') + |\mathcal{DES}(X, r')|$. If the lower bound is strictly positive, $\mathcal{F}(X\overline{Y}, r)$ is also strictly positive then non null and the pattern is k-free in r. If the upper bound is null, $\mathcal{F}(X\overline{Y}, r)$ is null and the pattern is not k-free in r.

Computed with Definition 8, the k-free patterns are then k-correct, i.e. they are k-free in every database completion. In [22,23], this correction is shown for the particular case when $k = 1$. These definitions of the k-freeness and the k-dependence allow to compute properties which are true in every completion: our definitions are **correct**. They are also *complete* because they characterize all k-free patterns in every completion:

Theorem 2 (k-freeness completeness). *Let r' be an incomplete database. If Z is k-free in every complete database r such that there exists a modeling operator $mv()$ with $mv(r) = r'$, then Z is k-free in r': the k-correct patterns of r' are k-free in r'.*

Proof. Suppose the converse, i.e. let Z be k-free in every database r such that $mv(r) = r'$ but non k-free in r'. $\exists XY = Z \mid \mathcal{F}(X\overline{Y}, r') - \mathcal{DES}(\wedge Y, r'_X) \leq 0$. Let r_0 be the database stemming from r' with replacing each missing value by an absent value, then $mv(r_0) = r'$. In r_0, the deactivation is null because r_0 is complete, and the computation of $\mathcal{F}(X\overline{Y}, r_0)$ gives the same result as in r' where it is done with the frequencies of the present attributes. $\mathcal{F}(X\overline{Y}, r_0)$ is then null and Z is not k-free is r_0 : contradiction.

In an incomplete database, every computed k-free pattern is k-correct and every pattern which is k-free in every completion of the database is covered by this definition.

4.5 Properties of the k-Freeness in Incomplete Databases

The k-freeness and the k-dependency are not complementary: some patterns will be neither k-free nor k-dependent because it is sometimes impossible to decide if they are present or not in an object. The table below details the computation of 1-freeness for the pattern a_4a_7:

X	Y	$\mathcal{F}(X\overline{Y}, mv(r))$	$|\mathcal{DES}(\wedge Y, mv(r)_X)|$	$|\mathcal{DES}(X, mv(r))|$	1-free?	1-dependent?
a_4	a_7	1	1	1	$1 - 1 \not> 0$: no	$1 + 1 \neq 0$: no
a_7	a_4	1	1	1	$1 - 1 \not> 0$: no	$1 + 1 \neq 0$: no

We now give a vital property for designing k-free patterns mining algorithms. It refers to the (anti)-monotonicity of the k-freeness or dependency. The k-freeness does not satisfy a property of (anti-)monotonicity, but Theorem 3 indicates that the k-dependency is monotone.

Theorem 3 (Monotonicity of the k-dependency property). *The k-dependency property is monotone, i.e. for all patterns Z and every database r', $Z \subseteq Z' \Rightarrow (kDepdt(Z, r')$ $\Rightarrow kDepdt(Z', r'))$.*

Proof. Let Z be a k-dependent pattern. $\exists XY = Z$, $\mathcal{F}(X\overline{Y}, mv(r)) + |\mathcal{DES}(X, mv(r))| = 0$ or $\mathcal{F}(X\overline{Y}, mv(r)) = 0$ and $|\mathcal{DES}(X, mv(r))| = 0$. $\mathcal{F}(X\overline{Y}, mv(r)) = 0$ means that for all object $o \in \mathcal{O}$, $X \subseteq o \Rightarrow Y \cap o \neq \emptyset$. A fortiori, $X \subseteq o \Rightarrow aY \cap o \neq \emptyset$ for all $a \in \mathcal{A}$, then $\mathcal{F}(X\overline{aY}, mv(r)) = 0$. By induction on all attributes of $Z' \backslash Z$, one deduces that Z' is also k-dependent.

With this result, the framework of the level-wise algorithms can be used with the negation of the k-dependency constraint, and we have written the MV-k-miner prototype.

4.6 Prototype MV-k-miner

We have designed the MV-k-miner prototype which returns the correct and complete collection of k-free patterns. It is based on the mining of k-dependent patterns. It runs on a two-step process: a classical level-wise scan of the search space (Algorithm 1) and the candidate process phase (Algorithm 2).

MV-k-miner stores $\mathcal{DES}(X, mv(r))$ and $\mathcal{DES}(\wedge Y, mv(r_X))$ for each pattern. This allows to compute two couples of bounds for $\mathcal{F}(X, mv(r))$ during the generation: the first couple is based on $\mathcal{DES}(X, mv(r))$ and stands for the k-dependency. The corresponding pruning criterion is only used during the generation phase, so these bounds are not stored. The second couple is related to $\mathcal{DES}(\wedge Y, mv(r_X))$ and stands for the k-freeness. It is used both during the generation phase and the scan phase, so these bounds are stored. The memory cost is finally higher than for a classical algorithm in complete databases, but the execution time is comparable. Our implementation should take benefit of recent development in k-free pattern mining [24].

5 Experiments on UCI Benchmarks

We show here the relevance of our missing values treatment by reproducing the experiments described in Section 3.1. We measure the number of 3-free

Data : an incomplete database $mv(r)$, a frequency minimum threshold γ, and
        $k > 0$ a rule depth
Result : the set $\mathcal{S}$ of the patterns satisfying $kFree$
$\mathcal{D}_l$ is the set of patterns of length l, k-dependent or non frequent ;
$l = 1$; initialize $Cand_1$ with the singletons ;
repeat
    /*compute the disqualifiers */
    $\mathcal{D}_l = \{X \in Cand_l \; s.t. \; kDepdt(X, mv(r)) \vee \neg frequent(X, mv(r))\}$;
    /*discard disqualiers */
    $\mathcal{S}_l = \{X \in Cand_l \backslash \mathcal{D}_l \mid kFree(X, mv(r))\}$;
    generate the candidates in $Cand_{l+1}$ (cf. algorithm 2);
    $l = l + 1$;
until $Cand_l = \emptyset$;
return $\mathcal{S} = \bigcup_l \mathcal{S}_l$;

Algorithm 1. MV-k-miner: k-free patterns miner in incomplete databases

Data : a set $\mathcal{S}_l$ of k-free patterns with length l
Result : the set $Cand_{l+1}$ of the pattern candidate to $kDepdt$
for *every candidate Z, generated by two patterns in $\mathcal{S}_l$ sharing the same*
$l - 1$-*prefix* **do**
    begin
        verify that all the $Z' \subsetneq Z$ of length $|Z| - 1$ are k-free ;
        /*compute the frequency bounds */
        build the tree of the patterns X and their frequencies such that $|Z \backslash X| \leq k$;
        for every X in the tree, compute the alternated sum of the frequency of its
        subsets, that constitutes a preliminary version of
        $\sigma(X, Y) = \sum_{\emptyset \subseteq J \subsetneq Y} (-1)^{|J|} \mathcal{F}(XJ)$ for bounding $\mathcal{F}(Z)$;
        compute $\sigma(X, \overline{Y}) - |\mathcal{DES}(\wedge Y, mv(r_X))|$ and $\sigma(X, Y) + |\mathcal{DES}(X, mv(r))|$;
        store the bound $\sigma(X, Y) + |\mathcal{DES}(X, mv(r))|$ pour $\mathcal{F}(Z)$;
        if the bounds are equal, decline the candidate ;
    end
end

Algorithm 2. $l + 1$-candidate generation

patterns computed with MV-k-miner in $mv(r)$, compared to r. The results for
solar-flare and zoo are reported in Figure 3. In the other datasets, the same
trends appear. For each dataset, the running time of the whole experience is
about 10 seconds.

As expected, the number of patterns recovered by our method decreases according to the number of missing values. Indeed, each pattern is k-correct or
k-free in every complete dataset, whose number is exponential in the number of
missing values. But MV-k-miner computes only k-correct patterns. While data
mining is known to produce a huge number of patterns, their correctness is essential. Missing values damages are then avoided and this result opens the way
for the uses of k-free patterns mentioned in Section 2.3. In particular, the future of this work has to address the interestingness of the correct k-free patterns

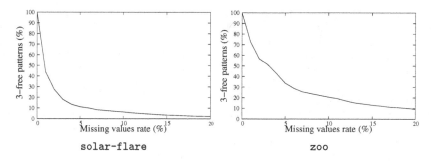

Fig. 3. Proportion of 3-free patterns in $mv(r)$ (r gives 100 %)

during a supervised classification process, according to the approach based on minimal k-free patterns, as outlined in Section 2.3.

6 Conclusion

Without any suitable treatment, missing values in incomplete databases lead the k-free pattern mining algorithms to produce incorrect patterns. With the help of a modeling operator, we have introduced the notion of k-correct patterns in an incomplete database. These patterns are k-free in every corresponding complete database. We have then proposed a new definition for the k-free property in an incomplete database. Thanks to this new definition, the mined patterns are k-correct, and all k-correct patterns are mined: this avoids damages due to missing values.

Our perspectives address now the classification with generalized associations and its application to missing values imputation. The first step of this project consists in studying how to compute generalized closures in incomplete databases.

References

1. Grzymala-Busse, J., Hu, M.: A comparison of several approaches to missing attribute values in data mining. In: Ziarko, W., Yao, Y. (eds.) RSCTC 2000. LNCS (LNAI), vol. 2005, pp. 378–385. Springer, Heidelberg (2001)
2. Calders, T., Goethals, B.: Minimal k-free representations of frequent sets. In: Lavrač, N., Gamberger, D., Todorovski, L., Blockeel, H. (eds.) PKDD 2003. LNCS (LNAI), vol. 2838, pp. 71–82. Springer, Heidelberg (2003)
3. Calders, T., Goethals, B.: Mining all non-derivable frequent itemsets. In: Elomaa, T., Mannila, H., Toivonen, H. (eds.) PKDD 2002. LNCS (LNAI), vol. 2431, Springer, Heidelberg (2002)
4. Agrawal, R., Srikant, R.: Fast algorithms for mining association rules. In: Intl. Conference on Very Large Data Bases (VLDB'94), Santiago de Chile, Chile, pp. 487–499 (1994)
5. Bykowski, A., Rigotti, C.: A condensed representation to find frequent patterns. In: ACM SIGMOD-SIGACT-SIGART symposium on Principles of database systems, Santa Barbara, USA, pp. 267–273. ACM Press, New York (2001)

6. Blake, C., Merz, C.: UCI repository of machine learning databases (1998)
7. Bastide, Y., Taouil, R., Pasquier, N., Stumme, G., Lakhal, L.: Mining minimal non-redundant association rules using frequent closed itemsets. In: International Conference on Deductive and Object Databases (DOOD'00), pp. 972–986 (2000)
8. Zaki, M.: Generating non-redundant association rules. In: ACM SIGKDD international conference on Knowledge discovery and data mining, Boston, USA, pp. 34–43. ACM Press, New York (2000)
9. Rioult, F.: Extraction de connaissances dans les bases de données comportant des valeurs manquantes ou un grand nombre d'attributs. PhD thesis, Université de Caen Basse-Normandie, France (2005)
10. Gunopulos, D., Mannila, H., Khardon, R., Toivonen, H.: Data mining, hypergraph transversals, and machine learning. In: ACM SIGACT-SIGMOD-SIGART Symposium on Principles of Database Systems (PODS'97), Tucson, USA, ACM Press, New York (1997)
11. Mannila, H., Toivonen, H.: Levelwise search and borders of theories in knowledge discovery. Data Mining and Knowledge Discovery 1(3), 241–258 (1997)
12. Antonie, M.L., Zaïane, O.: An associative classifier based on positive and negative rules. In: ACM SIGMOD Workshop on Research Issues in Data Mining and Knowledge Discovery (DMKD'04), Paris, France, ACM Press, New York (2004)
13. Antonie, M.L., Zaïane, O.: Mining positive and negative association rules: An approach for confined rules. In: Boulicaut, J.-F., Esposito, F., Giannotti, F., Pedreschi, D. (eds.) PKDD 2004. LNCS (LNAI), vol. 3202, pp. 27–38. Springer, Heidelberg (2004)
14. Jaroszewicz, S., Simovici, D.: Support approximations using bonferroni-type inequalities. In: Elomaa, T., Mannila, H., Toivonen, H. (eds.) PKDD 2002. LNCS (LNAI), vol. 2431, pp. 212–224. Springer, Heidelberg (2002)
15. Dyreson, C.E.: A Bibliography on Uncertainty Management in Information Systems. In: Uncertainty Management in Information Systems, Kluwer Academic Publishers, Dordrecht (1997)
16. Levene, M., Loizou, G.: Database design for incomplete relations. ACM Transactions on Database Systems 24(1), 80–126 (1999)
17. Ragel, A., Crémilleux, B.: Mvc - a preprocessing method to deal with missing values. Knowledge-Based Systems 12(5-6), 285–291 (1999)
18. Nayak, J., Cook, D.: Approximate association rule mining. In: Florida Artificial Intelligence Research Symposium, Key West, Florida, USA, pp. 259–263 (2001)
19. Jami, S., Jen, T., Laurent, D., Loizou, G., Sy, O.: Extraction de régles d'association pour la prédiction de valeurs manquantes. In: Colloque Africain sur la Recherche en Informatique (CARI) (2004)
20. Ragel, A., Crémilleux, B.: Treatment of missing values for association rules. In: Wu, X., Kotagiri, R., Korb, K.B. (eds.) PAKDD 1998. LNCS, vol. 1394, pp. 258–270. Springer, Heidelberg (1998)
21. Kryszkiewicz., M.: Association rules in incomplete databases. In: Zhong, N., Zhou, L. (eds.) Methodologies for Knowledge Discovery and Data Mining. LNCS (LNAI), vol. 1574, pp. 84–93. Springer, Heidelberg (1999)
22. Rioult, F., Crémilleux, B.: Condensed representations in presence of missing values. In: Berthold, M.R., Lenz, H-J., Bradley, E., Kruse, R., Borgelt, C. (eds.) IDA 2003. LNCS, vol. 2810, pp. 578–588. Springer, Heidelberg (2003)
23. Rioult, F., Crémilleux, B.: Représentation condensée en présence de valeurs manquantes. In: XXIIé congrés Inforsid, Biarritz, France, pp. 301–317 (2004)
24. Calders, T., Goethals, B.: Quick inclusion-exclusion. In: Bonchi, F., Boulicaut, J.-F. (eds.) KDID 2005. LNCS, vol. 3933, Springer, Heidelberg (2006)

Efficient Mining Under Rich Constraints Derived from Various Datasets

Arnaud Soulet[1], Jiří Kléma[1,2], and Bruno Crémilleux[1]

[1] GREYC, Université de Caen
Campus Côte de Nacre
F-14032 Caen Cédex France
{Forename.Surname}@info.unicaen.fr
[2] Department of Cybernetics
Czech Technical University, Prague
klema@labe.felk.cvut.cz

Abstract. Mining patterns under many kinds of constraints is a key point to successfully get new knowledge. In this paper, we propose an efficient new algorithm MUSIC-DFS which soundly and completely mines patterns with various constraints from large data and takes into account external data represented by several heterogeneous datasets. Constraints are freely built of a large set of primitives and enable to link the information scattered in various knowledge sources. Efficiency is achieved thanks to a new closure operator providing an interval pruning strategy applied during the depth-first search of a pattern space. A transcriptomic case study shows the effectiveness and scalability of our approach. It also demonstrates a way to employ background knowledge, such as free texts or gene ontologies, in the discovery of meaningful patterns.

Keywords: constraint-based mining, transcriptomic data.

1 Introduction

In current scientific, industrial or business data mining applications, the critical need is not to generate data, but to derive knowledge from huge and heterogeneous datasets produced at high throughput. In order to explore and discover new highly valuable knowledge it is necessary to develop environments and tools able to put all this data together. This involves different challenges, like designing efficient tools to tackle a large amount of data and the discovery of patterns of a potential user's interest through several datasets. There are various ways to interconnect the heterogeneous data sources and to express the mutual relations among the entities they address. Constraints provide a focus on the most promising knowledge by reducing the number of extracted patterns to those of a potential interest given by the user. Furthermore, when constraints can be pushed deep inside the mining algorithm, performance is improved, making the mining task computationally feasible and resulting in a human-workable output.

This paper addresses the issue of efficient pattern mining from large binary data under flexible constraints derived from additional heterogeneous datasets

S. Džeroski and J. Struyf (Eds.): KDID 2006, LNCS 4747, pp. 223–239, 2007.

synthetizing background knowledge (BK). Large datasets are characterized mainly by a large number of columns (i.e., items). This characteristic often encountered in a lot of domains (e.g., bioinformatics, text mining) represents a remarkable challenge. Usual algorithms show difficulties in running on this kind of data due to the exponential search space growth with the number of items. Known level-wise algorithms commonly fail in mining frequent or constrained patterns in such data [17]. On top of that, the user often would like to integrate BK in the mining process in order to focus on the most plausible patterns consistent with pieces of existing knowledge. BK is available in relational and literature databases, ontological trees and other sources. Nevertheless, mining in a heterogeneous environment allowing a large set of descriptions at various levels of detail is highly non-trivial. This paper solves the problem by pushing user-defined constraints that may stem both from the mined binary data and the BK summarized in similarity matrices or textual files.

The contribution of this paper is twofold. First we provide a new algorithm MUSIC-DFS which soundly and completely mines constrained patterns from large data while taking into account external data (i.e., several heterogeneous datasets). Except for specific constraints for which tricks like the transposition of data [14, 9] or the use of the extension [8] can be used, levelwise approaches cannot tackle large data due to the huge number of candidates. On the contrary, MUSIC-DFS is based on a depth first search strategy. The key idea is to use a new closure operator enabling an efficient interval pruning for various constraints (see Section 3). In [5], the authors also benefit from intervals to prune the search space, but their approach is restricted to the conjunction of one monotone constraint and one anti-monotone constraint. The output of MUSIC-DFS is an interval condensed representation: each pattern satisfying the given constraint appears once in the collection of intervals only. Second, we provide a generic framework to mine patterns with a large set of constraints based on several heterogeneous datasets like texts or similarity matrices. It is a way to take into account the BK. Section 4 depicts a transcriptomic case study. The biological demands require to mine the expression data with constraints concerning complex relations represented by free texts and gene ontologies. The discovered patterns are likely to encompass interesting and interpretable knowledge.

This paper differs from our work in [20] for a double reason. First, the framework is extended to external data. Second, MUSIC-DFS is deeply different from the prototype used in [20]: MUSIC-DFS integrates primitives to tackle external data and thanks to its strategy to prune the search space (new interval pruning based on prefix-free patterns, see Section 3), it is able to mine large data. Section 4 demonstrates the practical effectiveness of MUSIC-DFS in a transcriptomic case study and shows that other prototypes (including the prototype presented in [20]) fail. To the best of our knowledge, there is no other constraint-based tool to efficiently discover patterns from large data under a broad set of constraints linking the information distributed in various knowledge sources.

This paper is organized as follows. Section 2 introduces our framework to mine patterns satisfying constraints defined over several kinds of datasets. In Section 3, we present the theoretical essentials that underlie the efficiency of MUSIC-DFS and we provide its main features. Experiments showing the efficiency of MUSIC-DFS and the cross-fertilization between several sources of genomic information are given in Section 4.

2 Defining Constraints on Several Datasets

2.1 Integrating Background Knowledge Within Constraints

Usual data-mining tasks rarely deal with a single dataset. Often it is necessary to connect knowledge scattered in several heterogeneous sources. In constraint-based mining, the constraints should effectively link different datasets and knowledge types. In the domain of genomics, there is a natural need to derive constraints both from expression data and descriptions of the genes and/or biological situations under consideration. Such constraints require to tackle various data types - transcriptome data and background knowledge may be stored in the boolean, numeric, symbolic or textual format.

Let us consider the transcriptomic mining context given in Figure 1. Firstly, the involved data include a transcriptome dataset also called internal data. The dataset is in the transactional format - the items correspond to genes and the transactions represent biological situations. The occurrence of an item in a transaction signifies over-expression of the corresponding gene in the corresponding biological situation (genes A, E and F are over-expressed in situation s_1). Secondly, external data – a similarity matrix and textual resources – are considered. They summarize background knowledge that contains various information on items (i.e., genes). This knowledge is transformed into a similarity matrix and a set of texts. Each field of the triangular matrix $s_{ij} \in [0,1]$ gives a similarity measure between the items i and j. The textual dataset provides a description of genes. Each row of this dataset contains a list of phrases characterizing the given gene (details are given in Section 4.1). The mined patterns are composed of items of the internal data, the corresponding transactions are usually also noted (and possibly analyzed). The external data are used to further specify constraints in order to focus on meaningful patterns. In other words, the constraints may stem from all the datasets.

Table 1 provides the meaning of the primitive constraints applied in this text. The meaning of the primitives is also illustrated by their real values taken from the example in Figure 1. As primitives can address different datasets, the dataset makes another parameter of the primitive (for clarity not shown in Table 1).

A real example of the compound constraint $q(X)$ is given in Figure 1. The first part (a) of q addresses the internal data and means that the biologist is interested in patterns having a satisfactory size – a *minimal area*. Indeed, $area(X) = freq(X) \times length(X)$ is the product of the frequency of X and its length and means that the pattern must cover a minimum number of situations and contain a minimum number of genes. The other parts deal with the external data: (b) is used to discard ribosomal patterns (one gene exception per pattern is allowed), (c) avoids

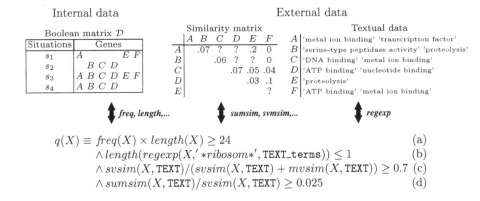

$$q(X) \equiv freq(X) \times length(X) \geq 24 \tag{a}$$
$$\wedge \, length(regexp(X,' *ribosom*', \texttt{TEXT\_terms})) \leq 1 \tag{b}$$
$$\wedge \, svsim(X, \texttt{TEXT})/(svsim(X, \texttt{TEXT}) + mvsim(X, \texttt{TEXT})) \geq 0.7 \tag{c}$$
$$\wedge \, sumsim(X, \texttt{TEXT})/svsim(X, \texttt{TEXT}) \geq 0.025 \tag{d}$$

Fig. 1. Example of a toy (transcriptomic) mining context and a constraint

Table 1. Examples of primitives and their values in the data mining context of Figure 1. Let us note that item pairs of the pattern ABC are (A, B), (A, C) and (B, C).

Primitives		Values
Boolean matrix		
$freq(X)$	frequency of X	$freq(ABC) = 2$
$length(X)$	length of X	$length(ABC) = 3$
Textual data		
$regexp(X, RE)$	items of X whose associated phrases match the regular expression RE	$regexp(ABC,' * ion *')$ $= AC$
Similarity matrix		
$sumsim(X)$	the similarity sum over the set of item pairs of X	$sumsim(ABC) = 0.13$
$svsim(X)$	the number of item pairs in X for which a similarity value is recorded	$svsim(ABC) = 2$
$mvsim(X)$	the number of item pairs in X for which a similarity value is missing	$mvsim(ABC) = 1$
$insim(X, min, max)$	the number of item pairs of X whose similarity lies between min and max	$insim(ABC, 0.07, 1) =$ 1

patterns with prevailing items of an unknown function and (d) is to ensure a minimal average gene similarity. Section 4 provides another constraint q'.

Let us generalize the previous informal description. Let $\mathcal{I}$ be a set of items. A pattern is a non-empty subset of $\mathcal{I}$. $\mathcal{D}$ is a transactional dataset (or boolean matrix) composed of rows usually called transactions. A pattern X is present in $\mathcal{D}$ whenever it is included in one transaction of $\mathcal{D}$ at least. The constraint-based mining task aims to discover all the patterns present in $\mathcal{D}$ and satisfying a constraint q. Unfortunately, real constraints adressing several datasets (the constraint q, for example) are difficult to mine because they have no suitable property as monotonicity [12] or convertibility [16].

2.2   Primitive-Based Constraints

This section presents our framework previously defined in [20] (and the declarative language) enabling the user to set compound and meaningful constraints. This framework naturally integrates primitives adressing external data (e.g., *sumsim* or *regexp*). Furthermore, in our framework constraints are freely built of a large set of primitives. Beyond the primitives mentioned earlier there are primitives such as $\{\wedge, \vee, \neg, <, \leq, \subset, \subseteq, +, -, \times, /, sum, max, min, \cup, \cap, \setminus\}$. The compound constraints of this framework are called *primitive-based constraints*. There are no formal properties required on the final constraints. The only property which is required on the primitives to belong to our framework is a property of monotonicity according to each variable of a primitive (when the others remain constant) [20]. We have already shown that the whole set of primitive-based constraints constitutes a super-class of monotone, anti-monotone, succinct and convertible constraints [19]. Consequently, the proposed framework provides a flexible and rich constraint (query) language. The user can iteratively develop complex constraints integrating various knowledge types.

Let us recall that the primitives and the constraints defined in [20] only address one boolean data set. Current constraints can consider properties taken from a wide scale of dataset types. In addition to the similarity and textual datasets, the framework also enables to access numerical datasets having items in rows and numerical attributes in columns. It implements the primitive X.val which gives the list of values of the attribute named *val* for the items contained in the pattern X.

We give below other examples of constraints belonging to primitive-based constraints and highlighting the generality of our framework:

$$\begin{cases} freq(X) \times length(X) \geq 6 & \text{minimal area (nothing)} \\ (min(X.val) + max(X.val))/2 \leq 50 & \text{maximal mean (loose anti-monotone [2])} \\ sum(X.val)/length(X) \geq 25 & \text{minimal average (convertible [16])} \\ AE \subseteq X & \text{having } AE \text{ (monotone [12])} \\ freq(X) \geq 2 & \text{minimal frequency (anti-monotone [1])} \end{cases}$$

A previous work [21] approximates primitive-based constraints by one anti-monotone and one monotone constraint which can be pushed by DUALMINER [5]. The next section describes an alternative solution in order to benefit from equivalence classes. This way is often more efficient because it avoids the enumeration of all the patterns which compose a particularly huge collection in the case of wide datasets. Besides, in context of wide datasets, previous algorithm MUSIC [20] is ineffective due to the breadth-first search approach (see experiments in Section 4.2). Then, Section 3 presents a new algorithm dedicated to primitive-based constraints in wide datasets.

3   MUSIC-DFS Tool

This section presents the MUSIC-DFS tool (Mining with a User-Specified Constraint, Depth-First Search approach) which benefits from the primitive-based constraints presented in the previous section. Efficiency is achieved thanks to the exploitation of the primitive and constraint properties. We start by giving the key idea of the safe pruning process based on intervals.

3.1 Main Features of the Interval Pruning

The pruning process performed by MUSIC-DFS is based on the key idea to exploit properties of the monotonicity of the primitives (see Section 2) on the bounds of intervals to prune them. This new kind of pruning is called *interval pruning*. Given two patterns $X \subseteq Y$, the interval $[X, Y]$, also called sub-algebra or sub-lattice, corresponds to the set $\{Z \subseteq \mathcal{I} \mid X \subseteq Z \subseteq Y\}$. Figure 2 depicts an example with the interval $[AB, ABCD]$ and the values of the primitives *sumsim* and *svsim*.

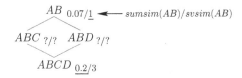

Fig. 2. Illustration of the interval pruning

Assume the constraint $sumsim(X)/svsim(X) \geq 0.25$. As the values associated to the similarities are positive, $sumsim(X)$ is an increasing function according X. Thus $sumsim(ABCD)$ is the highest *sumsim* value for the patterns in $[AB, ABCD]$. Similarly, all the patterns of this interval have a higher $svsim(X)$ value than $svsim(AB)$. Thereby, each pattern in $[AB, ABCD]$ has its average similarity lower or equal than $sumsim(ABCD)/svsim(AB) = 0.2/1$. As this fraction does not exceed 0.25, no pattern of $[AB, ABCD]$ can satisfy the constraint and this interval can be pruned. We say that this pruning is *negative* because no pattern satisfies the constraint. In the same way, if the values of proper combinations of the primitives on the bounds of an interval $[X, Y]$ show that all the patterns in $[X, Y]$ satisfy the constraint, then $[X, Y]$ is also pruned and this pruning is named *positive*. For instance, assuming that $sumsim(AB)/svsim(ABCD) \geq 0.02$, then all the patterns in $[AB, ABCD]$ satisfy the constraint.

In a more formal way, this approach is performed by two interval pruning operators $\lfloor . \rfloor$ and $\lceil . \rceil$ introduced in [20] (but only for primitives handling boolean data). The main idea of these operators is to recursively decompose the constraint to benefit from the monotone properties of the primitives and then to safely negatively or positively prune intervals as depicted above. This process is straightforwardly extended to all the primitives, no matter what kind of dataset they regard. This highlights the generic properties of our framework, as well as the feature of pushing all the parts of the constraint q into the mining step. Table 2 gives the description of the lower and upper bounding operators corresponding to the previous examples of primitives. In Table 2, the general notation

Table 2. The definitions of $\lfloor . \rfloor$ and $\lceil . \rceil$ with particular primitives

$e \in \mathcal{E}_i$	Primitive(s)	$\lfloor e \rfloor \langle X, Y \rangle$	$\lceil e \rceil \langle X, Y \rangle$
$e_1 \theta e_2$	$\theta \in \{\wedge, \vee, +, \times, \cup, \cap\}$	$\lfloor e_1 \rfloor \langle X, Y \rangle \theta \lfloor e_2 \rfloor \langle X, Y \rangle$	$\lceil e_1 \rceil \langle X, Y \rangle \theta \lceil e_2 \rceil \langle X, Y \rangle$
$e_1 \theta e_2$	$\theta \in \{>, \geq, \supset, \supseteq, -, /, \backslash\}$	$\lfloor e_1 \rfloor \langle X, Y \rangle \theta \lceil e_2 \rceil \langle X, Y \rangle$	$\lceil e_1 \rceil \langle X, Y \rangle \theta \lfloor e_2 \rfloor \langle X, Y \rangle$
θe_1	$\theta \in \{\neg, freq, \}$	$\theta \lceil e_1 \rceil \langle X, Y \rangle$	$\theta \lfloor e_1 \rfloor \langle X, Y \rangle$
$\theta(e_1.val)$	$\theta \in \{min\}$	$\theta(\lceil e_1 \rceil \langle X, Y \rangle.val)$	$\theta(\lfloor e_1 \rfloor \langle X, Y \rangle.val)$
$\theta(e_1)$	$\theta \in \{length\}$	$\theta \lfloor e_1 \rfloor \langle X, Y \rangle$	$\theta \lceil e_1 \rceil \langle X, Y \rangle$
$\theta(e_1.val)$	$\theta \in \{sum, max\}$	$\theta(\lfloor e_1 \rfloor \langle X, Y \rangle.val)$	$\theta(\lceil e_1 \rceil \langle X, Y \rangle.val)$
$\theta(e_1)$	$\theta \in \{sumsim, svsim, mvsim\}$	$\theta(\lfloor e_1 \rfloor \langle X, Y \rangle)$	$\theta(\lceil e_1 \rceil \langle X, Y \rangle)$
$\theta(e_1, m, M)$	$\theta \in \{insim\}$	$\theta(\lfloor e_1 \rfloor \langle X, Y \rangle, m, M)$	$\theta(\lceil e_1 \rceil \langle X, Y \rangle, m, M)$
$\theta(e_1, RE)$	$\theta \in \{regexp\}$	$\theta(\lfloor e_1 \rfloor \langle X, Y \rangle, RE)$	$\theta(\lceil e_1 \rceil \langle X, Y \rangle, RE)$
$c \in E_i$	-	c	c
$X \in \mathcal{L}_\mathcal{I}$	-	X	Y

E_i designates one space among $\mathfrak{B}$, $\mathfrak{R}^+$ or $\mathcal{L}_\mathcal{I} = 2^\mathcal{I}$ and $\mathcal{E}_i$ the associated expressions (for instance, the set of constraints $\mathcal{Q}$ for the booleans $\mathfrak{B}$).

The next section indicates how the intervals are built.

3.2 Interval Condensed Representation

As indicated in Section 1, levelwise algorithms are not suitable to mine datasets with a large number of items due to the huge number of candidates growing exponentially according to the number of items. We adopt a depth-first search strategy instead of enumerating the candidate patterns and avoiding subsequent memory failures. We introduce a new and specific closure operator based on a prefix ordering relation $\preceq$. We show that this closure operator is central to the interval condensed representation (Theorem 1) and enables efficient pruning of the search space.

The prefix ordering relation $\preceq$ starts from an arbitrary order over items $A < B < C < \ldots$ as done in [16]. We say that an ordered pattern $X = x_1 x_2 \ldots x_n$ (i.e., $\forall i < j$, we have $x_i < x_j$) is a prefix of an ordered pattern $Y = y_1 y_2 \ldots y_m$ and note $X \preceq Y$ iff we have $n \leq m$ and $\forall i \in \{1, \ldots, n\}$, $x_i = y_i$. For instance, the prefixes of $ABCD$ are the patterns A, AB, ABC and $ABCD$. On the contrary, $AD \npreceq ADC$ because the ordered form of ADC corresponds to ACD, and AD is not a prefix of ACD.

Definition 1 (Prefix-closure). *The prefix-closure of a pattern X, denoted* $\mathbf{cl}_\preceq(X)$, *is the pattern* $\{a \in \mathcal{I} | \exists Y \subseteq X$ *such that* $Y \preceq Y \cup \{a\}$ *and* $freq(Ya) = freq(Y)\}$.

The pattern $\mathbf{cl}_\preceq(X)$ gathers together the items occurring in all the transactions containing $Y \subseteq X$ such that Y is a prefix of $Y \cup \{a\}$. The fixed points of operator $\mathbf{cl}_\preceq$ are named the *prefix-closed patterns*. Let us illustrate this definition on our running example (cf. Figure 1). The pattern ABC is not a prefix-closed pattern because ABC is a prefix of $ABCD$ and $freq(ABCD) = freq(ABC)$. On the contrary, $ABCD$ is prefix-closed. We straightforwardly deduce that any pattern and its prefix-closure have the same frequency. For instance, as $\mathbf{cl}_{\preceq}(ABC) = ABCD$, $freq(ABC) = freq(ABCD) = 2$.

A closure operator is a function satisfying three main properties: extensivity, isotony, and idempotency [22]. Next property shows that $\mathbf{cl}_{\preceq}$ is a closure operator:

Property 1 (Closure operator). *The prefix-closure operator $\mathbf{cl}_{\preceq}$ is a closure operator.*

Proof. *Extensivity:* Let X be a pattern and $a \in X$. We have $\{a\} \subseteq X$ and obviously, $a \preceq a$ and $freq(a) = freq(a)$. Then, we obtain that $a \in \mathbf{cl}_{\preceq}(X)$ and $\mathbf{cl}_{\preceq}$ is extensive. *Isotony:* Let $X \subseteq Y$ and $a \in \mathbf{cl}_{\preceq}(X)$. There exists $Z \subseteq X$ such that $Z \preceq Za$ and $freq(Za) = freq(Z)$. As we also have $Z \subseteq Y$ (and $freq(Za) = freq(Z)$), we obtain that $a \in \mathbf{cl}_{\preceq}(Y)$ and conclude that $\mathbf{cl}_{\preceq}(X) \subseteq \mathbf{cl}_{\preceq}(Y)$. *Idempotency:* Let X be a pattern. Let $a \in \mathbf{cl}_{\preceq}(\mathbf{cl}_{\preceq}(X))$. There exists $Z \subseteq \mathbf{cl}_{\preceq}(X)$ such that $freq(Za) = freq(Z)$ with $Z \preceq Za$. As $Z \subseteq \mathbf{cl}_{\preceq}(X)$, for all $a_i \in Z$, there is $Z_i \subseteq X$ such that $freq(Z_i a_i) = freq(Z_i)$ with $Z_i \preceq Z_i a_i$. We have $\bigcup_i Z_i \preceq \bigcup_i Z_i a$ and $freq(\bigcup_i Z_i) = freq(\bigcup_i Z_i a)$ (because $freq(\bigcup_i Z_i) = freq(Z)$). As the pattern $\bigcup_i Z_i \subseteq X$, a belongs to $\mathbf{cl}_{\preceq}(X)$ and then, $\mathbf{cl}_{\preceq}$ is idempotent. □

Property 1 is important because it enables to infer results requiring the properties of a closure operator. First, this new prefix-closure operator designs *equivalence classes* through the lattice of patterns. More precisely, two patterns X and Y are equivalent iff they have the same prefix-closure (i.e., $\mathbf{cl}_{\preceq}(X) = \mathbf{cl}_{\preceq}(Y)$). Of course, as $\mathbf{cl}_{\preceq}$ is idempotent, the maximal pattern (w.r.t. $\subseteq$) of a given equivalence class of X corresponds to the prefix-closed pattern $\mathbf{cl}_{\preceq}(X)$. Conversely, we call *prefix-free patterns* the minimal patterns (w.r.t. $\subseteq$) of equivalence classes. Second, closure properties enable to prove that the prefix-freeness is an antimonotone constraint (see Property 2 in the next section).

Contrary to the equivalence classes defined by the Galois closure [4, 15], equivalence classes provided by $\mathbf{cl}_{\preceq}$ have a unique prefix-free pattern. This allows to prove that a pattern belongs to one interval only and provides the important result on the interval condensed representation (cf. Theorem 1). This result cannot be achieved without the new closure operator. Lemma 1 indicates that any equivalence class has a unique prefix-free pattern:

Lemma 1 (Prefix-freeness operator). *Let X be a pattern, there exists an unique minimal pattern (w.r.t. $\subseteq$), denoted $\mathbf{fr}_{\preceq}(X)$, in its equivalence class.*

Proof. Supposing that X and Y are two minimal patterns of the same equivalence class: we have $\mathbf{cl}_{\preceq}(X) = \mathbf{cl}_{\preceq}(Y)$. As X and Y are different, there exists $a \in X$ such that $a \notin Y$ and $a \leq min_{\leq}\{b \in Y \backslash X\}$ (or we swap X and Y). As X is minimal, no pattern $Z \subseteq X \cap Y$ satisfies that $Z \preceq Za$ and $freq(Za) = freq(Z)$. Besides, for all Z such that $Y \cap X \subset Z \subset Y$, we have $Z \npreceq Za$ because a is smaller than any item of $Y \backslash X$. So, a does not belong to $\mathbf{cl}_{\preceq}(Y)$ and then, we obtain that $\mathbf{cl}_{\preceq}(X) \neq \mathbf{cl}_{\preceq}(Y)$. Thus, we conclude that any equivalence class exactly contains one prefix-free pattern. □

Lemma 1 means that the operator $\mathbf{fr}_{\preceq}$ links a pattern X to the minimal pattern of its equivalence class, i.e. $\mathbf{fr}_{\preceq}(X)$. X is prefix-free iff $\mathbf{fr}_{\preceq}(X) = X$. Any equivalence class corresponds to an interval delimited by one prefix-free pattern and its prefix-closed pattern (i.e., $[\mathbf{fr}_{\preceq}(X), \mathbf{cl}_{\preceq}(X)]$). For example, AB (resp. $ABCD$) is the prefix-free (resp. prefix-closed) pattern of the equivalence class $[AB, ABCD]$.

Now let us show that the whole collection of the intervals formed by all the prefix-free patterns and their prefix-closed patterns provides an *interval condensed representation* where each pattern X is present only once in the set of intervals.

Theorem 1 (Interval condensed representation). *Each pattern X present in the dataset is included in the interval $[\mathbf{fr}_{\preceq}(X), \mathbf{cl}_{\preceq}(X)]$. Besides, the number of these intervals is less than or equal to the number of patterns.*

Proof. Let X be a pattern and $R = \{[\mathbf{fr}_{\preceq}(X), \mathbf{cl}_{\preceq}(X)] | freq(X) \geq 1\}$. Lemma 1 proves that X is exactly contained in $[\mathbf{fr}_{\preceq}(X), \mathbf{cl}_{\preceq}(X)]$. The latter is unique. As X belongs to R by definition, we conclude that R is a representation of any pattern. Now, the extensivity and the idempotency of prefix-closure operator $\mathbf{cl}_{\preceq}$ ensure that $|R| \leq |\{X \subseteq \mathcal{I} \text{ such that } freq(X) \geq 1\}|$. This proves Theorem 1. □

In the worst case the size of the condensed representation is the number of patterns (each pattern is its own prefix-free and its own prefix-closed pattern). But, in practice, the number of intervals is low compared to the number of patterns (in our running example, only 23 intervals sum up the 63 present patterns).

The condensed representation highlighted by Theorem 1 differs from the condensed representations of frequent patterns based on the Galois closure [4, 15]: in this last case, intervals are described by a free (or key) pattern and its Galois closure and a frequent pattern may appear in several intervals. We claim that the presence of a pattern in a single interval brings meaningful advantages: the mining is more efficient because each pattern is tested at most once. This property improves the synthesis of the output of the mining process and facilitates its analysis by the end-user. The next section shows that by combining this condensed representation and the interval pruning operators, we get an interval condensed representation of primitive-based constrained patterns.

3.3   Mining Primitive-Based Constraints in Large Datasets

When running, MUSIC-DFS enumerates all the intervals sorted in a lexicographic order and checks whether they can be pruned as proposed in Section 3.1. The enumeration benefits from the anti-monotonicity property of the prefix-freeness (cf. Property 2). The memory requirements grow only linearly with the number of items and the number of transactions.

Property 2. *The prefix-freeness is an anti-monotone constraint (w.r.t. $\subseteq$).*

The proof of Property 2 is very similar to those of the usual freeness [4, 15]:

Proof. Let X be a pattern which is not a prefix-free pattern. So, there is $Z \subset X$ such that $\mathbf{cl}_{\prec}(Z) = \mathbf{cl}_{\prec}(X)$. Let Y be a pattern with $X \subseteq Y$. First, we observe that $\mathbf{cl}_{\prec}(Y) = \mathbf{cl}_{\prec}(X \cup (Y \setminus X))$ and $\mathbf{cl}_{\prec}(X \cup (Y \setminus X)) = \mathbf{cl}_{\prec}(\mathbf{cl}_{\prec}(X) \cup \mathbf{cl}_{\prec}(Y \setminus X))$ (usual property of closure operators). As $\mathbf{cl}_{\prec}(Z) = \mathbf{cl}_{\prec}(X)$, we obtain that $\mathbf{cl}_{\prec}(\mathbf{cl}_{\prec}(X) \cup \mathbf{cl}_{\prec}(Y \setminus X)) = \mathbf{cl}_{\prec}(\mathbf{cl}_{\prec}(Z) \cup \mathbf{cl}_{\prec}(Y \setminus X))$ and then, $\mathbf{cl}_{\prec}(\mathbf{cl}_{\prec}(Z) \cup \mathbf{cl}_{\prec}(Y \setminus X)) = \mathbf{cl}_{\prec}(Z \cup (Y \setminus X))$. Finally, as Z is a proper subset of X, the pattern $Z \cup (Y \setminus X)$ is a proper subset of Y. Thus, we conclude that Y is not prefix-free. $\square$

In other words, the anti-monotonicity ensures us that once we know that a pattern is not prefix-free, any superset of this pattern is not prefix-free anymore [1, 12]. Algorithms 1 and 2 give the sketch of MUSIC-DFS.

Algorithm 1. GLOBALSCAN

Input: A prefix-pattern X, a primitive based constraint q and a dataset $\mathcal{D}$
Output: Interval condensed representation of constrained patterns having X as prefix
1: **if** $\neg PrefixFree(X)$ **then return** $\emptyset$ // *anti-monotone pruning*
2: **return** LOCALSCAN$([X, \mathbf{cl}_{\prec}(X)], q, \mathcal{D})$ // *local mining*
   $\cup \bigcup \{$GLOBALSCAN$(Xa, q, \mathcal{D}) | a \in \mathcal{I} \wedge a \geq \max_{\prec} X \}$ // *recursive enumeration*

Algorithm 2. LOCALSCAN

Input: An interval $[X, Y]$, a primitive based constraint q and a dataset $\mathcal{D}$
Output: Interval condensed representation of constrained patterns of $[X, Y]$
1: **if** $\lfloor q \rfloor \langle X, Y \rangle$ **then return** $\{[X, Y]\}$ // *positive interval pruning*
2: **if** $\neg \lceil q \rceil \langle X, Y \rangle$ **then return** $\emptyset$ // *negative interval pruning*
3: **if** $q(X)$ **then   return** $[X, X] \cup \bigcup \{$LOCALSCAN$([Xa, \mathbf{cl}_{\prec}(Xa)], q, \mathcal{D}) | a \in Y \setminus X \}$
4: **return** $\bigcup \{$LOCALSCAN$([Xa, \mathbf{cl}_{\prec}(Xa)], q, \mathcal{D}) | a \in Y \setminus X \}$ // *recursive division*

MUSIC-DFS scans the whole search space by running GLOBALSCAN on each item of $\mathcal{I}$. GLOBALSCAN recursively performs a depth-first search and stops whenever a pattern is not prefix-free (Line 1, GLOBALSCAN). For each prefix-free pattern X, it computes its prefix-closed pattern and builds $[X, \mathbf{cl}_{\prec}(X)]$ (Line 2, GLOBALSCAN). Then, LOCALSCAN tests this interval by using the operators $\lfloor . \rfloor$ and $\lceil . \rceil$ informally presented in Section 3.1. If the interval pruning can be performed, the interval is selected (positive pruning, Line 1 from LOCALSCAN) or rejected (negative pruning, Line 2 from LOCALSCAN). Otherwise, the interval is explored by recursively dividing it (Line 3 or 4 from LOCALSCAN). The decomposition of the intervals is done so that each pattern is considered only once. The next theorem provides the correctness of MUSIC-DFS:

Theorem 2 (Correctness). MUSIC-DFS *mines soundly and completely all the patterns satisfying q by means of intervals.*

Proof. Property 2 ensures us that MUSIC-DFS enumerates all the interval condensed representation. Thereby, any pattern is considered (Theorem 1) individually or globally with the safe pruning stemmed from to the interval pruning (see Section 3.1).   □

An additional anti-monotone constraint can be pushed in conjunction of prefix-freeness (Line 1, GLOBALSCAN). This constraint (e.g., minimal frequency constraint) optimizes the extraction by reducing more the search space. Such anti-monotone constraint is automatically deduced from the original constraint q in [21].

4   Mining Constrained Patterns from Transcriptomic Data

This section depicts the effectiveness of our approach on a transcriptomic case study. We experimentally show two results. First, the usefulness of the interval pruning strategy of MUSIC-DFS (the other prototypes fail for such large data, cf. Section 4.2). Second, BK enables to automatically focus on the most plausible candidate patterns (cf. Section 4.3). This underlines the need to mine constrained patterns by taking into account external data. If not mentioned otherwise, the experiments are run on the genomic data described in Section 4.1.

4.1   Gene Expression Data and Background Knowledge

In this experiment we deal with the SAGE (Serial Analysis of Gene Expression) [24] human expression data downloaded from the NCBI website (www.ncbi.nlm.nih.gov). The final binary dataset contains 11082 genes tested in 207 biological situations, each gene can be either over-expressed in the given situation or not. The biological details regarding gene selection, mapping and binarization can be seen in [10].

BK available in literature databases, biological ontologies and other sources is used to help to focus automatically on the most plausible candidate patterns. We have experimented with the gene ontology (GO) and free-text data. First, the available gene databases were automatically searched and the records for each gene were built (around two thirds of genes have non-empty records, there is no information available for the rest of them). Then, various similarity metrics among the gene records were proposed and calculated. More precisely, the gene records were converted into the vector space model [18]. A single gene corresponds to a single vector, whose components correspond to a frequency of a single term from the vocabulary. The similarity between genes was defined as the cosine of the angle between the corresponding *term-frequency inverse-document-frequency* (TFIDF) [18] vectors. TFIDF representation statistically measures how important a term is to a gene record. Moreover, the gene records were also simplified to get a condensed textual description. More details on text mining, gene ontologies and similarities are in [10].

4.2   Efficiency of MUSIC-DFS

Dealing with large datasets Let us show the necessity of the depth-first search and usefulness of the interval pruning strategy of MUSIC-DFS. All the experiments were conducted on a 2.2 GHz Xeon processor with 3GB RAM running Linux.

The first experiment highlights the importance of the depth-first search. We consider the constraint addressing patterns having an *area* $\geq$ 70 (the minimal area constraint has been introduced in Section 2) and appearing at least 4 times in the dataset. MUSIC-DFS only spends 7sec to extract 212 constrained patterns. In comparison, for the same binary dataset, the levelwise approach[1] presented in [20] fails after 963sec whenever the dataset contains more than 3500 genes. Indeed, the candidate patterns necessary to build the output do not fit in memory.

Comparison with prototypes coming from the FIMI repository (fimi.cs.helsinki.fi) shows that efficient implementations like KDCI [13], LCM (ver. 2) [23], COFI [25] or Borgelt's APRIORI [3] fail with this binary dataset to mine frequent patterns occuring at least 4 times. Borgelt's ECLAT [3] and AFOPT [11] which are depth-first approaches, are able to mine with this frequency constraint. But they require a post-processing step for other constraints than the frequency (e.g., area, similarity-based constraints).

The power of MUSIC-DFS can also be illustrated on any large benchmark dataset (i.e., containing many transactions). Let us consider the mushroom dataset taken from FIMI repository . Figure 3 presents the running times for the MUSIC-DFS, MUSIC, APRIORI and ECLAT algorithms with the constraints $freq(X) \times length(X) \geq \alpha$ (on the left) and $sum(X.val)/length(X) \geq \alpha$ (on the right). The latter is applied on item values (noted *val*) randomly generated within the range $[0, 100]$. An additional minimal frequency constraint $freq(X) \geq 100$ is used in order to make running of APRIORI and ECLAT feasible.

As APRIORI and ECLAT do not push the minimal area/average constraints into the mining, they require a post-processing step to select the right patterns

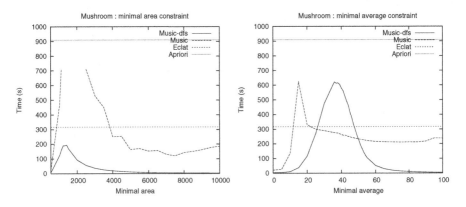

Fig. 3. Runtime performances with minimal area/average constraint on mushroom

---

[1] We do not use external data because this version does not deal with external data.

with respect to these constraints. Thus their curves (cf. Figure 3) do not depend on minimal area/average threshold α and are flat. Let us note that we neglect the time of the post-processing step therefore the total time spent by these methods is supposed to be even higher than shown. We observe that MUSIC-DFS clearly outperforms MUSIC and APRIORI. Moreover, MUSIC-DFS is often more efficient than ECLAT as it benefits from the constraint. The experimental study in [19] confirms that MUSIC-DFS is efficient with various constraints and various datasets.

Impact of interval pruning The next experiment shows the great role of the interval pruning strategy. For this purpose, we compare MUSIC-DFS with its modification that does not prune. The modification, denoted MUSIC-DFS-FILTER, mines all the patterns that satisfy the frequency threshold first, the other primitives are applied in the post-processing step. We use two typical constraints needed in the genomic domain and requiring the external data. These constraints and the time comparison between MUSIC-DFS and MUSIC-DFS-FILTER are given in Figure 4. The results show that post-processing is feasible until the frequency threshold generates reasonable pattern sets. For lower frequency thresholds, the number of patterns explodes and large intervals to be pruned appear. The interval pruning strategy decreases runtime and scales up much better than the comparative version without interval pruning and MUSIC-DFS becomes in the order of magnitude faster.

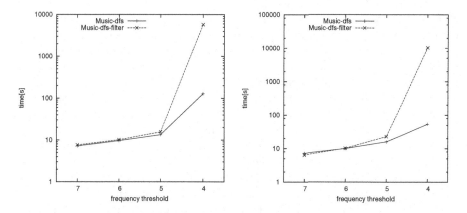

Fig. 4. Efficiency of interval pruning with decreasing frequency threshold. The left image deals with the constraint $freq(X) \geq thres \wedge lenght(X) \geq 4 \wedge sumsim(X)/svsim(X) \geq 0.9 \wedge svsim(X)/(svsim(X) + mvsim(X)) \geq 0.9$. The right image deals with the constraint $freq(X) \geq thres \wedge length(regexp(X,' *ribosom*', \texttt{GO\_terms})) = 0$.

4.3   Use of Background Knowledge to Mine Plausible Patterns

This transcriptomic case study demonstrates that constraints coming from the BK can reduce the number of patterns, they can express various kinds of interest and the patterns that tend to reappear are likely to be recognized as interesting by an expert. One of the goals of any pattern is to generalize the individual gene synexpressions observed in the individual situations. Although it seems that biologists focus on individual biological situations, they follow very similar generalization goals. The most valuable knowledge is extracted from the patterns that concern genes with interesting common features (e.g., process, function, location, disease) whose synexpression is observed in a homogeneous biological context (i.e., in a number of analogous biological situations). An example of this context is the cluster of medulloblastoma SAGE libraries discovered in one of the constrained patterns (see the end of this section). It is obvious that to get such patterns and to pursue the goals mentioned above, a tool dealing with external data is needed.

Let us consider all the patterns having a satisfactory size which is translated by the constraint $area \geq 20^2$. We get nearly half a million different patterns that are joined into 37852 intervals. Although the intervals prove to provide a good condensation, the manual search through this set is obviously infeasible as the interpretation of patterns is not trivial and asks for frequent consultations with medical databases. The biologists prefer sets with tens of patterns/intervals only.

Increasing the threshold of the area constraint to get a reasonable number of patterns is rather counter-productive. The constraint $area \geq 75$ led to a small but uniform set of 56 patterns that was flooded by the ribosomal proteins which generally represent the most frequent genes in the dataset. Biologists rated these patterns as valid but uninteresting.

The most valuable patterns expected by biologists – denoted as meaningful or plausible patterns – have non-trivial size containing genes and situations whose characteristics can be generalized, connected, interpreted and thus transformed into knowledge. To get such patterns, constraints based on the external data have to be added to the minimal area constraint just like in the constraint q given in Section 2. It joins the minimal area constraint with background constraints coming from the NCBI textual resources (gene summaries and adjoined PubMed abstracts). There are 46671 patterns satisfying the minimal area constraint (the part (a) of the constraint q), but only 9 satisfy q. This shows the efficiency of reduction of patterns brought by the BK.

A cross-fertilization with other external data is obviously favourable. So, we use the constraint q' which is similar to q, except that the functional Gene Ontology is used instead of NCBI textual resources and a similarity constraint is added (part (e) of q').

$$
\begin{aligned}
q'(X) &\equiv area(X) \geq 24 & \text{(a)}\\
&\wedge length(regexp(X,' *ribosom*', \texttt{GO\_terms})) \leq 1 & \text{(b)}\\
&\wedge svsim(X, \texttt{GO})/(svsim(X, \texttt{GO}) + mvsim(X, \texttt{GO})) \geq 0.7 & \text{(c)}\\
&\wedge sumsim(X, \texttt{GO})/svsim(X, \texttt{GO}) \geq 0.025 & \text{(d)}\\
&\wedge insim(X, 0.5, 1, \texttt{GO})/svsim(X, \texttt{GO}) \geq 0.6 & \text{(e)}
\end{aligned}
$$

---

[2] This threshold has been settled by statistical analysis of random datasets having the same properties as the original SAGE data. First spurious patterns start to appear for this threshold area.

Only 2 patterns satisfy q'. A very interesting observation is that the pattern[3] that was identified by the expert as one of the "nuggets" provided by q is also selected by q'. This pattern can be verbally characterized as follows: it consists of 4 genes that are over-expressed in 6 biological situations, it contains at most one ribosomal gene, the genes share a lot of common terms in their descriptions as well as they functionally overlap, at least 3 of the genes are known (have a non-empty record) and all of the biological situations are medulloblastomas which are very aggressive brain tumors in children. The constraints q and q' demonstrate two different ways to reach a compact and meaningful output that can be easily human surveyed.

5 Conclusion

Knowledge discovery from a large binary dataset supported by heterogeneous BK is an important task. We have proposed a generic framework to mine patterns with a large set of constraints linking the information scattered in various knowledge sources. We have presented an efficient new algorithm MUSIC-DFS which soundly and completely mines such constrained patterns. Effectiveness comes from an interval pruning strategy based on prefix free patterns. To the best of our knowledge, there is no other constraint-based tool able to solve such constraint-based tasks.

The transcriptomic case study demonstrates that our approach can handle large datasets. It also shows practical utility of the flexible framework integrating heterogeneous knowledge sources. The language of primitives applied to a wide spectrum of transcriptomic data results in constraints formalizing a viable notion of interestingness.

Acknowledgements. The authors thank the CGMC Laboratory (CNRS UMR 5534, Lyon) for providing the gene expression database and many valuable comments. This work has been partially funded by the ACI "masse de données" (French Ministry of research), Bingo project (MD 46, 2004-07).

References

[1] Agrawal, R., Srikant, R.: Fast algorithms for mining association rules. In: Proc. 20th Int. Conf. Very Large Data Bases, VLDB, pp. 432–444 (1994)
[2] Bonchi, F., Lucchese, C.: Pushing tougher constraints in frequent pattern mining. In: Ho et al. pp. 114–124 [7]
[3] Borgelt, C.: Efficient implementations of Apriori and Eclat. In: Goethals, Zaki [6]
[4] Boulicaut, J.F., Bykowski, A., Rigotti, C.: Free-sets: a condensed representation of boolean data for the approximation of frequency queries. Data Mining and Knowledge Discovery journal 7(1), 5–22 (2003)

---

[3] The pattern consists of 4 genes KHDRBS1 NONO TOP2B FMR1 over-expressed in 6 biological situations BM_P019 BM_P494 BM_P608 BM_P301 BM_H275 BM_H876. BM stands for brain medulloblastoma.

[5] Bucila, C., Gehrke, J., Kifer, D., White, W.M.: Dualminer: A dual-pruning algorithm for itemsets with constraints. Data Min. Knowl. Discov. 7(3), 241–272 (2003)

[6] Goethals, B., Zaki, M.J. (eds.): FIMI '03, Frequent Itemset Mining Implementations, Proceedings of the ICDM 2003 Workshop on Frequent Itemset Mining Implementations, 19 December 2003, Melbourne, Florida, USA, CEUR Workshop Proceedings, vol. 90 (2003), CEUR-WS.org

[7] Ho, T.-B., Cheung, D., Liu, H. (eds.): Advances in Knowledge Discovery and Data Mining, PAKDD 2005. LNCS (LNAI), vol. 3518. Springer, Heidelberg (2005)

[8] Hébert, C., Crémilleux, B.: Mining frequent δ-free patterns in large databases. In: Hoffmann, A., Motoda, H., Scheffer, T. (eds.) DS 2005. LNCS (LNAI), vol. 3735, pp. 124–136. Springer, Heidelberg (2005)

[9] Jeudy, B., Rioult, F.: Database transposition for constrained (closed) pattern mining. In: Goethals, B., Siebes, A. (eds.) KDID 2004. LNCS, vol. 3377, pp. 89–107. Springer, Heidelberg (2005)

[10] Kléma, J., Soulet, A., Crémilleux, B., Blachon, S., Gandrillon, O.: Mining plausible patterns from genomic data. In: Lee, D., Nutter, B., Antani, S., Mitra, S., Archibald, J. (eds.) CBMS 2006, the 19th IEEE International Symposium on Computer-Based Medical Systems, Salt Lake City, Utah, pp. 183–188. IEEE Computer Society Press, Los Alamitos (2006)

[11] Liu, G., Lu, H., Yu, J.X., Wei, W., Xiao, X.: AFOPT: An efficient implementation of pattern growth approach. In: Goethals, Zaki [6]

[12] Mannila, H., Toivonen, H.: Levelwise search and borders of theories in knowledge discovery. Data Mining and Knowledge Discovery 1(3), 241–258 (1997)

[13] Orlando, S., Lucchese, C., Palmerini, P., Perego, R., Silvestri, F.: kDCI: a multi-strategy algorithm for mining frequent sets. In: Goethals, Zaki [6]

[14] Pan, F., Cong, G., Tung, A.K.H., Yang, Y., Zaki, M.J.: CARPENTER: finding closed patterns in long biological datasets. In: Proceedings of the 9th ACM SIGKDD international conference on Knowledge discovery and data mining (KDD 2003), Washington, DC, USA, pp. 637–642. ACM Press, New York (2003)

[15] Pasquier, N., Bastide, Y., Taouil, T., Lakhal, L.: Discovering frequent closed itemsets for association rules. In: Beeri, C., Bruneman, P. (eds.) ICDT 1999. LNCS, vol. 1540, pp. 398–416. Springer, Heidelberg (1998)

[16] Pei, J., Han, J., Lakshmanan, L.V.S.: Mining frequent item sets with convertible constraints. In: ICDE, pp. 433–442. IEEE Computer Society, Los Alamitos (2001)

[17] Rioult, F., Robardet, C., Blachon, S., Crémilleux, B., Gandrillon, O., Boulicaut, J.-F.: Mining concepts from large sage gene expression matrices. In: Boulicaut, J.-F., Dzeroski, S. (eds.) KDID, pp. 107–118. Rudjer Boskovic Institute, Zagreb, Croatia (2003)

[18] Salton, G., Buckley, C.: Term-weighting approaches in automatic text retrieval. Information Processing Management 24(5), 513–523 (1988)

[19] Soulet, A.: Un cadre générique de découverte de motifs sous contraintes fondées sur des primitives. PhD thesis, Université de Caen Basse-Normandie, France, 2006 (to appear)

[20] Soulet, A., Crémilleux, B.: An efficient framework for mining flexible constraints. In: Ho,, et al. (eds.), pp. 661–671 (2005) [7]

[21] Soulet, A., Crémilleux, B.: Exploiting Virtual Patterns for Automatically Pruning the Search Space. In: Bonchi, F., Boulicaut, J.-F. (eds.) KDID 2005. LNCS, vol. 3933, pp. 98–109. Springer, Heidelberg (2006)

[22] Stadler, B.M.R., Stadler, P.F.: Basic properties of filter convergence spaces (2002)

[23] Uno, T., Kiyomi, M., Arimura, H.: LCM ver. 2: Efficient mining algorithms for frequent/closed/maximal itemsets. In: Bayardo Jr., R.J., Goethals, B., Zaki, M.J. (eds.) FIMI. CEUR Workshop Proceedings, vol. 126 (2004), `CEUR-WS.org`
[24] Velculescu, V., Zhang, L., Vogelstein, B., Kinzler, K.: Serial analysis of gene expression. Science 270, 484–487 (1995)
[25] Zaïane, O.R., El-Hajj, M.: COFI-tree mining: A new approach to pattern growth with reduced candidacy generation. In: Goethals, Zaki [6]

Three Strategies for Concurrent Processing of Frequent Itemset Queries Using FP-Growth

Marek Wojciechowski, Krzysztof Galecki, and Krzysztof Gawronek

Poznan University of Technology
Institute of Computing Science
ul. Piotrowo 2, 60-965 Poznan, Poland
marek@cs.put.poznan.pl

Abstract. Frequent itemset mining is often regarded as advanced querying where a user specifies the source dataset and pattern constraints using a given constraint model. Recently, a new problem of optimizing processing of sets of frequent itemset queries has been considered and two multiple query optimization techniques for frequent itemset queries: Mine Merge and Common Counting have been proposed and tested on the Apriori algorithm. In this paper we discuss and experimentally evaluate three strategies for concurrent processing of frequent itemset queries using FP-growth as a basic frequent itemset mining algorithm. The first strategy is Mine Merge, which does not depend on a particular mining algorithm and can be applied to FP-growth without modifications. The second is an implementation of the general idea of Common Counting for FP-growth. The last is a completely new strategy, motivated by identified shortcomings of the previous two strategies in the context of FP-growth.

1 Introduction

Discovery of frequent itemsets [1] is a very important data mining problem with numerous practical applications. Informally, frequent itemsets are subsets frequently occurring in a collection of sets of items. Frequent itemsets are typically used to generate association rules. However, since generation of rules is a rather straightforward task, the focus of researchers has been mostly on optimizing the frequent itemset discovery step.

Many frequent itemset mining algorithms have been developed. The two most prominent classes of algorithms are Apriori-like (level-wise) and pattern-growth methods. Apriori-like solutions, represented by the classic Apriori algorithm [3], perform a breadth-first search of the pattern space. Apriori starts with discovering frequent itemsets of size 1, and then iteratively generates candidates from previously found smaller frequent itemsets and counts their occurrences in a database scan. The problems identified with Apriori are: (1) multiple database scans, and (2) huge number of candidates generated for dense datasets and/or low frequency threshold (minimum support).

To address the limitations of Apriori-like methods, a novel mining paradigm has been proposed, called pattern-growth [8], which consists in a depth-first search of the

S. Džeroski and J. Struyf (Eds.): KDID 2006, LNCS 4747, pp. 240–258, 2007.

pattern space. Pattern-growth methods also build larger frequent itemsets from smaller ones but instead of candidate generation and testing, they exploit the idea of database projections. Typically, pattern-growth methods start with transforming the original database into some complex data structure, preferably fitting into main memory. A classic example of the pattern-growth family of algorithms is FP-growth [9][10], which transforms a database into an FP-tree stored in main memory using just 2 database scans, and then performs mining on that optimized FP-tree structure.

Frequent itemset mining is often regarded as advanced database querying where a user specifies the source dataset, the minimum support threshold, and optionally pattern constraints within a given constraint model [11]. A significant amount of research on efficient processing of frequent itemset queries has been done in recent years, focusing mainly on constraint handling (see [18] for an overview) and reusing results of previous queries [5][7][15][16].

Recently, a new problem of optimizing processing of sets of frequent itemset queries has been considered, bringing the concept of multiple-query optimization to the domain of frequent itemset mining. The idea was to process the queries concurrently rather than sequentially and exploit the overlapping of queries' source datasets. Sets of frequent itemset queries available for concurrent processing may arise in data mining systems operating in a batch mode or be collected within a given time window in multi-user interactive data mining environments. A motivating example from the domain of market basket analysis could be a set of queries discovering frequent itemsets from the overlapping parts of a database table containing customer transaction data from overlapping time periods.

Two multiple-query optimization techniques for frequent itemset queries have been proposed: Mine Merge [24] and Common Counting [22]. Mine Merge is a general strategy that consists in transforming the original batch of queries into a batch of intermediate queries operating on non-overlapping datasets, and then using the results of the intermediate queries to answer the original queries. Although Mine Merge does not depend on a particular mining algorithm, its efficiency has been evaluated only for Apriori, and it is unclear how it would perform with pattern-growth algorithms like FP-growth. Common Counting has been specifically designed to work with Apriori-like algorithms. The idea of Common Counting is concurrent execution of Apriori for each query, and integration of dataset scans required by Apriori so that the parts of the dataset shared by the queries are read only once per Apriori iteration.

In this paper, we (1) generalize the strategy applied by Common Counting and adapt it to work with FP-growth in the form of the Common Building method; (2) propose a completely new strategy of processing of batches of frequent itemset queries, aiming at integrating the data structures used by the queries, and implement it for FP-growth as the Common FP-tree method; (3) experimentally evaluate the three strategies in the context of FP-growth.

1.1 Related Work

Multiple-query optimization has been extensively studied in the context of database systems (see [21] for an overview). The idea was to identify common subexpressions and construct a global execution plan minimizing the overall processing time by executing the common subexpressions only once for the set of queries [4][12][19].

Data mining queries could also benefit from this general strategy, however, due to their different nature they require novel multiple-query processing methods.

To the best of our knowledge, apart from the Common Counting and Mine Merge methods mentioned above, multiple-query optimization for frequent pattern queries has been considered only in the context of frequent pattern mining on multiple datasets [14]. The idea was to reduce the common computations appearing in different complex queries, each of which compared the support of patterns in several disjoint datasets. This is fundamentally different from our problem, where each query refers to only one dataset and the queries' datasets overlap.

Earlier, the need for multiple-query optimization has been postulated in the somewhat related research area of inductive logic programming, where a technique based on similar ideas as Common Counting has been proposed, consisting in combining similar queries into query packs [6].

As an introduction to multiple-data-mining-query optimization, we can regard techniques of reusing intermediate or final results of previous queries to answer a new query. Methods falling into that category that have been studied in the context of frequent itemset discovery are: incremental mining [7], caching intermediate query results [17], and reusing materialized complete [5][15][16] or condensed [13] results of previous queries provided that syntactic differences between the queries satisfy certain conditions.

1.2 Organization of the Paper

The remainder of the paper is organized as follows. In Sect. 2 we review basic definitions regarding frequent itemset mining and we briefly describe the FP-growth algorithm. Section 3 contains basic definitions regarding frequent itemset queries and presents the previously proposed multiple-query optimization techniques: Mine Merge and Common Counting. In Sect. 4 we present the Common Building method as an adaptation of Common Counting to FP-growth. In Sect. 5 we introduce a new strategy for concurrent processing of frequent itemset queries and its implementation for FP-growth, called Common FP-tree. Section 6 presents experimental results. Section 7 contains conclusions and directions for future work.

2 Frequent Itemset Mining and Review of FP-Growth

Frequent itemsets. Let $L=\{l_1, l_2, ..., l_m\}$ be a set of literals, called items. Let a non-empty set of items T be called an *itemset*. Let D be a set of variable length itemsets, where each itemset $T \subseteq L$. We say that an itemset T *supports* an item $x \in L$ if x is in T. We say that an itemset T *supports* an itemset $X \subseteq L$ if T supports every item in the set X. The *support* of the itemset X is the percentage of T in D that support X. The problem of mining frequent itemsets in D consists in discovering all itemsets whose support is no less than a user-defined minimum support threshold *minsup*.

FP-growth. The initial phase of FP-growth is the construction of a memory structure called FP-tree. FP-tree is a highly compact representation of the original database (in particular for so-called dense datasets), which is assumed to fit into the main memory.

FP-tree contains only frequent items, each transaction has a corresponding path in the tree, and transactions having a common prefix share the common starting fragment of their paths. When storing a transaction in an FP-tree, only its frequent items are considered and are sorted according to a fixed order. Typically, frequency descending order is used as it is likely to result in a good compression ratio. The procedure of creating an FP-tree requires two database scans: one to discover frequent items and their counts, and one to build the tree by adding transactions to it one by one. An FP-tree for an example database represented by the first two columns of Table 1 and the minimum support threshold of 50% is presented in Fig. 1 (example from [9]).

Table 1. Example transaction database

TID	Items	Ordered frequent items
100	a;c;d;f;g;i;m;p	f;c;a;m;p
200	a;b;c;f;l;m;o	f;c;a;b;m
300	b;f;h;j;o	f;b
400	b;c;k;s;p	c;b;p
500	a;c;e;f;l;m;n;p	f;c;a;m;p

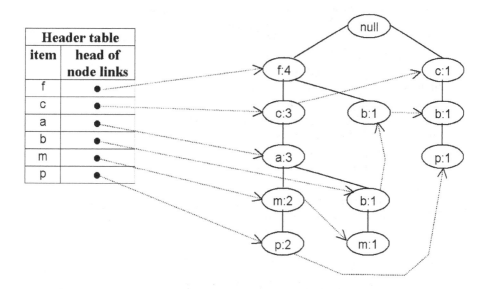

Fig. 1. An FP-tree for an example database

After an FP-tree is built, the actual FP-growth procedure is recursively applied to it, which discovers all frequent itemsets in a depth-first manner by exploring projections (called conditional pattern bases) of the tree with respect to frequent prefixes found so far. The projections are stored in memory in the form of FP-trees (called conditional FP-trees). FP-growth exploits the property that the support of an itemset $X \cup Y$ is equal to the support of Y in the set of transactions containing X (which forms the conditional pattern base of X). Thus, FP-growth builds longer patters from previously found shorter ones. Part of the FP-tree structure is the header table containing pointers to the lists containing all occurrences of given items in a tree, which facilitate the projection operation. It should be noted that after the FP-tree is created, the original database is not scanned anymore, and therefore the whole mining process requires exactly two database scans. The FP-growth algorithm is formally presented in Fig. 2, together with its initial tree-building phase. Our formulation differs slightly from that from [9] because we assume that *minsup* is relative to the total number of transactions. Therefore, in the first scan of the dataset we calculate the minimum required number of occurrences *mincount*, corresponding to *minsup* provided in a query. The *mincount* value is passed as a parameter to the FP-growth procedure. The term "frequent" within the algorithm implicitly refers to this *mincount* threshold.

Input: database D, minimum support threshold *minsup*
Output: the complete set of frequent itemsets
Method:
1. scan D to calculate *mincount* and discover frequent items and their counts
2. create the root of *FP-tree* labeled as *null*
3. scan D and add each transaction to *FP-tree* omitting non-frequent items
4. call *FP-growth(FP-tree, null, mincount)*

procedure *FP-growth(FP-tree, α, mincount)* {
  if *FP-tree* contains a single path P
  then for each combination β of nodes in P **do**
    generate frequent itemset $\beta \cup \alpha$
    with $count(\beta \cup \alpha, D) =$ min *count* of nodes in β;
  else for each a_i in header table of *FP-tree* **do** {
    generate frequent itemset $\beta = a_i \cup \alpha$
    with $count(\beta, D) = count(a_i, FP\text{-}tree)$;
    construct β's conditional pattern base and then
    β's conditional *FP-tree$_\beta$*;
    if *FP-tree$_\beta$* $\neq \varnothing$ **then** *FP-growth(FP-tree$_\beta$, β, mincount)*;
  }
}

Fig. 2. FP-growth algorithm

FP-growth has been found more efficient than Apriori for dense datasets (i.e., containing numerous and/or long frequent itemsets) and for low support thresholds. Moreover, as stated in [18], FP-growth can incorporate more types of pattern constraints than Apriori. In particular, a class of convertible constraints has been identified, representing the constraints that can be handled by FP-growth by properly ordering the items when storing a transaction in a tree (instead of "default" frequency descending order).

3 Multiple-Query Optimization for Frequent Itemset Queries

3.1 Basic Definitions and Problem Statement

Frequent itemset query. A frequent itemset query is a tuple $dmq = (R, a, \Sigma, \Phi, minsup)$, where R is a database relation, a is a set-valued attribute of R, Σ is a condition involving the attributes of R called *data selection predicate*, Φ is a condition involving discovered itemsets called *pattern constraint*, and *minsup* is the minimum support threshold. The result of *dmq* is a set of itemsets discovered in $\pi_a\sigma_\Sigma R$, satisfying Φ, and having support $\geq minsup$ (π and σ denote relational projection and selection operations respectively).

Example. Given the database relation $R_1(a_1, a_2)$, where a_2 is a set-valued attribute and a_1 is of integer type. The frequent itemset query $dmq_1 = (R_1, "a_2", "a_1>5", "|itemset|<4", 3\%)$ describes the problem of discovering frequent itemsets in the set-valued attribute a_2 of the relation R_1. The frequent itemsets with support of at least 3% and length less than 4 are discovered in the collection of records having $a_1>5$.

Elementary data selection predicates. The set $S=\{s_1, s_2, ..., s_k\}$ of data selection predicates over the relation R is a set of elementary data selection predicates for a set of frequent itemset queries $DMQ = \{dmq_1, dmq_2, ..., dmq_n\}$ if for all u,v we have $\sigma_{su}R\cap\sigma_{sv}R =\emptyset$ and for each dmq_i there exist integers $a, b, ..., m$ such that $\sigma_\Sigma R=\sigma_{sa}R\cup\sigma_{sb}R\cup..\cup\sigma_{sm}R$. The set of elementary data selection predicates represents the partitioning of the database determined by overlapping of queries' datasets.

Example. Given the relation $R_1=(attr_1, attr_2)$ and three data mining queries: $dmq_1=(R_1, "attr_2", "5 <attr_1<20", \emptyset, 3\%)$, $dmq_2=(R_1, "attr_2", "0<attr_1<15", \emptyset, 5\%)$, $dmq_3=(R_1, "attr_2", "5<attr_1<15$ or $30<attr_1<40", \emptyset, 4\%)$. The set of elementary data selection predicates is then $S=\{s_1="0<attr_1<5", s_2="5<attr_1<15", s_3="15<attr_1<20", s_4="30<attr_1<40"\}$.

Problem Statement. Given a set of frequent itemset queries $DMQ = \{dmq_1, dmq_2, ..., dmq_n\}$, the problem of *multiple-query optimization* of *DMQ* consists in generating an algorithm to execute *DMQ* that minimizes the overall processing time.

In general, it is assumed that after collecting the queries to be concurrently executed using any strategy, duplicated queries are eliminated in a pre-processing step. It is also advisable to combine queries operating on exactly the same dataset (at least the ones that have the same data selection predicate) into one query, whose results can be used to answer the original queries by simple checking of pattern constraints and/or support. Such a new query should have the support threshold equal to the smallest threshold among the queries to be replaced and the pattern constraint in the form of a disjunction of their pattern constraints.

3.2 Mine Merge

Mine Merge employs the property that for a database divided into a set of disjoint partitions, an itemset frequent in a whole database, must also be frequent in at least one partition of it. This important property has been proved in [20] and served as the basis for a frequent itemset mining algorithm called Partition. The difference between Partition and Mine Merge is that Partition uses memory-based partitions, determined by the amount of available main-memory, while Mine Merge operates on disk-based partitions, which are the consequence of overlapping between queries' datasets.

/* Generate intermediate queries $IDMQ = \{idmq_1, idmq_2, ...\}$ */
   $IDMQ \leftarrow \varnothing$
   for each $s_j \in S$ **do begin**
    $Q \leftarrow \{dmq_i \in DMQ \mid \sigma_{sj}R \subseteq \sigma_{\Sigma i}R \}$
    $intermediate\_minsup \leftarrow min\{minsup_i \mid dmq_i=(R, a, s_i, \Phi_i, minsup_i) \in Q\}$
    $intermediate\_\Phi \leftarrow \Phi_1 \vee \Phi_2 \vee ... \vee \Phi_{|Q|}, \forall i=1..|Q|, dmq_i=(R, a, s_i, \Phi_i, minsup_i) \in Q$
    $IDMQ \leftarrow IDMQ \cup idmq_j=(R, a, s_j, intermediate\_\Phi, intermediate\_minsup)$
   end
/* Execute intermediate queries */
   for each $idmq_i \in IDMQ$ **do**
    $IF_i \leftarrow execute(idmq_i)$
/* Generate results for original queries $DMQ = \{dmq_1, dmq_2, ...\}$ */
   for each $dmq_i \in DMQ$ **do**
    $C^i \leftarrow \{c \mid c \in \bigcup_k IF_k, \sigma_{sk}R \subseteq \sigma_{\Sigma i}R, c.support \geq minsup_i, c \text{ satisfies } \Phi_i\}$
   for each $s_j \in S$ **do begin**
    $CC \leftarrow \{C^i \mid \sigma_{sj}R \subseteq \sigma_{\Sigma i}R \}$; /* select the candidates to count now */
    if $CC \neq \varnothing$ **then** $count(CC, \sigma_{sj}R)$;
   end
   for $(i=1; i<=n; i++)$ **do**
    $Answer^i \leftarrow \{c \in C^i \mid c.support \geq minsup_i\}$ /* generate final results */

Fig. 3. Mine Merge method

Mine Merge first generates a set of *intermediate queries*, in which each frequent itemset query is based on a single elementary data selection predicate only. The intermediate queries are derived from those original queries that are sharing a given elementary data selection predicate. The minimum support thresholds and pattern constraints for the intermediate queries are chosen so that their results are guaranteed to include all locally frequent itemsets for all the original queries that refer to the database partition corresponding to a given intermediate query, i.e., (1) the support threshold of an intermediate query is the smallest minimum support threshold value from all the relevant original queries, (2) the pattern constraint of an intermediate query is a disjunction of the pattern constraints of the relevant original queries.

Next, the intermediate queries are executed sequentially using any frequent itemset mining algorithm (Apriori, FP-growth, etc.). The pattern constraints that the chosen algorithm can incorporate are pushed into the mining process, the remaining ones are verified in a post-processing phase.

The results of intermediate queries are merged to form global candidates for the original queries. For each of the original queries the set of its global candidates is a union of frequent itemsets from all the intermediate queries operating on subsets of its dataset. Since intermediate queries correspond to elementary data selection predicates, these intermediate queries represent a partitioning of the original query's dataset into a set of disjoint partitions. Thus, the set of global candidates is guaranteed to contain all frequent itemsets thanks to the property that in a partitioned dataset a pattern can be frequent only if it is frequent in at least one partition.

Finally, a database scan is performed to count the global candidate supports and to answer the original queries. The pseudocode of Mine Merge is shown in Fig. 3.

Obviously, efficiency of Mine Merge depends on the presence of efficient access paths to dataset partitions corresponding to elementary data selection predicates. In fact, Mine Merge must exploit ordering and/or indexing of the database relation containing the mined datasets. Otherwise, each of the intermediate queries would perform full relation scans, similarly as in sequential processing of the original queries. This would lead to worse performance of Mine Merge than in case of sequential processing because the number of intermediate queries generated by Mine Merge is greater than the number of original queries. Another problem with Mine Merge is that it introduces an extra database scan to generate final results from the results of the intermediate queries, and therefore requires significant overlapping of queries' datasets in order to outperform sequential processing. Finally, Mine Merge is not appropriate for large batches of queries as the number of intermediate queries in the worst case is 2^n-1, where n is the number of queries (all subsets of the set of queries except the empty set). In such worst-case scenarios gains thanks to I/O reduction may not compensate the increased amount of computations.

Although Mine Merge is independent of the mining algorithm used to execute intermediate queries, one can expect that its performance relative to sequential processing will depend on the chosen mining algorithm. For instance, the efficiency of Mine Merge for Apriori strongly depends on data distribution which has an impact on the number of Apriori iterations required for the intermediate queries. The same should be true for FP-growth, i.e., the size of FP-tree and processing time of the recursive FP-growth procedure for each intermediate query will depend on data distribution. Additionally, one can expect that in case of FP-growth, which requires exactly only two database scans, it will be more difficult for Mine Merge to compensate the cost of its extra database scan with the reduction of I/O thanks to dataset overlapping between the queries than it was for Apriori.

3.3 Common Counting

Common Counting was specifically developed for the Apriori algorithm. It consists in concurrent execution of a set of frequent itemset queries using Apriori and integrating their dataset scans. The method iteratively generates and counts candidates for all the data mining queries, storing candidates generated for each query in memory (in separate hash-tree structures). For each elementary data selection predicate, its corresponding database partition is scanned once per iteration, and candidates for all the queries referring to that partition are counted.

An advantage of Common Counting over Mine Merge is that it does not introduce any significant computations and I/O operations apart from these performed by Apriori executions. Therefore, Common Counting outperforms sequential processing if any overlapping between queries' datasets occurs and in general is more predictable than Mine Merge. Another positive feature of Common Counting is that, contrary to Mine Merge, in order to outperform sequential processing it does not require efficient access paths to dataset partitions corresponding to elementary data selection predicates. Moreover, if full scans of database relation are necessary to identify datasets for each query, Common Counting is particularly efficient compared to sequential processing as it performs one full scan per Apriori iteration, serving all the queries. (Transactions are read sequentially and each of them is processed by the queries, whose data selection predicates it satisfies.)

One problem with Common Counting is that it needs to maintain data structures (candidate hash-trees) of several queries in main memory at the same time. If the candidates of all the queries do not fit into memory, the counting process is divided into phases, and queries are scheduled into phases so that an overall I/O cost is minimized [23][25].

4   Common Building: Adaptation of Common Counting for FP-Growth

Common Counting as formulated for Apriori cannot be applied directly to FP-growth because FP-growth does not perform candidate generation and counting. However, we can exploit the general strategy of Common Counting, which is integration of operations performed by a set of queries during the scan of the common part of the dataset. In case of FP-growth, the database is scanned 2 times (during the FP-tree building phase), and these two scans can be integrated for the collection of queries for which FP-trees are to be built. Thus, our adaptation of Common Counting to FP-growth will consist in concurrent building of FP-trees in main memory for a batch of queries, and therefore will be called Common Building. The Common Building method for FP-growth for two concurrent queries dmq_1 and dmq_2 can be formalized as presented in Fig. 4. Generalization of the procedure for an arbitrary number of queries is straightforward.

Integration of common I/O operations takes place only during the tree-building step, the FP-growth recursive procedure is not affected by the multiple-query processing strategy. D^1 and D^2 denote parts of the database read by dmq_1 and dmq_2 respectively. Similarly, $mincount^1$ and $mincount^2$ are minimum required numbers of occurrences for an itemset to be frequent for dmq_1 and dmq_2 respectively. $FP\text{-}tree^1$ and $FP\text{-}tree^2$ are separate FP-tree structures containing compressed datasets for dmq_1 and dmq_2 as proposed in [9].

It should be noted that Common Building for FP-growth preserves one of the crucial positive features of Apriori Common Counting as it also does not rely on the presence of efficient access paths to dataset partitions corresponding to elementary data selection predicates for its efficiency, and is even more advantageous if full scans are the only (or the most efficient) choice. If full scans of the database relation are necessary, Common Building will build FP-trees for all the queries using two scans, whereas in case of sequential processing each query would need its own two scans.

1. scan D to calculate $mincount^1$ and $mincount^2$,
   and discover frequent items for dmq_1 and dmq_2
2. create the root of $FP\text{-}tree^1$ labeled as $null$
3. create the root of $FP\text{-}tree^2$ labeled as $null$
4. scan $D^1 - D^2$ and add each transaction to $FP\text{-}tree^1$,
   omitting items not frequent for dmq_1
5. scan $D^1 \cap D^2$ and add each transaction to both $FP\text{-}tree^1$ and $FP\text{-}tree^2$,
   omitting items not frequent for dmq_1 and dmq_2 respectively
6. scan $D^2 - D^1$ and add each transaction to $FP\text{-}tree^2$,
   omitting items not frequent for dmq_2
7. call $FP\text{-}growth(FP\text{-}tree^1, null, mincount^1)$
8. call $FP\text{-}growth(FP\text{-}tree^2, null, mincount^2)$

Fig. 4. Common Building method

Common Building does not explicitly consider pattern constraints, which are an important elements of frequent pattern queries, and had to be considered by Mine Merge (when generating intermediate queries). This is due to the fact that constraints are taken into account by FP-growth when sorting the frequent elements from a transaction before adding it to an FP-tree and within the recursive FP-growth procedure. With Common Building, these operations are performed independently for each query, and therefore the constraints can be handled as described in [18].

Common Building as an adaptation of Common Counting inherits not only its advantages but also its disadvantage, which is the need for maintaining the data structures (FP-trees in case of Common Building) for several queries at the same time in main memory. If fact, this is even a more serious problem for Common Building than it was for original Common Counting for the following two reasons. Firstly, an initial FP-tree serving as a compressed and compact representation of the source dataset is not the only memory structure used by FP-growth. The recursively called FP-growth procedure builds conditional FP-trees, which especially in early calls require significant amounts of main memory. Secondly, if datasets are sparse then the FP-tree structure does not offer significant compression and storing initial FP-trees for several queries simultaneously in main memory may be infeasible. To address the above problem, in the next section we propose a novel, memory-saving strategy for concurrent processing of frequent itemset queries using FP-growth.

5 Common FP-Tree: Integration of Queries' FP-Trees into One Data Structure

Common Building builds a separate initial FP-tree for each query. If data distribution is uniform and/or the queries' datasets significantly overlap, FP-trees built by Common Building will have a significant number of paths in common. Motivated by this observation, we propose a new strategy, named Common FP-tree, aiming at integration of FP-trees of several queries into one data structure, and thus reducing memory consumption.

The basic idea is to extend the FP-tree structure so that instead of just one counter, each tree node will contain a vector of counters – one per frequent itemset query. We will call this extended FP-tree *CFP-tree*. CFP-tree must contain all the information needed for answering all the frequent itemset queries whose datasets its represents. In order to guarantee that, when storing a transaction in CFP-tree, items frequent in *any* of the queries referring to this transaction (referred to as *locally frequent*) have to be preserved. However, for each tree node the counter of a given query is incremented only provided that both following conditions are fulfilled: (1) the item represented by the node is frequent for the query *and* (2) the query refers to the transaction being processed. If a new node is introduced to the tree, counters of the queries for which the above two conditions hold are set to 1 and the remaining counters are set to 0.

One remaining implementation detail regarding CFP-tree is the ordering of items. In general, the supports of items can be different for different queries and therefore finding an order-preserving frequency descending order for locally frequent items for all the queries is not possible. As a sensible compromise, we propose to use global frequency descending order when storing a transaction in a CFP-tree. These global supports can be counted in the same database scan as local item supports for the queries (when counting these global supports only parts of the database relevant for at least one query are considered).

Table 2. Example transaction database

TID	Items	Ordered relevant locally frequent items
100	a;c;d;f;g;i;m;p	f;c;a;m;p
200	a;b;c;f;l;m;o	f;c;a;b;m
300	b;f;h;j;o	f;b
400	B;f;k	f;b
500	b;c;k;s;p	C;b;p;s
600	a;c;e;f;l;m;n;p	f;c;a;m;p
700	c;f;m;p;s	f;c;p;s
800	a;c;f;s	f;c;s

To illustrate the structure of CFP-tree let us consider an example database represented by the first two columns of Table 2 (which will be referred to by the queries as relation R_1) and two frequent itemset queries $dmq_1 = (R_1, "Items", "100 \le TID \le 600", "\varnothing", 40\%)$ and $dmq_2 = (R_1, "Items", "400 \le TID \le 800", "\varnothing", 50\%)$. The first query refers to the first six transactions, the second – to the last five. Three transactions are shared by the queries. For both queries an item (and any itemset) is frequent if it is contained in at least three transactions.

In the first scan of the database frequent items for dmq_1 and dmq_2 are discovered and global supports of all the items are registered. The frequent items for dmq_1 are {a, b, c, f, m, p} and for dmq_2: {c, f, p, s}. The global item supports are used to descendingly order the list containing all items frequent for at least one query[1]. In our

---

[1] If two or more items have equal global support, they can be ordered arbitrarily. However, this order has to be fixed and used for all the transactions.

case: <(f:7), (c:6), (a:4), (b:4), (m:4), (p:4), (s:3)>. This list will be used to sort transactions before storing them in the CFP-tree. The third column of Table 2 shows the form in which each transaction will be inserted into the CFP-tree. For example, from transaction 500, which belongs to the datasets of both queries, items frequent for at least one query are preserved, while for transaction 800, which is referred only by the second query, only its frequent items are preserved.

The resulting CFP-tree for the database from Table 2 and the two example queries is depicted in Fig. 5. Note that, as explained earlier, some of the counters have the value of 0, which means that either a given item is not frequent for a given query or a given path in the tree represents only transactions that do not belong to the source dataset of a given query. For instance, the rightmost branch of the CFP-tree represents only transaction 500. The transaction belongs to the datasets of both considered queries, so items frequent for any of them are preserved and ordered according to descending global supports: <c, b, p, s>. However, since b and s are frequent only for one of the queries, only one of the counters in their nodes on the path is non-zero.

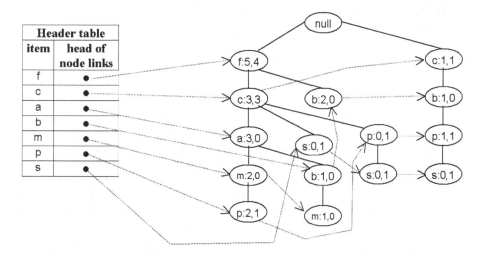

Fig. 5. CFP-tree for an example database and two queries

The Common FP-tree method for two concurrent queries: dmq_1 and dmq_2 is formally presented in Fig. 6. Similarly as with Common Building, generalization of the procedure for an arbitrary number of queries is straightforward.

Steps 1-6 represent the process of building the CFP-tree structure, described earlier in detail. In steps 7 and 8 actual in-memory mining is performed for the two queries sequentially. In the first call to the FP-growth procedure the FP-tree of a given query, "embedded" in the CFP-tree structure has to be "logically extracted". This logical extraction, for brevity represented in the algorithm as a call to *extractFPtree* function, is performed on-line, while traversing the tree, according to the following set of rules:

a) for query dmq_i, only i-th counters in tree nodes are considered;
b) when analyzing a path in a tree, nodes whose counters are 0 are ignored, but their descendants are considered;

c) when using the header table for projections, the items infrequent for a given query are omitted;
d) when following the list connecting all the nodes representing the same item (starting from the header table), nodes whose counters are 0 are ignored, but the traversal from such nodes continues.

The above rules are applied only in the first call to FP-growth as conditional FP-trees passed to further recursive calls are classic FP-tree structures.

---

1. scan D to calculate $mincount^1$ and $mincount^2$, discover frequent items for dmq_1 and dmq_2, and count global support of the locally frequent itemsets
2. create the root of CFP-tree labeled as $null$
3. scan $D^1 - D^2$ and add each transaction to CFP-tree,
   omitting items not frequent for dmq_1
5. scan $D^1 \cap D^2$ and add each transaction to CFP-tree,
   omitting items not frequent for both dmq_1 and dmq_2
6. scan $D^2 - D^1$ and add each transaction to CFP-tree,
   omitting items not frequent in for dmq_2
7. call FP-$growth(extractFPtree(dmq_1, CFP$-$tree), null, mincount^1)$
8. call FP-$growth(extractFPtree(dmq_2, CFP$-$tree), null, mincount^2)$

Fig. 6. Common FP-tree method

Similarly to Common Building, Common FP-tree performs exactly two scans of the database for the whole batch of queries, reading parts shared by the queries once per scan. Common FP-tree also does not rely on the presence of efficient access paths to dataset partitions corresponding to selection predicates for its efficiency, and is more advantageous over sequential processing if full scans are required.

As for constraint handling, Common FP-tree has one drawback compared to Common Building. Handling convertible constraints, which require specific ordering of items before storing a transaction in a tree, is possible only for one of the concurrently processed queries, due to the fact that the same fixed order has to be used by all the queries[2]. This problem definitely can be a subject of further study.

6   Experimental Results

In order to evaluate performance of Mine Merge using FP-growth, Common Building, and Common FP-tree we performed several experiments using synthetic datasets generated with GEN [2]. The datasets were stored in flat files on a disk. The transactions forming a dataset were ordered according to the transaction identifier. The dataset selection predicates had a form of range predicates on transaction identifiers. To facilitate access to database partitions determined by overlapping between queries' datasets, the data files were accompanied with simple sequential indexes. The experiments were conducted on a PC with Intel Pentium M 1,6 GHz processor and 1024 MB of main memory, running Microsoft Windows XP.

---

[2] Unless, of course, two or more queries would benefit from the same ordering.

In the experiments we varied the minimum support threshold and the overlapping between the queries' datasets. Although neither of the methods requires this, in all the experiments all the queries to be concurrently processed used the same support threshold, so as to make the potential influence of the support threshold easier to observe.

In the first series of experiments we used a small dataset (denoted as GEN1) generated using the following parameters: number of transactions = 50000, number of different items = 1000, average number of items in a transaction = 5, number of patterns = 500, average pattern length = 3. The size of this dataset was 2.5 MB. Figure 7 presents the execution times for Mine Merge using FP-growth (MM), Common Building (CB), Common FP-tree (CT), and sequential processing using FP-growth (SP) of two queries for minimum support thresholds of 1% and 2% respectively. The thresholds where experimentally selected so that they resulted in significantly different sizes of FP-trees (on average by the factor of 40). For both values of the support threshold the level of overlapping varied from 0% to 100%.

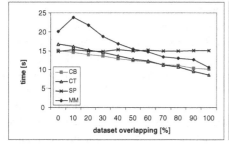 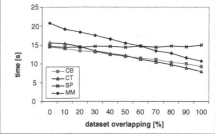

Fig. 7. Execution times on the GEN1 dataset for Mine Merge (MM), Common Building(CB), Common FP-tree (CT), and sequential processing (SP) for 2 overlapping queries with minsup=1% (left) and minsup=2% (right)

The experiments show that Common Building reduces the overall processing time if any overlapping between queries' datasets occurs (the same was true for Apriori as reported in [22]). However, Mine Merge to outperform sequential processing with FP-growth required the overlapping of about 60%, and still was beaten by Common Building and Common FP-tree in each tested case. Execution time of Common FP-tree was shorter than that of Common Building if the overlapping between the queries' datasets was greater than about 50%. The different support threshold values did not significantly influence the relative performance of the compared methods.

Comparing the above results with the ones reported for concurrent processing of frequent itemset queries using Apriori in [24], we observe that using FP-growth, Mine Merge requires much more significant overlapping between the queries and exhibits worse relative performance to Common Building than to Common Counting in case of Apriori. This can be explained by the fact that FP-growth uses only 2 database scans, typically much fewer then Apriori, and therefore for FP-growth Mine Merge needs more I/O reduction during the integrated scans to compensate the extra scan of database that it performs after collecting results of intermediate queries.

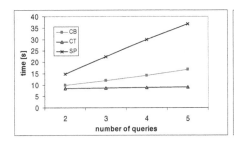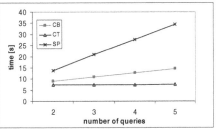

Fig. 8. Execution times on the GEN1 dataset for Common Building(CB), Common FP-tree (CT), and sequential processing (SP) for 2-5 identical queries with minsup=1% (left) and minsup=2% (right)

We also experimented with sets containing more than two queries using Common Building, Common FP-tree, and sequential processing. Mine Merge was excluded from these tests as it was found to be clearly the worst strategy for sets of two queries, and our theoretical analysis (Sect. 3.2) indicated that it is not suitable for large batches of queries. In general, it is hard to compare the performance of our methods for different numbers of queries in a batch because the more queries the more overlapping configurations possible. Therefore, in order to assess the influence of the number of queries on their performance we "benchmarked" the methods on sets of identical queries. Figure 8 shows the execution times for the batches of 2 to 5 queries and support thresholds of 1% and 2%. The results indicate that the greater the number of queries the bigger advantage of Common Building and Common FP-tree over sequential processing. This is due to the fact that the more queries, the greater relative reduction of I/O. The execution time of Common FP-tree stays almost constant with the increase of the number of identical queries as its tree structure stays the same and the time required to handle additional node counters is negligible.

Apart from measuring processing times of the tested methods, we also investigated main memory consumption by the two most efficient methods: Common Building and Common FP-tree[3]. For these two methods, Figure 9 shows the number of tree nodes[4] for different levels of overlapping and support thresholds of 1% and 2% respectively. The values for Common Building are sums of the number of nodes for both queries[5]. The experiments show that Common FP-tree requires significantly less memory than Common Building, and as expected memory savings increase with the level of overlapping.

---

[3] Note that Mine Merge does not introduce any specific memory management issues compared to sequential processing as it uses unmodified FP-tree structure and by processing intermediate queries sequentially never needs to maintain FP-trees of more than one query at the same time.

[4] For the case of two queries comparing the numbers of tree nodes provides a satisfactory approximation of the relation between the actual tree sizes as in that case the nodes consist mostly of pointers with one extra integer counter per node in case of Common FP-tree.

[5] The number of nodes measured for Common Building was not constant due to the fact that in our experiments changing the level of overlapping resulted in different parts of the generated dataset being mined and the items were not uniformly distributed.

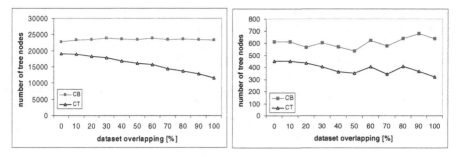

Fig. 9. Number of tree nodes for Common Building (CB) and Common FP-tree (CT) for 2 overlapping queries on GEN1 with minsup=1% (left) and minsup=2% (right)

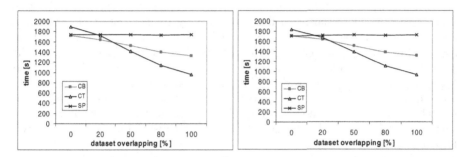

Fig. 10. Execution times on the GEN2 dataset for Common Building(CB), Common FP-tree (CT), and sequential processing (SP) for 2 overlapping queries with minsup=0.9% (left) and minsup=1.05% (right)

In the second series of experiments, aiming at testing scalability of the proposed methods, we used a significantly larger and more dense dataset (denoted as GEN2) generated using the following parameters: number of transactions = 2500000, number of different items = 10000, average number of items in a transaction = 8, number of patterns = 1500, average pattern length = 4. The size of this dataset was 260 MB. Figure 10 presents the execution times for the two most promising methods: Common

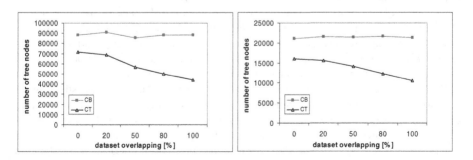

Fig. 11. Number of tree nodes for Common Building (CB) and Common FP-tree (CT) for 2 overlapping queries on GEN2 with minsup=0.9% (left) and minsup=1.05% (right)

Building (CB) and Common FP-tree (CT), compared to the execution times of sequential processing using FP-growth (SP) for two queries and minimum support thresholds of 0.9% and 1.05% respectively. For both values of the support threshold the level of overlapping varied from 0% to 100%. The thresholds where again experimentally selected so that they resulted in significantly different sizes of FP-trees (on average by the factor of 4). The numbers of tree nodes for Common Building (CB) and Common FP-tree (CT) are shown in Fig. 11. The results obtained for the large GEN2 dataset are consistent with the ones on the small GEN1 dataset both in terms of relative execution times and sizes of tree structures.

7 Conclusions

We have addressed the problem of concurrent processing of frequent itemsets queries. While previous studies analyzed this problem only in the context of the Apriori algorithm, in this paper we focused on FP-growth, which represents a newer, pattern-growth family of data mining algorithms. We considered and experimentally evaluated three multiple-query processing strategies for FP-growth. The first was Mine Merge, originally proposed for Apriori, consisting in transforming the original set of queries into the set of intermediate queries on non-overlapping datasets. The second, inspired by Common Counting for Apriori, was based on integration of dataset scans performed by the queries on shared parts of the database, and was formulated for FP-growth as the Common Building method. The third was a completely new strategy, aiming at integrating memory structures used by the queries, and was implemented in the context of FP-growth as the Common FP-tree method.

The experiments show that Common Building reduces the overall processing time compared to sequential processing if any overlapping between queries' datasets occurs (the same was true for Apriori Common Counting). On the other hand, Mine Merge to be successful with FP-growth requires much more significant overlapping between the queries than in case of Apriori. Finally, the novel strategy, applied by Common FP-tree, outperformed Common Building if queries' datasets overlapped by more than 30% to 50% depending on the nature of the dataset, and in all cases had smaller memory requirements, which makes it an optimal solution for highly overlapping queries and environments with limited memory. For queries that do not overlap significantly, Common Building is more appropriate.

For each of the proposed methods we analyzed the influence of the presence of efficient access paths to queries' source datasets and briefly discussed the possibility of integrating pattern constraints into the mining process. Handling pattern constraints within Mine Merge and Common Building is trivial but their incorporation into Common FP-tree leaves some open questions for future research.

Another direction for further research, which we are currently investigating, is concurrent processing of frequent itemset queries using Apriori by integrating candidate hash-trees of the queries, resulting in a method analogous to Common FP-tree for FP-growth. Finally, we also plan to investigate further possibilities of computation sharing between the concurrently processed queries, going beyond sharing disk accesses and memory data structures.

Acknowledgments. Part of this work has been published by the authors as "Concurrent Processing of Frequent Itemset Queries Using FP-Growth Algorithm" in the Proceedings of the 1st ADBIS Workshop on Data Mining and Knowledge Discovery (ADMKD'05), Tallinn, Estonia, 2005.

References

1. Agrawal, R., Imielinski, T., Swami, A.: Mining Association Rules Between Sets of Items in Large Databases. In: Proc. of the 1993 ACM SIGMOD Conf. on Management of Data, ACM Press, New York (1993)
2. Agrawal, R., Mehta, M., Shafer, J., Srikant, R., Arning, A., Bollinger, T.: The Quest Data Mining System. In: Proc. of the 2nd Int'l Conference on Knowledge Discovery in Databases and Data Mining (1996)
3. Agrawal, R., Srikant, R.: Fast Algorithms for Mining Association Rules. In: Proc. of the 20th Int'l Conf. on Very Large Data Bases (1994)
4. Alsabbagh, J.R., Raghavan, V.V.: Analysis of common subexpression exploitation models in multiple-query processing. In: Proc. of the 10th ICDE Conference (1994)
5. Baralis, E., Psaila, G.: Incremental Refinement of Mining Queries. In: Mohania, M.K., Tjoa, A.M. (eds.) DaWaK 1999. LNCS, vol. 1676, pp. 173–182. Springer, Heidelberg (1999)
6. Blockeel, H., Dehaspe, L., Demoen, B., Janssens, G., Ramon, J., Vandecasteele, H.: Improving the Efficiency of Inductive Logic Programming Through the Use of Query Packs. Journal of Artificial Intelligence Research 16 (2002)
7. Cheung, D.W., Han, J., Ng, V., Wong, C.Y.: Maintenance of Discovered Association Rules in Large Databases: An Incremental Updating Technique. In: Proc. of the 12th ICDE (1996)
8. Han, J., Pei, J.: Mining Frequent Patterns by Pattern-Growth: Methodology and Implications. SIGKDD Explorations (December 2000)
9. Han, J., Pei, J., Yin, Y.: Mining frequent patterns without candidate generation. In: Proc. of the 2000 ACM SIGMOD Conf. on Management of Data, ACM Press, New York (2000)
10. Han, J., Pei, J., Yin, Y., Mao, R.: Mining Frequent Patterns without Candidate Generation: A Frequent-pattern Tree Approach. Data Mining and Knowledge Discovery: An International Journal 8(1) (2004)
11. Imielinski, T., Mannila, H.: A Database Perspective on Knowledge Discovery. Communications of the ACM 39(11) (1996)
12. Jarke, M.: Common subexpression isolation in multiple query optimization. In: Kim, W., Reiner, D.S. (eds.) Query Processing in Database Systems, Springer, Heidelberg (1985)
13. Jeudy, B., Boulicaut, J-F.: Using condensed representations for interactive association rule mining. In: Elomaa, T., Mannila, H., Toivonen, H. (eds.) PKDD 2002. LNCS (LNAI), vol. 2431, pp. 225–236. Springer, Heidelberg (2002)
14. Jin, R., Sinha, K., Agrawal, G.: Simultaneous Optimization of Complex Mining Tasks with a Knowledgeable Cache. In: Proc. of the 11th ACM SIGKDD International Conference on Knowledge Discovery and Data Mining, ACM Press, New York (2005)
15. Meo, R.: Optimization of a Language for Data Mining. In: Proc. of the ACM Symposium on Applied Computing - Data Mining Track, ACM Press, New York (2003)
16. Morzy, T., Wojciechowski, M., Zakrzewicz, M.: Materialized Data Mining Views. In: Zighed, A.D.A., Komorowski, J., Żytkow, J.M. (eds.) PKDD 2000. LNCS (LNAI), vol. 1910, Springer, Heidelberg (2000)

17. Nag, B., Deshpande, P.M., DeWitt, D.J.: Using a Knowledge Cache for Interactive Discovery of Association Rules. In: Proc. of the 5th KDD Conference (1999)
18. Pei, J., Han, J.: Can We Push More Constraints into Frequent Pattern Mining? In: Proceedings of the 6th ACM SIGKDD International Conference on Knowledge Discovery and Data Mining, ACM Press, New York (2000)
19. Roy, P., Seshadri, S., Sundarshan, S., Bhobe, S.: Efficient and Extensible Algorithms for Multi Query Optimization. ACM SIGMOD Intl. Conference on Management of Data (2000)
20. Savasere, A., Omiecinski, E., Navathe, S.: An Efficient Algorithm for Mining Association Rules in Large Databases. In: Proc. 21th Int'l Conf. Very Large Data Bases (1995)
21. Sellis, T.: Multiple-query optimization. ACM Transactions on Database Systems 13(1) (1988)
22. Wojciechowski, M., Zakrzewicz, M.: Evaluation of Common Counting Method for Concurrent Data Mining Queries. In: Kalinichenko, L.A., Manthey, R., Thalheim, B., Wloka, U. (eds.) ADBIS 2003. LNCS, vol. 2798, Springer, Heidelberg (2003)
23. Wojciechowski, M., Zakrzewicz, M.: Data Mining Query Scheduling for Apriori Common Counting. In: Proc. of the Sixth International Baltic Conference on Databases and Information Systems (2004)
24. Wojciechowski, M., Zakrzewicz, M.: Evaluation of the Mine Merge Method for Data Mining Query Processing. In: Benczúr, A.A., Demetrovics, J., Gottlob, G. (eds.) ADBIS 2004. LNCS, vol. 3255, Springer, Heidelberg (2004)
25. Wojciechowski, M., Zakrzewicz, M.: On Multiple Query Optimization in Data Mining. In: Ho, T.-B., Cheung, D., Liu, H. (eds.) PAKDD 2005. LNCS (LNAI), vol. 3518, Springer, Heidelberg (2005)

Towards a General Framework for Data Mining

Sašo Džeroski

Jožef Stefan Institute, Jamova 39, 1000 Ljubljana, Slovenia

Abstract. In this paper, we address the ambitious task of formulating a general framework for data mining. We discuss the requirements that such a framework should fulfill: It should elegantly handle different types of data, different data mining tasks, and different types of patterns/models. We also discuss data mining languages and what they should support: this includes the design and implementation of data mining algorithms, as well as their composition into nontrivial multi-step knowledge discovery scenarios relevant for practical application. We proceed by laying out some basic concepts, starting with (structured) data and generalizations (e.g., patterns and models) and continuing with data mining tasks and basic components of data mining algorithms (i.e., refinement operators, distances, features and kernels). We next discuss how to use these concepts to formulate constraint-based data mining tasks and design generic data mining algorithms. We finally discuss how these components would fit in the overall framework and in particular into a language for data mining and knowledge discovery.

1 Introduction: The Challenges for Data Mining

While knowledge discovery in databases (KDD) and data mining have enjoyed great popularity and success in recent years, there is a distinct lack of a generally accepted framework for data mining. The present lack of such a framework is perceived as an obstacle to the further development of the field. For example, at the SIGKDD-2003 conference panel "Data Mining: The Next 10 Years" (Fayyad et al. 2003), U. Fayyad emphasizes in his position statement that "the biggest stumbling block from the scientific perspective is the lack of a fundamental theory or a clear and well-understood statement of problems and challenges".

Yang and Wu (2006) collected the opinions of a number of outstanding data mining researchers about the most challenging problems in data mining research (and presented them at ICDM-2005). Among the ten topics considered most important and worthy of further research, the development of a unifying theory is listed first. The article states: "Several respondents feel that the current state of the art of data mining research is too ad-hoc. ... a theoretical framework that unifies different data mining tasks ..., as well as different data mining approaches ..., would help the field and provide a basis for future research."

High on the list of important research topics is mining complex data (Yang and Wu 2006). We will take complex data here to mean structured data that depart from the format most commonly used in data mining, namely the format

S. Džeroski and J. Struyf (Eds.): KDID 2006, LNCS 4747, pp. 259–300, 2007.

of a single table. This will include sequences and graphs, but also text, images, video, and multi-media data. From this viewpoint, much of the current research in data mining is about mining complex data, e.g., text mining, link mining, mining social network data, web mining, multi-media data mining. Many of the grand challenges for data mining are perceived to be in this area, cf. the SIGKDD-2006 conference panel (Piatetsky-Shapiro et al. 2006). An additional challenge is to treat the mining of different types of structured data in a uniform fashion, which is becoming increasingly more difficult, as somewhat separate research (sub)communities are evolving around text/link/tree/graph mining.

Hand in hand with the above go the problems of mining complex patterns and the incorporation of domain knowledge (Yang and Wu 2006; Aggrawal's comments in Fayyad et al. 2003). As the complexity of the data analyzed grows, more expressive formalisms are needed to represent patterns found in the data. The use of such formalisms has been proposed within relational data mining (Džeroski and Lavrač 2001) and statistical relational learning (Getoor and Taskar, 2007); these are now used increasingly more often in link mining, web mining and mining of network data.

The last set of methodological questions that we want to emphasize here concerns knowledge discovery as a process, rather than individual data mining tasks and approaches. Data preparation typically takes significant time and different data mining operations need to be applied and composed in practical applications. Arguably, there is insufficient support for humans carrying out the knowledge discovery process as a whole. Integration and compositionality of data mining operations/algorithms are called for.

At a KDD-03 panel discussion (Fayyad et al. 2003), Fayyad states: "In a typical data mining session, I spend most of my time extracting and manipulating data, not really doing data mining and exploration. The trail of 'droppings' I leave behind in any given data mining session is enormous, and it seems every time it is replicated and repeated, almost from scratch, again." Ramakrishnan (at the same panel) follows suit and identifies as technical challenges the following: "(1) Finding ways to address the real bottleneck in data mining, which is the human cycles spent in analyzing data. ... Real advances will come from techniques that lead to more efficient management of the process of data mining, and that reduce the cycle time in arriving at useful insights. (2) Data mining is often perceived as a bag of tricks. We need to at least provide a vision of how these tricks fit into a coherent tool-kit." In the same article, Uthurusamy makes the point that: "Even obvious and immediate needs like ... the core need of integration have not received their much-deserved attention... The original process centric view of KDD espoused the three 'I's (Integrated, Iterative, and Interactive) as basic for KDD. These are central to the ideas of 'Computer Assisted Human Discovery' and 'Human Assisted Computer Discovery.' There has been very little work on these in recent years." Yang and Wu (2006) also point out the need to support the composition of data mining operators, as well as the need to have a theory behind this.

In the remainder of this article, we first discuss (Section 2) inductive databases and inductive queries, one of the most promising approaches to formulating a general framework for data mining, then discuss the desirable properties of such a framework (Section 3). Section 4 defines the basic concepts of data mining, including data, patterns/models, and data mining tasks. Section 5 discusses the dual nature of patterns/models, which can be viewed both as data and as functions. Section 6 introduces constraint-based data mining and discusses the types of constraints considered therein. Section 7 introduces the key ingredients of data mining algorithms (i.e., refinement operators, distances, features and kernels). Section 8 revisits constraint-based data mining and treats it in the context of the basic ingredients from Section 7. Section 9 discusses the design of generic data mining algorithms for structured data. We finally discuss how all of the above components would fit in the overall framework and in particular into a language for data mining and knowledge discovery in Section 10. The article closes with a brief discussion of related work.

2   Inductive Databases and Inductive Queries

Inductive databases (IDBs, Imielinski and Mannila 1996, De Raedt 2002a) are an emerging research area at the intersection of data mining and databases. In addition to normal data, inductive databases contain patterns (either materialized or defined as views). Besides patterns (which are of local nature), models (which are of global nature) can also be considered. In the IDB framework, patterns become "first-class citizens" and can be stored and manipulated just like data in ordinary databases.

Inductive databases embody a database perspective on knowledge discovery, where knowledge discovery processes become query sessions. Ordinary queries can be used to access and manipulate data, while inductive queries (IQs) can be used to generate (mine), manipulate, and apply patterns. KDD thus becomes an extended querying process (Imielinski and Mannila 1996) in which both the data and the patterns that hold (are valid) in the data are queried. IDB research thus aims at replacing the traditional KDD process model, where steps like pre-processing, data cleaning, and model construction follow each other in succession, by a simpler model in which all data pre-processing operations, data mining operations, as well as post-processing operations are queries to an inductive database and can be interleaved in many different ways.

Given an inductive database that contains data and patterns, several different types of queries can be posed. Data retrieval queries use only the data and their results are also data: no pattern is involved in the query. In IDBs, we can also have cross-over queries that combine patterns and data in order to obtain new data, e.g., apply a predictive model to a dataset to obtain predictions for a target property. In processing patterns, the patterns are queried without access to the data: this is what is usually done in the post-processing stages of data mining. Data mining queries use the data and their results are patterns: new patterns are generated from the data and this corresponds to the traditional data mining step. When we talk about inductive queries, we most often mean data mining queries.

A general statement of the problem of data mining (Mannila and Toivonen 1997) involves the specification of a language of patterns and a set of constraints that a pattern has to satisfy. The latter can be divided in two parts: language constraints and evaluation constraints. The first part only concerns the pattern itself, while the second part concerns the validity of the pattern with respect to a given database. Constraints thus play a central role in data mining and constraint-based data mining is now a recognized research topic (Bayardo 2002). The use of constraints enables more efficient induction and focusses the search for patterns on patterns likely to be of interest to the end user.

In the context of inductive databases, inductive queries consist of constraints. Inductive queries can involve language constraints (e.g., find association rules with item A in the head) and evaluation constraints, formed by using evaluation functions. The latter express the validity of a pattern on a given dataset. We can use these to form evaluation constraints (e.g., find all item sets with support above a threshold) or optimization constraints (e.g., find the 10 association rules with highest confidence).

Different types of data and patterns have been considered in data mining, including frequent itemsets, episodes, Datalog queries, and graphs. Designing inductive databases for these types of patterns involves the design of inductive query languages and solvers for the queries in these languages, i.e., constraint-based data mining algorithms. Of central importance is the issue of defining the primitive constraints that can be applied for the chosen data and pattern types, that can be used to compose inductive queries. For each pattern domain (type of data, type of pattern, and primitive constraints), a specific solver is designed, following the philosophy of constraint logic programming (De Raedt 2002b).

The IDB framework is an appealing approach towards a theory for data mining, because it employs declarative queries instead of ad-hoc procedural constructs. As such, it holds the promise of facilitating the formulation of an "algebra" for data mining, along the lines of Codd's relational algebra for databases (Calders et al. 2006b, Johnson et al. 2000). The IDB framework is also appealing for data mining applications, as it supports the entire KDD process (Boulicaut et al. 1999). In inductive query languages, the results of one (inductive) query can be used as input for another: nontrivial multi-step KDD scenarios can be thus supported in IDBs, rather than just single data mining operations.

The state-of-the-art in IDBs (Boulicaut et al. 2006) is that there exists some theory for and various effective approaches to constraint-based mining (inductive querying) of local patterns, such as frequent itemsets and sequences. There is an obvious lack of a theory for and practical approaches to inductive querying of global models. This issue has only recently began to attract some attention through the research on constrained induction of tree-based (Garofalakis et al. 2003, Struyf and Džeroski 2006) and equation-based (Džeroski et al. 2006) predictive models.

More importantly, most of the existing approaches to constraint-based data mining and inductive querying work in isolation and are not integrated with databases or other data mining tools. Only few attempts at integration have been made, such as the approach of mining views (Calders et al. 2006a). Answering complex inductive queries that involve different pattern domains and supporting complex KDD scenarios has also barely been studied.

3 Desiderata for a General Data Mining Framework

In this section, we briefly discuss the requirements that a general framework for data mining should fulfill. In our opinion, such a framework should elegantly handle different types of data, different data mining tasks, and different types of patterns/models. These should be orthogonal dimensions, so that combinations should be facilitated, e.g., tree-based approaches for classification of images (where the type of data is image(s), the task is classification and the model type is decision tree(s)).

One of the distinguishing features of data mining is its concern with analyzing different types of data. Besides data in the format of a single table, which is most commonly used in data mining, complex data are receiving increasing amounts of interest. These include data in the form of sequences and graphs, but also text, images, video, and multi-media data. Much of the current research in data mining is about mining such complex data, e.g., text mining, link mining, mining social network data, web mining, multi-media data mining. A major challenge is to treat the mining of different types of structured data in a uniform fashion.

Many different data analysis tasks have been considered so far within the field of data mining. By far the most common is the task of predictive modelling, which includes classification and regression. Mining frequent patterns is the next most popular, with the focus shifting from mining frequent itemsets to mining frequent patterns in complex data. Clustering, which has strong roots in the statistical community, is also commonly encountered in data mining, with distance-based and density-based clustering as the two prevailing forms. A variety of other tasks has been considered, such as change and deviation detection, but it is not clear whether these are of fundamental nature or can be defined by composing some of the tasks listed here.

Finally, different kinds/representations of patterns/models may be used for the same data mining task. This is most obvious for predictive modelling, where a variety of methods/approaches exist, ranging from rules and trees, through support vector machines, to probabilistic models (such as Naive Bayes or Bayesian networks for classification). The different types of models are interpreted in different ways, and different algorithms may exist for building the same kind of model (cf. the plethora of algorithms for building decision trees).

A general framework for data mining should define a set of basic concepts that cover the dimensions outlined above. Through combining these basic concepts, one should be able to obtain most of the diversity present in data mining approaches today. Hopefully, it would also facilitate the derivation of new approaches and insights. The basic concepts would be a keystone in the development of data mining languages, which should support the design and implementation of data mining algorithms, as well as their composition into nontrivial multi-step knowledge discovery scenarios relevant for practical application. In the latter case, we can speak of knowledge discovery languages.

4   The Basic Concepts of Data Mining

"Knowledge discovery in databases (KDD) is the non-trivial process of identifying valid, novel, potentially useful, and ultimately understandable patterns in data", state Fayyad et al. (1996). According to this definition, data mining (DM) is the central step in the KDD process concerned with applying computational techniques (i.e., data mining algorithms implemented as computer programs) to actually find patterns in the data. To arrive at a general theory/framework for data mining, we need to have general definitions for the above terms, including data, patterns and validity.

The basic concepts of data mining include data, data mining tasks, and patterns/models. The validity of a pattern/model on a given set of data is related to the data mining task considered. Below we discuss these in some detail.

4.1   Data

Let us start with data: This is the most basic ingredient of data mining. A data mining algorithm takes as input a set of data. An individual datum in the data set has its own structure, e.g., consists of values for several attributes, which may be of different types or take values from different ranges. We typically assume that all data items are of the same type and share the same structure.

More generally, we are given a data type T and a set of data D of this type. We will not discuss in detail what a data type is and how to formally define it: any standard textbook on data structures (e.g., Aho et al. 1983) covers this topic, while a more formal treatment in the context of logic is given by Lloyd (2003). It is important to notice, though, that a set of basic/primitive types is typically taken as a starting point, and more complex data types are built by using type constructors. As argued above, it is of crucial importance to be able to deal with structured data, as these are attracting an increasing amount of attention within data mining.

Assume we are given a set of primitive data types, such as Boolean or Real. Other primitive data types might include Discrete(S), where S is a finite set of identifiers, or Integer. In addition, we are given some type constructors, such as Tuple and Set, that can be used to construct more complex data types from existing ones. For example, Tuple(Boolean,Real) denotes a data type where each datum consists of a pair of a Boolean value and a real number, while Set(Tuple(Boolean,Real)) denotes a data type where each datum is a set of such pairs.

Other type constructors might include Sequence(T), which denotes a sequence of objects of type T, or LabeledGraph(VL,EL), which denotes a graph where vertex labels are of type VL and edge labels are of type EL. With these, we can easily represent the complex data types that are of practical interest. For example, DNA sequences would be of type Sequence(Discrete($\{A, C, G, T\}$)), while molecules would be labeled graphs with vertices representing atoms and edges representing bonds between atoms: atoms would be labeled with the type of element (e.g., nitrogen, oxygen) and edges would be labeled with the type of bond (e.g., single, double, triple).

4.2 Patterns and Models

Here we will consider four types of patterns/models, which are directly related to the data mining tasks discussed later in this section. These are probability distributions, patterns (in the sense of frequent patterns), predictive models and clusterings. All of these are defined on a given type of data, except for predictive models, which are defined on a pair of data types. Note that we allow arbitrary (arbitrarily complex) data types. The most typical case in data mining would consider a data type $T = \text{Tuple}(T_1, \ldots, T_k)$, where each of $T_1, \ldots, T_k$ is Boolean, Discrete(S) or Real.

A **probability distribution D on type T** is a mapping from objects of type T to non-negative Reals, i.e., has the signature $\mathbf{d} :: \mathbf{T} \to \mathbf{R}^{0+}$. For uncountably infinite types, probability densities are used instead. The sum of all probabilities (the integral of the probability densities) over T is constrained to amount to one.

A **pattern P on type T** is a Boolean function on objects of type T, i.e., has the signature $\mathbf{p} :: \mathbf{T} \to \mathbf{bool}$. A pattern on type T is true or false on an object of type T. Frawley et al. (1991) define a pattern as a statement (expression) in a given language, that describes (relationships among) the facts in (a subset of) the data. In the broadest sense, the word pattern is used to describe the output of a variety of data mining algorithms and includes probability distributions, predictive models and clusters/clusterings; however, we restrict it here to the sense that it is most commonly used, i.e., in the sense of frequent pattern mining.

A **predictive model M for types $\mathbf{T}_d, \mathbf{T}_c$** is a function that takes an object of type T_d and returns one of type T_c, i.e., has the signature $\mathbf{m} :: \mathbf{T}_d \to \mathbf{T}_c$. Most often, predictive modelling is concerned with classification, where T_c would be Boolean (for binary classification) or Discrete(S) (for multi-class classification), or regression, where T_c would be Real. In our case, we allow both T_d (description) and T_c (class/target) to be arbitrarily complex data types.

A **probabilistic predictive model P for types $\mathbf{T}_c, \mathbf{T}_d$** is a function that takes an object of type T_c and returns a probability distribution over type T_d, i.e., has the signature $\mathbf{p} :: \mathbf{T}_c \to (\mathbf{T}_d \to \mathbf{R}^{0+})$. For discrete T_c, the probability of each possible class value is given by a prediction. For real-valued T_c, the probability distribution can be, for example, assumed to be normal and its mean and standard deviation can be given by the prediction.

A **clustering C on a set of objects S of type T** is a function from S to $\{1, \ldots, k\}$, where k is the number of clusters, which has to obey $k \leq |S|$. Unlike all the previously listed types of patterns, a clustering is not necessarily a total function on T, but rather a partial function defined only on objects from

S. Overlapping and soft clusterings, where an element can (partially) belong to more that one cluster have the signature $\mathbf{T} \to (\ \{1, \ldots, k\} \to \mathbf{R}^{0+})$.

We can think of C as a matrix B, where $B(e, c)$ states to which degree datum e belongs to cluster c. In conventional clustering $B(e, c) = 1$ if datum e belongs to cluster c and 0 otherwise; only one "1" entry is allowed in each row of B. In overlapping clustering, there can be more than one "1" in each row of B. In soft clustering, the sum of the entries in each row should amount to one.

In predictive clustering, C is a total function on T. In addition, we have $T = (T_d, T_c)$ and we have a predictive model associated with each cluster through a mapping $M :: \{1, \ldots, k\} \to (T_d \to T_c)$. Performing the function composition of M and C, i.e., applying first C and then M, we get a predictive model on T.

4.3 Data Mining Tasks

In essence, the task of data mining is to produce a generalization from a given set of data. A plethora of data mining tasks has been considered so far in the literature. Here we will focus on four tasks, according to the generalizations produced: approximating the (joint) probability distribution, learning predictive models, clustering and finding valid (frequent) patterns.

Estimating the (Joint) Probability Distribution. A set of data (of type T) is often assumed to be a sample taken from a population according to a probability distribution. A probability distribution/density function assigns a non-negative probability/density to each object of type T. Probably the most general data mining task (Hand et al. 2001) is the task of estimating the (joint) probability distribution D over type T from a set of data items or a sample drawn from that distribution.

As mentioned above, in the most typical case we would have $T = \text{Tuple}(T_1, \ldots, T_k)$, where each of $T_1, \ldots, T_k$ is Boolean, Discrete(S) or Real. We talk about the joint probability distribution to emphasize the difference to the marginal distributions of each of the variables of type $T_1, \ldots, T_k$: the joint distribution captures the interactions among the variables.

Representing multi-variate distributions is a non-trivial task. Two approaches are commonly used in data mining. In the density-based clustering paradigm, mixtures of multi-variate Gaussian distributions are typically considered (Hand et al. 2001). Probabilistic graphical models, most notably Bayesian networks, represent graphically the (in)dependencies between the variables: Learning their structure and parameters is an important approach to the problem of estimating the joint probability distribution.

Learning a (Probabilistic) Predictive Model. In this task, we are given a dataset that consists of examples of the form (d, c), where each d is of type T_d and each c is of type T_c. We will refer to d as the description and c as the class or target. To learn a predictive model means to find a mapping from the description to the target, $\mathbf{m} :: \mathbf{T}_d \to \mathbf{T}_c$, that fits the data closely. This means that the observed target values and the target values predicted by the model, i.e., c and $\hat{c} = m(d)$, have to match closely.

In the case of learning probabilistic models, we need to find a mapping of the form $\mathbf{m} :: \mathbf{T}_d \rightarrow (\mathbf{T}_c \rightarrow \mathbf{R}^{0+})$. In a more general formulation of the problem, the training examples can have probability distributions over the c values instead of individual c values: This can represent uncertainty in the observations. Few (if any) actual data mining approaches take this stand; most assume that a single value for the target is given for each example.

Many different kinds of predictive models have been considered in data mining. Some examples include classification rules, decision trees and (generalized) linear models. We postpone the discussion on different model kinds (classes) until later in the chapter.

The present task can be viewed as a special case of the task of estimating the probability distribution. If we solve the latter and obtain $P((d, c))$, an estimate of the probability of observing the example (d, c), we can derive the conditional distribution $P(c|d)$, which is a predictive probabilistic model.

Clustering. Clustering in general is concerned with grouping objects into classes of similar objects (Kaufman and Rousseeuw 1990). Given a set of examples (object descriptions), the task of clustering is to partition these examples into subsets, called clusters. The notion of a distance (or conversely, similarity) is crucial here: examples are considered to be points in a metric space (a space with a distance metric). The goal of clustering is to achieve high similarity between objects within individual clusters (intra-cluster similarity) and low similarity between objects that belong to different clusters (inter-cluster similarity).

In clustering, the examples do not contain a target property to be predicted, but only an object description. Note that a prototype (prototypical example) may be used as a representative for a cluster. This may be, e.g., the mean or the medoid of the examples in the cluster (which are examples with lowest average distance to all the examples in the cluster).

Clustering is known as cluster analysis in statistics, as customer segmentation in marketing and customer relationship management, and as unsupervised learning in machine learning. Conventional clustering focusses on distance-based cluster analysis. In conceptual clustering (Michalski 1980), a symbolic representation of the resulting clusters is produced in addition to the partition into clusters: we can thus consider each cluster to be a concept (much like a class in classification). In predictive clustering (Blockeel et al. 1998), a predictive model is associated with the clustering, so that new instances can be immediately associated with one of the created clusters and its prototype, which can be considered as a representative of the cluster.

In density-based clustering (Hand et al. 2001), clusters correspond to different components of the joint probability distribution, which is assumed to be a mixture model. An example belongs to each cluster to a different degree, determined by the probability that the corresponding component of the mixture assigns to it. In this context, clustering is clearly a special case of the task of estimating the joint probability distribution.

Pattern Discovery. In contrast to the previous three tasks, where the goal is to build a single global model describing the entire set of data given as input, the task of pattern discovery is to find all local patterns from a given pattern language that satisfy the required conditions. A prototypical instantiation of this task is the task of finding frequent itemsets (sets of items, such as $\{bread, butter\}$), which are often found together in a transaction (e.g., a market basket) (Aggrawal et al 1993). The condition that a pattern (itemset) has to satisfy in this case is to appear in (hold true for) a sufficiently high proportion (called support and denoted by s) of the transactions in the input dataset.

With the increasing interest in mining complex data, mining frequent patterns is also considered for structured data. We can thus talk about mining frequent subsequences or mining frequent subgraphs in sequence or graph data. We can consider as frequency the multiple occurrences of a pattern in a single data structure (e.g., sequence or graph) or the single occurrences of a pattern in multiple data structures.

The task of finding frequent itemsets (patterns) is typically performed in the context of association analysis (Han and Kamber 2001). After all frequent itemsets are found, one looks for association rules of the form $X \rightarrow Y$, where X and Y are frequent itemsets and the confidence of the rule passes a threshold c. The confidence of the rule $X \rightarrow Y$ is the percentage of transactions containing X that also contain Y. Generalizations of the task of pattern discovery include the discovery of clauses in first order logic (Dehaspe and De Raedt 1997) and the discovery of frequent Datalog queries and query extensions (Dehaspe and Toivonen 1999), the latter being generalizations of finding frequent itemsets and association rules to first order logic.

While the original formulation of the problems of frequent itemset and association rule mining reports all itemsets and rules that pass the support respectively confidence threshold, we can think of these tasks also as ranking tasks, where the itemsets and rules are ordered according to support, respectively confidence. One can then imagine asking for the top-k most frequent itemsets or most confident association rules. This formulation bears an important similarity to the problem of feature ranking and selection, which is often encountered in the context of global (mostly predictive) modelling. Top-k queries of this kind also appear in the context of correlated itemsets and association rules, which can be used for constructing classifiers. In fact, there is an increasing body of research that uses the results of local pattern mining/discovery to build global (predictive) models.

In this context, we can view the tasks of bump hunting (Friedman and Fisher 1999) and subgroup discovery (Kloesgen 2002, Lavrač et al. 2004) as special cases of pattern discovery. Both involve finding groups of examples where the (probability distribution of) the values of a designated target is unusual. Here unusual can be taken to mean unusually large or small, or, more generally, significantly different from the average (or the distribution) over the entire dataset/population. It is in addition desired that these regions be describable in an interpretable form involving simple statements (rules).

Note, finally, that finding frequent patterns can be viewed as a special case of estimating the joint probability distribution. If we think of the joint probability distribution as a surface in multi-dimensional space, then the frequent patterns (and the groups of examples for which they are true) would correspond to peaks of the surface. The threshold on the frequency would correspond to a hyperplane that would cut off patterns below the given frequency.

5   The Dual Nature of Patterns and Models

Patterns and models inherently have a dual nature. According to the definitions from the previous sections, they are functions that take as input data points and map them to probabilities, Booleans, class predictions or probabilities thereover, or cluster assignments. On the other hand, they can be treated as data structures and as such represented, stored and manipulated.

Let us illustrate this with a simple example. Suppose we have a frequent itemset consisting of the items bread and butter. We can view this as a set, namely $\{bread, butter\}$, and store it in a database. In this fashion, we can store the frequent itemsets derived from a set of transactions. On the other hand, from the functional viewpoint, the itemset represents a mapping from transactions to Booleans. The transactions which contain the itemset, i.e., both bread and butter, are assigned the value true, i.e., the pattern holds true for such transactions. For example, the transaction $\{bread, butter, milk\}$ subsumes our itemset and yields the value true, while $\{beer, peanuts, butter\}$ does not and yields the value false.

5.1   The Data Aspect: Classes of Patterns and Models

Many different kinds of predictive models have been considered in the data mining literature. Classification rules, decision trees and linear models are just a few examples. We will refer to these as model classes. In the case of patterns we will talk about pattern classes.

A class of patterns C_P on type T is a set of patterns P on type T, expressed in a language L_P. Similarly, a class of models C_M on types T_d, T_c is a set of models M on types T_d, T_c, expressed in a language L_M. In the same fashion, we can define classes of probability distributions C_D and clusterings C_C.

The languages $L_P/L_M/L_D/L_C$ refer to the data part of the patterns and models. They essentially define data types for representing the patterns and models. For example, if we have data types $T_d = $ (Real, Real) and $T_e = $ Real, linear models would be represented by three real-valued coefficients and would need a data type $T_l = $ (Real, Real, Real) to be represented.

Suppose we have a dataset where data items correspond to descriptions of individuals, each individual being described by a tuple of the form (Gender, Age, HairColor), where Gender = Discrete($\{M, F\}$), Age = Real, HairColor = Discrete($\{Blond, Brown, Black, Red, Other\}$), and the target is of type Education = Discrete($\{None, Elementary, High, College, BSc, MSc, PhD\}$). The language of decision trees for this case would be the language of tree structures with tests like HairColor=Blond in the internal nodes and predictions like Education=PhD in the leaves. The elements of this language (its alphabet) depend on the attributes and their values, and vary with the underlying data type.

5.2   The Function Aspect: Interpreters

There is usually a unique mapping from the data part of a pattern/model to the function part. This takes the data part of a pattern/model as input, and returns the corresponding function as an output. The mapping we refer to is inherently second/higher order (Lloyd 2003) since it has a function as an output.

This mapping can be realized through a so-called interpreter. An interpreter takes as input (the data part of) a pattern and an example, and returns the result of applying the (function part) of the pattern to the example. Given a data type d, an example E of type d, and a pattern P of type $\mathbf{p} :: \mathbf{d} \to \mathbf{bool}$, an interpreter I returns the result of applying P to E, i.e., $I(P, E) = P(E)$.

The signature of the interpreter is $\mathbf{i} :: \mathbf{p} \to \mathbf{d} \to \mathbf{bool}$. If we apply the interpreter to a pattern and an example, we obtain a Boolean value. In functional programming (Thompson 1999), we can evaluate the interpreter only partially, i.e., apply it only to the data part of a pattern, obtaining as a result the function part of the pattern. The partial evaluation $\mathbf{i}\ \mathbf{p}$ has a signature $\mathbf{d} \to \mathbf{bool}$.

The interpreters map from the data part of a pattern/model to the function part. Suppose we are given a linear model with coefficients a, b, and c. The interpreter of linear models I_l would, given a, b, and c, and a data tuple of the form (x, y), return the value of the linear combination $ax + by + c$. A partial evaluation/application of the interpreter to the tuple of constant coefficients of the linear model I_l (a, b, c) would yield the linear function $aX + bY + c$: This linear function can then be applied to specific tuples (x, y) to yield predictions.

The interpreter is crucial for the semantics of a class patterns/models: a class of patterns/models is only completely defined when the corresponding interpreter is defined (e.g., I_P/I_M for patterns/models are parts of the definition of the class C_P/C_M). To illustrate this, consider rule sets, which may be ordered or unordered. Both can actually be represented by the same list of rules: It is the interpreter that treats the rules as ordered or unordered. In the first case, the rules are considered in the order they appear in the list and the first rule that applies to a given example is taken to make a prediction. In the second case, all rules from the list that apply to a given example are taken, and their predictions combined to obtain a final prediction.

6   Constraints in Data Mining: Introduction

Let us recall briefly that data mining is concerned with finding patterns/models that are valid in a given set of data. The key ingredients of data mining thus include data, data mining tasks, and patterns/models, which we have elaborated on in some detail in the previous sections. We now turn to the issue of pattern/model validity. Essentially, we say that a pattern is valid if it satisfies a given set of constraints. The constraints considered depend heavily on the data mining task at hand, and so does the concept of validity. In this section, we introduce the notion of constraints and discuss the different types of constraints.

A view generally held is that constraints are Boolean functions on patterns/models. A constraint is either satisfied or not satisfied. Given that patterns and models have a dual nature, i.e., have both a data and a function aspect, we can have constraints on each of these aspects.

6.1 Language Constraints

Language constraints concern the data part of a pattern/model. Boolean language constraints define a subclass/sublanguage of the class of patterns/models considered. For example, in the context of mining frequent itemsets, we might be interested only in itemsets where a specific item, e.g., *beer* occurs. Or, in the context of learning predictive models, we may be interested only in decision trees that have a specific attribute in the root node and, in addition, do not have more than seven leaves.

These are language constraints and refer to the data part only. We can check whether they are satisfied or not without accessing the data that we have been given as a part of the data mining task. If we are in the context of inductive databases and queries, queries on the data part of patterns/models are composed of primitive language constraints.

Language constraints may also involve (cost) functions on the data part of patterns/models. An example of these is the size of a decision tree, mentioned above. Another example would be the cost of an itemset (market basket), in the context where each item has a price. The cost functions as discussed here are mappings from the data part of a pattern/model to non-negative reals and Boolean language constraints can put thresholds on the values of these functions.

6.2 Evaluation Constraints

Evaluation constraints correspond to inductive queries that concern the function aspect of patterns/models. Evaluation constraints are typically Boolean functions, i.e., statements, involving evaluation functions and comparing them to constant thresholds. Evaluation functions measure the validity of patterns/models on a given set of data.

Evaluation functions are functionals, i.e., they take a function (in this case a pattern or a model) as input and return a scalar (real) value as output. The set of data is an additional input to the evaluation functions. For example, the frequency of a pattern on a given dataset is a typical evaluation function. Similarly, the classification error of a predictive model is also an evaluation function. Evaluation constraints typically compare the value of an evaluation function to a constant threshold, e.g., minimum support or maximum error.

Constraints on the function part of a pattern/model may also involve some general property of the function, which does not depend on the specific dataset considered. For example, we may only consider functions that are convex or symmetric or monotonic in certain variables. These properties are usually defined over the entire domain of the function, i.e., the corresponding data type, but may be checked for the specific dataset at hand.

6.3 Optimization Constraints

Many Boolean constraints are obtained by imposing a threshold on the value of a function(al). This can be a threshold on a cost function over the data part of a pattern/model or on an evaluation function(al) on the function part of the model. Boolean constraints are either satisfied or not.

On the other hand, optimization constraints ask for (a fixed-size set of) patterns/models that have a maximal/minimal value for a given cost or evaluation function. Example queries involving such constraints would ask for the k most frequent itemsets or the top k correlated patterns. Alternatively, we might ask for the most accurate decision tree of size five, or the smallest decision tree with classification accuracy of at least 90%.

In this context, optima for the cost/evaluation function at hand are searched for over the entire class of patterns/models considered, in the case the optimization constraint is the only one given. But, as illustrated above, optimization constraints often appear in conjunction with (language or evaluation) Boolean constraints. In this case, optima are searched for over the patterns/models that satisfy the given Boolean constraints.

6.4 Soft Constraints

If we define language and evaluation constraints as Boolean functions, we view them as hard constraints. A constraint is either satisfied or not satisfied by a pattern. The fact that constraints actually define what patterns are valid or interesting in data mining, and that interestingness is not a dichotomy (Bistarelli and Bonchi 2005), has lead to the introduction of so-called soft constraints.

Instead of dismissing a pattern for violating a constraint, we might consider the pattern incurring a penalty for violating a constraint. In the cases where we typically consider a larger number of binary constraints, such as must-link and cannot-link constraints in constrained clustering (Wagstaff and Cardie 2000), a fixed penalty may be assigned for violating each constraint. In case we are dealing with evaluation constraints that compare an evaluation function to a threshold, the penalty incurred by violating the constraint may depend on how badly the constraint is violated. For example, if we have a size threshold of five, and the actual size is six, a smaller penalty would be incurred as compared to the case where the actual size is twenty.

In the hard constraint setting, a pattern/model is either a solution or not. In the soft constraint setting, all patterns/models are solutions to a different degree. Patterns that satisfy the constraint(s) get zero penalty: This leads to an optimization problem where we look for patterns with minimum penalty.

6.5 The Task(s) of (Constraint-Based) Data Mining

Having set the scene, we can now attempt to formulate a very general version of the problem addressed by data mining. We are given a dataset D, drawn according to some probability distribution P, consisting of objects of type T. We are also given a data mining task, one of the four listed in a previous section (estimating the probability distribution P, learning a predictive model, clustering or pattern discovery). We are further given a class of generalizations C_G (patterns/models/clusterings/probability distributions), from which to find solutions to the data mining task at hand. Finally, a set of constraints C is given, which can include both language and evaluation constraints.

The problem addressed by constraint-based data mining is to find a set of generalizations G from C_G that satisfy the constraints in C, if C is boolean, or optimize the constraints in C, if C contains optimization or soft constraints. A desired cardinality on the solution set is usually specified.

In the above formulation, all of data mining is really constraint-based data mining. We argue that the 'classical' formulations of and approaches to data mining tasks, such as clustering and predictive modelling, are a special case of the above formulation. A major difference between the 'classical' data mining paradigm and the 'modern' constraint-based one is that the former typically consider only one optimization constraint, such as minimize predictive error or intra-cluster variance, and requires only one solution (predictive model or clustering).

A related difference concerns the fact that most of the 'classical' approaches to data mining are heuristic and do not give any guarantees regarding the solutions. For example, a decision tree generated by a learning algorithm is typically not guaranteed to be the smallest or most accurate tree for the given dataset. On the other hand, constraint-based mining approaches have typically been concerned with the development of so-called 'optimal solvers', i.e., data mining algorithms that return the complete set of solutions that satisfy a given set of constraints or the truly optimal solutions (e.g., the k itemsets with highest correlation to a given target) in the context of optimization constraints.

7   The Key Ingredients of Data Mining Algorithms

7.1   Generality and Refinement Operators

The notion of generality is a key notion in data mining, in particular for the task of pattern discovery. To find patterns/models valid in the data, data mining algorithms search the space of patterns defined by the class of patterns/models considered, possibly additionally restricted by language constraints. To make the search efficient, the space of patterns/models is typically ordered by a generality or subsumption relation. A generality relation on a set (of patterns/models) is a partial order on that set.

The generality relation typically refers to the function part of a pattern/model. The corresponding notion for the data part is that of refinement. A typical example of a refinement relation is the subset relation on the space of itemsets. This relation is a partial order on itemsets and structures itemsets into a lattice structure, which is typically explored during the search for, e.g., frequent itemsets. The refinement relation is typically the closure of a refinement operator, which performs minimal refinements. In the case of itemsets, it takes an itemset and adds an item to it: if all possible items are *beer, diapers, milk* and *peanuts*, the refinements of the itemset $i_1 = beer$ are $i_2 = beer, diapers, i_3 = beer, milk$ and $i_4 = beer, peanuts$. Starting with the empty itemset, we can obtain any itemset through a sequence of refinements (applications of the refinement operator).

We can think of refinement and generality as expressing the same relation between patterns at the data (or syntax) level and the function (or semantics) level. In logic, we talk about subsumption in the first case and logical entailment (implication) in the second (Džeroski 2007). For example, if we take the itemsets from the above paragraph, i_2 is a refinement of i_1 at the data level means $i_1 \subseteq i_2$. At the function level, i_1 and i_2 are Boolean functions over transactions, $i_1(t)$ and $i_2(t)$. Generality here has the following meaning: i_1 is more general than i_2 at the function level means $\forall t : i_2(t) \models i_1(t)$, where $\models$ denotes logical implication.

In the ideal case, the notions of refinement at the syntactic and generality at the semantic level (resp. the data and function level) coincide. Whether this is actually the case depends on the interpreter for the class of patterns considered. These issues have received considerable attention in the area of inductive logic programming (Lavrač and Džeroski 1994, Džeroski 2007), where both data and patterns are represented in first order logic. The notions of generality and refinements are also directly relevant to and ubiquitously used in mining predictive models and other forms of generalizations. However, the notion of semantic generality does not transfer in a straightforward manner to the case of functions that are not binary/Boolean (i.e., to clusterings, probability distributions and predictive models in general).

7.2   Distances and Prototypes

Distance functions are of crucial importance for the design of many data mining algorithms, most notably for clustering and predictive modelling. A distance function d for type T is a mapping from pairs of objects of type T to non-negative reals: $d :: \mathbf{T} \times \mathbf{T} \to \mathbf{R}^{0+}$. A distance function has to satisfy three properties: (1) $d(x, y) \geq 0$, (2) $d(x, y) = 0$ if and only if $x = y$, and (3) $d(x, y) = d(y, x)$.

Note that the distance between two objects should be zero if and only if the two objects are identical (this property is called discernibility) and that a distance function should be symmetric. Properties (1) and (2) taken together produce positive definiteness. An additional property of interest for distance functions is the triangle inequality: (4) $d(x, z) \leq d(x, y) + d(y, z)$. A distance function that satisfies the triangle inequality is called a metric.

While it is immediately obvious that we need distances for distance-based clustering (where by definition we want to minimize the distance between objects in a cluster), it is may be less obvious why we need them for predictive modelling. The primary reason is the need to assess the predictions of a model: we need to compare the true value of the target to the predicted one, for any given example. In most predictive modelling approaches, it is assumed that the error/penalty incurred by predicting x instead of y is the same as the one incurred by predicting y instead of x, and equal to some distance function $d(x, y)$.

For any type of data we can easily define the distance function δ, which takes the value zero for pairs of identical data points and one for all other pairs: $\delta(x, x) = 0$ and $\delta(x, y) = 1$ for $x \neq y$. In fact, this is the distance function most commonly used for discrete/nominal data types in data mining algorithms. For real numbers, we can use $|x - y|$ as the distance between x and y.

Related to the notion of distance is the notion of a prototype. A prototype is something that is representative of a category of things, in this case of all the objects in a given set S. The prototype of a set of objects (defined in the context of a given distance d) is the object o that has the lowest average square distance to all of the objects in S: $o = \operatorname{argmin}_q \sum_{X \in S} d^2(X, q)$. Note that the quantity that we want to minimize in this formula is a generalization of the notion of variance from a set of real numbers to a set of arbitrary objects.

A prototype function p for objects of type T, takes as input a set S of objects of type T, and returns an object of type T, i.e., the prototype: $p :: \mathbf{Set(T)} \to \mathbf{T}$. We can consider two possibilities here: (a) the prototype is an arbitrary object of type T or (b) the prototype is one of the objects from S. In the case (b), the prototype can be computed with $|S|^2$ distance computations by substituting q with each of the objects in s. In the case (a), the space of candidate prototypes may easily be infinite. We thus need to have a closed algebraic form of the prototype or should resort to approximative algorithms to compute it.

In vector spaces, such as the Euclidean spaces $\mathbf{R}^n$, where objects may be scaled or added, the prototype of a set of objects can be defined in closed form as the centroid of the set. The notion of centroid generalizes the notion of mean from sets of real numbers to multidimensional spaces. The centroid is defined as the (weighted) mean / average of the vectors in the set: by default each vector has an equal weight $(1/|S|)$, although different weights may be assigned to different vectors. For example, given a set S of vectors x_i in the Euclidean space $\mathbf{R}^n$, each of the form $x_i = (x_{i1}, \ldots, x_{ik})$, the centroid $\overline{x}$ is defined as $\overline{x} = (\overline{x}_1, \ldots, \overline{x}_i)$, where $\overline{x}_j = \sum_{i=1}^{|S|} x_{ij}/|S|$. The centroid can be computed by $|S|$ addition computations and one scaling computation.

Prototypes and prototype functions are directly relevant to the clustering task of data mining, as well as the task of predictive modelling. Quite often, a prototype is associated with each cluster. In predictive modelling approaches which partition the space of training examples, such as tree-based and rule-based methods, the prediction of a rule/tree leaf is typically obtained by constructing a prototype of the (target part) of the examples covered by the rule/leaf.

7.3   Features and Background Knowledge

The term 'feature' is heavily used in pattern recognition (Bishop 2006), where features are individual measurable properties of a phenomena or object being observed. Features are usually numeric, but structural features (such as strings and graphs) are used in syntactic pattern recognition. While different areas of pattern recognition (such as image analysis or speech recognition) obviously use different features, once the features are decided upon, a relatively small set of algorithms is used to analyze the resulting data table. These algorithms include, e.g., linear discriminants / regression and probabilistic (naive Bayes) approaches.

Some approaches to data mining do not explicitly rely on a feature-based representation of the data analyzed. For example, many distance-based approaches to prediction (e.g., nearest neighbor methods) and clustering (e.g., hierarchical agglomerative/divisive clustering or k-medoids) only need a distance function on the underlying data (type). However, even for these, the distances are most commonly calculated through a set of features. The majority of data mining algorithms, though, crucially depend on the use of features (linear regression, naive Bayes, decision trees, classification rules, to name the most common ones).

Defining an appropriate set of features for a data mining problem at hand is still much of an art. However, it is also a step of key importance for the successful use of data mining. In the following, we try to formalize the notion of a feature and briefly discuss principled approaches to generating features.

Suppose d is a datum (structured object) of type T. Note that d can be, e.g., an image represented by an array of real numbers, or a recording of speech, represented by a sequence of real numbers. A feature f of objects of type T is a mapping from objects of type T to a primitive data type (Boolean, Discrete or Real) and $f(d)$ refers to the value of the feature for the specific object d.

There are at least three ways to arrive at features for a given object d of type T. First, the feature may have been directly observed and thus be a part of the representation of d. For example, if we have a molecule represented by its molecular weight, hydrophobicity and activity against a given species of bacteria, hydrophobicity as a bulk property is typically measured directly and is a feature of the molecule.

The other two ways are related to background knowledge concerning the structure of the object or concerning domain knowledge. Suppose molecules are represented by labeled graphs with vertices representing atoms and edges representing bonds between atoms: atoms would be labeled by the type of element (e.g., nitrogen, oxygen) and edges would be labeled by the type of bond (e.g., single, double, triple). In this context, a (simple) structural feature might indicate the presence/absence of a carbon and oxygen atom connected by a double bond (a $C = O$ group) in a given molecule. To illustrate how a feature may be derived through the use of some domain knowledge, consider molecules again. The presence of (complex) structures, such as certain functional groups (alcohols) or complexes thereof (triple fused rings) might be used as features. Connectivity indices calculated on the entire graph might also be used as features.

Background knowledge can be thought of as a set of mappings that generate new features, either directly, as in the case of connectivity indices on graphs mentioned above, or indirectly. In the second case, a mapping from the background knowledge would map an object from one representation to another, and features can be generated from the latter. For images, such a mapping might perform image segmentation and describe each segment with a new set of features, thus transforming the learning problem to a completely different representation.

From the latter, new features can then be generated directly or through the further use of domain knowledge.

7.4 Kernels

Kernel Methods (KMs, Shawe-Taylor and Cristianini 2004) in general, and Support Vector Machines (SVMs) in particular, are among the most successful recent developments within the machine learning and data mining communities. KMs can be used to address different tasks of data mining, such as clustering, classification, and regression, for general types of data, such as sequences, text documents, sets of points, vectors, images, etc. KMs (implicitly) map the data from its original representation into a high dimensional feature space, where each coordinate corresponds to one feature of the data items, transforming the data into a set of points in a Euclidean / linear space. Linear analysis methods are then applied (such as separating two classes by a hyperplane), but since the mapping can be nonlinear, nonlinear concepts can effectively be captured.

Technically, a kernel k corresponds to the inner product in some feature space. The computational attractiveness of kernel methods comes from the fact that quite often a closed form of these feature space inner products exists. The kernel can then be calculated directly, thus performing the feature transformation only implicitly without ever computing the coordinates of the data in the 'feature space'. This is called the kernel trick.

Whether, for a given function k with signature $k :: \mathbf{T} \times \mathbf{T} \to \mathbf{R}$, a feature transformation ϕ exists from $\mathbf{T}$ to a Hilbert space H, such that $k(x, x') = \langle \phi(x), \phi(x') \rangle$ for all x, x' can be checked by verifying that the function is positive definite. A symmetric function k on pairs of data points of type T is a positive definite kernel on T if, for all positive integers n, $x_1, \ldots, x_n \in T$ and $c_1, \ldots, c_n \in R$, it holds that $\sum_{i,j \in 1,\ldots,n} c_i c_j k(x_i, x_j) \geq 0$. While it is not always easy to prove positive definiteness for a given kernel, positive definite kernels do have nice closure properties. In particular, they are closed under sum, direct sum, multiplication by a scalar, product, tensor product, zero extension, pointwise limits, and exponentiation (Shawe-Taylor and Cristianini 2004).

Probably the simplest kernel is the linear one, defined for tuples of real numbers (x, x') as $k(x, x') = \langle x, x' \rangle$, where $\phi(x) = x$. If we have $x = (x_1, x_2)$ and $x' = (x'_1, x'_2)$, then $k(x, x') = x_1 x'_1 + x_2 x'_2$. Other kernels include the polynomial $k(x, x') = (\langle x, x' \rangle + 1)^p$ and the exponential $k(x, x') = e^{-\gamma \|x - x'\|^2}$ kernel.

At the conceptual level, kernels elegantly relate to both features and distances. As mentioned above, a kernel k (implicitly) defines a mapping from the original space to a Hilbert space $x \to \phi(x)$, the latter being the feature space implicitly associated with the kernel. A (pos. def.) kernel also defines a distance: if k is a kernel, then $d(x, y) = \sqrt{k(x, x) - 2k(x, y) + k(y, y)}$ is a (pseudo)metric.

At the practical level, kernel functions have been introduced for different types of data, such as vectors, text, and images, including structured data, such as sequences and graphs (Gaertner 2003). There are also many algorithms capable of operating with kernels: these include SVMs, Fisher's linear discriminant analysis

(LDA), principal components analysis (PCA), ridge regression, spectral clustering, and many others. Since any kernel can be used with any kernel-algorithm, it is possible to construct many combinations, such as regression over DNA sequences, classification of documents, and clustering of images.

8   Constraints in Data Mining: Revisited

8.1   Evaluation Functions for the Basic Data Mining Tasks

The evaluation functions used in evaluation constraints are tightly coupled with the data mining task at hand. If we are solving a predictive modelling problem, the evaluation function used will most likely concern predictive error. If we are solving a frequent pattern mining problem, the evaluation function used will definitely concern the frequency of the patterns.

For **predictive models** with a signature $\mathbf{m} :: \mathbf{T}_d \to \mathbf{T}_c$, we need a distance (or cost) function d_c on objects of type T_c to define the notion of predictive error. For a given model m and a dataset D, the average predictive error of the model is defined as $1/|D| \times \sum_{e=(a,t) \in D} d_c(t, m(a))$. For each example $e = (a, t)$ in the dataset, which consists of a descriptive (attribute) part a and target (class) part t, the prediction of the model $m(a)$ is obtained and its distance to the true class value t is calculated. Analogously, the notion of mean squared error would be defined as $1/|D| \times \sum_{e=(a,t) \in D} d_c^2(t, m(a))$.

The notion of cost-sensitive prediction has been recently gaining increasing amounts of attention in the data mining community. In this setting, the errors incurred by predicting x instead of y and predicting y instead of x, are typically not the same. The corresponding misprediction (analogous to misclassification) cost function is thus not symmetric, i.e., is not a distance. The notion of average misprediction cost can be defined as above, where the distance $d(x, y)$ is replaced by a cost function $c(x, y)$.

In the case of **probabilistic models**, which predict a probability distribution over the target type and are of the form $\mathbf{m} :: \mathbf{T}_d \to (\mathbf{T}_c \to \mathbf{R}^{0+})$, we need a distance function on probability distributions over the target data type T_c. When T_c is discrete and takes values from $S = \{s_1, \ldots, s_k\}$, we can represent a probability distribution on T_c with a vector $p = (p_1, \ldots, p_k)$ of probabilities of its possible values. We can then use distances on vectors of reals. However, distances or cost functions that explicitly take into account the fact that we are dealing with probability distributions can also be taken, such as the likelihood-ratio defined for two distributions p and q as $\sum_{i=1}^{k} p_i log(p_i/q_i)$. The latter is a special case of the Kullback-Leibler divergence, defined also for probability distributions / densities over continuous variables.

For the task of **estimating the probability distribution** of objects of type T, we need a scoring function for distributions / densities. The most commonly used ones are based on likelihood or log-likelihood (Hand et al. 2001). Given a dataset D and a probability distribution p, the likelihood function is defined as $L(p) = \prod_{e \in D} p(e)$ and the log-likelihood function as $logL(P) = \sum_{e \in D} logp(e)$.

Another possibility for evaluating a candidate probability distribution p is to calculate the integrated (average) squared error between p and the true distribution p^*. This is defined as $\int_x (p(x) - p^*(x))^2 dx$. We can ignore terms that do not depend on p, yielding $\int_x p^2(x) dx - \int_x p^*(x)p(x) dx = \int_x p^2(x) dx - E(p(x))$, where each of the terms can be approximated to obtain an estimate of the true integrated (average) squared error for p: $E(p(x))$ denotes the expectation of $p(x)$.

Density-based **clustering** is a direct special case of the task of estimating the joint probability distribution, where clusters correspond to different components of the joint probability distribution, which is assumed to be a mixture model. A mixture model has the form $p(x) = \sum_{i=1}^k \pi_k p_k(x)$ and decomposes the overall density (or distribution) for x into a weighted linear combination of k component or class densities. In this case, the same evaluation functions as for the task of estimating the probability distribution can be applied.

For the traditional partition-based clustering approach, the quality of a clustering is typically evaluated with intra-cluster variance (ICV). For a clustering with k clusters C_i with $D = \cup_{i=1}^k C_i$, we have $\mathrm{ICV} = \frac{1}{|D|} \sum_{i=1}^k |C_i| Var(C_i)$, where C_i is the set of elements of cluster i. $Var(C_i)$ is the intra-cluster variance of cluster i and is defined as $Var(C_i) = \sum_{e \in C_i} d^2(e, \overline{C_i})$, where $\overline{C_i}$ is the prototype of cluster C_i with respect to the distance d.

Finally, for the task of **pattern discovery**, with the discovery of frequent patterns as the prototypical instantiation, the primary evaluation function is frequency. Recall that patterns are Boolean functions and have the signature $\mathbf{p :: T \to bool}$. For a dataset D of objects of type T, the frequency of a pattern p is defined as $f(p, D) = |\{e | e \in D, p(e) = true\}|$.

8.2 Cost Functions for Language Constraints

The cost functions that are used in language constraints concern the data part of generalizations (patterns/models/...). Most often, these functions are related to the size/complexity of the generalizations. They are different for different classes of generalizations, e.g., for itemsets, mixture models of Gaussians, linear models or decision trees. For itemsets, the size is the cardinality of the itemset, i.e., the number of items in it. For decision trees, it can be the total number of nodes, the number of leaves or the depth of the tree. For linear models, it can be the number of variables (with non-zero coefficients) included in the model.

More general versions of cost functions involve costs of the individual language elements, such as items or attributes, and sum/aggregate these over all elements appearing in the pattern/model. These are motivated by practical considerations, e.g., costs for items in an itemset and total cost of a market basket. In the context of predictive models, e.g., attribute-value decision trees, it makes sense to talk about prediction cost, defined as the total cost of all attributes used by the model. For example, in medical applications where the attributes correspond to expensive lab tests, it might be useful to upper-bound the prediction cost of a decision tree.

Language constraints as commonly used in constraint-based data mining involve thresholds on the values of cost functions (e.g., find a decision tree of size at most ten leaves). They are typically combined with evaluation constraints, be it threshold or optimization (e.g., find a tree of size at most 10 with classification error of at most 10% or find a tree of size at most 10 and the smallest classification error). Also, optimization constraints may involve the language-related cost functions, e.g., find the smallest decision tree with classification error lower than 10%.

In the 'classical' formulations of and approaches to data mining tasks, scoring functions often combine evaluation functions and language cost functions. The typical score function is a linear combination of the two, i.e., $Score(G, D) = w_E \times Evaluation(G.function, D) + w_L \times LanguageCost(G.data)$, where G is the generalization (pattern/model) scored and D is the underlying dataset. For predictive modelling, this can translate to $Score = w_E \times Error + w_S \times Size$.

8.3 Monotonicity and Closedness

The notion of monotonicity of an evaluation (or cost) function on a class of generalizations is often considered in constraint-based data mining. In mathematics, a function $f(x)$ is monotonic (monotonically increasing) if $\forall x, y : x < y \rightarrow f(x) \leq f(y)$, i.e., the function preserves the $<$ order. If the function reverses the order, i.e., $\forall x, y : x < y \rightarrow f(x) \geq f(y)$, we call it monotonically decreasing.

In data mining, in addition to the order on Real numbers, we also have a generality order on the class of generalizations. The latter is typically induced by a refinement operator. We say that $g_1 \leq_{ref} g_2$ if g_2 can be obtained from g_1 through a sequence of refinements (and thus g_1 is more general than g_2): we will refer to this order as the refinement order.

An evaluation (or cost) function is called monotonic if it preserves the refinement order or anti-monotonic if it reverses it. More precisely, an evaluation function f is called monotonic if $\forall g_1, g_2 : g_1 \leq_{ref} g_2 \rightarrow f(g_1) \leq f(g_2)$ and anti-monotonic (or monotonically decreasing) if $\forall g_1, g_2 : g_1 \leq_{ref} g_2 \rightarrow f(g_1) \geq f(g_2)$.

Note that the above notions are defined for both evaluation/cost functions that refer to the function part of a generalization and for functions that refer to the data part. In this context, the frequency of itemsets is anti-monotonic (it decreases monotonically with the refinement order). The total cost of an itemset and the total prediction cost of a decision tree, on the other hand, are monotonic.

In the constraint-based data mining literature (Boulicaut and Jeudy 2006), the refinement order considered is typically the subset relation on itemsets ($\leq_{ref}$ is identical to $\subseteq$). A constraint C (taken as a Boolean function) is considered monotonic if $i_1 \leq_{ref} i_2 \wedge C(i_1)$ implies $C(i_2)$. A maximum frequency constraint of the form $freq(i) \leq \theta$, where θ is a constant, is monotonic. Similarly, minimum frequency/support constraints of the form $freq(i) \geq \theta$, the ones most commonly considered in data mining, are anti-monotonic. A disjunction or a conjunction of anti-monotonic constraints is an anti-monotonic constraint. The negation of a monotonic constraint is anti-monotonic and vice versa.

The notions of monotonicity and anti-monotonicity are important because they allow for the design of efficient constraint-based data mining algorithms. Anti-monotonicity means that when a pattern does not satisfy a constraint C, then none of its refinements can satisfy C. It thus becomes possible to prune huge parts of the search space which can not contain interesting patterns. This has been studied within the learning as search framework (Mitchell, 1982) and the generic levelwise algorithm from (Mannila and Toivonen, 1997) has inspired many algorithmic developments.

Finally, let us mention the notion of closedness. A pattern (generalization) is closed, with respect to a given refinement operator $\leq_{ref}$ and evaluation function f, if refining the pattern in any way decreases the value of the evaluation function. More precisely, x is closed if $\forall y, x \leq_{ref} y : f(y) < f(x)$. While this notion has primarily been considered in the context of mining frequent itemsets, where it plays an important role in condensed representations (Calders et al. 2005), it can be defined analogously for other types of patterns, as indicated above.

8.4 Multi-objective Optimization and Constraint-Based Data Mining

The moment we consider more than one evaluation or cost function in the context of a single data mining task, we are dealing with a multi-objective optimization problem. In multi-objective optimization we wish to simultaneously optimize several (possibly conflicting) objectives. More precisely, we want to minimize each component of a vector of objective/evaluation functions $\mathbf{f} = (f_1, \ldots, f_m)$ simultaneously.

In the context of multi-objective optimization, the notions of Pareto dominance and Pareto optimality are important. We say that a vector of values of the objective functions g weakly dominates another vector h iff $g_i \leq h_i$ for all i. If, in addition, $g_j < h_j$ for at least one j, we say that g dominates h. If $g_i < h_i$ for all i, we are talking about strict Pareto dominance.

The weak Pareto dominance is a natural generalization of the $\leq$ relation on real numbers. While $\leq$ induces a total order on reals, the weak Pareto dominance induces only a partial order on vectors of reals. This means that two objective vectors (and therefore two solutions) can be incomparable: In case of conflicting objectives the multi-objective optimization problem can have multiple optimal solutions. A solution and its corresponding vector of objective function values are Pareto optimal if they are not Pareto dominated by any other solution/vector in the space considered. All Pareto optimal solutions compose the Pareto optimal set, while the corresponding objective vectors constitute the Pareto optimal front.

The typical approach to multi-objective optimization taken within the data mining community, as indicated earlier in this section, is to transform the multi-objective optimization problem into a single-objective problem, by combining the individual objectives using a weighted sum. A single solution (e.g., predictive model) is then acquired by solving the corresponding single-objective problem (e.g., optimizing the weighted sum of error and complexity of the predictive model). This approach is recognized in multi-objective optimization as an application of the 'preference-based principle' (Deb 2001), where the user explicitly specifies her preference for the different objectives (e.g., weights) in advance.

In contrast, using the 'ideal principle', the multi-objective problem is first solved and only then the user selects a single solution among several alternatives, using preference information. The ideal principle is ideal in the sense that it does not demand from the user to set a preference for the objectives before optimization. Only when several tradeoff solutions are known, the user chooses the preferred one among them.

The ideal principle for multi-objective optimization seems very suitable in the context of inductive databases/queries and constrained based data mining, where multiple objectives are often employed and multiple solutions are usually expected. After a set of solutions has been obtained, this can be the input for further (inductive) queries that would allow the user to express her preference and select a solution. Unfortunately, few approaches in data mining and machine learning employ the ideal approach, with the notable exception of Tušar (2007). This leaves ample space for the development of truly multi-objective approaches to constraint-based data mining and inductive querying, which we believe is a promising direction for further research.

9   Generic Algorithms for Mining Structured Data

Early on in this article, we have stated that a unifying approach to mining different types of data would be a significant step towards a general data mining framework. Having elaborated on the different types of data, different data mining tasks and the basic components of data mining algorithms, we can now outline what such a unifying approach would look like. Essentially, it should provide an elegant mechanism for defining the key ingredients of data mining algorithms, such as generality/refinement operators, distances, features and kernels, for the different types of data considered.

The key data mining notions have been studied extensively and are reasonably well understood for primitive data types. The basic idea of the unified approach to mining structured data is to derive the key components of data mining algorithms for a complex data type (built through using type constructors) from information on the structure of that type (what constructors on what simpler data types) and the key components for the simpler data types. For example, a distance function d on tuples of type $\text{Tuple}(T_1, \ldots, T_n)$ can be composed from distance functions d_i on types T_i by adding up the distances for each tuple component $d(x,y) = d((x_1, \ldots, x_n), (y_1, \ldots, y_n)) = \sum_{i=1}^{n} d_i(x_i, y_i)$.

Note that there are several degrees of freedom when constructing the distance for a more complex data type from distances on simpler types. One dimension is the type constructor, which besides Tuple() may also be Set() or Sequence(). Even if we fix the type constructor to Tuple(), there are alternative ways to combine the distances on the simpler types: for example, we can take the square root of the sum of squared distances for each tuple component $d(x,y) = \sqrt{\sum_{i=1}^{n} d_i^2(x_i, y_i)}$ instead of the above. Finally, different distances may exist for the same simpler type (e.g., d_{11} and d_{12} on type T_1, instead of just d_1).

The approach we have outlined above for distances can be also applied for generality/refinement operators, features and kernels. In the remainder of this section, we outline how this would be done. We also discuss generic data mining algorithms that would work on arbitrary types of data: These would be parameterized with the key components mentioned above.

9.1 Distances and Distance-Based Algorithms

Distances. We have already discussed how distances for simpler data types can be combined to derive distances for more complex data types created with the Tuple() constructor: this is done in a straightforward fashion by adding up the distances along each component. For the Set() constructor, the situation is more complicated. Many proposals exist in the literature for constructing a distance on sets of objects of type T from a distance on objects of type T. A concise, yet comprehensive, overview is given by Kalousis et al. (2007).

The simpler option of constructing a distance on sets is to calculate the distances for all pairs of elements $D(A, B) = \{d(a_i, b_j)|(a_i, b_j) \in A \times B\}$, then aggregate this $d(A, B) = f(D(A, B))$: Here A and B are sets, a_i/b_j are elements thereof, and f an aggregation function. The three options of $f = min, max$ or *average* give rise to the so-called single, complete and average linkage, which are in common use, e.g., in hierarchical clustering. Even if $d(a, b)$ is a metric, none of the three variants here is a metric and only single linkage is a true distance function, as the other two are not reflexive. The Hausdorff distance, defined as $d_H(A, B) = max(max_{a_i}\{min_{b_j}\{d(a_i, b_j)\}\}, max_{b_i}\{min_{a_j}\{d(b_i, a_j)\}\})$, one of the most well known distances for sets, is a metric if $d(a, b)$ is a metric.

The more complicated option is to consider a set of relations between elements of A and B, $R = \{R_i|R_i \subseteq A \times B\}$ and compute the distance between A and B based on the relation $R_i \in R$ that minimizes a distance on the elements of R_i. Here the relations may be surjections, fair surjections, linkings, or matchings (Kalousis 2007). Of these, the proposal by Ramon and Bruynooghe (2001) is a metric: as R it considers matchings in which each element of the two sets is associated with at most one element of the other set. The distance, defined as $d(A, B) = min_{R_i \in R}(\sum_{(a_i, b_j) \in Ri} d(a_i, b_j) + (|B - R_i(A)| + |A - R_i^{-1}(B)|)\frac{M}{2})$ adds a $M/2$ penalty for the elements of A and B that do not participate in the relation R_i, where M is the maximum possible distance between two elements.

For the Sequence() type constructor, the edit-distance approach can be used. While this has typically been used for sequences of alphabet symbols, i.e., Sequence(Discrete(Alphabet))), Kalousis et al. (2007) have recently suggested an extension towards sequences of arbitrary complex objects on which a distance d is defined. Given two sequences $A = [a_1 \ldots, a_m]$ and $B = [b_1 \ldots, b_m]$, an alignment of A and B is a pair of sequences A' and B' of equal length $l \geq max(n, m)$, constructed from the initial sequences by insertion of gaps, $-$. In an alignment, an element from A/B can be aligned to a gap (insert/delete operation) or two elements from A resp. B can be aligned with each other (replace operation).

The cost of an alignment is simply the sum of the cost of all operations used to derive the alignment, where the cost of the replace operation is $c(x, y) = d(x, y)$

and the cost of the insert and delete operations is a constant, i.e., $c(x, -) = c(-, y) = \alpha$, called the gap penalty. The alignment-based edit distance, $d_E(A, B)$, of two sequences A and B is then simply the minimum cost overall possible alignments of the two sequences, i.e., the cost of the lowest cost sequence of operations that turns the first sequence into the second. The edit distance can be computed using dynamic programming (Durbin et al., 1998) in time $O(mn)$.

Generic Distance-Based Algorithms. It is quite easy to formulate generic distance-based algorithms for data mining, which have the distance as a parameter. For example, hierarchical agglomerative clustering only makes use of the distances between the objects clustered and distances between sets of such objects. The latter can be based on single, complete or average linkage.

Clustering algorithms that make use of cluster prototypes, such as the k-means/medoids algorithm, require in addition a prototype function to be defined on the type of objects clustered. A closed-form prototype is desirable since its computation is more efficient and supports the version of the k-means algorithm parameterized with the distance and prototype functions. If no closed-form is known, the prototype of a cluster can be computed as the element of the cluster that has the lowest average (squared) distance to the other objects in the cluster, and the distance-parameterized version of (k-means like) k-medoids applies.

Distance-based prediction algorithms are also easy to formulate in a generic way. For a predictive problem of type $T_i \rightarrow T_j$, the nearest neighbor method applies as long as we have a distance on T_i. To make a prediction for a new instance, the distance between the (descriptive part of the) new instance and the training instances is calculated. The target part is copied from the nearest training instance and returned as a prediction. To use the k-nearest neighbor algorithm, we also need a prototype function on the target data type: the prediction returned is the prototype of the target parts of the k nearest (in the description space) instances.

9.2   Kernels and Kernel Methods

Kernels for a complex data type T can be derived from kernels for the simpler data types used to form T, analogously to distances. The manner in which the kernels for the simpler types are combined depends on the type constructor used to form T. As for distances, the easiest case is the one for tuples. A kernel function k on tuples of type $Tuple(T_1, \ldots, T_n)$ can be composed from kernel functions k_i on types T_i by adding up the kernels for each tuple component $k(x, y) = k((x_1, \ldots, x_n), (y_1, \ldots, y_n)) = \sum_{i=1}^{n} k_i(x_i, y_i)$.

One possibility for kernels on sets is the product kernel, defined as $k(A, B) = \sum_{x \in A, y \in B} k(x, y)$. This is a special case of the convolution kernel proposed by Haussler (1999), which defines kernels of composite objects based on a relation between an object and its parts. Sets and multi-sets are also a special case of abstractions, which are mappings to the set of (non-negative) reals: sets are mappings to $\{0, 1\}$ ($A(x) = 1$ if $x \in A$), while multi-sets are mappings to non-negative integers ($B(x) = 2$ if x occurs in B twice). Kernels for abstractions can be defined by $k(A, B) = \sum_{x \in A, y \in B} A(x)B(y)k(x, y)$ (Lloyd 2003).

Analogously to the manner in which edit-distances on strings have been adapted to work on sequences on structured objects (Kalousis et al. 2006), kernels on strings have been adapted to work on sequences on structured objects (Woznica et al. 2006). In particular, the "Contiguous Sublist" and the "Longest Common Sublist" kernels have been adapted to structured objects. A more detailed treatment of kernels on structured data is given by Gaertner (2003).

Kernel methods are also generic in the sense that any kernel can be used with any kernel algorithm, thus the kernel function can be seen as a parameter to the algorithm. We will not discuss here in detail any of the kernel methods, except to mention the most commonly used methods: support vector machines (SVMs), ridge regression and spectral clustering. As we have seen, kernels for structured data can be derived in a principled manner. In addition, special kernels have been designed for text, images, sequences and graphs, thus making kernel methods applicable to many kinds of data.

9.3 Features and Feature-Based Methods

The vast majority of data mining methods operate on a feature-based representation of data. These include, among others, decision trees and rules, linear equations and discriminants, and probabilistic methods (naive Bayes, Bayes nets). We will not discuss these here, but all of them assume that data reside in a single table, with columns representing features and rows representing data points (also referred to as instances and examples). Methods from machine learning, pattern recognition and statistics alike make use of this representation.

In this (sub)section, we briefly discuss how to derive features for structured objects in a principled manner. So far, this issue has been considered in more detail by subcommunities dealing with the analysis of more specific forms of data, such as image processing. The notable exception has been the relational data mining (Džeroski and Lavrač 2001) community, where propositionalization, introduced by Lavrač and Džeroski (1994), explicitly deals with the construction of features from (possibly structured) data represented relationally.

A large body of work exists in the machine learning and data mining communities that goes under the heading of feature construction and feature extraction (Liu and Motoda 1998), jointly referred to as feature discovery or feature transformation. Feature transformation is defined as the process in which a new set of features is constructed. If the new features are constructed by logical operations (e.g., conjunction or disjunction) on the original features, we speak about feature construction. If functional mappings are used instead (e.g., linear combinations), we speak about feature extraction. The crucial assumption is that the set of objects is originally already represented by a set of features, which are further combined to obtain new features. In our discussion, we do not make this assumption; rather the objects considered are of an arbitrary data type.

To construct the features for a type T, we proceed as follows. If the type T is primitive (Boolean, Discrete(S) or Real), a single feature of that type is generated; we write $Features(T) = \{UniqueID : T\}$, where the feature of type T is assigned a unique identifier $UniqueID$. For a type $\text{Tuple}(T_1, \ldots, T_n)$, the set of features generated is the union of the set of features derived for each of the component types, i.e., $Features(T) = \cup_{i=1}^n Features(T_i)$.

To describe a set of objects $t = \{t_1, \ldots, t_k\}$ of type T, the most general approach would be to view t as a sample from a probability distribution p_T and specify the (joint) probability distribution as approximated from that sample. To describe t in terms of features, we need to consider features for describing probability distributions. If we assume the objects of type T can be described by a set/vector of features over the space $Features(T)$, we need to specify a probability distribution over that space. A simplified approach to this problem is to specify the marginals of this distribution, i.e., the distributions of the values for each feature.

For features of type Discrete(S), where $S = \{s_1, \ldots, s_m\}$, m features suffice to describe the distribution completely, namely $P(s_i)$, $i = 1, \ldots, m$. Oftentimes, the mode of the distribution would be included as a feature, which is also of type Discrete(S). The cardinality of the set $|t|$ is also a feature to be included. For real-valued features, their minimum and maximum values can be used as features, as well as the mean, standard deviation, and median: these are known as aggregates in relational databases. Histograms may be used if a more accurate description of the distribution is necessary.

For strings (sequences of objects of type Discrete(S)), n-grams are often used as features. These count the number of occurrences of each of the letters in the alphabet (1-grams), pairs of letters (2-grams), triplets of letters (3-grams), and so on. For time series (sequences of objects of type Real), many different features can also be constructed by using techniques from signal processing, such as the Fourier transform (Bracewell 1965) to the frequency domain or by wavelet analysis (Mallat 1999).

For objects of type Sequence(T), assume we can represent objects of type T with $Features(T)$. We hence consider feature construction on an object of the type Sequence(Tuple($F_1, \ldots, F_k$)), where F_i are the types of the features from $Features(T)$. In analogy to the approach taken for sets, where the marginals were used to represent the probability distribution, we replace the type Sequence(Tuple($F_1, \ldots, F_k$)) with Tuple(Sequence(F_1), ..., Sequence(F_k)) and derive features from this, resulting in the feature set $Features(Sequence(T)) = \cup_{i=1}^n Features(Sequence(F_i))$.

We have already mentioned earlier that features may be derived through the use of domain or background knowledge. Background knowledge can be thought of as a set of mappings. Assuming we are given a data type T for the data we are analyzing, as well as some additional data types T_i, as well as background knowledge consisting of a set of mappings $b_i : T \to T_i$.

In addition to the features $Features(T)$ that can be derived from T directly as discussed earlier in this section, features can be generated also from each of the types T_i. Suppose each of T_i gives rise to $Features_i(T_i)$. For an object t

of type T, besides $Features(t)$, the feature-based representation would include $Features_i(b_i(t))$.

For simplicity we have assumed one level of background knowledge only: all mappings apply to type T and yield an object of a type other than T. We can easily imagine that the background knowledge mappings apply to, as well as, yield objects of different types. The mappings would then be composed according to their type signatures. In that case, objects such as $b_i(b_j(t))$ and features thereof will have to be considered.

Let us conclude by noting that a huge number of features may be generated in this fashion. Hence we expect such feature generation to be used in conjunction with feature ranking and selection, where pattern discovery can be viewed as a form of the latter. For example, instead of using all possible n-grams as features to describe a sequence, only those that occur with a frequency exceeding a certain threshold may be used. There is a strong link between feature construction and (frequent) pattern discovery: the latter has been used to generate features for predictive modelling both in the context of frequent itemsets (Cheng et al. 2007) and frequent Datalog queries (King et al. 2001).

9.4 Refinement Orders and (Frequent) Pattern Discovery

In the most general formulation of pattern discovery, we can have an arbitrary language/class of patterns, a matching/covering relationship which corresponds to the interpreter for the given class of patterns, and an arbitrary evaluation function to optimize. In practice, the most commonly encountered pattern discovery task is the task of mining frequent patterns, where the evaluation function is frequency. For this task, the language of patterns is commonly the same (or very close) to the language of the data (type) considered.

When we mine frequent itemsets, the patterns - itemsets - are expressed in exactly the same language as the data - transactions. The same holds when mining frequent (sub)strings, (sub)sequences of structured terms or (sub)graphs. Consequently, the matching relationship used is a syntactic subsumption relationship, defined on the data type in question. For frequent itemsets this is the subset relation (on transactions), for the other data types this is analogously the substring, subsequence, and subgraph relationship.

The prototypical algorithm for mining frequent patterns starts its search with the empty pattern (set/sequence/graph), which is always frequent. It then proceeds levelwise, considering at each level the refinements of the patterns from the previous level and testing their frequencies. Only frequent patterns are kept for further refinement: Due to the anti-monotonicity of frequency, no refinement of an infrequent pattern can be frequent.

The key to a generic algorithm for mining frequent patterns that would work for arbitrary data types is to derive a subsumption/refinement relation from the definition of the type and subsumption relations for the component types, in much the same fashion we discussed above for distances, kernels and feature sets. For the primitive data types, subsumption is defined as follows. For the type Discrete(S), a pattern is a subset of S and the $\leq_{ref}$ relation corresponds to the $\subseteq$

relation. The data type Boolean can be viewed as a special case of Discrete(S), with $S = \{false, true\}$ ($\{0,1\}$). For the type Real, a pattern is an interval of the form (a, b): we say $(a, b) \leq_{ref} (c, d)$ iff $a \geq c$ and $b \leq d$, i.e., $(a, b) \subseteq (c, d)$ if we view the intervals as sets of real numbers.

For two tuples x and y of type $\text{Tuple}(T_1, \ldots, T_n)$, such that $x = (x_1, \ldots, x_n)$ and $y = (y_1, \ldots, y_n)$, we have $x \leq_T y = \wedge_{i=1}^{n}(x_i \leq_{T_i} y_i)$. For two sets X and Y of objects of type T, we have $X \leq_{ref} Y$ iff there is a subset Y' of Y such that each element $x_i \in X$ can be paired with an element $y_i \in Y'$ such that $x_i \leq_T y_i$. For two sequences X and Y of objects of type T, we have $X \leq_{ref} Y$ iff there is a subsequence Y' of Y of the same length as X, such that $(x_i \leq_T y_i')$ for all i.

10   Towards a Language for Data Mining and Knowledge Discovery

Based on the elements presented above, we outline here a vision of a language for data mining and knowledge discovery. First-order citizens of the language would include data types, data sets, and generalizations (patterns, models, clusterings, probability distributions), as well as data mining algorithm components, such as distance/cost functions, feature sets, kernels and refinement operators.

We envisage an interpreted language of declarative nature, incorporating some features from both functional programming (Thompson 1999) and logic programming (Lloyd 1987). For example, storing and querying structured data, database style, would be nicely supported by the logic programming side of the language. The same would hold for materialized collections of patterns/models, when queries concern the data part thereof.

On the other hand, the functional programming side would support the manipulation of the function aspects of patterns/models, such as the retrieval of the function aspect of a pattern/model from the data aspect or deriving predictions through the application of a given predictive model to new data. It would support operations on patterns and models, such as creating a mixture model from a given set of probability distributions. It would also support the derivation of the basic data mining algorithm ingredients for more complex data types from those of the component types. Finally, it would support the composition of different data mining operations into knowledge discovery scenarios.

10.1   Data and Background Knowledge

The data part of the language would be close in spirit to deductive databases (Lloyd 1983). A database in this setting would contain a set of data types $T_1, \ldots, T_n$, as well as (some) datasets D_{ij} of objects of (each of) these types T_i. Background knowledge, consisting of a set of mappings $b : T_i \rightarrow T_j$, can also be included.

Each dataset can be viewed as a predicate. Each background knowledge mapping can be also viewed as a predicate $b(T_i, T_j)$. Assuming that the data are represented relationally (in a flattened form), queries on data would be very similar to Datalog queries.

In our setting, data types are represented explicitly and can also be the object of manipulation. Recall that types are constructed from primitive data types (Boolean, Discrete(S), and Real) using type constructors (Tuple, Set, Sequence). In this context, it is important to note the relationships between different data types, which can lead to a taxonomy/ontology of data types.

For example, we can have a data type molecule, which is a special case of labeled graphs. Molecular fragments, which can also be defined as a type, are substructures (linear paths) in such graphs. Explicitly representing and reasoning with such information can be very useful, for example, to determine the applicability of different data mining algorithms to different data types: an algorithm for mining frequent subgraphs can be used for finding frequent molecular fragments.

10.2   Generalizations

Patterns, models, clusterings and probability distributions (which we collectively refer to as generalizations) are first-class citizens in this framework. Recall that they all have both a data and a function part. Classes of generalizations can be defined, for which an interpreter can map the data part of a generalization to its function part.

The function part of a generalization is typed according to the underlying data type(s), for example, Sequence($\{A, C, T, G\}$) $\rightarrow$ Boolean. For the data part, a type definition needs to be given, so that the generalizations can be explicitly stored and queried as data objects. The symbols that can appear in the type definition depend on the underlying data type(s), as well as the class of generalizations. If we consider classification trees that classify tuples of Boolean features $X = (x_1, \ldots, x_n)$ into a Boolean class, internal nodes of the trees would be labeled with a feature name $x_i \in X$ while leaves will be labeled with one of $\{true, false\}$.

We can imagine sets of decision trees stored in a 'dataset' of the appropriate type. For example, the set of trees in a random forest can be stored in such a dataset. The trees need not all be generated by machine: we can give students, as part of their machine learning exam, the task to generate a decision tree for a certain (small) set of examples. All of the answers we get from the class of students would form such a dataset of decision trees as well.

Datasets of generalizations of the kind outlined above can be queried in much the same fashion as ordinary datasets. For example, datasets of decision trees can be queried much like datasets of ordinary trees. We might ask, e.g., for all the trees that contain a certain feature at the root node.

The set of solutions to a data mining query, i.e., the set of generalizations of a certain class satisfying a given set of constraints would also constitute a dataset of generalizations. For example, all the decision trees of size at most 10 leaves with classification error of at most 10% would form a dataset of trees. Another example would be the set of all itemsets with frequency higher than 10% and cost lower than 100$: Note that the latter also refers to a cost function on the data part of the pattern. Additional queries, called post-processing queries, can be posed after the data mining results have become part of a dataset.

10.3   Cross-Over Queries

Cross-over queries apply generalizations to a given datum or a dataset. If the source data type is T_d and the generalization maps to type T_c, we can think of cross-over queries as producing pairs of type (T_d, T_c). Recall that patterns map to Booleans, clusterings to integers in the range $1, \ldots, k$ (where k is the number of clusters), probability distributions/densities to non-negative Reals, and predictive models to an arbitrary data type T_c. Since cross-over queries most often involve predictive models, we refer to the application as a prediction join.

More specifically, the application of a generalization to a given datum refers to the function part of the generalization. If the function part is explicitly stored (e.g., as a stored procedure), it would be called directly. Otherwise we would make use of the interpreter for the particular class of generalizations.

Once we have the results of applying a generalization to a dataset, the value of an evaluation function can be computed for that generalization. For example, for a classification model, the classification error can be computed. For a clustering, the intra-cluster variance can be calculated.

10.4   Generic Data Mining: Components and Algorithms

We also propose that the basic components of data mining algorithms, i.e., distance and prototype functions, kernel functions, feature sets, and refinement operators, are also first-class citizens of our language. Suppose we have a set of distance functions, e.g., a set of weighted Euclidean distances over tuples of reals, each represented by a tuple of weights. We can query this set and look for distances that give a very high weight (over a threshold) to a selected feature.

Generic data mining algorithms, such as the ones for distance-based prediction discussed in the previous section, could then be used, parameterized with the selected basic components. We envisage several generic algorithms for each of the major approaches (distance-based, kernel, and feature based). For example, distance-based methods would include hierarchical clustering (agglomerative and divisive), k-means/medoids clustering, and k-nearest neighbor prediction.

Generic feature-based algorithms for predictive data mining would be parameterized with feature sets on the descriptive side and distance functions for the target side. If the prediction problem is predicting objects of type T_c from objects of type T_d, the algorithm will need a set of features $Features(T_c)$ and a distance on T_d as input. Algorithms for learning predictive clustering trees (Blockeel et al. 1998) and rules (Ženko et al. 2006) have come closest to this paradigm.

We expect default basic components to be associated with each data type and/or generic algorithm. For example, a default distance can be associated with each data type. For the primitive data types, these have been discussed earlier (Section 7.2). For compound data types, if not specified explicitly, default distances can be derived using the methodology outlined in Section 9.1.

10.5   Constraints and Data Mining Queries

Once we have defined a data mining task and selected the associated basic components, we can define precisely the evaluation function(s) to be used. For example, we can only define predictive error once we have defined a distance/cost function on the target data type of a predictive modelling task. Different evaluation functions can be defined by selecting different basic components (distances). For probabilistic classification, one can optimize squared loss or log loss, depending on the underlying distance on probability distributions over discrete variables. Note that the above are independent of the class of predictive models used.

Besides evaluation constraints, language constraints, which can be subsumption-based or based on cost functions, can also be used. These are defined for a specific class of generalizations. Subsumption constraints involve the generality/refinement order on the data part of the generalization. For example, a specific item has to appear in the discovered frequent itemsets or the classification tree has to include a given subtree at the root. Examples of cost functions for language constraints include the size or depth of a decision tree and the cost of an itemset. Note that we can also have evaluation constraints that are specific for a given class of generalizations. For instance, we can require each leaf of a decision tree to cover at least 10 examples, have accuracy of its majority class higher than a threshold, or have a majority class frequency higher by a given margin than the frequency of any other class (Nijssen and Fromont 2007).

Similar to the ontology of data types mentioned above, we can imagine having a hierarchy/an ontology on generalizations. Evaluation and language cost functions can be defined at different levels in this ontology. The most general ones will apply, say, for all models, while more specific ones will apply for a given class of models only, e.g., for decision trees.

When a user defines a data mining task, she will then have available a choice of primitives (evaluation functions, language cost functions, and subsumption relations) appropriate to the task at hand. The primitives can be used to form individual constraints, which can then be combined to form inductive (data mining) queries. Recall that we have Boolean (hard) constraints, optimization constraints and soft constraints. Boolean constraints can be combined via logical operations to form complex queries. Note that the use of multiple evaluation/language cost functions entails a multi-objective optimization problem, to which different approaches can be applied as outlined in Section 8.4.

The design of data mining algorithms to solve arbitrary inductive queries composed along the lines described above is still much of an open issue. So far, most of the algorithms for constraint-based data mining have focussed on mining frequent patterns (in structured data) under frequency constraints (Boulicaut et al. 2005). Mining closed patterns and mining under (language) cost constraints has also been considered in this setting. Since all of the above are anti-monotonic, combinations thereof are also anti-monotonic and the generic algorithm for mining frequent patterns (discussed in Section 9.4) applies.

Interest in the constraint-based mining of predictive models has increased recently. A number of methods have been proposed that take into account accuracy and size constraints in decision trees (Garofalakis et al. 2003), as well as subsumption constraints (Struyf and Džeroski 2006). Constraints (including subsumption and accuracy) have also been considered in the context of learning polynomial equations (Džeroski et al. 2005). However, unlike 'complete' frequent pattern mining approaches, which return the complete/optimal set of solutions, these approaches are heuristic and give no guarantees. Only recently have 'complete' approaches been considered for predictive models, e.g., for learning optimal decision trees (Nijssen and Fromont 2007).

10.6   Re-using the Results of Learning

Recall that the set of solutions to an inductive query produced by a data mining algorithm constitutes a dataset of generalizations (e.g., patterns/models) and can be stored as such. It then becomes available for further queries, be it post-processing queries, cross-over queries or inductive queries. Actually, post-processing queries can be viewed as just data queries on the data part of the generalizations.

One way to use cross-over queries is to apply learned models (patterns) on a new set of data to produce a new (feature-based) representation. For example, as discussed in Section 9.3 frequent patterns (discovered by data mining) have already been used as features for predictive modelling. This has been done both for itemsets/propositional representations (Cheng et al. 2007) and for structured objects/relational representations (King et al. 2001).

Models can also be used to generate new features, either directly or indirectly. If the target type of a model is a primitive type or a vector thereof, the model's predictions can be used directly as features. If it is structured, feature construction thereon can be applied as outlined in Section 9.3. The above can be done for any model, irrespective of its representation.

For some classes of models, features can be generated from the structure of the data part of the model. For instance, if we have a decision tree, we can take fragments thereof, such as paths which represent a conjunction of conditions, and make these new features. A similar approach has been used by Srinivasan and King (1999) to extract features from a logic program, then use these for predicting biological activity of molecules.

We can also pose inductive queries on sets of patterns/models. We take as input the data part of the patterns/models. It is important to note that the ability to mine structured data is of crucial importance here. Namely, patterns and models are often structured objects, even if the data they were generated from is flat/propositional: Take for example decision trees and Bayesian networks derived from a propositional dataset.

Termier et al. (2006) first learn gene networks from microarray data through a process that generates many different networks. They then apply frequent pattern mining to extract DAGs (directed acyclic graphs) which commonly occur in the networks. A human expert then only needs to look at and assess the biological meaning of these smaller components of the gene networks.

The above discussion addresses directly issues raised by Siebes (2006) as priority issues to be solved in order to achieve truly inductive database functionality. The paragraphs immediately above refer to what Siebes calls 'Models on Models' or 'Mining on Models and Patterns'. The earlier part of the discussion refers to what Siebes calls 'Models for Models'. Both are related to meta-learning (Vilalta and Drissi 2002), where the results of (base-level) learning are used as input to a further learning process.

More complicated ways are possible of re-using learned patterns and models. In some ways, these would depart from the basic data mining tasks that we have addressed earlier in this article. For example, a given set of data can be used to improve an existing predictive model: This task is referred to as theory revision. Here we want to find an improved model, which however is not discovered from scratch but is based on the given model. One possibility is to formulate this in terms of subsumption constraints. Džeroski et al. (2005) discuss a scenario in which a previously discovered polynomial is used in a sub-polynomial constraint in the discovery of more complex polynomials. In general, we want the revised model to be similar to the original model, and constraints based on (syntactic or semantic) similarity of patterns/models might prove to be useful.

10.7   Operations on Generalizations

It would be desirable to support some operations on generalizations in a data mining language. An example would be the operation that combines a set of regression models by taking the average prediction of individual models. A set of classification models would be combined via majority voting and a set of probabilistic classification models by probability distribution voting/summation. Another example would be the weighted summation of a number of probability distributions to obtain a mixture model. Finally, clustering aggregation (Gionis et al. 2005) takes as input a set of clusterings and finds a clustering that agrees as much as possible with the given clusterings.

The first two examples above are easy to implement, especially in functional programming languages. We can operate on the functional part of the generalizations directly, and obtain, e.g., $r(x) = (r_1(x) + \ldots + r_k(x))/k$ in the first example, where $r_i(x)$ are the individual regression models (the function parts thereof). For certain classes of generalizations, these operations can be done on the data part thereof in closed form: if $r_i(x)$ were linear models represented by the coefficients for each of the features x_j used, we could simply add these up.

Defining operations on generalizations with a clear semantics goes in the direction of defining an algebra for data mining, analogous to relational algebra. Mannila (2001) outlined a proposal of an algebra for probabilistic (mixture) models, with the basic operations of projection, selection, union and join analogues to the operations in the relational model. A probabilistic model is viewed as a relation: selection corresponds to partial evaluation of the model, projection to marginalization over the variables projected away, union corresponds to mixing, and applying a model to an ordinary relation to (prediction) join.

10.8   Integration Aspects, Compositionality, and Scenarios

So, how would a user go about solving a specific data mining problem in the framework outlined here? She would start with the data: Define data type(s), or choose from pre-defined ones, then load a dataset. Along with the data type(s), distances/prototypes, features, kernels and refinements may be defined (either directly by the user or in a semi-automated fashion from the definitions of the data types).

The data mining task has to be specified next: This can be one of pattern discovery, estimating a probability distribution, clustering or prediction. A different type of generalization (a set of patterns, a probability distribution, a clustering or a predictive model) is produced as output, depending on the task. These are parameterized in the first instance with the types of data they operate on.

Once a data mining task and the underlying data types are selected, a class of generalizations has to be selected. We expect that some generic classes (e.g., trees) will be predefined, parameterized with the appropriate basic components (e.g., feature sets). Evaluation/language cost functions and constraints have to be selected next, based on distance/cost functions and refinement orders on the underlying data/generalization types: These constitute an inductive query.

Integration. The language we envision would support the creation of data mining algorithms capable of solving a variety of inductive queries on a variety of data types involving a variety of evaluation and language constraints. The key to this would be the support for different data types, the explicit treatment of generalizations as both data objects and functions, the explicit representation and manipulation of basic components of data mining algorithms, as well as constraint primitives (evaluation an language cost functions). Data mining algorithms implemented in this environment would be tightly integrated into an overall knowledge discovery language, where outputs of one data mining operation can be used as input to another.

Loose integration of externally developed data mining algorithms would also be possible. For an algorithm to be plugged in, we would need a precise specification of the data mining task addressed, the underlying data type(s), and the class of generalizations considered. If the algorithm is constraint-based, the evaluation and language primitives used, and the types of constraints supported should also be specified. For example, MolFea (Kramer and De Raedt 2001) addresses the task of finding frequent patterns in the form of linear molecular fragments in data that consists of molecular structures in the form of labeled graphs and takes into account subsumption language constraints and frequency evaluation constraints.

Compositionality. Compositionality is the technique of constructing complex analyses by using a collection of standard operations as building blocks, with the outputs of some operations serving as inputs to other operations (Ramakrishnan et al. 2005). Relational algebra, for example, includes the operations of selection, projection, join, union and difference that take as input tables and produce tables as output. In the context of data mining, it has so far been a largely open issue what are the operators of interest, their inputs and outputs.

We argue that data mining operators corresponding to the data mining tasks we have defined and discussed here should definitely be included in an algebra for data mining. Whether or not (and which) operations of lower granularity should be included can be debated on further and depends on whether we want to focus on knowledge discovery or data mining. In a knowledge discovery language a coarser granularity may be preferred, while for data mining a finer granularity might be necessary.

We have described data mining tasks/operations, as well as the basic ingredients of data mining algorithms, in terms of their signatures, i.e., the domain and ranges of the functions they are computing. Not all operations can be meaningfully combined in all possible ways and signatures provide us with some guidance on what combinations are meaningful. For example, the output of a frequent pattern mining algorithm for data type T applied to a dataset D_1 of objects of type T can be used as the input to a cross-over operation (together with another dataset D_2 of objects of type T).

The signatures of data mining operators can be organized in a hierarchy (Ramakrishnan et al. 2005). At the higher level, the signatures are described in general terms, such as pattern or model. In the lower levels they may be specialized for certain types/classes of patterns or models. Following the same approach makes sense in our case as well. We propose to lift the hierarchy described there, which works only for propositional data, to the case of mining structured data. The ontology of structured data types would be taken into account as well.

Scenarios. Real-life applications of data mining typically require interactive sessions and involve the formulation of a complex sequence of inter-related inductive queries (including data mining operations), which we will call a KDD scenario (Boulicaut et al. 1999). Some of the inductive queries would generate or manipulate patterns, others would apply these patterns to a given dataset to form a new dataset, still others would use the new dataset to to build a predictive model. The ability to formulate and execute such sequences of queries crucially depends on compositionality, the ability to use the output of one query as the input to another.

KDD scenarios can be described at different levels of detail and precision and can serve multiple purposes. At the lowest level of detail, the specific data mining algorithms used and and their exact parameter settings employed would be included, as well as the specific data analyzed. Moving towards higher levels of abstraction, details can be gradually omitted, e.g., first the parameter setting of the algorithm, then the actual algorithm may be omitted but the class of generalizations produced by it can be kept, and finally the class of generalizations can be left out (but the data mining task kept). On the data side, one might move from the specification of an actual dataset to a specification of the underlying data type and further to data types that are higher in the hierarchy/ontology of data types. Having ontologies of data types, data mining tasks, generalizations and data mining algorithms would greatly facilitate the description of scenarios at higher abstraction levels: the abstraction can proceed along each of the respective ontologies.

At the most detailed level of description, KDD scenarios can serve to document the exact sequence of data mining operations undertaken by a human analyst on a specific task. This would facilitate, for example, the repetition of the entire sequence of analyses after an erroneous data entry has been corrected in the source data. At higher levels of abstraction, the scenarios would enable the re-use of already performed analyses, e.g., on a new dataset of the same type. We thus argue that the explicit storage and manipulation of scenarios (e.g., by reducing/increasing the level of detail) would greatly facilitate the KDD process as a whole, reduce human effort and thus alleviate a major bottleneck in applying KDD in practice.

11   Related Work

When attempting to formulate a general framework for data mining, the potential set of related work items is dangerously large. Here we will give a biased sample of what we consider related work. Parts of it have been mentioned previously, while others have not been explicitly mentioned above even though they have made an intellectual influence during the writing of this article.

Let us start with inductive databases and constraint-based data mining. Since the notion of inductive databases was introduced, a significant body of research has grown on these two topics: A survey can be found in the book edited by Boulicaut et al. (2005). An earlier collection of papers focussing on constraint-based data mining was edited by Bayardo (2002).

Data mining query languages are also directly relevant: A survey article is presented by Boulicaut and Masson (2005). A more recent proposal for an SQL-based data mining query languages, which allows for the integration of various data mining operations at the data level, has been given by Kramer et al. (2006). Finally, the IQL language proposed by Nijssen and De Raedt (2007/this volume), is very close in spirit to the discussion presented here: it recognizes the importance of functions and extends tuple relational calculus with a function and a typing system. However, it only allows for loose integration of data mining algorithms and does not support the creation of new algorithms.

Another way to recognize the importance of functions is to use higher-order logic or functional programming to facilitate the implementation of data mining algorithms (for mining structured data). Lloyd (2003) uses higher-order logic to define structured data types and principled ways of constructing distances, features (which he calls predicates) and kernels. Allison (2004) uses functional programming to define data types and type classes for models (where models include probability distributions, mixture models and decision trees) that allow for models to be manipulated in a precise and flexible way.

Formulating an algebra for data mining that would be the equivalent of Codd's relational algebra for databases is probably the most ambitious goal in the context of the discussion presented here. The 3W-model (Johnson et al. 2000) was among the first to take an algebraic view on data mining: A refined version has been presented recently by Calders et al. (2006b). Mannila (2001) presented an algebraic view on operations with mixture models. Siebes (2006) discusses how to lift relational algebra to patterns and models. Finally, the compositionality of data mining operators, as discussed by Ramakrishnan et al. (2005), can be expected to play a crucial role in the general framework.

Acknowledgments. This work was supported by the IQ project (IST-FET FP6-516169). Thanks are due to the members of the project for providing the intellectual background for this work, as well as numerous discussions on related issues. Special thanks to Jan Struyf, who helped with this article in various ways, which among other things included a detailed proofreading and search for references. Thanks also to Alexandros Kalousis and Ljupčo Todorovski for reading this text at short notice, as well as Marko Bohanec and Bernard Ženko for commenting on portions thereof. Thanks as well to Martin Erwig and John Lloyd for the useful discussions on functional programming languages and their use for data mining.

References

1. Agrawal, R., Imielinski, T., Swami, A.: Mining association rules between sets of items in large databases. In: Proc. of the ACM SIGMOD Conf. on Management of Data, pp. 207–216. ACM Press, New York (1993)
2. Aho, A.V., Ullman, J.D., Hopcroft, J.E.: Data Structures and Algorithms. Addison-Wesley, Reading, MA (1983)
3. Allison, L.: Models for machine learning and data mining in functional programming. Journal of Functional Programming 15(1), 15–32 (2004)
4. R. Bayardo (ed.) Constraints in data mining. Special issue of SIGKDD Explorations, 4(1) (2002)
5. Bishop, C.M.: Pattern Recognition and Machine Learning. Springer, Berlin (2006)
6. Bistarelli, S., Bonch, F.: Interestingness is not a Dichotomy: Introducing Softness in Constrained Pattern Mining. In: Jorge, A.M., Torgo, L., Brazdil, P.B., Camacho, R., Gama, J. (eds.) PKDD 2005. LNCS (LNAI), vol. 3721, Springer, Heidelberg (2005)
7. Blockeel, H., De Raedt, L., Ramon, J.: Top-down induction of clustering trees. In: Proc. of the 15th Intl. Conf. on Machine Learning, pp. 55–63. Morgan Kaufmann, San Mateo, CA (1998)
8. Boulicaut, J.-F., Jeudy, B.: Constraint-based data mining. In: Maimon, O., Rokach, L. (eds.) The Data Mining and Knowledge Discovery Handbook, pp. 399–416. Springer, Berlin (2005)
9. Boulicaut, J.-F., Masson, C.: Data mining query languages. In: Maimon, O., Rokach, L. (eds.) The Data Mining and Knowledge Discovery Handbook, Springer, Berlin (2005)
10. Boulicaut, J.-F., Klemettinen, M., Mannila, H.: Modeling KDD processes within the inductive database framework. In: Mohania, M.K., Tjoa, A.M. (eds.) DaWaK 1999. LNCS, vol. 1676, pp. 293–302. Springer, Heidelberg (1999)

11. Boulicaut, J.-F., De Raedt, L., Mannila, H. (eds.): Constraint-Based Mining and Inductive Databases. LNCS (LNAI), vol. 3848. Springer, Heidelberg (2006)
12. Bracewell, R.N.: The Fourier Transform and Its Applications. McGraw-Hill, New York (1965)
13. Calders, T., Rigotti, C., Boulicaut, J.-F.: A survey on condensed representations for frequent sets. In: Boulicaut, J-F., De Raedt, L., Mannila, H. (eds.) Constraint-Based Mining and Inductive Databases. LNCS (LNAI), vol. 3848, pp. 64–80. Springer, Heidelberg (2006)
14. Calders, T., Goethals, B., Prado, A.B.: Integrating pattern mining in relational databases. In: Fürnkranz, J., Scheffer, T., Spiliopoulou, M. (eds.) PKDD 2006. LNCS (LNAI), vol. 4213, pp. 454–461. Springer, Heidelberg (2006a)
15. Calders, T., Lakshmanan, L.V.S., Ng, R.T., Paredaens, J.: Expressive power of an algebra for data mining. ACM Transactions on Database Systems 31(4), 1169–1214 (2006b)
16. Cheng, H., Yan, X., Han, J., Hsu, C.-W.: Discriminative frequent pattern analysis for effective classification. In: Proc. 23nd Intl. Conf. on Data Engineering, pp. 716–725. IEEE Computer Society Press, Los Alamitos (2007)
17. Deb, K.: Multi-Objective Optimization Using Evolutionary Algorithms. Wiley & Sons, New York (2001)
18. De Raedt, L., Dehaspe, L.: Clausal discovery. Machine Learning 26, 99–146 (1997)
19. Dehaspe, L., Toivonen, H.: Discovery of frequent Datalog patterns. Data Mining and Knowledge Discovery 3(1), 7–36 (1999)
20. De Raedt, L.: A perspective on inductive databases. SIGKDD Explorations 4(2), 69–77 (2002a)
21. De Raedt, L.: Data mining as constraint logic programming. In: Kakas, A.C., Sadri, F. (eds.) Computational Logic: Logic Programming and Beyond. LNCS (LNAI), vol. 2408, pp. 113–125. Springer, Heidelberg (2002b)
22. Durbin, R., Eddy, S.R., Krogh, A., Mitchison, G.J.: Biological Sequence Analysis: Probabilistic Models of Proteins and Nucleic Acids. Cambridge University Press, Cambridge (1998)
23. Džeroski, S.: Inductive logic programming in a nutshell. In: Getoor, L., Taskar, B. (eds.) Statistical Relational Learning, MIT Press, Cambridge, MA (2007)
24. Džeroski, S., Lavrač, N. (eds.): Relational Data Mining. Springer, Berlin (2001)
25. Džeroski, S., Todorovski, L., Ljubič, P.: Inductive queries on polynomial equations. In: Boulicaut, J-F., De Raedt, L., Mannila, H. (eds.) Constraint-Based Mining and Inductive Databases. LNCS (LNAI), vol. 3848, pp. 127–154. Springer, Heidelberg (2006)
26. Fayyad, U., Piatetsky-Shapiro, G., Uthurusamy, R.: Summary from the KDD-2003 panel – "Data Mining: The Next 10 Years". SIGKDD Explorations 5(2), 191–196 (2003)
27. Friedman, J.H., Fisher, N.I.: Bump hunting in high-dimensional data. Statistics and Computing 9(2), 123–143 (1999)
28. Fayyad, U., Piatetsky-Shapiro, G., Smyth, P.: From data mining to knowledge discovery: An overview. In: Fayyad, U., Piatetsky-Shapiro, G., Smyth, P., Uthurusamy, R. (eds.) Advances in Knowledge Discovery and Data Mining, pp. 495–515. MIT Press, Cambridge, MA (1996)
29. Frawley, W.J., Piatetsky-Shapiro, G., Matheus, C.J.: Knowledge discovery in databases: An overview. In: Knowledge Discovery in Databases, pp. 1–30. AAAI/MIT Press, Cambridge
30. Gaertner, T.: A survey of kernels for structured data. SIGKDD Explorations 5(1), 49–58 (2003)

31. Garofalakis, M., Hyun, D., Rastogi, R., Shim, K.: Building decision trees with constraints. Data Mining and Knowledge Discovery 7(2), 187–214 (2003)
32. Getoor, L., Taskar, B. (eds.): Statistical Relational Learning. MIT Press, Cambridge, MA (2007)
33. Gionis, A., Mannila, H., Tsaparas, P.: Clustering aggregation. In: Proc. of the 21st Intl. Conf. on Data Engineering, pp. 341–352. IEEE Computer Society Press, Los Alamitos (2005)
34. Han, J., Kamber, M.: Data Mining: Concepts and Techniques. Morgan Kaufmann, San Francisco, CA (2001)
35. Hand, D.J., Mannila, H., Smyth, P.: Principles of Data Mining. MIT Press, Cambridge, MA (2001)
36. Haussler, D.: Convolution kernels on discrete structures. UC Santa Cruz, Technical Report UCS-CRL-99-10 (1999)
37. Imielinski, T., Mannila, H.: A database perspective on knowledge discovery. Communications of the ACM 39(11), 58–64 (1996)
38. Johnson, T., Lakshmanan, L.V., Ng, R.: The 3W model and algebra for unified data mining. In: Proc. of the Intl. Conf. on Very Large Data Bases, pp. 21–32. Morgan Kaufmann, San Francisco, CA (2000)
39. Kalousis, A., Woznica, A., Hilario, M.: A unifying framework for relational distance-based learning founded on relational algebra. Technical Report, Computer Science Department, University of Geneva (2006)
40. Kaufman, L., Rousseeuw, P.J.: Finding Groups in Data: An Introduction to Cluster Analysis. Wiley & Sons, New York (1990)
41. King, R.D., Karwath, A., Clare, A., Dehaspe, L.: The utility of different representations of protein sequence for predicting functional class. Bioinformatics 17(5), 445–454 (2001)
42. Kloesgen, W.: Data mining tasks and methods: Subgroup discovery: deviation analysis. In: Kloesgen, W., Zytkow, J.M. (eds.) Handbook of Data Mining and Knowledge Discovery, pp. 354–361. Oxford University Press, Oxford (2002)
43. Kramer, S., Aufschild, V., Hapfelmeier, A., Jarasch, A., Kessler, K., Reckow, S., Wicker, J., Richter, L.: Inductive Databases in the Relational Model: The Data as the Bridge. In: Bonchi, F., Boulicaut, J-F. (eds.) KDID 2005. LNCS, vol. 3933, pp. 124–138. Springer, Heidelberg (2006)
44. Lavrač, N., Kavšek, B., Flach, P.A., Todorovski, L.: Subgroup Discovery with CN2-SD. Journal of Machine Learning Research 5, 153–188 (2004)
45. Lavrač, N., Džeroski, S.: Inductive Logic Programming: Techniques and Applications. Ellis Horwood, Chichester (1994)
46. Liu, H., Motoda, H.: Feature Extraction, Construction and Selection: A Data Mining Perspective. Kluwer, Dorderecht (1998)
47. Lloyd, J.W.: Foundations of Logic Programming. Springer, Berlin (1987)
48. Lloyd, J.W.: An introduction to deductive database systems. Australian Computer Journal 15(2), 52–57 (1983)
49. Lloyd, J.W.: Logic for Learning. Springer, Berlin (2003)
50. Mallat, S.: A Wavelet Tour of Signal Processing. Academic Press, London (1999)
51. Inductive databases vision: Relational operations on models. Unpublished slides. In: Presented at the meeting of the cInQ project (December 2001)
52. Mannila, H., Toivonen, H.: Levelwise search and borders of theories in knowledge discovery. Data Mining and Knowledge Discovery 1(3), 241–258 (1997)
53. Michalski, R.S.: Knowledge acquisition through conceptual clustering: A theoretical framework and an algorithm for partitioning data into conjunctive concepts. Intl. Jrnl. of Policy Analysis and Information Systems 4, 219–244 (1980)

54. Mitchell, T.M.: Generalization as search. Artif. Intell. 18(2), 203–226 (1982)
55. Nijssen, S., Fromont, E.: Mining optimal decision trees from itemset lattices. In: Proc. of The 13th ACM SIGKDD Intl. Conf. on Knowledge Discovery and Data Mining, ACM Press, New York (to appear, 2007)
56. Piatetsky-Shapiro, G., Djeraba, C., Getoor, L., Grossman, R., Feldman, R., Zaki, M.: What are the grand challenges for data mining? KDD-2006 Panel report. SIGKDD Explorations 8(2), 70–77 (2006)
57. Ramakrishnan, R., et al.: Data Mining: The Next Generation. In: Ramakrishnan, R., Agrawal, R., Freytag, J.-C. (eds.) Perspectives Wshp. – Data Mining: The Next Generation. Intl. Begegnungs- und Forschungszentrum fuer Informatik (IBFI), Schloss Dagstuhl, Germany (2005)
58. Ramon, J., Bruynooghe, M.: A polynomial time computable metric between point sets. Acta Informatica 37(10), 765–780 (2001)
59. Shawe-Taylor, J., Cristianini, N.: Kernel Methods for Pattern Analysis. Cambridge University Press, Cambridge (2004)
60. Siebes, A.: Data mining in inductive databases. In: Bonchi, F., Boulicaut, J-F. (eds.) KDID 2005. LNCS, vol. 3933, pp. 1–23. Springer, Heidelberg (2006)
61. Srinivasan, A., King, R.D.: Feature construction with inductive logic programming: A study of quantitative predictions of biological activity aided by structural attributes. Knowledge Discovery and Data Mining 3(1), 37–57 (1999)
62. Struyf, J., Džeroski, S.: Constraint based induction of multi-objective regression trees. In: Bonchi, F., Boulicaut, J-F. (eds.) KDID 2005. LNCS, vol. 3933, pp. 222–233. Springer, Heidelberg (2006)
63. Termier, A., Tamada, Y., Imoto, S., Washio, T., Higuchi, T.: From closed tree mining towards closed DAG mining. In: Proc. of the Intl. Wshp. on Data Mining and Statistical Science, pp. 1–7 (2006)
64. Thompson, S.: Haskell: The Craft of Functional Programming. Add. Wesley, Reading (1999)
65. Tušar, T.: Design of an Algorithm for Multiobjective Optimization with Differential Evolution. M.Sc. Thesis. Faculty of Computer and Information Science, University of Ljubljana, Slovenia (2007)
66. Vilalta, R., Drissi, Y.: A perspective view and survey of meta-learning. Artificial Intelligence Review 18(2), 77–95 (2002)
67. Wagstaff, K., Cardie, C.: Clustering with instance-level constraints. In: Proc. 17th Intl. Conf. on Machine Learning, pp. 1103–1110. Morgan Kaufmann, San Francisco, CA (2000)
68. Woznica, A., Kalousis, A., Hilario, M.: Kernels on lists and sets over relational algebra: an application to classification of protein fingerprints. In: Ng, W-K., Kitsuregawa, M., Li, J., Chang, K. (eds.) PAKDD 2006. LNCS (LNAI), vol. 3918, pp. 546–551. Springer, Heidelberg (2006)
69. Yang, Q., Wu, X.: 10 Challenging problems in data mining research. Intl. Jrnl. of Information Technology & Decision Making 5(4), 597–604 (2006)
70. Ženko, B., Džeroski, S., Struyf, J.: Learning predictive clustering rules. In: Bonchi, F., Boulicaut, J-F. (eds.) KDID 2005. LNCS, vol. 3933, pp. 234–250. Springer, Heidelberg (2006)

Author Index

Arimura, Hiroki 152

Besson, Jérémy 11
Bistarelli, Stefano 24
Blockeel, Hendrik 81
Bonchi, Francesco 24, 42
Boulicaut, Jean-François 11

Crémilleux, Bruno 208, 223

De Raedt, Luc 11, 189
Džeroski, Sašo 63, 134, 259

Fromont, Élisa 81

Galecki, Krzysztof 240
Gallo, Arianna 97
Gawronek, Krzysztof 240
Giannotti, Fosca 42
Gjorgjioski, Valentin 63

Kaufman, Kenneth A. 116
Kléma, Jiří 223
Kocev, Dragi 134

Lucchese, Claudio 42

Meo, Rosa 97
Michalski, Ryszard S. 116
Minato, Shin-ichi 152

Nanni, Mirco 170
Nijssen, Siegfried 189

Orlando, Salvatore 42

Perego, Raffaele 42
Pietrzykowski, Jarosław 116

Rigotti, Christophe 170
Rioult, François 208
Robardet, Céline 11

Slavkov, Ivica 63
Soulet, Arnaud 223
Struyf, Jan 63, 81, 134

Trasarti, Roberto 42

Wagstaff, Kiri L. 1
Wojciechowski, Marek 240
Wojtusiak, Janusz 116

Lecture Notes in Computer Science

Sublibrary 3: Information Systems and Application, incl. Internet/Web and HCI

For information about Vols. 1– 4312
please contact your bookseller or Springer

Vol. 4797: M. Arenas, M.I. Schwartzbach (Eds.), Database Programming Languages. VIII, 261 pages. 2007.

Vol. 4796: M. Lew, N. Sebe, T.S. Huang, E.M. Bakker (Eds.), Human–Computer Interaction. X, 157 pages. 2007.

Vol. 4777: S. Bhalla (Ed.), Databases in Networked Information Systems. X, 329 pages. 2007.

Vol. 4761: R. Obermaisser, Y. Nah, P. Puschner, F.J. Rammig (Eds.), Software Technologies for Embedded and Ubiquitous Systems. XIV, 563 pages. 2007.

Vol. 4747: S. Džeroski, J. Struyf (Eds.), Knowledge Discovery in Inductive Databases. X, 301 pages. 2007.

Vol. 4740: L. Ma, M. Rauterberg, R. Nakatsu (Eds.), Entertainment Computing – ICEC 2007. XXX, 480 pages. 2007.

Vol. 4730: C. Peters, P. Clough, F.C. Gey, J. Karlgren, B. Magnini, D.W. Oard, M. de Rijke, M. Stempfhuber (Eds.), Evaluation of Multilingual and Multi-modal Information Retrieval. XXIV, 998 pages. 2007.

Vol. 4723: M. R. Berthold, J. Shawe-Taylor, N. Lavrač (Eds.), Advances in Intelligent Data Analysis VII. XIV, 380 pages. 2007.

Vol. 4721: W. Jonker, M. Petković (Eds.), Secure Data Management. X, 213 pages. 2007.

Vol. 4718: J. Hightower, B. Schiele, T. Strang (Eds.), Location- and Context-Awareness. X, 297 pages. 2007.

Vol. 4717: J. Krumm, G.D. Abowd, A. Seneviratne, T. Strang (Eds.), UbiComp 2007: Ubiquitous Computing. XIX, 520 pages. 2007.

Vol. 4715: J.M. Haake, S.F. Ochoa, A. Cechich (Eds.), Groupware: Design, Implementation, and Use. XIII, 355 pages. 2007.

Vol. 4714: G. Alonso, P. Dadam, M. Rosemann (Eds.), Business Process Management. XIII, 418 pages. 2007.

Vol. 4704: D. Barbosa, A. Bonifati, Z. Bellahsène, E. Hunt, R. Unland (Eds.), Database and XML Technologies. X, 141 pages. 2007.

Vol. 4690: Y. Ioannidis, B. Novikov, B. Rachev (Eds.), Advances in Databases and Information Systems. XIII, 377 pages. 2007.

Vol. 4675: L. Kovács, N. Fuhr, C. Meghini (Eds.), Research and Advanced Technology for Digital Libraries. XVII, 585 pages. 2007.

Vol. 4674: Y. Luo (Ed.), Cooperative Design, Visualization, and Engineering. XIII, 431 pages. 2007.

Vol. 4663: C. Baranauskas, P. Palanque, J. Abascal, S.D.J. Barbosa (Eds.), Human-Computer Interaction – INTERACT 2007, Part II. XXXIII, 735 pages. 2007.

Vol. 4662: C. Baranauskas, P. Palanque, J. Abascal, S.D.J. Barbosa (Eds.), Human-Computer Interaction – INTERACT 2007, Part I. XXXIII, 637 pages. 2007.

Vol. 4658: T. Enokido, L. Barolli, M. Takizawa (Eds.), Network-Based Information Systems. XIII, 544 pages. 2007.

Vol. 4656: M.A. Wimmer, J. Scholl, Å. Grönlund (Eds.), Electronic Government. XIV, 450 pages. 2007.

Vol. 4655: G. Psaila, R. Wagner (Eds.), E-Commerce and Web Technologies. VII, 229 pages. 2007.

Vol. 4654: I.-Y. Song, J. Eder, T.M. Nguyen (Eds.), Data Warehousing and Knowledge Discovery. XVI, 482 pages. 2007.

Vol. 4653: R. Wagner, N. Revell, G. Pernul (Eds.), Database and Expert Systems Applications. XXII, 907 pages. 2007.

Vol. 4636: G. Antoniou, U. Aßmann, C. Baroglio, S. Decker, N. Henze, P.-L. Patranjan, R. Tolksdorf (Eds.), Reasoning Web. IX, 345 pages. 2007.

Vol. 4611: J. Indulska, J. Ma, L.T. Yang, T. Ungerer, J. Cao (Eds.), Ubiquitous Intelligence and Computing. XXIII, 1257 pages. 2007.

Vol. 4607: L. Baresi, P. Fraternali, G.-J. Houben (Eds.), Web Engineering. XVI, 576 pages. 2007.

Vol. 4606: A. Pras, M. van Sinderen (Eds.), Dependable and Adaptable Networks and Services. XIV, 149 pages. 2007.

Vol. 4605: D. Papadias, D. Zhang, G. Kollios (Eds.), Advances in Spatial and Temporal Databases. X, 479 pages. 2007.

Vol. 4602: S. Barker, G.-J. Ahn (Eds.), Data and Applications Security XXI. X, 291 pages. 2007.

Vol. 4601: S. Spaccapietra, P. Atzeni, F. Fages, M.-S. Hacid, M. Kifer, J. Mylopoulos, B. Pernici, P. Shvaiko, J. Trujillo, I. Zaihrayeu (Eds.), Journal on Data Semantics IX. XV, 197 pages. 2007.

Vol. 4592: Z. Kedad, N. Lammari, E. Métais, F. Meziane, Y. Rezgui (Eds.), Natural Language Processing and Information Systems. XIV, 442 pages. 2007.

Vol. 4587: R. Cooper, J. Kennedy (Eds.), Data Management. XIII, 259 pages. 2007.

Vol. 4577: N. Sebe, Y. Liu, Y.-t. Zhuang, T.S. Huang (Eds.), Multimedia Content Analysis and Mining. XIII, 513 pages. 2007.

Vol. 4568: T. Ishida, S. R. Fussell, P. T. J. M. Vossen (Eds.), Intercultural Collaboration. XIII, 395 pages. 2007.

Vol. 4566: M.J. Dainoff (Ed.), Ergonomics and Health Aspects of Work with Computers. XVIII, 390 pages. 2007.

Vol. 4564: D. Schuler (Ed.), Online Communities and Social Computing. XVII, 520 pages. 2007.

Vol. 4563: R. Shumaker (Ed.), Virtual Reality. XXII, 762 pages. 2007.

Vol. 4561: V.G. Duffy (Ed.), Digital Human Modeling. XXIII, 1068 pages. 2007.

Vol. 4560: N. Aykin (Ed.), Usability and Internationalization, Part II. XVIII, 576 pages. 2007.

Vol. 4559: N. Aykin (Ed.), Usability and Internationalization, Part I. XVIII, 661 pages. 2007.

Vol. 4558: M.J. Smith, G. Salvendy (Eds.), Human Interface and the Management of Information, Part II. XXIII, 1162 pages. 2007.

Vol. 4557: M.J. Smith, G. Salvendy (Eds.), Human Interface and the Management of Information, Part I. XXII, 1030 pages. 2007.

Vol. 4541: T. Okadome, T. Yamazaki, M. Makhtari (Eds.), Pervasive Computing for Quality of Life Enhancement. IX, 248 pages. 2007.

Vol. 4537: K.C.-C. Chang, W. Wang, L. Chen, C.A. Ellis, C.-H. Hsu, A.C. Tsoi, H. Wang (Eds.), Advances in Web and Network Technologies, and Information Management. XXIII, 707 pages. 2007.

Vol. 4531: J. Indulska, K. Raymond (Eds.), Distributed Applications and Interoperable Systems. XI, 337 pages. 2007.

Vol. 4526: M. Malek, M. Reitenspieß, A. van Moorsel (Eds.), Service Availability. X, 155 pages. 2007.

Vol. 4524: M. Marchiori, J.Z. Pan, C.d.S. Marie (Eds.), Web Reasoning and Rule Systems. XI, 382 pages. 2007.

Vol. 4519: E. Franconi, M. Kifer, W. May (Eds.), The Semantic Web: Research and Applications. XVIII, 830 pages. 2007.

Vol. 4518: N. Fuhr, M. Lalmas, A. Trotman (Eds.), Comparative Evaluation of XML Information Retrieval Systems. XII, 554 pages. 2007.

Vol. 4508: M.-Y. Kao, X.-Y. Li (Eds.), Algorithmic Aspects in Information and Management. VIII, 428 pages. 2007.

Vol. 4506: D. Zeng, I. Gotham, K. Komatsu, C. Lynch, M. Thurmond, D. Madigan, B. Lober, J. Kvach, H. Chen (Eds.), Intelligence and Security Informatics: Biosurveillance. XI, 234 pages. 2007.

Vol. 4505: G. Dong, X. Lin, W. Wang, Y. Yang, J.X. Yu (Eds.), Advances in Data and Web Management. XXII, 896 pages. 2007.

Vol. 4504: J. Huang, R. Kowalczyk, Z. Maamar, D. Martin, I. Müller, S. Stoutenburg, K.P. Sycara (Eds.), Service-Oriented Computing: Agents, Semantics, and Engineering. X, 175 pages. 2007.

Vol. 4500: N.A. Streitz, A.D. Kameas, I. Mavrommati (Eds.), The Disappearing Computer. XVIII, 304 pages. 2007.

Vol. 4495: J. Krogstie, A. Opdahl, G. Sindre (Eds.), Advanced Information Systems Engineering. XVI, 606 pages. 2007.

Vol. 4480: A. LaMarca, M. Langheinrich, K.N. Truong (Eds.), Pervasive Computing. XIII, 369 pages. 2007.

Vol. 4473: D. Draheim, G. Weber (Eds.), Trends in Enterprise Application Architecture. X, 355 pages. 2007.

Vol. 4471: P. Cesar, K. Chorianopoulos, J.F. Jensen (Eds.), Interactive TV: A Shared Experience. XIII, 236 pages. 2007.

Vol. 4469: K.-c. Hui, Z. Pan, R.C.-k. Chung, C.C.L. Wang, X. Jin, S. Göbel, E.C.-L. Li (Eds.), Technologies for E-Learning and Digital Entertainment. XVIII, 974 pages. 2007.

Vol. 4443: R. Kotagiri, P. Radha Krishna, M. Mohania, E. Nantajeewarawat (Eds.), Advances in Databases: Concepts, Systems and Applications. XXI, 1126 pages. 2007.

Vol. 4439: W. Abramowicz (Ed.), Business Information Systems. XV, 654 pages. 2007.

Vol. 4430: C.C. Yang, D. Zeng, M. Chau, K. Chang, Q. Yang, X. Cheng, J. Wang, F.-Y. Wang, H. Chen (Eds.), Intelligence and Security Informatics. XII, 330 pages. 2007.

Vol. 4425: G. Amati, C. Carpineto, G. Romano (Eds.), Advances in Information Retrieval. XIX, 759 pages. 2007.

Vol. 4412: F. Stajano, H.J. Kim, J.-S. Chae, S.-D. Kim (Eds.), Ubiquitous Convergence Technology. XI, 302 pages. 2007.

Vol. 4402: W. Shen, J.-Z. Luo, Z. Lin, J.-P.A. Barthès, Q. Hao (Eds.), Computer Supported Cooperative Work in Design III. XV, 763 pages. 2007.

Vol. 4398: S. Marchand-Maillet, E. Bruno, A. Nürnberger, M. Detyniecki (Eds.), Adaptive Multimedia Retrieval: User, Context, and Feedback. XI, 269 pages. 2007.

Vol. 4397: C. Stephanidis, M. Pieper (Eds.), Universal Access in Ambient Intelligence Environments. XV, 467 pages. 2007.

Vol. 4380: S. Spaccapietra, P. Atzeni, F. Fages, M.-S. Hacid, M. Kifer, J. Mylopoulos, B. Pernici, P. Shvaiko, J. Trujillo, I. Zaihrayeu (Eds.), Journal on Data Semantics VIII. XV, 219 pages. 2007.

Vol. 4365: C.J. Bussler, M. Castellanos, U. Dayal, S. Navathe (Eds.), Business Intelligence for the Real-Time Enterprises. IX, 157 pages. 2007.

Vol. 4353: T. Schwentick, D. Suciu (Eds.), Database Theory – ICDT 2007. XI, 419 pages. 2006.

Vol. 4352: T.-J. Cham, J. Cai, C. Dorai, D. Rajan, T.-S. Chua, L.-T. Chia (Eds.), Advances in Multimedia Modeling, Part II. XVIII, 743 pages. 2006.

Vol. 4351: T.-J. Cham, J. Cai, C. Dorai, D. Rajan, T.-S. Chua, L.-T. Chia (Eds.), Advances in Multimedia Modeling, Part I. XIX, 797 pages. 2006.

Vol. 4328: D. Penkler, M. Reitenspiess, F. Tam (Eds.), Service Availability. X, 289 pages. 2006.

Vol. 4321: P. Brusilovsky, A. Kobsa, W. Nejdl (Eds.), The Adaptive Web. XII, 763 pages. 2007.

Vol. 4317: S.K. Madria, K.T. Claypool, R. Kannan, P. Uppuluri, M.M. Gore (Eds.), Distributed Computing and Internet Technology. XIX, 466 pages. 2006.